FINDING THE SOURCE

FINDING THE SOURCE

ONE MAN'S QUEST FOR HEALING IN WEST
AFRICA

DAVE KOBRENSKI

ARTEMISIA BOOKS
NEW HAMPSHIRE, USA

Publisher's Cataloging-in-Publication Data
provided by Five Rainbows Cataloging Services

Names: Kobrenski, Dave, author.
Title: Finding the source : one man's quest for healing in West Africa / Dave Kobrenski.
Description: North Conway, NH : Artemisia Books, 2022.
Identifiers: LCCN 2021924591 (print) | ISBN 978-0-9826689-8-6 (paperback) | ISBN 979-8-9854287-0-4 (ebook) | ISBN 979-8-9854287-1-1 (audiobook)
Subjects: LCSH: Africa, West--Description and travel. | Drug addiction. | Autoimmune diseases. | Shamanism. | Spiritual healing, | Autobiography. | BISAC: BIOGRAPHY & AUTOBIOGRAPHY / Personal Memoirs. | TRAVEL / Africa / West. | BODY, MIND & SPIRIT / Healing / General. | HEALTH & FITNESS / Diseases / Immune & Autoimmune.
Classification: LCC DT12.25 .K64 2022 (print) | LCC DT12.25 (ebook) | DDC 916.604/33--dc23.

Paperback ISBN: 978-0-9826689-8-6
eBook ISBN: 979-8-9854287-0-4

Library of Congress Control Number: 2021924591

10 9 8 7 6 5 4 3 2 1

For L.C., who still guides me

The life of every man is a diary in which he means to write one story, and writes another; and his humblest hour is when he compares the volume as it is with what he vowed to make it.

— J.M. BARRIE

ACKNOWLEDGEMENTS

Stories are wild things. This particular story arose like a tempest, and howled in my dreams until it was properly told. My telling of it sticks to the truth, at least according to my own memory. Memory has its own wildness, however, and I'm grateful to Doug Santaniello, Julie Ellerbeck, Kerri Biller, Sayon Camara, and Lanciné Condé for their contributions in preserving or correcting details that would have been otherwise lost or skewed in the sandstorm of time.

I have done my best to present all personages fairly and accurately. Certain names have been changed.

A big thanks goes to my editor, Emily Krempholtz, for helping me negotiate the twists and turns of the narrative, and emerge mostly unscathed.

Here's to wild stories and to the adventures that inspire them.

Dave Kobrenski
December 14, 2021

∿

Additional photos and content for this book are available at:

davekobrenski.com/fts

PRONUNCIATION KEY

Malinké names:

Lanciné Condé: LAHN-see-nay COHN-day
Daouda: DOW-dah
Sako Gbè: SAH-ko gbway
Mousso: MOO-so
Sayon: SY-oh(n)
Famoudou Konaté: FAH-moo-doo ko-NAH-tay
Aminata: ah-mee-NAH-ta
Lamine: lah-MEEN

PART I

Elmina Castle, Ghana

1

A DEPARTURE

THE PAIN IS SEARING. It radiates from the center of my spine, up my neck and down to my hips, flaring outward like the thorns of a brittle acacia branch along its route. This fiery serpent in my body consumes the whole of my being: I am the pain, and the pain is me. It is my curse to bear.

I shift my weight in the rickety wooden chair and brace myself for the oncoming surge, which hits me like a jolt of electricity. I grip the seat, my face contorting in agony. After a few moments, my invisible assailant lightens its grip, but the fear lingers. There will be more.

At least no one can see me here. Yes, that would be worse. To suffer like this publicly would be even more unbearable.

For now, I can be alone. In my hiding place behind the small round hut, chickens peck idly at the ground. The occasional lizard scurries past me. A little further, a spindly fence made of sticks separates me from the main compound. On the other side, women are pounding millet, unaware of my presence. A few children pass by the fence, a little too closely, pulling a reluctant goat by a rope. I stay perfectly still. I don't want to jeopardize this moment of solitude. These moments are scarce here.

Rhythmic blows of the mortar and pestle resound from nearby. A woman breaks into song, softly at first, and then she is joined by another:

Eh Daouda lè! Dunin timba, tinya maka, Daouda!

The short song is followed by laughter. I recognize my name in their song, though I'm frustrated I can't understand all the words. Are they mocking me? The intricacies of the language still elude me, even after all these years.

I turn my thoughts inward. The sun, though not yet at its apex, is already scorching and blindingly bright. The dry season is at its peak, that dust-choked time of year when rain seems like an impossible dream. The leaves of the giant kapok and baobab trees are brown, as desperate for relief as I am. Only the river brings respite now, and it is shrinking daily. The dry season has reduced even the mighty Djoliba River to a feeble current.

The rains will return, perhaps in a month, they say. *A month!* Clouds are building on the horizon, but hold only a vague promise of rain. I wonder if I'll still be here when the first drops fall from the sky. I imagine thirsty leaves turning upward, quavering with anticipation to catch the first plump droplets. When they overflow and roll off, they'll bead up on an earth still too dry to receive them. Small pools will form, and the cracked soil will yield, softening, allowing the water to penetrate. The thought of it quenching the land is soothing, in the way that I want to soothe the fire in my spine. Well, a month might as well be an eternity. How much more of this can I take? That rain might never fall for me.

I close my eyes and let the sensation of the sun's heat take me over, trying to focus on anything besides my burning spine. The memory of the old shaman arises, her weathered face illuminated by firelight a world away from here. I recall her words that night: *If you do not do this, the pain they will inflict on you will only grow worse.*

I shudder at the thought. I'm doing everything I can to appease them.

Sweat rolls down my neck and onto my bare chest. My shirt, still stained with blood, lies crumpled at my feet. I remember the pool of blood spreading on the ground, shockingly red in the midday sun. The smooth feel of the wooden shaft of the blade in my hand. The prayers and chants uttered in languages unintelligible to me. Under the hot African sun, the deed had been done.

You are in the fold now, on the inside, the old woman had said, *and as such, you are beholden to the customs of the people.*

A bolt of lightning crackles through my spine. My entire body convulses in response. *Christ, it's bad!* I wince and ride it out with gritted teeth, clutching the chair. *It's not supposed to be like this.* I'm following their instructions. Why are they still torturing me like this?

From within me, the familiar voice of doubt and self-criticism chimes up. *Idiot. You deserve to die in Africa.* What the hell am I doing here? I've staked so much on this journey. Was the life I left behind *that* bad? Sure, I had thoughts of ending it all before; at times, it seemed the only way to be free of this curse. But wasn't there still so much good in my life, too?

I remember one late summer night at home, sprawled out on the lawn behind our house in the mountains. The pain was coursing through my body as I gazed at the stars overhead. *Oh, the stars!* Too infinite to grasp, too numerous to comprehend. I had the almost casual thought that I could slip away into that inky blackness and leave this torment behind. People would understand, I was certain. I was only a burden to them anyway, unlovable, surely, in my wretched state of never-ending anguish. I wouldn't be missed for long. They'd go about their lives like they had before.

The ease with which these thoughts arose that night jolted me: *No, no, NO! How could you?!* I remembered a time before the curse began. I had dreams then, and an insatiable vigor for life. What became of that young man? If I ended it all, those dreams would never come to fruition. The vision I once had for my art and music, left to wither on the vine. But what if there truly *was* a way to end this nightmare? How could I not at least try?

My awareness drifts back to the path set before me by an old shaman and a council of elders. I must complete all the tasks to have any hope of redemption. If I fail, the consequences are unthinkable.

I let out a deep breath and prepare myself for what is next. I must still reckon with the blacksmith's wife—if I can find her, that is, if even she is still alive. I pray she is, though the thought of facing her terrifies me. The old blacksmith himself died some years before. I had taken a photograph of him dancing in the *numuw* festival, the dance of the blacksmiths. In the old days, the blacksmiths were reputed to be sorcerers, and Sako Gbè was no exception. Sako "the Pure," they called him. He was from the old tradition, a leader of the secret societies. He *knew* things—mysterious things, perhaps even dark things. Back home in my art studio, I had captured his likeness in paint. I remember the way his image came to life on my easel, how his painted eyes had looked back at me. What secrets did those eyes keep? Shortly after, old Sako Gbè left this world to rejoin the world of his ancestors, those spirits who oversee the world of the living. The ancestors are a bridge between the realms of death and life. It is *them* I must ultimately contend with.

The ancestors are not to be fooled with, the shaman had said. *It would have been much better for you if this man was still alive.*

Somewhere on the outskirts of the village, I am told, Sako's wife is still alive. She is my last remaining hope, and now I *have* to find her. What will the encounter with the old sorceress be like? I never knew her, but my mind conjures an image of a formidable African woman, sitting on the dirt floor of a small hut. Her face deep with lines, like a road map of her years carved into her ebony skin. Around her, there would be jars of herbs and potions, collections of amulets and horns, beaks and feathers, bones and strange powders. All part of her magic, her *gris-gris.* I picture her dark eyes piercing my soul, scrutinizing my worthiness. I would be a strange apparition to her eyes, with my pale skin reddening beneath a hostile sun, a weathered fedora shading a brow furrowed by worry. What would she think of this man who had left his culture and ventured too close to their secrets? I had crossed a line, and now I was in trouble. Would she help this outsider? Would she have the power to release me from this curse?

If only there was some way out of it, I think, though I know such thoughts are futile now. But still, for a moment, I long for my old life, the *normal* one with a house and a yard and a proper bed to sleep in. I think wistfully about the forest path that leads to my beloved mountains. My family, who pleaded with me not to come here. Friends who are carrying on without me, and the one I couldn't save.

And of course, there is Kerri. The love I took for granted. A lump rises in my throat, and I strain to hold back unwanted tears. An empty house is all that remains of the home that once held so many dreams.

The images of that old life recede, like a curtain closing on a play in which I once had a part. The characters onstage hadn't understood, perhaps couldn't. They wanted an ordinary life for me, to save me from my reckless adventures. But life had led me down the path of the extraordinary, and I couldn't turn my back on it. Not then, and not now. I will have to take this journey to whatever end. Perhaps some unknowable magic will lift this curse and reveal the cure. Or maybe Africa will finally claim me—and then, too, I will be free from this pain.

Time is running out.

One way or another, I sense that I will not see the return of the rains in Africa.

Almost unconsciously, I reach into my pocket for the small plastic container. I listen for the familiar rattle inside. *Good,* I think, *there are still some left.* I've long since depleted my rations of the dried, powdered leaves I used to numb the agony in my spine. While it lasted, the soothing tea made from that green powder had helped keep the dragon at bay. Now, only the pills remain. I dump two of them into my dirty palm, and stare at the shapes. Their perfect round whiteness is out of place here, so unnatural. I hate the pills, and myself for taking them.

I can't go on this way forever. I have to stop…

My attacker lashes at me, catching me off guard. My torso contorts and a moan escapes me unbidden.

Oh, fuck it. The pain decides it. I wash the pills down with some tepid water and wait for the chemical endorphins that will soon flood my body, allowing me to ignore my throbbing joints for a time. Just as importantly, they'll numb the sorrow residing in my heart, the sorrow that collected over the years like a dark pool in a cave, one little drop at a time.

I sit waiting for some blessed relief as the sun climbs. The heat rises off the baked earth in waves. At least the forest path between villages will offer some shade.

A sound puts me on alert: the shuffling of feet from behind me. From inside the hut, a familiar voice calls out, searching.

"Daouda?" It's Lanciné. "*T'es là?*" He's looking for me.

I pull myself together. *"Oui, Lanciné, j'arrive,"* I respond, my voice cracking. "I'm coming." I try to sound confident, but I wish I had just a few more moments to myself. I close my eyes, my fears and doubts buzzing around me like a swarm of angry bees.

"Daouda, *il faut y aller.* It is time to go. *Maintenant."* There is urgency in his voice.

I can't linger any longer. With a deep breath, I stand shakily, turn the corner, and approach the hut. I brush aside the curtain that hangs from the narrow door frame, and enter.

Inside, the temperature is cooler by several degrees, and dim enough that I have to pause to let my eyes adjust. The interior is sparse and dusty. On my left is the small table that holds the few items we use at mealtime: two spoons, two mugs, the thermos for hot water, a canister of instant coffee. The plastic bowl, almost always filled with rice, is now covered with a towel to keep the flies off. Two steps further is the wooden frame with the clumpy straw mattress reserved for me. After months of agonizing tossing and turning, however, I've taken to sleeping on the dirt floor, trying hard not to wake anyone with my groans. A thin cot flanks the opposite wall. Two plastic chairs face each other in the center of the room, a contrast to the ancient-looking wooden flutes that lie beside them, each decorated with strips of leather and cowry shells. Against the far wall is the small, black portfolio case that carries my drawings. This is home, for now.

Lanciné stands in the opposite doorway, his tall frame silhouetted against the thin curtain that barely filters the sunlight. In the afternoons, when a breeze blows, we pull the curtains aside at either end of the hut, allowing for a pleasant cross-draft to ease the stifling heat. Today, there is no breeze.

Lanciné is silent, unmoving. The woven straw fedora he's taken to wearing recently is cocked to one side, and his calm temperament makes me all the more aware of the wild tempest that rages inside me. His stature too, strong and almost imposing, is a contrast to my frailty. I carry the weight of my curse on my back, and that burden pushes my posture ever downward into a hunch I can no longer hide.

My eyes adjust to the light, and I catch Lanciné's gaze. Like always, he's studying me, ever trying to make sense of me and the strange world I come from. Over the years, we've formed an unlikely relationship that is something like brotherhood: he the big brother and I the little brother. The master of the *tambin*, the three-holed Malinké flute, and his devoted apprentice from a world away. My quest of healing now forces us to reckon with our differences, our beliefs, our identities. I am challenging to him, with all of my questions, all of my *whys*. The trip has stretched our friendship to its breaking point—but still, something else unites us. He committed to helping me and has been unwavering thus far. Perhaps he seeks his redemption, either here on this Earth or in the ʾ*ākhirah*, the afterlife. Whatever his reasons, I am grateful. Without him, I would not have survived in this strange, often hostile landscape—and we both know it.

I hesitate before collecting my gear.

"And what about Famoudou?" I ask. "Has there been any word?" I've been awaiting the old master's arrival in the village for two months now. The waiting has been torturous. My respect for the old man borders on reverence, and it's not just because he bears the title of *djembefola*, one who makes the djembé speak. He too had been my teacher for more than a decade, but time has altered that relationship, deepened it. Bonds of family are unexpected motivators now, and I need him here.

I picture the soft creases in Famoudou's weathered face, the kindness in his bright, playful eyes when we last saw each other.

I shall see you again before the rains come, he had said to me then. *You will wait for me in the village.*

He gave instructions, and I followed them diligently. I am not to undertake the final steps without him. But the months that have passed without word have made me nervous: the trip here is long, filled with many dangers, and he would be traveling alone. I worry for his safety. And if the old man doesn't make it, all will be for naught.

Lanciné pauses before responding. "I have no news about Famoudou. But we must go on. You remember we agreed—"

I hold up my hand and cut him off, suddenly annoyed.

"I know what we agreed, Lanciné." I don't like it, but I can ask no more of him. Without Famoudou here, my tasks are more daunting. I need his encouragement, his guidance. I want assurance I am doing the right thing. But I know that Lanciné is right: time has run out. We must go on without him.

Lanciné just nods, assessing me. Both the pain and the narcotic medication cause my mood to shift unexpectedly like a gust of wind kicking up the harsh sands of the harmattan.

"Do you have the book?" he asks.

"It's in my backpack."

My doubts surface again. Can I get out of what I have to do next? The question is absurd, though my mind still searches for an answer.

I muster up my resolve. *Courage.* That simple word. In Malinké, they say, *Kewó jusôo nánta benná le:* One's heart must be courageous. It's like a mantra to the people here. Life is hard. The strong keep going, one day into the next.

When this is all over…I'll stop taking the pills. I promise. But not now.

"*An nye wa,*" Lanciné says, switching now to Malinké. *Let's go.*

I brace myself against the pain, and sling my pack onto my back with a grimace. I feel the weight of the book inside. Before turning to go, I pick up the small black portfolio case. I have to guard it now. The drawings are all I have left.

With a deep breath, I walk out of the hut and into the bright sunlight. There is no turning back now.

2

THE CASTLES OF YOUTH

SOME MEMORIES ARE VAGUE NOW. I try to recall the chain of events that led me here, to a village in West Africa where I limp along a dirt path with a man named Lanciné. Certain details bring the memories into focus: in my backpack, I carry a book infused with ancient magic. The portfolio case in my hand contains artwork of immeasurable value to me. But most of all, it is the pain that reminds me why I'm here. Though the invisible enemy is now a constant, I remember a time when it wasn't there.

The memories drift closer, like a familiar melody playing somewhere in the distance. I strain to hear the song, and try to recall that person who was me, who must have been me, though he might as well have been someone else. But I have proof. In a box somewhere, old Polaroids and Kodak prints show a younger man who was still healthy, hiking in the mountains of Virginia or Vermont, or perched on a rocky cliff somewhere in New Mexico or California. The photos reveal the wildness within him. He was always searching for the next adventure. Pushing the limits. Tempting fate. If I could step into those photographs and warn that kid of all that was to come, of the pain and heartache his adventures would cause, would he still go on? Probably. Because he was bold. Unafraid. He would have said that he could take whatever came. *Bring it,* he would have growled with a devilish grin, a glint in his eye.

Naïve as he may have been, life was fresh and exciting for that kid—for me—in my teens and early twenties. Before the *curse*. The whole world was outside my door, waiting to be explored. I remember the simple thrill of being alive, the rush of the open road, and having nowhere and everywhere to go. Life was exhilarating, and the possibilities were endless.

One of my best friends growing up was a guy named Erik, who was even wilder than me. He was the leader of our gang of misfits, an unruly group bound together by deep friendship and an unspoken pact: we were rebels, and would never succumb to the trappings of the modern world. So we pushed the boundaries. We skipped school to go surfing, and posited existential theories while balanced on surfboards. We experimented with substances and explored the untapped regions of the mind. We got into all manner of mischief too, but always in the name of our righteous cause of saving the world from its shortsightedness. Erik was the ringleader, all right, and his boundless energy and unbridled enthusiasm were hard to keep up with sometimes. When Erik got an idea in his head, he couldn't be stopped. Despite his reckless behavior and affinity for mind-altering substances, I never had to worry about Erik. He was a superhero. And he was invincible.

Erik's motto was direct and memorable: "Fuck the dumb shit." Crude as it was, the mantra encapsulated our desire to differentiate between the "made-up" priorities of society and the "real" experiences of life—and to give precedence to the latter. It was a face-off between daring and safe, exhilarating versus mundane.

In high school, my conversations with Erik would sometimes go like this:

"Erik, you gonna finish that paper tonight?"

"Nah, fuck the dumb shit. Let's go surfing."

I didn't need a lot of convincing. Sometimes it would be a whole crew of us, or sometimes just Erik and me, but we'd cruise full tilt down the highway toward the ocean, leaving a trail of weed smoke behind us. Erik was always the first one suited up and in the water, the first to catch a sweet wave, and the last one out, even after it was full dark. It was thus that he earned the nickname, *Salty Dog*.

"Hey Salty Dog, ocean's flat today. You gonna study for tomorrow's SATs?"

"Nah, fuck the dumb shit. Let's drop acid and stay up all night."

Me, I was somewhere between recklessly spontaneous and minimally responsible. I wasn't ready to throw *all* caution to the wind and sabotage my future. That's not to say Erik didn't think about life after graduation. On the contrary, he was already planning to literally ride into his future on his most formidable talent: after high school, he was headed west to train with the U.S. Olympic ski team. He was a badass skier in those days. Although I had abundant artistic talents and liked to write, I was unsure what I'd actually do next. So instead of blowing off the SATs, I did the responsible thing and showed up for the test on time —still tripping on the prior night's hallucinogens. I hadn't slept yet. Nonetheless, with my brain all lit up by LSD, I finished the test in record time and scored high enough to earn a partial scholarship to the college of my choice. Plus, I wouldn't have to take any of the boring prerequisite courses once I got there. I would make art full-time. Fuck the dumb shit, indeed.

Despite doing well in school, it was no joy for me. I craved raw experiences to satisfy the burning curiosity that drove me. The educational system hadn't managed to squelch that flame; by the time I headed off for college, a roaring fire of passion blazed within me. I was ready for my real education to begin. I sought experiences, and mentors to guide me to the good stuff. But in the end, I wouldn't find what I needed in the halls of academia. Something else called to me, a wild voice that sang to my heart. I had to follow.

My schedule in art school was flexible, and my professors gave me the freedom to come and go as I pleased, as long as I produced good work, on time. I did. When I wasn't painting, I climbed mountains and slept beneath the stars. I woke to heavenly vistas, and pondered my own flittering existence, tiny and exposed beneath the universe. As these excursions became more frequent, their durations lengthened. I needed time to explore the seed growing within me, and only in the absolute silence of a morning on a windswept summit could I fully engage with the voice in my heart. But I was never alone. My trekking backpack always had room for a few books, and thus my companions on those traverses were a diverse bunch: J. Krishnamurti, Gary Snyder, Lao Tzu, Khalil Gibran, Thich Nhat Hanh, Black Elk, and John Lame Deer. They shed light on my experience of the world, helped make sense of it.

In the summers, I was free to ramble further. The world was opening up to me. I always had friends along the way, kindred spirits who shared the same vigor for life, and who just might have a couch to crash on. I'd check around to see who was up for a wild adventure, and who could take off at a moment's notice. *Who's got a car? Hop in, let's go!* And the miles would pass almost unnoticed, the windows down and the scenery zipping by, until we reached wherever we were going, which was usually no place in particular.

I roamed the country, fancying myself a mystic vagabond poet of days past. I dreamt of seeing the world in its purest form—and shunned the middle-class white existence I was born into. I was sure that some cosmic mistake had been made. Surely, I was supposed to have been born Navajo or Hopi, Zulu or Maasai, maybe Quechua or Aborigine— anything but the descendant of white European conquerors, those agents of Manifest Destiny. I wanted nothing to do with the legacy of the West. The history that had transpired in my country horrified me: native lands stolen, buffalo slaughtered, cultures destroyed. My white- ness linked me to that history. My middle-class privilege had been bought with the lives of native peoples, and further paid for by the turmoil of Africans stolen from their homeland.

Freedom was bittersweet. Though free to roam wherever I chose, I had no identity of my own. I rejected the offerings of the modern world on philosophical grounds, but in reality, I couldn't escape them. I was modern. And it was terrible.

So in the bookstores and libraries of small-town America, I sought to learn everything I could about the indigenous peoples of the world. Undoubtedly, I thought, these cultures were the continuation of the branch of humanity that *hadn't* gotten off track. Learning about their legacy just might open a door into a larger human identity to which I could connect, and feel proud.

Looking back, the native peoples I found in books lacked any real context. At that age, I had only a superficial understanding of the varied ways of life represented there. But still, it was more than a fanciful look back at what humanity once was—it was a look ahead to what humanity could be. A different orientation within the world was possible, and a worldview could be malleable and evolving. These ideas were a complete contradiction, and refreshingly so, to the absolutism of my Roman Catholic upbringing.

As I grew older, I knew I needed a new worldview to help me navigate the rest of my time on Earth. I didn't know *what* that worldview was, or how to find it. But in light of the increasingly shaky ground of my inner foundations, I had little recourse. I would have to first deconstruct, then rebuild that foundation, one brick at a time. I didn't suppose I'd find a manual on how to do this. But *hey-ho, here we go!*—it was an inner romp through the uncharted wilds of mind and spirit to rival the outer adventures I was already having.

Naturally, I found it difficult to function in society while the process was ongoing. I probably should have worn a sign on my back: *Pardon the mess! Renovations in progress!* Was I a freak, wandering around the country with a backpack full of books? Perhaps. If so, I was utterly harmless; I mean, the only possible threat I posed was to the epistemological foundations of Western culture itself. Ha! But who would suspect it? I was always smiling and friendly, and in any case, I was disassembled and embarrassingly imperfect, which rendered whatever tiny intellectual hand grenade I held quite null. Plus, I had no idea where I *belonged*—and for a young man in the springtime of his life, these were bigger problems.

But these weren't all dark times. The curse of pain had not yet been cast on me. Africa was still a place that had nothing to do with me, or I with it. Though I was stumbling through that embarrassingly self-conscious state of post-adolescence, life held so much promise. I was young after all, and there was love. Oh, sweet love, that divine nectar, so delightfully intoxicating!

My first real love was with a fellow art student named Camille. In truth, I didn't think much of her when we first met. She was skinny and gangly and maybe a little tomboyish. We were practically kids, still finding ourselves, and we were both more than a little awkward. But

Camille had a vision for her future, as well as for her art. She was serious about it, and maybe it started to rub off on me. While I bumbled around the country trying to find my identity, Camille was finishing her art degree and already making a name for herself. She had a plan to get somewhere, and I suspected it might be better than the nowhere I was currently headed.

Then, one day something else changed in my perception of her. Maybe it was the way she leaned back and laughed, or the way the light caught her long hair as it cascaded down her slender back. Suddenly, she was something else: a Woman. Divinely Feminine. And the first time we leaned in to kiss, her scent, her breath, the way my trembling hands found the small of her back, and ventured nervously to the swell of her petite breasts, all sent my heart pounding through my chest. The world melted away when we were together. When we weren't, I gushed poems about the virtues of love onto pages of home-made journals. With my reckless heart wide open—dear God help me —I was all in.

～

During that time, another maiden had set her sights on me. Unbeknownst to me, she was casting her net. Her name was Africa.

It started with an event whose future significance I could not have guessed. But now, decades later, as I walk painfully with Lanciné through his village, I know that history binds us to our fate in strange ways.

As a Fine Arts student, I wavered between various disciplines. I thought I'd either major in Painting, or take the more practical path, Illustration. Seriously, what does one actually *do* with a *Painting* degree, I wondered? And then there was music, my other lifelong passion. I grew up playing music, and in college, I earned my pocket cash playing guitar and singing in local coffee shops. Since I had plenty of room in my schedule for elective courses, I filled it with jazz theory and improv classes, and started developing some halfway decent guitar chops. When it came time to choose a major, however, I settled on the Illustra-tion program, thinking it was a sound bet. This proved to be fortuitous.

In my sophomore year, a friend in the Anthropology program pulled me aside.

"Hey Dave, the head of the Anthropology Department just announced an internship open only to Illustration majors. He asked me if I knew anyone that might want to apply. I thought of you."

"Oh yeah?" My interest was piqued. An internship would impress Camille, and show her I could actually do something serious. "What's the deal?" I asked.

"The guy is leading a dig on the coast of West Africa. Somewhere in Ghana, I think. He's writing a textbook. *Smithsonian's* gonna publish it. He needs illustrators to crank out drawings—maps, artifacts, stuff like that. I could put a good word in for you if you're interested."

Seemed cool. Why not? I met with the esteemed professor, and showed him my portfolio. Without much fanfare, I got the internship. Africa began to pull in her net.

The subject of the book was a village on the Gold Coast of Ghana. To this day, a strange castle looms over this village, casting its ominous shadow from its perch high above the pounding surf of the Atlantic Ocean. *Castelo de São Jorge da Mina*, or St. George of the Mine Castle, was constructed by the Portuguese in the late 1400s. Back then, it was known simply as *Mina*, in the town that later became Elmina. For the Portuguese, the fortress was the heart of a lucrative gold trade in West Africa, but its use was destined to change.

The professor was passionate about the place. Maps, sketches, and notes littered his desk as we spoke about the internship in detail.

"You see, before the Portuguese arrived," he explained, "the area was populated by native fishing and farming communities. When the Portuguese announced their plans for a fortress, the locals were not pleased. Actually, they were pretty pissed off."

He leaned back in his cushy office chair and stroked his short beard. His third-story office smelled like old books and had a view of the whole campus. I was less drawn to the air of prestige he exuded than to the fact that this guy had been places I hadn't yet dreamt of going. I wondered if he was some kind of Indiana Jones, exploring the jungles of Africa when he wasn't in the halls of academia. The image appealed to me.

"The big problem for the locals," he went on, "was that the Portuguese planned to quarry the stone for the castle from a local sacred site. Not good. The Portuguese offered gifts and promises, but the villagers were still reluctant. So the Portuguese resorted to thinly veiled threats."

The professor mimed holding a rifle up, and pointed it straight at me. I got his point.

"The chief was in a tight spot. Conflict would be disastrous for the village. He reluctantly agreed to allow the quarrying to proceed. The Portuguese wasted no time. A fleet of twelve ships was already waiting offshore, carrying supplies for construction of the fort. None other than Christopher Columbus stepped ashore."

As the professor spoke, a new side of history unfolded before me. This wasn't the boring stuff we learned in social studies class. I was on the edge of my chair, aligning his words with the artifacts and scribbled notes all around us.

"When construction began, the gifts promised to the villagers were never delivered." He saw my expression change, and laughed heartily. "What, you weren't surprised, were you? Yes, the Portuguese went back on their word—and proceeded to destroy all the homes standing in the path of the fort. The angry residents waged an attack, killing several Portuguese. The Portuguese, not to be outdone, burned the entire village in retaliation."

Such were the beginnings of the first European fort in Sub-Saharan Africa. I asked him to tell me more, though I suspected the situation would not improve for the locals. He could see I was hanging on his every word.

"It didn't take long before the Dutch began to eye the castle. Its location offered access to a region renowned for its gold. If the coast could be controlled, the riches were immeasurable—and could fuel the expansion of an empire."

The professor thought for a moment, searching for a date. He fumbled through the chaos of papers on his desk.

"It was...let's see. 1637, I believe. After two decades of fighting, the Dutch finally overtook the Portuguese, and seized the castle. They made Elmina the capital of what was renamed the *Dutch Gold Coast*. But the name became a misnomer. Empire building required labor, and slaves proved to be more lucrative than gold. Elmina Castle ultimately became one of the most important stops in the trans-Atlantic slave trade, and changed the world forever."

He let his words sink in, and I understood now the historical importance of the castle. During the internship that followed, I learned how the castle held slaves captured from other kingdoms in West Africa. As I worked on drawings and site maps under his guidance, I became familiar with the castle's layout. Slaves were loaded onto ships through the infamous "Door of No Return." The holding areas were nothing short of dungeons. The windowless fortresses held up to fifteen hundred slaves at a time. Lacking sanitation or water, slaves stood shoulder-to-shoulder in pitch-black spaces that filled with their own waste. Slaves waited in these conditions for up to three months until a ship arrived to transport them across the dreaded Middle Passage of the Atlantic, to their final destination in the New World. Present-day visitors to the remains of the castle can see marks on the walls from prisoners attempting to claw their way out. Above the dungeons, luxurious chambers for the officers and governor, replete with parquet floors, overlook the scenic coastline.

During the internship, I thought about Elmina night and day. I read research papers and articles, and talked to the professor until I became somewhat of an expert myself. I spoke to my friends about it, and told them stories. It was a history that, prior, we had all only known in vague terms.

During the peak of the slave trade, an estimated thirty thousand slaves a year moved through Elmina Castle. It was the epicenter of an enormous global system of supply and demand. The demand was for a labor force to support the growth of empires elsewhere; the supply was found in the peoples of West Africa, where opportunistic bands of traders from hostile tribes were willing to profit from providing that supply. It was a dirty affair all around, and one that is hard to deconstruct even today.

In Elmina, the castle's use as a slave fortress continued until the abolition of the trans-Atlantic slave trade in 1807. When the slave trade ended, the village itself was rebuilt into the thriving town of Elmina.

Even with the slave trade behind them, however, the problems were not yet over for the locals. In 1837, the native Ashanti refused to submit to British colonial rule. From warships situated in the adjacent Benya Lagoon, the British opened fire on Elmina with heavy artillery, leaving it once again in flames. In subsequent fighting, the British killed more than two hundred Ashanti natives, who were armed only with spears.

I remember sitting in my cramped art studio, sifting through photos and artifacts from this once desolate place. The image of the current-day village, with the white-walled castle looming assertively above, was burned into my memory. It was a reminder that the enterprises of slavery and colonialism had left their mark. From them was borne the racism that still haunts us today.

Beyond fanning the flames of my youthful discontent, a peculiar thing happened while working on illustrations for the book: I became enthralled by the people living in Elmina today. The faces of the men and women in the photographs revealed resilience and pride. These were a people who had persevered through unimaginable adversities and remained rooted in their traditions. Perhaps it was even because of those traditions that they persevered. And something else in those photos kept me awake at night, for it was something I sorely lacked: an *identity*.

Though not in the scope of my internship, I pulled out my oil paints and set about to stretch a canvas. A particular image jumped out at me. It was of two Ghanaian women, adorned with colorful headdresses. The vibrant colors of their traditional *kente* cloth were a striking contrast against their dark skin. Ignoring my deadlines, I painted feverishly into the night. The portrait leapt from the canvas. Broad brush strokes conveyed the richness of emotions I saw in them: in their eyes, a light shone. Was it joy? Yes, there it was, *joy*, amidst even their poverty. How was this possible? I lived in the wealthiest nation on Earth. But at that moment, I would have traded it all for the richness of joy in those eyes. I felt poor in comparison.

In hindsight, this painting—my first portrait of African peoples—was the first glow of an ember that would burn slowly for many years. Its first real flames wouldn't emerge until...when? Ah, but wait, I still had to finish the internship. I showed the painting to the professor. He too was excited, and freed me from the chore of rendering ceramic fragments in black ink. He set me instead to the mission of re-creating, in full color, the village as it would have appeared before its destruction by the British. I set about the task with newfound vigor, performing my research with the diligence of an anthropologist.

Combining archeological evidence with photographs of modern Ghanaians, I painted, this time in watercolor, a scene that depicted the imposing white castle above a bustling African village. I was proud of the resulting painting, and there was talk of using it for the book's cover. Imagine my excitement! I was a second-year art student who had stumbled into a lowly internship. I now had the opportunity to have a published work, via the *Smithsonian* no less. Camille was proud of me, and I beamed with accomplishment.

But it was not to be. The professor's disgruntled secretary pulled me aside one day.

"You know the museum has offered the professor a generous stipend for the book cover, right? Is he even paying you for this?"

The blood ran from my face. I hadn't considered it.

"He's taking you for a ride. You should ask to get paid."

My internship was academic, of course, but it had veered from its initial scope. Broke and hungry, I confronted the professor. The completed painting already leaned against his oversized desk. The professor scoffed at the suggestion, leaning back in his chair and putting his feet up on the desk. I eyed his fancy leather boots, which probably cost more than a whole month's rent for me. He would offer me no money. My pride swelled, and the old fiery rebellion flared up. I refused to let him use the painting. My internship ended abruptly as I walked out of his office with the painting under my arm.

I stormed back to Camille's apartment, still indignant about the injustice of it all. She was just returning from class, and I told her what happened.

"Seriously, can you *believe* this guy?" I asked. "I mean, who does he think he is?" Camille shook her head woefully, and I knew she'd be proud that I had stood up to him. I folded my arms and awaited her commiseration.

"I love you man, but you're a fucking idiot. Don't be stupid. Just let him use the damn painting."

I was shocked, and hurt. We fought about it, but in the end, I knew she was probably right. But what was done, was done. I wasn't about to crawl back to the professor and beg for forgiveness.

Needless to say, the book was published without me (and with an inferior cover, if I may say so). I sold the painting for a hundred bucks—a small fortune for me at the time—and I victoriously stocked up on ramen noodles and beer. I sure showed him!

Life went on. I soon forgot the incident, and the specter of Elmina Castle faded into memory. But fate was still at work, and Africa would not be done with me so easily.

Life shifted my attention elsewhere. Love continued to blossom with Camille, though my disillusionment with college, and with society in general, grew rapidly. These two forces—love and discontent—pulled at each other. I had decisions to make. Two weeks into my junior year, the fire inside me became too great to contain. I marched into my academic advisor's office and hastily signed the paperwork declaring my intention to drop out. The ink was barely dry before I was off on another adventure, liberated to pursue life on my own terms. I was twenty-two. I never looked back.

Erik's future hadn't gone quite to plan, either. While training for the Olympics, his substance use turned to abuse and got out of control. Finally, an injury dashed his hopes for an Olympic appearance. But Erik still had other ideas, and as always, he wasn't about to let a setback slow him down. Fuck the dumb shit, right?

Erik had taken a strong interest in organic farming and permaculture, seeing in it the possibility of escaping the trappings of modern society. Plus, his family had a few hundred acres of unused farmland in upstate New York. The property was north of the Adirondacks, a stone's throw from the Canadian border. It was an ideal hideout. Erik set about learning everything he could about organic farming, with the goal of starting his own farm. He took out agricultural loans, secured a few grants, and purchased tractors and equipment. His project was ambitious, and he needed help doing it. He recruited a couple of friends to live and work there. Since my own future was uncertain, I signed on as a farmhand and moved north, visiting Camille on the weekends.

I settled into the farm, working the land by day, and pursuing art and music by night. In the farm's little bunkhouse, I spent hours every evening composing songs on my guitar, and drawing in the quiet hours. In the absolute tranquility of north country nights, I filled sketchbooks and then put them aside to start new ones. I started a small counter-culture magazine for which I was the sole writer. In the woods behind the farm's crop fields, we grew an abundance of fresh marijuana. After a long day's work of planting, tilling, and harvesting, our wine glasses were always full. Oh, how the creativity flowed! These were just like the good ol' days again, with Erik at the helm. We channeled our fiery discontent into our projects. Erik and I had big plans to change the world.

After each growing season, we'd go our separate ways for the winter. Erik went off traveling to this place or that, seeking new and ever wilder adventures. I eventually moved in with Camille. She had become as fiery and passionate as me, though she was funneling it into her art. It would prove to be a hard mix. After two stormy years of an on again, off again relationship, things came to a head. While driving across the country, our disparate views were a powder charge that eventually ignited. One chilly, clear night in the desert of New Mexico, a full moon bathed our campsite with light. It should have been beautiful, but instead we pelted each other with angry words. I was frustrated, lost, and envious of her direction in life. She had wearied of my impulsive temperament. We decided to part ways. When she drove off the next morning at first light, her tires kicked up a great cloud of dust that resembled a sand storm. I was quite alone in a barren landscape, and as I hitched my way back to civilization, I knew we would not see each other again.

My fire had burned out of control, and the damage was done. My heartbreak was absolute. I had failed at love, and that was unacceptable. I now filled my diaries with laments, scores of poems both sad and beautiful, the ink smeared by my tears. When all the tears had fallen, I turned defiant, vowing to build a fortress—my own Elmina Castle of the heart. Only it was *me* who became its prisoner. *I don't need her,* I thought. *I don't need anyone.* This became my new truth. Over time, I learned to wield this new independence with ferocity. I could do anything, and I could do it alone. I built walls to shield myself from the pain of love, from the rupture of being a flawed human who didn't belong anywhere, and from a cold world that had no place for the likes of me anyway.

Though other feeble attempts at relationships came and went, I sincerely doubted I could be loved in my current state of imperfection. I had hard work to do to correct what I was sure were glaring flaws, and to render myself a human worthy of love. In the meantime, my heart would need to remain closed.

Back at the farm the next year, Erik introduced me to his latest passion.

"Behold, nature's gift," he declared. "You're going to like this."

He held out a container filled with tiny seeds.

"Poppy seeds?" I asked.

"Not just any poppy seeds. These are from Afghanistan." He flashed his trademark grin. "We're gonna grow opium."

Over the winter, he had developed a taste for smoking the resin that oozes from that beautiful and beguiling flower—and by midsummer when our first harvest was ready, I did too.

Our days on the farm now passed in an opium-induced haze. In the evening, we sliced the flower pods with a sharp razor. In the morning, we had only to scrape the resin. A whole field of poppies was at our disposal. It was medicine for my troubled heart. I had neither love nor an identity, and I was disconnected from a sense of community. But I had learned how to numb the resulting discord.

3

MEETING AFRICA

I PULL myself out of remembrance, and glance down at my feet. A shadow flickers across the path as a bird passes overhead. The sun is white-hot and blinding, and my spine is on fire.

Lanciné turns to look at me over his shoulder. My limp is making it hard to keep up with him, and he slows his pace. We pass beneath the *bandan* tree at the center of the village, and dry branches rattle above me like bones. The sound makes me think about ancestor spirits. The words of the shaman echo in my head.

The ancestors are never far away. Your work in Africa has brought you very close to them. You have penetrated the surface. They have noticed.

Lanciné urges me on. We have a lot of distance to cover, and I hope the painkillers will kick in before we reach *la brousse*, the wild territory. The walk through it will be slow and arduous. Beyond there, we'll come to the village of the late Sako Gbè.

As we walk, I feel the scars of my past. I think back to the rugged coast where Elmina Castle still stands like a sentinel of the dark past. It is hard to forget that place, for it is where the curse began.

∾

When I first stepped onto African soil in August 2001, I had no sense of the tumultuous romance that lay ahead. Africa confounds me. When I'm with her, Africa charms me with her beauty and grace, and I must paint her. When I'm not with her, I dream of her heat and sensuality, the coolness of her dark gaze, and I long to go back to her. But Africa is a seductress and a deceiver. When she turns hostile, she is a dangerous battleground of war and poverty from which I must escape. But never for long. Her magic spell always pulls me to her. I apologize for ever having left, and beg her to take me back.

In hindsight, returning from my first trip to Africa in a wheelchair should have clued me in to the danger that lay ahead. But I was too enamored to see it. Africa had something I needed, and that need blinded me. *But I was young! I was just a child!* I insist. To which she replies, *You knew what you were getting into. Don't deny this is what you always wanted.*

And so, I suppose it was.

The small New England town I grew up in was, culturally speaking, about as flavorful as the Wonder Bread that lined the shelves of its Market Basket grocery store. By the time I left college and was coming of age, as they say, the town was a cluster of generic shopping centers and chain stores, the neatly packaged and cleverly marketed product version of the American dream. A trip to the mall on a Saturday night was about as richly cultural as it got.

So when I caught a glimpse of her again—of Africa, I mean, or at least the thrilling prospect of becoming acquainted with her—I had to meet her. What caught my eye was a listing in a brochure for a West African drumming course in Boston, but it might as well have been a seductive personals ad in the newspaper. I enrolled, got myself spruced up for the big date, and went to meet her.

When I arrived for the class, I was dismayed to find there were no actual Africans. A bit of a letdown, for sure. But oh, there were these *drums!* And we learned these rhythms, real traditional-sounding pieces. Not that I could have distinguished a traditional African rhythm from something that wasn't, any more than I can distinguish a piece of cheese made in Camembert from one made in Vermont—but these rhythms were dynamic, exciting, alive. The drums we played came from

Guinée, a country I knew almost nothing about. The rhythmic patterns lit my brain on fire like never before.

The interweaving of the whole drum ensemble enthralled me. For starters, there was the *djembé*: this is the goblet-shaped hand drum covered with a tightly stretched goat skin. I remember running my hands over the skin for the first time, feeling its soft texture, with the animal's fur still around the rim. There was a wildness to it. I learned to play the tones and slaps that make the *djembé* speak. When my hands danced over this drum, rhythms exploded from it like pure magic.

Add to that the intricate melodies produced by the *dunun*, the three cylindrical bass drums. From low to high, they are the *dununba*, *sangban*, and *kenkeni*. These powerful beauties are covered at both ends with cowhide, and are played with a stick in the right hand. An iron bell is positioned atop each drum, and this is played by the left hand, producing a rhythmic chattering that keeps time for the whole ensemble. The three *dunun* drums work together to create a conversation that is both melodic and rhythmically complex.

The *djembé* and *dunun* drums became my passion. I practiced day and night. I sought out other teachers—musicians from Guinée, Mali, and Senegal—who taught me authentic music, as well as the culture behind it. I attended classes and workshops wherever I could find them, and took private lessons whenever I had the money. I became more of an apprentice than a casual student, and sat in with the African players during advanced dance classes. Those classes pushed me beyond the basics, and I reveled in playing with musicians who had lived and breathed the music their whole lives. I was hooked.

It is said that to really get good at something, teach it. And so I did. I began teaching beginner classes whenever they needed an instructor. Teaching rhythms to a room of twenty or thirty students was transformative for me. I poured my heart and soul into it. And I wanted more.

I organized my own classes up north in the mountains, where I had taken up residence with a bunch of friends in a cabin in the woods. I approached the local college, and began teaching courses through their Adult Education program. I bought drums—lots of them. The classes caught on, and each semester we added more classes to accommodate the growing interest.

It seemed I had a knack for teaching the stuff. The way music is taught in West Africa is different from how we approach it in the West. But as someone who understood both, I could be an intermediary. I absorbed the knowledge from my African teachers and presented it in a way that was accessible to even the most rhythmically challenged middle-aged white ladies (who, much to my chagrin as a twenty-something, represented the majority of my clientele).

Within a year, teaching *djembé* was my full-time job. Group classes were filled to capacity, and I worked with nearly a hundred students every week. Like me, these budding drummers were people who never knew they *needed* these rhythms until they started playing. Once they had a taste, they too were hooked. Schools contacted me, and soon I was presenting workshops to kids. I thought it was a great twist of fate: a college dropout who despised the rigidity of education was now teaching in elementary schools. But I loved being an entertainer, and was always eager to put on a show. I eventually convinced some of the better adult students to join me as assistants. In this way, both the program and the community around it grew.

These were happy times. My brain was constantly on fire with rhythms, rhythms, *rhythms!* My hands grew calluses as thick as leather from playing the *djembé* forty hours a week. And my technique got sharp. While students worked on the *djembé* and *dunun* parts, I was free to explore and improvise. It was like having my own band with which to practice soloing, as long as I kept the group from drifting. At times, the whole rhythm would fall apart; we'd laugh and start it up again, and I'd drill them on the fundamentals. Then, I would tear back into *djembé* solos like my life depended on it. Maybe it did.

It was through these drumming classes that I met a young woman named Kerri. She was one of my very first students, before the program took off. She was pretty and lean, with long brown hair that hung down over muscular shoulders. We took notice of one another immediately, but I had no intention of risking being seen for what I really was—a messy work-in-progress—by getting involved in an actual relationship.

Camille had taught me that I still had work to do, and I hadn't yet finished the job. Besides, I was having a blast being independent and free. But Kerri's outgoing personality made me take to her right away. She came across as fearless, the kind of person who wanted to grab life and soak up its experiences. Just my kind of gal. And she was direct about what she wanted. After a few sessions, she approached me.

"These classes are good, but I learn better in a one-to-one situation. You offer private lessons?" She wasn't fooling me. I played along, suddenly very alert.

"Yeah, I can do private lessons," I said. "I mean, if you're serious about it." She was close enough that her sweet scent reached me. It was mildly intoxicating.

"Oh yeah, I'm serious." She leaned in closer.

"Then I could teach you a lot."

"When do we start?" She smiled, her eyes dancing with light. I wasn't fooling her, either.

"How about this Friday evening?" My heart was beating fast, and I panicked that it was audible from a mile away. *What the hell am I doing?* I wondered. This was unexpected. *She* was unexpected.

She nodded. "Come to my place." I was at least relieved for that, because I was currently couch-surfing without a place of my own. I wasn't ready to admit that.

"Sure, that's cool," I said. "We can work on *djembé* technique and some more challenging rhythms, whatever you like." I was suddenly not sure what I had just done. I was being tricked at my own game.

At the first lesson, we uncorked a bottle of wine and didn't play much music. Thereafter, our weekly "lessons" turned into an excuse to drink red wine and talk late into the night. She loved a good Merlot or a Zinfandel. We talked about music, our love for nature, and the current state of the world. We did play music, too, and as it turned out, she was quite serious about learning, and a natural when it came to drumming. Kerri was soon one of my best students, a feat she pulled off without ever practicing. She just had it.

As we spent more time together, I began to see that this was a woman who was anything but one-dimensional. Kerri had a passion for languages and had backpacked in Central America. She was an avid rock climber, an activity that scared me shitless given that I'm terrified of heights. Since I was already putting my better judgment aside anyway, I let her strap a harness onto me, and I forced myself to scale the sides of cliffs—all the while trying not to embarrass myself by puking from fear. She also sang and played guitar, white-water kayaked, and organized a yearly trip to Nicaragua to do community service projects in Managua along with students at the high school where she taught. So, yeah. Here was a lady who had a thing or two to teach me, and who could push me out of my comfort zone—something I thought few people could do.

A romance ignited, despite the dire warnings from my heart. Soon, it was a five-alarm blaze, and I needed all the help I could get putting it out before I got burned. The scars from my failed relationship with Camille were still too fresh, and the thought of entering the arena of love again scared me. My defenses were only partially built, and vulnerable to this fresh attack. I could go on with the metaphors, really. Suffice it to say, things were most certainly *not* going to plan on my rocky ascent to absolute independence. My protective anchor was coming loose from the rock, and I had no active belayer. I now feared I'd be unable to stop the free fall toward certain doom in the messy shrapnel of love littered at the base of the cliff.

As our relationship progressed, I guarded my heart. I played it safe, letting little drips of love in, and regulated the outflow carefully. In spite of me, however, love found the chinks in the dam, and I suspected that when it blew, I'd drown in the flood. But Kerri was assuring and confident, tender and patient. I somehow knew our paths needed to join, and eventually it became too much effort to resist it. Those efforts had been futile, anyway. Love was a mightier force than I had imagined. I just hoped we were both strong enough for it.

Just a few months into our relationship, we took our first trip to Nicaragua together, and it sealed the deal. The walls of the dam broke free, and instead of drowning, I was swimming in a sea of bliss. I wasn't sure I deserved it, and was hesitant to trust it. But as we rattled down a back road in a crowded bus toward the tiny coastal town of San Juan del Sur, I knew this was the kind of life I wanted—and together, Kerri and I could have it.

◠

Shortly after our return from Central America, Africa contacted me directly, like I always knew she would. When the phone rang, it might as well have been destiny calling.

It was about three in the morning when a befuddled roommate answered the phone. She roused me from my slumber.

"Some guy is asking for you," she said, offering me the receiver. "I can't understand his accent. I thought it was a prank call, so I hung up on him the first time. But he called back."

I put the receiver to my ear, still half asleep.

"Hello?"

"Hello, Dave—I am Nii Tetteh Tettey, from Ghana," he announced. I sat up, full alert. I brought the cordless phone outside so I didn't wake anyone else up.

"Yeaaah," he continued, the phone line echoing from four thousand miles away, "I want talk you some thing." I strained to hear his broken English through the echo.

He had gotten my number from a friend in New York who had heard about my music program. Tetteh, as I came to know him, was building a cultural center a few hours up the coast of Ghana from the capital city of Accra. He envisioned teaching the youth of the area about their own cultural traditions.

"These kids, they only want to be like Americans," he explained. "They no want old traditions. We lose our heritage if that no change. That is why I build culture center."

To fund his cultural center, Tetteh planned on dedicating part of the year to drum and dance workshops for Americans and Europeans. He hoped these workshops would demonstrate to the youth of Ghana that their culture had value to the outside world.

"It sounds like a great idea," I said, not quite sure where the conversation was heading. I was still wrapping my head around the fact that this guy from *Ghana* had called *me* at 3 a.m. to discuss this.

Tetteh was direct. "Dave, you come to Africa." The way he said *Ah-free-ca*, drawing the word out in his thick accent, made my heart race.

"Yeaaah, you come, you stay my house. I teach you. In trade, you help me with culture center."

The phone call didn't last long. It didn't need to. A week later, a package arrived containing a CD of Tetteh's music. I played it in my car as I drove away from the post office. The music was glorious. Until this point, the music I studied was from Mali and Guinée. Tetteh's music featured the softer but no less complex *kpanlogo* drums of the Ga people from Ghana, accompanied by Tetteh's flute and vocals.

I couldn't get enough of his music. It was both exotic yet familiar, like a language I sort of spoke. The thought of going to Africa tantalized me. Was I crazy to even consider it? He seemed credible, but I didn't know much else about this stranger from Ghana.

But this, *this*—it was a bonafide *invitation*. Africa was beckoning. Tetteh and I spoke several more times on the phone. I liked him. But I had to consider the implications. Could I drop everything and go to Africa?

I never doubted I would go, of course, right from that first phone call with Tetteh. What surprised me was the brief conversation with Kerri about it.

"How long will you be gone?" she asked. We were lying in bed, and I turned to look at her as I responded.

"Two months, at least." I figured it would be a solo expedition, since she'd be teaching high school that time of year. But there was something about the way she looked at me, or perhaps it was how the silence hung in the air. In the end, I think maybe I was scared to go alone, and needed her there. In any case, the words slipped out without my brain's explicit consent.

"Will you come with me?"

She didn't hesitate. "Yes."

We hadn't even known each other a year. Like it was meant to be all along, we were going to Africa. The wheels of fate were turning.

Three months later, Kerri and I departed for the African continent.

We touched down in Accra late one night in early August, and the heat hit us like a wave. Outside the Kotoka International Airport, throngs of people made their way through the streets. The smell of wood smoke was thick in the air. Though it was well after midnight local time, vendors sold fried plantains, skewers of meat, and *chichinga* kebabs. Street kids sold bags of water and bottles of Orange Fanta. Strangers tugged at us, asking for money. *Goro boys*, the unofficial porters at the airport, grasped our suitcases. We attempted to maintain control over our possessions amidst utter mayhem. Taxi drivers cajoled us with their favorite catchphrase:

My friend, my friend! For you, a good price!

Once outside, we hauled our luggage and searched for Tetteh in a panic. My only image of him was from the photo on his CD. In the sea of dark faces, we stood out uncomfortably. Unfamiliar eyes probed us. At the main road, cars drove this way and that in a strange symphony of disorder, driving over sidewalks and swerving around each other. *Tro-Tro* drivers yelled out the windows of overcrowded minibuses, honking at goats and pedestrians who scrambled to avoid them.

"Kerri," I said, as a one-armed kid carrying a monkey skipped by, "I have a feeling we're not in Kansas anymore."

I paused for a moment to make sense of it all, wanting to freeze the scene around me, to preserve these first sensations of Africa. But stopping was a bad idea; crowds of people swarmed us immediately. Kerri and I exchanged a bewildered look and laughed. We were in it now.

Keep moving!

We forged our way through the crowds. I was sweating profusely, and breathless from hauling so much stuff. I struggled to find my composure. I tried imagining that I *belonged* here, as if I might fool anyone into thinking I wasn't a foreigner. Fat chance. Outwardly, I was still a scrawny white kid laden with baggage. Inwardly, however, I noticed a change in how I felt. I wasn't just a *traveler*, I thought to myself—I was an *adventurer*. An *explorer*. I suppose it was the start of something like an identity, because the thought made me feel about seven feet tall.

Tetteh materialized like an apparition. We locked eyes for a moment through the crowd. He appeared cool and confident in a woven tunic that hung down over blue jeans, plastic sandals on his feet. A thick gold chain hung around his neck. He was a striking blend of modern and traditional. And he wasn't breaking a sweat, despite it being almost a hundred degrees.

Tetteh stepped forward to greet us, flashing a huge grin that revealed a gold tooth and a generous gap between his two front teeth.

"Welcome to *Ah-free-ca!*" he laughed.

Tetteh drove us away from the city. Cook fires and torches illuminated the rugged coastline of the former Dutch Gold Coast. The night air was sweet and salty, and the ocean glimmered in the moonlight.

Exhaustion gave way to exhilaration. My life's next adventure had begun, as had my relationship with Africa. I didn't know yet that this particular adventure would consume the next two decades of my life. And neither Kerri nor I could have any way of suspecting how much pain and suffering awaited me in Africa.

4

A TEMPEST IN GHANA

WHEN I ARRIVED at Tetteh's house in Ghana, I had not yet acquired the experiences to give the concept of a *curse* any weight whatsoever. It certainly had no part to play in my understanding of illness and healing. For me, these belonged solely to the departments of science and Western medicine, which were obviously infallible.

So when Amaa first proposed it as a possible explanation for the sudden onslaught of my disturbing symptoms, I couldn't support the logic. But nonetheless, I was intrigued. His reasoning, surely, was part of his own integrated view of the world, and as such, went beyond mere superstition. Or did it?

But let me back up.

~

Our first weeks staying in Tetteh's seaside village passed easily, like a sweet dream. The coastal region of Ghana varied between ethereal and substantial. Sandy, palm-fringed paradises gave way to impassable rocky headlands. The surf pounded ceaselessly, and a fine mist hung in the air. From the beach, unpredictable Atlantic currents swirled in an enchanting chaos that revealed sharp rocks beneath the surface; the mischievous rising tide concealed their danger just as quickly.

Inland, Kerri and I explored on foot and by bicycle. Banana and orange trees grew among the twisting limbs of giant ficus, and small farm plots appeared here and there. Over the ocean, the sky presented an impossibly rich shade of blue. The locals wore hand-spun *kente* cloth with orange and red patterns that accentuated the ebony skin beneath it. On the fringe of wild garden plots grew patches of red *Nyameduo*, the aptly named Blood of Jesus Plant. It was all a feast for our eyes, accustomed as we were to the drab gray of New England winters.

Everywhere we went, remnants of the colonial period mingled with the Africa of old. In Accra, large European-style buildings with white-washed walls receded abruptly to ramshackle lean-tos. Roadside *chop-bars* served local cuisine for mere pennies, while upscale restaurants catered to politicians and wealthy tourists. Outside of Accra, traditional round huts became the norm. The roadways in ever-smaller coastal towns were bordered with open gutters, through which sewage ran freely. Along the route, mud-brick buildings housed local enterprises that ranged from hair salons to internet cafés, carpentry workshops to tumbledown supply shacks.

The construction of Tetteh's cultural center was already well underway by the time we arrived. The guest house was nearly finished, and we were staying in one of the rooms on the ground floor. Up the stairs, we had access to a spacious patio overlooking the Atlantic, where we could have our morning coffee while enjoying tropical breezes. Tetteh and his family made us feel right at home.

If a nobler and more charismatic person than Tetteh exists, I have not yet met them. Tetteh had the air of a king. He exuded a confident joy, and was never without a song. He was quick to share a wise anecdote too, even when he was busy organizing people and materials for the new cultural center. Which he usually was. Tetteh was on a mission, and as we found out, he was unstoppable when he set his mind to a goal. While he worked, he sang a particular song that I remember well. Its unforgettably cheery refrain went, "Do some-thing before you die!"

"My philosophy, it is very simple," he explained. "Life is short. One day, each of us, we all go away. No person can know when. You have to make something of you life! You have to *do some-thing*—before you die."

All that remained for the new cultural center was to complete the thatched-roof structures where classes would be held. After raising the frames, Kerri and I were assigned to thatching duty. A dreadlocked Rastafarian named Yanoba was our mentor.

"You take the strands in your hand, like this," he explained, as we balanced on the roof's beams in the blazing afternoon sun. I was struggling to see what Yanoba was doing with his nimble fingers. In a flash, he had woven the strands of grass together into a tight band and tied them off to the mat that was forming beside him.

Yanoba had become our friend over the past weeks. He was funny and free of cares. "Worry" was a state of being that had no apparent use to him. His name, *Ya-no-ba*, literally means "comes and goes." This pretty much summed him up. Like the winds, he was there one day, gone the next. Nobody really knew where he disappeared to, or why he would unexpectedly show up again.

"You see? Very easy," he said, deftly finishing another section of roofing. This thatching work was second nature to him, but it would take me some time. I was having a hard time focusing for other reasons.

As it turned out, Yanoba was equally adept at rolling the giant spliffs that he smoked throughout the day. Between thatching, he produced several of these massive cone-shaped joints, one for each of us. Kerri and I soon fell prone to fits of giggles, as much from the African *ganja* as from the recognition that we were thatching roofs in an African village.

I looked over at Kerri, who had caught on to this thatching business pretty quickly. I felt like I had three thumbs, and they were all getting in the way.

"How are you doing that so easily?" I asked her.

"It's simple. Watch." She spun up another strand. I leaned over to see her fingers. As I did, I teetered on the open beams and glimpsed the ground below us, and the vast ocean sprawling out just beyond. I caught my breath and let out a little gasp.

"Oh my god, we're so high up."

"Dude, no—*you're* high. We're like twelve feet up. Relax." She snickered. She knew I was terrified of heights from our rock-climbing outings. I groaned, which only made Kerri laugh harder. While I gripped the beams, she finished up another section of thatching.

"Show off."

Yanoba joined in. "My friend, enjoy the view from up here! All of Africa reaches out that way. Perhaps one day, you will explore all of it." He spread out his hands, and I viewed the countryside reaching into the horizon. "And there, somewhere across the ocean, is the land from where you come." I looked at the expanse of blue, which eventually melted into sky. Home was a long ways away.

Yanoba turned his attention to the unfinished bundle of grass in my hands, a spliff still dangling from his mouth. He took my hands and guided them until I had finished a bundle of roofing, and exhaled a cloud of smoke.

"Ah, I see," I said, coughing on the wispy remnants of the cloud. "I think I get it now." Once I had it, Yanoba left me to my work, which soon became mindless. We fell into a comfortable silence, and the hours passed like minutes. The roofs progressed rapidly. Tetteh came to check on our progress, and satisfied, returned to other business. As we thatched, I heard him singing:

Do some-thing before you die!

We also became friends with a young man named Amaa, whom I mentioned earlier. Amaa was a talented dancer who had grown up in a traditional family, surrounded by local beliefs and customs. His family was poor and Amaa had suffered in his lifetime. His gentle character sometimes slipped into wistful sadness.

"One day," he said in a voice that was soft and melodic, "I will become a professional dancer. I will leave Ghana and see the world. I will bring home many riches for my family!"

He had the talent and work ethic to do it, too. Each morning, we watched Tetteh's group rehearsing in the courtyard, and Amaa was a standout. His acrobatics were breathtaking, his dancing full of character.

Amaa graciously acted as our personal tour guide, showing us around the village and pointing out details we might have otherwise missed.

"This is the road that leads to the palace of the Mantse, or paramount chief," he said as we strolled through the village. We crossed over a courtyard where women were preparing large kettles of food.

"And here, the women prepare for the upcoming festival of Homowo. The word Homowo means 'jeering at hunger.' A long time ago, a great famine fell over the land, and many people died. Our people prayed to the ancestors. When the rains arrived and the crops began to grow again, the festival of Homowo was created. Today, the festival commemorates the day that hunger was defeated and ridiculed. The rituals performed during Homowo usher in a new season, and we implore the gods for health and good crops."

Amaa shared his numerous opinions on the state of Ghana and the world as he saw it. In doing so, he revealed a modest wisdom. He was worldly in the truest sense: he belonged to the world. Amaa wore his African pride without any sneer of nationalism.

"The current ruler of the traditional Ga state," he explained, "is Nii Amugi II. He has been Mantse since 1965. He is a good man and well loved, but his health is failing. When he dies, we all fear for the power struggle that will occur when a new Mantse is installed." He clucked, and shook his head. "It is like this the world over. Nowadays, it is power and control of wealth that drives politics, and not the well-being of the citizens. To me, the well-being of one is the well-being of us all. It is that simple. How can one man hoard so much when his neighbor is hungry? It makes no sense."

On our daily excursions, Amaa guided us over winding pathways to a truer Africa than can be seen from the roadside. With Amaa as our guide, the village became visible through the eyes of someone steeped in the traditions of his people. Amaa's Africa held an air of mystery— and it wasn't long before some of those mysteries rose to the surface.

One morning, Amaa came to find us. He called us by the Ghanaian names that had recently been bestowed upon us.

"Adotey, Adoleh—come! We go visit some relatives today."

Amaa led us to the place. Upon arriving and greeting his relatives, we entered the house. Wooden statues adorned the interior. Many were decorated with rope or feathers, some with cowry shells. Some had horns, and nails protruded from others, with red paint—or perhaps it was blood? In either case, the effect was vaguely disturbing. Framed portraits of what appeared to be Christian saints hung above the figurines. My curiosity was piqued. I inquired with Amaa.

Amaa hesitated before responding.

"In Africa, we have *vodoun*." He said the word quietly, *voh-doon*. Before I could reply, he added, "It's not what you are thinking. Many people think they know about voodoo, but the voodoo from the white people's movies is a made-up version of it. *Vodoun* simply means *spirit*. This spirit is in everything, even the ground you walk on. It is not black magic like in movies. It is a spiritual practice, a way of life as old as the Earth."

I had read about Haitian *vodoun* and knew that it had its roots in West Africa. The island of Saint Dominique—only later renamed Haiti, its original Arawak name—was largely populated with slaves taken from Ghana, Guinée, Togo, and Benin. I hadn't expected to encounter *vodoun* on my trip to Ghana—though it shouldn't have surprised me. Its roots were here, after all.

"What are the statues used for?" I asked.

"These statues, they are very powerful. Each statue contains a spirit, sometimes from the forest, or that of a dead relative. Our ancestors, they are like gods to us. We pray to them for guidance and protection."

I was still puzzled by the pictures of Christian saints alongside the statues. The influence of Christianity here was strong, and the area had an abundance of small churches. Local businesses often bore signs like *God Rules Internet Café*, or *Jesus is the Answer Carpentry Workshop*, or *The Anointed Plumber*. But I wondered how Christianity and traditional religions coexisted. The *vodoun* statues were the first I had seen.

"But aren't a lot of people here Christian?" I asked.

Amaa laughed softly. "There are many, many Christians here, yes. The missionaries came long ago and said we did not know God. They called us heathens. They came to save us, to bring us their religion. The early colonialists banned our shrines and practices, and demonized us as witches."

Amaa's face grew serious. The history of colonialism had left irreversible scars. The colonialists made every effort to reduce entire belief systems to the occult, and suppressed any practices that threatened their rule. Subsequent waves of missionaries condemned "everything African" —and primarily anything that fell under the category of religion. Viewing the natives as primitive and backward was, of course, part of the justification for the colonialist movement in the first place. But it also laid the roots of racism that has since spread throughout the Western world.

Amaa went on.

"There are those who converted to Christianity, who believed the colonialists when they said the traditional practices were wrong. Others felt they had to accept the new religion to appease the missionaries. But for many people, the belief in the spirits of nature and in the powers of our ancestors is strong, and can never be taken away. The values of our traditional religions have always helped us. They bring balance with the spirit powers in the world."

I wondered how this dichotomy of worldviews played out in modern-day life. As has happened the world over, attempts at suppressing traditional practices mostly succeed in driving them underground.

"So how do the two religions coexist now?"

"You see, *vodoun* is more than religion. It is *life*. But Christianity is part of life, too. For some, the idea of the white man's Jesus and the Christian saints can fit into the traditional view. To us, they are ancestor spirits. They remind us of our local gods. So today, we practice Christianity in our own way. There are many independent *African* churches. But the spirits of *vodoun* are present regardless of your faith. As long as the Earth exists, *vodoun* will always be here."

I was still skeptical. I grew up around devout Christians for whom there was no room for deviation. Here in Ghana, the presence of Christianity was apparent. But though people frequently spoke about *juju*, or magic, I hadn't yet seen much outward sign of it. Perhaps it remained an undercurrent for good reason. Ghana had a history of witch-hunts— even recently.

I remarked to Amaa about it, though I sensed I was pushing.

"Appearances are one thing," he replied. "Reality is another. You shall soon see!" He was done with the conversation, for now.

∽

Several days later, I found out what Amaa was talking about. We were making our morning rounds together, and the village was strangely deserted. Where was everyone? We kept walking.

Soon, drums sounded in the distance. We rounded a corner and drew closer to the sound. A rhythmic fury exploded around us. Excited shrieks blended with a chorus of singing. It sounded like a mix of gospel music and chanting.

Then it dawned on me. It was Sunday morning. Of course! We had arrived at one of the small churches. But this was not the Sunday mass I had experienced in Catholic school, no sir. The small building was packed to capacity, and the overflow spilled into the adjacent courtyard. The drumming was deafening. The church was shaking from the reverberations—I thought the quavering building might take off like a rocket.

Inside, the practitioners wore white, and many had adorned themselves with cowry shell necklaces. Some had white paint on their bodies. The interior of the tiny church was hot; it had to be well over a hundred degrees in there. Sweat dripped from undulating bodies. A young woman at the front of the dancers appeared to be the center of attention. Her arms flailed, and her head tilted back as she writhed and danced. On either side, two women were prepared to catch her. I caught a brief glimpse of her face. Only the whites of her eyes were showing. The drums controlled her body in a form of ecstatic communication. She was in trance.

Amaa was beside me. "You see, the white people, they say we do not know God. When the missionaries go to church, they pray and talk *about* God. Here, we dance and *become* God."

∽

After a few weeks, the cultural center was ready. International guests arrived at Tetteh's compound, students who came from Australia and

New Zealand, various parts of Europe, and America. When the workshops began, the once quiet guest house was transformed into a lively multicultural collection of travelers united by music and dance. It was exciting to witness Tetteh's vision coming to life before us.

The first morning of classes, I awoke to a courtyard filled with dozens of *kpanlogo* and *djembé* drums. It was a divine sea of beautifully carved instruments, each one covered with a goat or antelope skin. Many bore carvings of traditional *Adinkra* symbols, visual representations of various proverbs and traditional wisdom.

Tetteh instructed us. "Each person will choose two drums: one *kpanlogo* and one *djembé*. These will be yours to keep."

With the eagerness of a kid on Christmas morning, I selected a *djembé* with a nice high pitch, and then searched for a *kpanlogo* drum that called to me. I found one that bore an intricate symbol carved into its body. I was examining it closely when Tetteh came up beside me.

"This symbol, it is called *Gye nyame*—it means 'except for God.'" Tetteh explained. "It is for us a symbol that only God can make something happen. You see, the symbol shows a person wrapped in a hand. This is the hand of God, or *Ataa-Naa Nyonmo*—who is both the Grandfather, *Ataa*, and the Grandmother, *Naa*, of all things. We are all in the hands of the creator *Ataa-Naa Nyonmo*." He spread his hands in a caring gesture.

Envisioning an all-powerful creator as both a grandmother and grandfather was comforting to me. My Catholic school upbringing had left me with the notion that "God" was a source of constant guilt and fear. Pious, God-fearing nuns had impressed upon me the idea that humans were eternally flawed, and as such, I was a sinful and shameful creature. I was always suspicious of these pasty nuns, who never went outside into nature and who often threatened us little kids with long sticks. It was a perpetual source of stress for me, given that I was predisposed to perfectionism, even at a tender young age.

Ataa. Naa. Nyonmo. I turned the words over a few times while running my hands over the drum. Grandfather and grandmother. *Yeah,* I liked this. I pulled the drum toward me; this was to be my *kpanlogo*. In the months that followed, its significance grew every time I played it.

Later that morning, a special event was to occur. Tetteh had planned a traditional ceremony beneath the structures we had helped thatch, for this is where we would hold our classes. To bring the workshop and the participants good luck, a blessing would take place.

"This morning, we sacrifice one chicken," Tetteh informed us. "We spill its blood to appease the spirits of the Earth where we will drum. We must ask ancestors for permission to hold workshop here."

Anyone who wasn't comfortable with this, he explained, was free to stay at the guest house. *Hey! You kidding me?* I wasn't going to miss this, not for the world.

Down at the beach, Tetteh and his drummers were dressed in ceremonial robes, accompanied by local priests. A chicken was brought forth. Prayers were uttered in the *Ga* language to the *dzemawodzii*, the local gods who are the mediators between the people and *Ataa-Naa Nyonmo*. Every region, and sometimes every family, has their own local gods they can communicate with. They are intermediaries to the Almighty, and it is these *dzemawodzii* who handle all the day-to-day stuff. While my Catholic school nuns would have hit me with a frying pan for uttering such blasphemy, this made perfect sense to me. I mean, how can one God possibly manage all the inane requests that come in? Surely, the all-knowing and wise creator was smart enough to delegate some of the more tedious crap. It was proof of God's genius, really. Bring on the *dzemawodzii!*

I was startled out of my divine realizations. The drums started up, fast and full of energy. The drummers were skilled and precise, and the rhythms surged into a resplendent wall of sound. The priest raised the chicken. He cut its throat quickly, and its blood flowed as he uttered the benedictions. The spirits were thus invoked as the drumming reached a crescendo. Libations to the ancestors were poured. It was a potent reminder of the traditions from which this music arose—and of which I still knew so little.

Back in the States, I had been spending my time in classrooms lit by fluorescent lights, teaching hand patterns to my students. But here, the rhythms came alive in a totally new way to me. I was in *Africa*, the birthplace of humanity, where life and death dance freely, and where the living and the dead communicate every day. *Sacrifices. Spirits. Ancestors, and the encompassing hand of God.* The scene before me sent shivers up my spine. I felt deeply humbled.

For me, the event was a sort of initiation. A rite of passage even. My drumming would henceforth be infused with an awareness, however vague, of these unknown ancestors from whom this music had come. In Ghana, my relationship with the drums transformed into something— dare I say?—*spiritual.* It was hard to predict what that feeling would grow into, as it was yet young and fragile. But I had departed from the shore and was now venturing out to the open seas of something far greater than me. And there was no turning back.

Ah, but to be immersed in rhythms again! During the next month, the sound of *kpanlogo, gome, djembé,* and *dunun* drums resounded. In the evenings, highlife music filled the air while palm wine flowed into our glasses.

Do some-thing before you die!

This was living, and I was doing it. I happily pounded the skins of drums as dancers performed the traditional steps in an expressive conversation. My hands were light, moving freely as if powered by a new spirit. Rhythms became my new language.

Those first months in Ghana were a whirlwind of cultural experiences. The cultural center was buzzing and alive, and Tetteh was beaming. We attended nearby festivals several times a week, and I learned more than I ever thought possible. Students exchanged notes on the rhythms and dances we learned. I was diligent in notating every rhythmic phrase, knowing I would bring them home to teach my students. I would also be returning with a new respect for the people and culture in which they were rooted.

Kerri in turn focused her attention on learning the traditional dances.

"When we get home," she said one evening, "let's offer dance classes, too. You can teach the rhythms, and I can teach the dances. We can put together a group. Think of the possibilities."

I did think about them. It sounded fantastic. We talked about it late into the night. Together, we could start our very own cultural program, and bring in guest teachers from Africa. The next day, I spoke to Tetteh about it, too, and inquired whether he and his whole group would want to come to America for a residency. I didn't want our program, theoretical as it still was, to be an appropriation. I wanted it to connect cultures, and to introduce people back home to the *real* traditions of Africa.

Tetteh and I discussed it while watching a dance class that afternoon.

"Dave, this idea very good. We make plan over winter. We come to America and stay in you house. Together, we teach drum and dance."

Just like that, it was settled. We returned to watching the dance class, which was picking up in intensity. Kerri was at the center, with a huge grin on her face.

"You wife, she very good dancer," Tetteh remarked.

Hearing Tetteh call her my *wife* made me break out into a cold sweat. It was little more than a year into our relationship. Kerri and I had already weathered a trip to Central America, and were now in Africa discussing a project partnership. But *wife?* I didn't want things to move *that* quickly, I mean, *sheesh.* She really was beautiful to watch though, with her long brown hair falling over her shoulders. She picked up the dance moves as easily as she learned the rhythms. She had taken to wearing Ghanaian dresses, woven from fabrics carefully selected in the market. The colorful fabrics looked radiant on her, with skin darkening from daily exposure to the intense sun. Her smile lit up the courtyard. Or at least it did for me. Wait, was I...? Oh, *shit.* Yes, despite all my precautions, I was falling deeper in love.

One morning at breakfast, Tetteh came into our little dining hall. To my disappointment, he announced to the whole lot of us, "Today, no classes! We go see some-thing." But Tetteh was our fearless leader, and if he had something in mind, I was sure it would be good. Perhaps another festival?

After breakfast, we readied ourselves for a day trip up the coast. We all piled into Tetteh's van—Ghanaians and Aussies and Kiwis and Swiss and a handful of us Americans all crammed in together. On the way, we sang and laughed and played the *kpanlogo* drums we'd brought. Raucous rhythms and exuberant singing poured out of the bus like we were a traveling carnival. I barely noticed the trip go by. When we arrived at our destination, I stumbled out of the van, punch-drunk on music and laughter.

I sobered quickly, and stared at the scene in front of me with disbelief. My mind raced to comprehend where I was. Before me, an enormous white castle loomed over a bustling village. A long row of cannons flanked the castle's outer wall, which rose straight up from a cliff. Beneath it, the waves of the Atlantic sprayed foam high into the air. The sense of *déjà vu* was overwhelming.

"Oh my god," I muttered to Kerri.

"What? What is it?"

"I know this place." I hadn't thought about it in years. It was like something out of a dream, or—

"What do you mean?"

"I painted this place. This castle. The village. All of it."

It was Elmina Castle. This was what Tetteh had brought us to see. It was a landmark that all Ghanaians were familiar with, a part of the dark history that had transpired not two centuries ago. No one here wanted the world to forget.

We approached the castle, and a sense of foreboding came over me as we went inside. The air inside the stone walls of the fortress was cool and damp. We slowly descended corridors that led deeper into the castle's interior. The hair on my neck stood up as we approached the holding cells where slaves had been kept, and a chill ran down my spine. At some point, Kerri and I were split from the group. Alone, we continued deeper. In a narrow passageway, we made room for a group of local school kids. Our white skin was a horrible insignia of all that had occurred here.

The corridor brought us to a cold dungeon. Above the entryway a sign read, "The Door of No Return." *So this was it*, I thought, *the final place one would see before being loaded like cargo onto a ship.* Our eyes adjusted to the dim light, and the desperate marks on the wall became clear, signs of futile attempts at escape. The school group was now here with us. Kerri and I were the only white faces among this group of young Africans. I was trapped in a dark corner, and the stale air made it hard to breathe.

The school kids soon made their way out of the dungeon, and Kerri and I lingered behind in reverent silence. Without warning, the great wooden door swung shut with a loud *bang!* that echoed through the chamber.

Kerri let out a shriek as total darkness took us over. I couldn't see my hands in front of me. My heart thudded in my chest like a drum. I fumbled for the wall, found its cold, rough surface, and grappled for the exit. At last, I found the wooden door, and put my weight against it. Light came flooding back in.

For us, the fear and confinement was a momentary sensation. We had but to push the door to escape. I imagined the horror of being trapped for weeks or months, awaiting an unknown future, never again to see my home and family.

The past cannot be undone, I thought. *But we all have an obligation to learn from it.*

~

Most of Tetteh's guests would stay for a month or so. Kerri and I had decided to come early and stay late, for a total of about three months. As excited as I was to immerse myself in the music at Tetteh's, I was also eager to take in as much of the country as possible.

"Let's just head north," I said to Kerri. "We've got time. I'm dying to see more of the country. The north gets really remote. We could camp, or stay in other villages..."

It would be a real adventure, crossing the Ghanaian countryside, seeing the savannah and experiencing the more remote wilderness areas. What's more, Yanoba agreed to accompany us.

"I am from the North," he said. "That is my home. My family lives there, and you are welcome to stay with us. We can even visit Mole National Park, our largest wildlife refuge." The park is home to elephants, antelope, baboons, and dozens of other mammals, not to mention over three hundred species of birds. I was practically trembling with excitement.

Kerri was on board in theory, but had some reservations. She had managed to take time off from school, arguing that the Africa experience would benefit her students. But she would have to return on time and get right back to teaching.

"I dunno, the timing's gonna be tight," she said. I didn't want to admit it, but I feared she was right. Our return flight from Accra to New York was already booked with SwissAir. Once we reached the north of Ghana, we would have little time to hop a plane in Tamale back to Accra. From there, we would have a layover in Zurich before reaching the States.

I thought about it. I was determined to make it happen. "No, I think we can do it. Barring any mishaps, of course. But we're here now! When will we have this chance again?"

It was already the 10th of September, and I felt the time slipping away. Part of me wanted to stay here forever. We had a few short days to decide our plans before the workshops ended.

The next day, Kerri and I were running late for class. Tiring of the overcrowded guest house, we were dying for a chance to slip away unnoticed, and taste the fruits of our blossoming love. Oh, that sweet nectar! Giggling and disheveled, we emerged from our little hideaway and realized that everyone had long since departed. We were going to be very late for class.

It was a fifteen-minute walk, so we took the bikes instead. I was still flushed from our little escapade in paradise, but I didn't want to miss a single moment of the drumming. We were working on some particularly complex stuff, and I was just starting to wrap my head around it.

We didn't make it far. No sooner had we left than voices called for us.

"Come, come! You Americans, you must come now!" I wondered what was up. Perhaps my family was trying to reach us; could there be some issue back home?

When we reached the guest house, a crowd of Ghanaians huddled around a small black and white television. One of the older kids fumbled with the antenna, trying to get better reception. The sound of the broadcast came in and out. Static occasionally disrupted the picture. I struggled to make sense of what they were showing us.

"America, it is under attack!" someone cried out, pointing to the screen. This seemed unlikely to me; nobody attacks America. But the tiny screen showed a building on fire. I recognized the building, of course; we had visited the World Trade Center before we flew out of New York. But it was now crumbling into a billowing cloud of dust. An airplane crashed directly into the next building, and I gasped. The screen went to static, and the television was silent.

I wanted to throw up. What the hell was going on? We were half a world away. Disconnected. I instantly thought about my friends and family. Was all of America under attack? What other madness was transpiring?

The nearest phone was not near at all. To place a call, we'd have to use an internet café in town. Kerri and I grabbed our bikes and pedaled furiously through the village. Locals with whom we had recently shared lunch came out of their houses to wave to us, unaware of our frantic mission.

When we finally connected with our families, it was with great relief. They were safe at home, and filled us in. In the local Cyber Café, strangers watched our outpouring of emotions and grief that 11th day of September. We cried for the tragedy that was occurring, but also for being so far away, so isolated. Should we go home and be with our families? Would there be more attacks? *Could* we even go home? No one knew. The world had been changed, forever.

We walked our bikes towards the guest house, and weighed our options. We had no way of knowing that dark clouds were still forming on our horizon, and that a new tempest was about to be unleashed upon us.

5

ILLNESSES AND CURSES

"YOU HAVE BEEN CURSED," Amaa said. "This curse was perhaps not meant for you, but you have received it nonetheless."

The illness had come on suddenly, and did not relent for the next forty-eight hours. But that was just the beginning.

"Here, when someone wants to place a curse on somebody," Amaa continued, "they sprinkle a powder in the doorway of the house, on the ground. The somebody walks over it with their bare feet, and they receive the curse. Since it was a sorcerer who made the curse, it is only a sorcerer who can remove it."

I was reclining on the patio the evening it came on. A month had passed since the morning of September 11th. International travel was tenuous at best in this new world, and our scheduled flight home was canceled. We tried to negotiate with the airline, but it was futile. Then, SwissAir went bankrupt. There would be no more flights and no refunds. The price of the same ticket on other airlines tripled. We couldn't afford it, so we waited.

The days passed, and turned into weeks.

When the first wave of nausea hit me, I rushed down to our room on the first floor. I barely reached the toilet before the gut-wrenching vomiting came on. It was like a demon was trying to escape from deep inside me. Over and over. Evening turned to night, receded into day, and gave way to night again. The demon did not cease its thrashing inside me.

By the third night, I still hadn't moved. Kerri was by my side, using a damp cloth to wash my face. Amaa stood over me, talking.

"Sometimes, the wrong person, someone for whom the curse was not intended, can walk across the doorway. They can receive the curse." Amaa was sullen. It was the dark side of *vodoun*.

The ferocious retching took over my whole body. I had barely enough strength to hold myself over the toilet. I implored God through choked sobs to end my life, *pleeease…*

Tetteh came too. They discussed what to do.

"Is there a hospital nearby?" Kerri asked. "If he doesn't get to a doctor soon…" She trailed off. Nobody wanted to finish that thought, but we all feared it.

"We have only small medical center here," Tetteh said. "Closed now." It was late at night. "In Accra, we have hospital, one hour away. But no transport until morning."

Kerri paced the floor, then sat on the edge of the bed and put her face in her hands. Amaa sat and put his arm around her.

"He *must* see a traditional healer," he urged her in a low voice, "and soon. It is the only way."

Kerri was perplexed. "I mean, it *could* just be something he ate, or—"

"No, it is not that. I know Africa's sicknesses. This is different. This is black magic. He need powerful remedy. A hospital will not know what to do. I do not have any doubt about this."

Kerri sighed deeply, and tears leaked from her eyes. She didn't bother brushing them away. A fresh barrage of full body retching came over me, though my stomach had nothing left in it. Once again, I wished I would die.

"For now, we can only wait," Tetteh said. "In morning, we make decision."

∾

During the night, I lost all sense of time. My head spun as the concrete floor beneath me formed waves. The walls closed in around me. A bright light formed at the center of my vision, and steadily grew to encompass all but my periphery. I lost consciousness several times, and occasionally came to and felt Kerri's hand on my back.

Sometime in the pre-dawn hours, the intervals between my body's self-purging grew wider. I slept intermittently at the base of the toilet, in a delusional dream state. At some point—I don't remember why—I crawled outside on my hands and knees. All was quiet, and the village still slept. A dog barked somewhere far off. I pulled myself to an open gutter by the edge of the street. The smell of sewerage hit me, and I began to vomit anew. I didn't care that I was lying in the dirt; nothing mattered. I heard the shuffling of feet. A man approached, silhouetted in the dim moonlight. He made the sign of the cross when he saw me on the ground, and hurried away to escape the touch of death.

Above me, the night sky was filled with stars, and the space of the whole universe opened up before me. I wondered what ancestor spirits walked about silently, unseen. I was sure they were close by. Then, the physical world faded, and I was alone with God. I remembered the *gye nyame* symbol carved into my drum. I was now in the hand of *Ataa-Naa Nyonmo*, the Grandfather and Grandmother of all things. A sense of peace came over me. I was ready to let go.

I closed my eyes and waited to cross into the realm of the ancestors.

But it was not my time. Instead of dying, I was jolted back into confused awareness by what felt like an electric shock.

A terrible force took hold of me, and my body seized up uncontrollably. The pain was unfathomable. Under attack, I recoiled but couldn't escape. It was like the giant hand of some terrible god was gripping me. I thought my organs would be crushed by the force. In the stillness of dawn, I let out a terrible cry, something between a moan and a scream.

When morning's first light appeared on the horizon, unpredictable spasms of full-body pain now replaced the retching. A new terror had been awoken like an angry demon unearthed from its fiery depths, and it took hold of me. It was not going to let go.

∼

A new day emerged slowly, and the peaceful seaside village resumed its casual dance with life. The whisking of brooms mixed with the sound of pots and pans clinking, a baby crying, and familiar voices that spoke in unfamiliar languages. I focused on the sounds and rhythms of Africa as I sat on the edge of the bed, bracing myself against the savage onslaught of pain. I couldn't fathom what was happening to me. Death would have been better.

An entourage of Africans surrounded me to discuss my situation, including a concerned Tetteh, along with Amaa, Yanoba, and members of Tetteh's family.

Our options were limited. Amaa argued that a nearby healer would be best. Tetteh was considering it, and rubbed his chin in thought. With a scarcity of choices, Kerri and I were considering it, too. But we had questions. We were way out of our league here, and scared. Could a local healer actually be our best bet? Was it our only option?

One of Tetteh's companions spoke up, an elder named Ataa—*Grandfather*. He stroked a long gray beard as he talked. He was well versed in the healing traditions.

"We first must determine if this sickness, what we call *hela*, is a simple illness, *hela keke*, or a spiritual illness, *mumo hela*," he began. The others nodded in agreement. "If he simply has an *adeboo* within him, then any doctor will do. This *adeboo* will be chased away by the medicine."

He paused, studying me carefully. None of this made any sense to me.

Amaa joined in to explain. "In the traditional view, all illnesses have a physical component and a spiritual component. When you get sick, sometimes it is a natural sickness, what we call *adeboo*—this means a 'creation' disease, because these types of illnesses have existed since the world was created."

"All people have *adeboo* inside them," Tetteh interjected. "This means that every person have sickness already inside them, and can fall ill to an *adeboo*. When you do not feel well, normally you just take medicine, you wash *adeboo* out."

"This *adeboo* can be malaria, typhoid, and other such conditions," said Amaa. "They have natural causes, and are *hela keke*, natural sicknesses. There are many medicines to treat them. We have herbal remedies, and Western medicines, too. If taken right away, most people recover."

I grimaced as another spasm overtook me, and moaned loudly. My torso convulsed so hard it took the breath out of me.

Ataa, the grandfather, frowned. "I have seen many sicknesses. But I do not think this is *adeboo*. It is not a common sickness. I think your Western medicine would do no good here. Surely, this is *mumo hela*—a supernatural sickness. But we need to find out what kind."

I tried hard to keep up, but was having difficulty deciphering the information in my weakened state.

"There are many kinds of *mumo hela*," Amaa explained. "They are not natural sicknesses. We say that they are *mumo*, or 'spirit breath,' because spiritual forces cause them."

A lengthy discussion followed. According to tradition, these *mumo hela* range widely in variety and form, based on their causation. For starters, illnesses caused by witchcraft are called *aye hela*. *Aye* is a power that is not inherently evil, but can cure or do harm depending on the intentions of the individual who possesses the power. If one falls sick through ill-meaning *aye*, then they can be cured by well-intentioned *aye*.

Sorcery, or *suu*, on the other hand, is much more serious, for it is always evil in nature. *Suu hela* are thus more difficult to treat. Sorcerers often employ curses in the form of "medicines" laid across an unsuspecting person's doorstep. Amaa suspected this could have happened to me, although other possibilities existed. If this were the case, we would need to find the medicine originally employed.

"It could also be *sisa hela*," grandfather Ataa suggested. His eyes met mine as he spoke, his brow furrowed. "An ancestor shade could be speaking to you through this illness."

The Ga people refer to their ancestor spirits as "shades," for when a person dies, their soul or *susuma* turns into a shade, or *sisa*. These shades intervene in the daily affairs of the living, and can cause *sisa hela* —a shade illness—as a way of drawing one's attention to a particular spiritual imbalance. It is through the illness that the ancestor shades speak.

It is common knowledge here that when you fall ill, you visit a healer to determine if this is the case. One can only recover from *sisa hela* by correcting the imbalance. But there's a catch: the *sisa hela* might never fully go away. Often, it remains in the body to serve as a reminder. To illustrate, Tetteh recounted the story of a stingy man who withheld money owed to his family. Subsequently, the man suffered a stroke. This was deemed *sisa hela*. Though he lived, he had been warned. Half his face remained contorted for the rest of his life as a reminder.

I shifted my weight, uncomfortable with this type of talk. It only caused another jolt of excruciating pain.

The final category of illnesses was explained. These were the "judgment illnesses," or *looma hela*. *Looma* is also a type of curse, but it is the *dzemawodzii*, the local gods, who invoke these. In a type of "supernatural trial," the local community brings forth a certain individual who has disrupted the community. The *dzemawodzii* might cast judgment in the form of an illness. If the infraction is serious enough, these illnesses can lead to death.

"The *dzemawodzii* have no business with you," Ataa assured me. A murmur of agreement went through the room. "You are in good standing here." He put a comforting hand on my shoulder.

The room fell quiet. I looked around me. Just a short time ago, Tetteh was a stranger who had telephoned in the night. The other people in the room were strangers until recently. But now, I counted many of them as friends. I felt their eyes on me. I was their guest, and the responsibility of my care was on their shoulders.

Ataa broke the long silence. "Yes, only a healer can determine what type of *hela* this is. And until you know, you cannot treat this. Normal medicines will never work against *mumo hela*. But it is you who must decide now."

His words were final. At that, the company rose solemnly, and Kerri and I were left alone with our thoughts.

The pain continued to radiate from my hips and up my spine. My ribs were bruised and swollen from the convulsions.

I was ready to try anything. I didn't know why my life's path had led me here, but here I was. For the second time today, I let go, and waited for the gods to hand down their decision.

In my head, Tetteh's song played: *Do some-thing before you die...*

~

A miraculous thing happened while I sat on my bed, racked with a mysterious and violent condition.

Far away, beyond the realm of our control—well, somewhere in Zurich, to be exact—the Swiss government convened to determine the fate of its national airline. The economy was hurting, since no one was flying in the wake of 9-11. Without its major air carrier in operation, the economic situation in Switzerland was getting bleaker each passing day. Long negotiations ensued.

While I was exploring the various types of spiritual afflictions with a council of Ghanaians, the Swiss government reached an agreement. It was in the country's best interest to bail SwissAir out of bankruptcy. Flights would resume immediately.

Later that afternoon, Kerri heard the news. She made calls frantically from the internet café down the street. A plane might be arriving in Accra, but nothing was certain. If a plane arrived, our old airline tickets would be honored. The best advice the airline could offer was to go to the airport and wait. Demand for seats would be fierce. It would be first-come, first-served. We wouldn't want to be far away.

The news of the SwissAir bailout was monumental. Up to that moment, I was considering a trip to a traditional healer. But now...could it be true? Was home so far away after all? I looked down at my shirt, which was still stained with dirt and puke. Suddenly, Africa lost a little bit of its charm. *Oh yes, fuck this place!* I thought. In all honesty, I was scared shitless of all this spiritual illness talk. I hadn't bargained for this particular tour of traditional Africa. Though I'm ashamed to admit it, what I wanted was for my middle-class, American white-dude privilege to swoop down and save my sorry ass. I wanted a real hospital, and a fucking top-notch doctor to make this nightmare stop. I wasn't sure how I'd pay for it, but I didn't care.

My choice was made, and Fate turned its wheels. But it wasn't going to let me off *that* easy.

~

The news came. A plane was arriving in the next day or two. Kerri hastily packed our bags. The next day, we organized transport to the city. Tetteh and Amaa agreed to accompany us.

"Well, I'm just about ready for *this* trip to be over," Kerri said, rubbing her eyes as we waited for the driver to arrive. "How about you?"

"Nah, I could have stayed a while longer. I still think we should visit the north for a few days before we leave."

"*What?* Are you—" She saw my face. "Oh," she giggled. "Thank God you're only joking. I was about to put you out of your misery myself."

I tried laughing, but my body promptly stifled it with another spasm.

It was nearly dark when we reached the Kotoka airport in Accra. Hordes of people waited outside. It was a circus of street vendors and travelers. We spoke to an airline representative, who assured us a flight was still on its way—but it was delayed. SwissAir was struggling to keep up with demand, and airplanes were shuffled around like playing cards on a global poker table. Ghana wasn't high on the list. Still, our best bet was to stay put and wait.

The outbound terminal of the airport was more akin to a hangar than the kind of airport we were accustomed to. There wasn't even seating inside. We parked ourselves at a picnic table in a large field nearby, surrounded by anxious travelers. They were in the same boat as us—minus the curses of sorcerers, I surmised.

Kerri and I said our goodbyes to Tetteh and Ama. They both looked at me somewhat pitifully.

"Dave..." Tetteh started. His look said it all. It was a strange departure for what had been a wild trip. The music brought us together, and bound us in a sort of kinship. He had imparted his knowledge and culture to me. I had honored him by embracing it earnestly.

"Perhaps we will meet again, Dave. No person can know what future bring." To this he added a Ga blessing, "*Yaaba jogbann.*" Go, and return well.

"*Omanye aba,*" I replied. May the gods give you success. He would succeed in whatever he endeavored; this I knew.

Amaa took my hand and held it for a long time. We had become good friends, and it must have hurt him to see me in my current state.

He shook his head. "You *must* see a healer," he implored. "I am very worried for you."

"Amaa," I said. "I'm going home." It was all I could say.

His expression remained unchanging, and he held my gaze for a long moment. At last, he spoke again.

"You will find a wise medicine person in your land of America." I didn't know if it was a command or a prediction. He squinted his eyes, as if trying to see beyond me. "Or perhaps, a healer will find you." He let the words linger before turning away.

They embraced Kerri warmly and wished us luck. Moments later, Tetteh and Amaa vanished in a sea of people.

Night fell. Flaming torches cast an eerie light around us. Shadows danced and jumped, like impish spirits. As the hours passed, my pain rose to unimaginable levels.

By midnight, I could take it no more. A plane hadn't yet arrived. I sat on a wooden bench, writhing in agony. Horrible moans escaped from me unbidden. A crowd of onlookers eyed me nervously.

"We're going to a hospital," Kerri said. "There *has* to be one nearby." She looked around. "There's gotta be a taxi, or…"

At this time of night, there weren't many cars about. Kerri left me on the bench to explore the possibilities. I watched her go, admiring her fortitude through all of this.

She disappeared into the darkness, and I thought about how she had danced in the courtyard, young and beautiful and full of life. She had charmed everyone with her enthusiasm and good humor. *If I survive this trip*, I thought, *I'm going to marry this woman.*

The crowds outside dispersed. Kerri was gone a long time, and I worried. I had no way of getting in touch with her—and realized I had no way of getting in touch with Tetteh or Amaa either. A new fear gripped me.

An eternity seemed to pass. My groans became forceful as my body convulsed, squeezing the breath out of me.

Kerri arrived at last, out of breath. I heaved a sigh of relief.

"Oh my *god*," she said. "All the taxis are gone or full. I found us a bush taxi that can take us somewhere, but I don't know what we'll find this late at night."

The driver approached. He was an older man in simple garb, and he greeted me with a wary nod. He hauled our luggage to the curb and loaded it into a tiny car, which was barely holding together. I choked back tears as they helped me into the back seat. We pulled away from the airport, and our chances for departure grew smaller. If a plane arrived, we wouldn't know about it.

Every bump in the road caused me to convulse. The driver glanced at me in the mirror. Kerri sat beside him, in the passenger's seat.

"We have to get him to a hospital fast," she urged. "Whichever one is closest to the airport, please."

The driver's English was not good.

"I am man of tradition," he explained, "and no have need of hospital. I only know Ghana medicine."

Kerri persisted. "But you must know of *something* around here?"

The driver thought. "It very late. *Yeeah*, I think all you hospital, they be closed now. But we have military hospital. It not far. Maybe open, maybe not."

He glanced at me in the mirror one more time.

"This man—your husband? He no need hospital. He need *traditional* medicine." We approached an intersection, and he slowed down to propose an alternate solution. "I think military hospital no good. We take him instead to my grandfather. He know *Ghana* medicine."

Kerri was slow to answer. "What will your grandfather do to help him?" It had been a long night already, and we were desperate.

"My grandfather, he find source of curse. He take sharp knife, he make many small cuts in your husband's back. Then, he place herbs on cuts. Very strong medicine. He draw out curse."

I took a moment to imagine this scene: me lying on a straw mat in the darkness, writhing in pain while a strange old man sliced my back with a rusty blade. While it wouldn't ordinarily be my first choice, my options were currently a bit slim.

Fortunately, Kerri spoke on my behalf. "How far is that military hospital? I think maybe we'd like to give that a try."

The driver shrugged. "It is your loss. My grandfather is very good healer. But hospital only a few miles away."

~

The sign outside read, "37 Military Hospital: Armed Forces Base Hospital." Dim lights illuminated the grounds, and mahogany trees surrounded the courtyard outside the hospital. A canopy of leaves extended above the entrance.

To our relief, the hospital was open, and had staff on duty. A nurse brought out a wheelchair, and the driver wheeled me in while Kerri dealt with our mountains of luggage. Beneath the old mahogany trees, the walkway was thick with droppings that crunched beneath us. Above us, the trees were alive with a curious rattling. When we reached the entrance, the taxi driver pushed me through the doorway. The wheelchair caught the door frame sharply. I screamed. It was thus that I made my grand entrance to the 37.

The 37 Military Hospital was no ordinary hospital. Built during World War II to provide treatment for injured troops, it was the 37th hospital of its kind in the British colonies of West Africa, hence its name. Years after the war, it opened to the public, but it remained staffed by military personnel. And it had its own local mythology.

The taxi driver summed it up bluntly. "This hospital, it is haunted."

Kerri was busy checking in at the reception. The driver glanced around nervously.

"What I tell you is true," he whispered. "Many years ago, there is great chief from the east, in Kibi. He fall ill to mysterious illness—much like you." He pointed at my chest, and I recoiled. "This chief, he very powerful. He know many magic. But now, he at end of life, and no cure found for sickness. He come to this hospital. To guard his spirit, he bring his *nankwaasere*—very large bats. But the chief, he die here at hospital. And the *nankwaasere,* they never leave—they are here, waiting his return. The bats wait in trees outside, and stay until chief come back."

The story had at least some basis in the truth. Years ago, a colony of fruit bats arrived inexplicably at the 37 Military Hospital. Though they normally dwell in caves, they took up residence in the mahogany trees outside the hospital. Over a million bats live in those trees today, and no efforts to remove them have yet succeeded. Each evening at dusk, the sky turns to black as the massive colony takes flight above the hospital. The bats return before morning, and have for decades. This explained the droppings that crunched beneath us as we entered, and the commotion above us in the trees.

"At night, the *nankwaasere,*" he went on. "It is said they feed on blood of patients at hospital. Every person who dies at hospital joins the *nankwaasere* in trees outside. And always, they search for their chief."

He stood up to leave. "One day, the chief shall return." And then as he departed, he added, "You should not have come here."

Haunted or not, the lobby of the 37 Military Hospital was surprisingly busy for this time of night. I saw people in that room who looked pretty darn sick, and I thought I might want to change my seat, to give myself some distance. But another spasm of pain hit me, and I screamed involuntarily. Everyone moved away from me right quick. What's more, I was admitted ahead of everyone, since I was making people nervous.

A nurse wheeled me out of the waiting room and into an open space that reminded me of the old TV show, M*A*S*H. It was a warehouse of hospital beds, each occupied by a motionless body. Sheets covered the lifeless forms.

"Not a very lively bunch," Kerri remarked.

"All I can think about is bats," I replied.

"Huh?"

"I'll tell you later."

The doctor arrived and examined me. He was perplexed. I was feverish, but beyond that, I didn't exhibit any signs of common tropical diseases. Unfortunately, the hospital's lab wasn't open this late at night, so a blood test wouldn't be possible until morning. Just to be safe, he treated me for malaria and typhoid with pills he had on site.

A particularly strong wave of pain gripped me. The doctor scribbled up a prescription. Kerri would need to fill it at the 24-hour pharmacy, which was within walking distance. He drew a map that showed her which alleyways to go down and which turns to make. He urged her to hurry. So off she went again, into the night. I joined the rows of motionless bodies and waited for the bats to take me to their chief.

Kerri returned a half-hour later. She had quite the adventure finding the pharmacy, with only a headlamp on the dark streets of Accra. Out of breath and victorious, she held a bag in her hand. From this, the doctor pulled out a syringe and numerous vials.

The morphine entered my bloodstream like a rocket. I felt its warmth in my veins. It was like liquid God. My eyes rolled back in my head, and all my muscles let go at once. The pain dissipated rapidly, but within moments, I was too *gone* to even notice. My last thought before I disappeared into myself was of the *vodoun* adepts dancing in church that Sunday morning not long ago. I remembered the woman in trance, with only the whites of her eyes showing. She, too, had been *gone*, flooded by the spirit of some ancestral god. I had chosen a different path of healing. Only chemicals flooded my body now.

A shiny curtain of synthetic bliss covered me. And that is all I remember.

My eyes fluttered, and I awoke slowly, cautiously. I was sitting upright in a wheelchair. I don't know how much time had passed. Morphine still coursed through my veins. I couldn't see too well because I was no longer wearing my glasses. *God*, I was as high as a bat's ass.

Kerri was nearby. Her voice was soft and soothing, her hand warm on mine. She handed my glasses to me. I slipped them on, and the whole world came into focus. My new surroundings startled me.

"Welcome back, buddy," Kerri said with a grin.

She was sipping a glass of red wine. We were in Zurich.

6

THE NECTAR OF THE GODS

LANCINÉ AND I WALK, and the memories become clear. Too clear. I remember that first trip to Ghana, and think about how life has changed in the two decades since then. My thoughts turn to Kerri, but now is not the time for the tears that well in my eyes. I must be strong. I know not what challenges await me when Lanciné and I reach our destination, and we still have far to go.

The old friend who walks beside me is quiet. Gone, for the moment, is the playful chatter that normally accompanies our time together. Absent, too, is the sound of music. This trip is like no other I have taken.

The book weighs on me. The shaman's words haunt my thoughts, and drive me forward:

They will hold your feet to the fire until you have accomplished all that you need to.

The journey behind me has been long. When I trace my footsteps along the path of life that has led me here, I see a line that points me to what I must do.

One way or another, it will all be over soon.

∿

My first trip to Africa passed into the realm of memory, though the pain did not. Ghana left me with two new realities: drumming and Africa were now my identity, and pain was the new lens through which all other things were filtered.

In Africa, they called my condition a curse. Whether it was caused by sorcery, a spiritual imbalance, or even ancestor spirits, the treatment is the same, and starts with finding the source of the imbalance. For healing to take place, harmony must be restored between body and spirit, the self and the community, the earthly and the divine.

In America, they had two words for my painful condition: *Ankylosing Spondylitis*. In Latin, it means simply a fusing of the spine. And as X-rays showed, that is exactly what my spine was doing, one painful vertebrae at a time.

The violent onset of my symptoms likely coincided with a severe infection or poisoning in Ghana. But Western doctors deemed this irrelevant. And none attempted to divine my emotional or spiritual state. Nor would I have expected them to. This is not their realm, and it sure wasn't mine. Like a good adept of the church of Western progress, I believed unquestioningly that science knows everything—or will, eventually. I was confident that doctors would find out exactly what was wrong with me, then fix it.

Doctors in the States offered no real explanation for my illness, save a rare genetic marker known as HLA-B27. The best I could hope for was to manage the symptoms. The most obvious of these was extreme pain, so they prescribed medicines to make me feel less of it. I was grateful for this, in the short term.

Blind faith is a road fraught with perils. My path of healing led me not toward harmony and balance, but rather into a centuries-old, profit-driven system of pain management. And it all centered around a flower that I knew well.

∾

The first pain medications prescribed to me were various forms of the narcotic oxycodone, a synthetic derivative of opium. My days at the farm reading books on the subject had made me somewhat of an expert on its history.

I remember sitting before a vast field of colorful poppies with Erik, years before I had ever ventured into Africa. The sun was just setting, painting the field in a golden hue, and we had come to collect our prize.

"God, how are they so *beautiful?*" Erik mused, supporting a delicate flower in his open palm.

"I know, right?" I delicately sliced a pod with a sharp razor, and milky white resin oozed out. "Nectar of the gods."

The delicate beauty of the brightly colored poppy belies the potent medicinal properties found within it. At the farm that summer, we conducted research and learned how to consume its nectar. Whether it was poppy-head smoothies mixed with lime and 7UP, tea made from dried poppies, or "chasing the dragon"—a term used to describe the inhalation of vapor from heated opium resin—we found out quickly its remarkable ability to erase pain and obliterate depression.

Chalk it up to coincidence, an evolutionary twist, or the work of the gods, but this otherwise unassuming plant produces chemicals identical to ones produced by our brains. In response to pain or stress, our bodies produce endogenous opioids, known loosely as endorphins, that act upon opioid receptors in our brain. The word endorphin itself is a contraction of the words *endogenous*, meaning "internal," and *morphine*. Indeed, endorphins are the body's own internal morphine. They are the reason behind the natural high we feel when we engage in aerobic exercise, eat delicious food, have sex, listen to music, laugh, or eat chocolate (or for the gluttonous, all those things at once). How it came to be that a simple flower is capable of producing the same pain-relieving compound as our bodies is a biological marvel we may never fully understand. Suffice it to say that the opium poppy, or *Papaver somniferum*, has held a special place in the lives—and brains—of humans around the world since ancient times.

Opium from the poppy flower contains several active constituents. The most active of these is morphine, named after the Greek god of dreams, *Morpheus*. In the 1800s, scientists succeeded in extracting morphine from opium in a pure form. This potent extract was ten times stronger than opium itself, and was used as a painkiller during the American Civil War. The unexpected result was that as many as four hundred thousand soldiers on both sides became quite addicted to it. The South was hit the hardest. In some areas, as many as one out of every hundred people were addicted to opium or morphine following the Civil War. It was the nation's first widespread opioid epidemic.

During this time, opium and morphine were both legal items on the apothecary's shelves. Recreational use of opium was widespread throughout the Western world. As a commercial item, opium was an economic force that would ultimately lead to conflicts across the globe —and change the course of Western medicine forever.

In eighteenth century Britain, high demand for Chinese goods such as tea and silk had created a major trade imbalance. In an effort to counter this imbalance, the British East India Company began to grow opium in India, from where it was then smuggled into China.

As imports rose, the number of addicts in China grew rapidly. So did profits for the East India Company. Soon, the East India Company was sending nearly four thousand chests of opium to China yearly. Each chest weighed nearly one hundred seventy pounds. American companies wanted in on the deal too, and grew opium in Turkey. The number of opium chests sent to China each year rose to thirty thousand. It was lucrative business for both the Brits and the Yankees—as long as it was allowed to continue.

To counter its rising addiction problem, however, the Chinese government attempted to place bans on opium coming into the country. But this jeopardized the profits of the East India Company, so the British government proposed that opium should instead be legalized and taxed. The Daoguang Emperor rejected Britain's proposition wholesale. Enormous profits were at stake. If China didn't comply, the entire British economy itself would be at risk.

In 1839, China seized twenty thousand chests of illegal opium at the port. The Daoguang Emperor asserted the country's moral responsibility to stop the opium trade, for the sake of its citizens—millions of whom were now addicted. The British responded by sending warships. Tensions grew as Britain employed "gunboat diplomacy" and inflicted serious casualties on the Chinese. Thus began the first of two Opium

Wars, based solely on Britain's alleged right to continue its illegal trafficking of opium into China.

At the outset of the wars, China's economy had been the largest in the world. By 1858, the two wars left China severely weakened, its economy decimated. The victorious British enforced the legalization of opium on China. They mandated that China open ten additional ports to accommodate the ships that would soon be arriving with more opium than China would know what to do with.

The precedent had been set: commercial opium was too profitable to be stopped. The cornerstone of its profitability was the little-studied chemistry of addiction. And it wasn't about to end there, for opium had great medicinal potential that would prove to be equally lucrative.

In the late 1800s, a German company named Bayer created a product from opium that they claimed was a less addictive form of morphine. Their new derivative was called Heroin, based on the ancient Greek word *heros*, meaning "heroic and strong." It was aggressively marketed as a safe morphine replacement, useful as a cough suppressant—particularly for children.

Remarkably, Bayer's labs had actually produced a derivative that was two times stronger than morphine. Nonetheless, the American Medical Association approved Bayer's brand-name Heroin in 1906 for general use. It was soon available over the counter in packages that included an "emergency kit" of hypodermic syringes and needles.

By 1914, shooting up was both legal and medically accepted. Addiction rates escalated in the United States. In what appeared to be a response to the addiction problem, Uncle Sam passed an act aimed at opiates and their derivatives, including Heroin. But the infamous Harrison Narcotics Tax Act was not a prohibition of any sort. Rather, it set up a framework through which the government could tax and control the sale of opium-based products. In a brash misplacement of blame that had racist undertones, the creators of the Harrison Act stated that it "aimed to solve the opium problems of the Far East"—implying that China was the source of the problem. Furthermore, the act set a precedent with which we still live today: it redirected the blame of addiction from drug manufacturers to users. Patients were refused access to medicines formerly prescribed or purchased over the counter.

Addicts were criminalized and imprisoned. The drugs were forced underground, and a black market formed. In one fell swoop, the War on Drugs had begun.

The Harrison Act's economic effects eventually forced Bayer to stop production of Heroin. But researchers didn't stop there. Opium products were too profitable, and they would soon find commercially viable alternatives.

In 1916, two years after the Harrison Act was passed, scientists succeeded in synthesizing a new drug called oxycodone from thebaine, another of opium's minor alkaloids. Its proponents claimed it was less addictive. They were, of course, quite wrong. In the 1930s, oxycodone was combined with the stimulant ephedrine and used as a battlefield medication. The combination was heralded in Europe as the "Miracle Drug of the 1930s." The only miracle was how many people became addicted to it. Historical records show that Hitler himself was addicted to oxycodone and suffered severe withdrawals when he couldn't obtain it.

Oxycodone hit U.S. markets in 1939. The first commercial product was a combination of oxycodone and aspirin, sold by Endo Pharmaceuticals under the name of Percodan. The stuff was both highly effective and wildly popular. By the 1960s, Percodan accounted for one third of all drug addiction cases in the state of California. Elvis Presley was one of its reported abusers.

Endo Pharmaceuticals was later sold to DuPont, the nation's top chemical maker. They formulated a closely related drug called Percocet, which substituted only the companion element, aspirin, for *acetaminophen*, the anti-inflammatory drug found in Tylenol. Although oxycodone had been placed on the Schedule II drug list in 1970, the Food and Drug Administration approved Percocet just four years later.

The newly recharged Endo Pharmaceuticals, now under DuPont, had big plans for their line of painkillers. The big thinkers at Endo saw the potential to maximize their profits by developing a companion line of addiction treatments. As it turned out, perpetuating a cycle of addiction and treatment resulted in profits that were equally endless.

From here, we need only to follow the money trail straight into the healthcare system of today.

Once oxycodone had been listed as a controlled substance, drug producers needed to get it in the hands of doctors who could prescribe it. To do so, they waged a campaign of systematic misinformation. Poorly cited articles in shoddy medical journals claimed narcotic-based painkillers were non-addictive. Some went so far as to argue that *not* prescribing them was cruel and amounted to medical negligence. In 1977, a benign-sounding organization called the American Pain Society began to advocate the use of opioid pain medicines. The pharmaceutical industry provided most of its funding.

Companies like Purdue Pharma—the creators of OxyContin—used sophisticated data to target physicians who were the highest prescribers of opioids. A nationwide force of six hundred sales reps enticed these doctors on all-expenses paid trips to exotic locations to hear their sales pitch. Patients received coupons for a free thirty-day supply of OxyContin. It was marketed as a "less addictive opioid" painkiller, with the enticing slogan, "smooth and sustained pain control all day and all night." A thirty-day supply was just enough to leave patients wanting more, and knowing exactly where to get it. Purdue's head of marketing, Richard Sackler, exuberantly proclaimed that OxyContin's release would "be followed by a blizzard of prescriptions that will bury the competition."

Indeed, doctors prescribed more to their patients, and the profits followed. In its first year on the market, OxyContin sales reached $48 million. By the year 2000, the number had skyrocketed to $1.1 billion in a single year.

∽

By the time I weathered my first trip to Africa in 2001, the U.S. medical system was embroiled in a century-long pain management protocol that centered around opioid-based painkillers. The American public itself was steeped in a culture of non-tolerance to pain, and well accustomed to taking pills to alleviate even the slightest notion of it. And I was no different.

For months after my return, I could not stand or walk without help. Fierce spasms of pain ripped through my body, and every joint in my spine, hips, and neck burned like a wildfire. I slept upright in a chair. The torment I experienced had no bounds. I wanted relief, and I wanted it fast.

My doctors saw the extent of my suffering. They prescribed oxycodone liberally. I washed the little white pills down eagerly, two at a time, every four to six hours. When the bottles were empty, my pain returned with a vengeance. I ran back to my doctors, begging for more. They willingly obliged.

Perhaps I would have done better to remain in Ghana. Any hope of harmony and balance vanished into a dark gray haze of narcotics.

I had chosen my path.

Meanwhile, Africa pulled at me constantly, for some part of my heart had remained there. She continued to work on me from the inside out, fashioning me into a new kind of person. My worldview was changing. I no longer felt at home in America. Technology was moving too fast. The modern world raced ahead, unaware of the richness it was leaving behind. It trampled both the biological and cultural diversity of the planet underfoot as it marched steadily toward what appeared to be its demise.

A year later, when I was on my feet again and able to manage the pain, Africa's pull became too much to resist. An endless supply of pain pills helped me shove the pain aside just enough to tolerate travel. Africa had cast her spell on me, and I would endure anything to stand on her shores again.

7

THE MASTERS AND THEIR APPRENTICE

LANCINÉ and I reach the sacred grove on the outskirts of the village, where the spirits of the ancestors are said to reside. Although at other times I walked here alone in silent reverence, today I'm not eager to venture in. I hope we can tiptoe past it, and avoid drawing the attention of spirit entities I don't understand. A reckoning of another sort awaits me.

Thankfully, our route takes us around the grove, and we draw nearer to the opening that leads into wild country. The painkillers have barely started to kick in, but the thunder rumbling in my spine and hips outpaces it. I try to hide my limp from Lanciné's eyes. I don't want to raise any more arguments about our mode of transportation—or lack of it. He'd rather take our old jalopy down the forest path to the next village, and continue on foot from there. But I want to walk, not drive. I need time to remember, and to feel the significance of every step, no matter how painful.

Maybe I'm delaying the inevitable. Whether I accept it or not, time has grown short. The seasons are changing. The old man Famoudou had been clear that we must wait for him in the village, but after months of biding our time, we're taking the final steps of the quest—without him.

I'm still not sure whether it's the right decision, but I'm carried forward helplessly now, like a stick in the current.

As we walk, the fear in my gut leaves me feeling disconcerted. Something isn't right.

The rains will come, perhaps in a month, they say. But dark clouds are already forming in the distance. I fear the rains will come early.

It was in the spring of 2003 that I first met Famoudou Konaté, a respected Malinké elder and the grand master of the *djembé* in Guinée. He is one of the few living links to the old traditions of the Malinké people. It is hard to forget that first meeting with the old man, as it altered the course of my life. Without him, I would never have met Lanciné Condé.

It took me a year to recuperate from my first trip to Africa. During that period of forced convalescence, I thought about music and Africa constantly. Laid up and unable to walk, I listened to my field recordings and pored over my transcriptions with the fervor of a student preparing for an exam. My brain was on fire with rhythms. Adding narcotics to that blaze was like pouring gasoline on a bonfire.

At night, Africa filled my dreams with vivid images. I fought to interpret their meaning upon waking, but had only the vague feeling that something important—something sacred, even—had transpired beyond the reach of my conscious mind. Phantom drums resounded in those dreamscapes, too. Complex polyrhythms I normally struggled with became crystal clear in dreams, and the next day, I could play them with ease. Rhythms were my savior from the oppression of now-constant pain. Without them, the depression lurking in the shadows might have seized me sooner. But this was my *work* now, and I couldn't be slowed down.

As soon as I was well enough, I resumed teaching. My students were eager to start classes again, and I was eager to hear the rhythms come alive. I *needed* the classes, quite simply because I needed other drummers to complete the polyrhythmic ensemble. Drumming alone is antithetical to its purpose.

Kerri continued honing the dances she learned in Ghana, and became adept at performing the sequences that went with the rhythms I taught. Together, we started a series of weekend dance classes at a local studio. I invited a handful of my advanced drum students to provide the music, and I orchestrated it carefully to respect the tradition. An ensemble was born.

By summer, the drum and dance program was in full swing. I held two classes every night of the week. Kerri's dance classes were a hit, and brought together a community of people that started to feel like family. Though I now hobbled around on a cane, I played and taught the *djembé* and *kpanlogo* drums non-stop. Soon, the new ensemble was performing at small festivals and clubs. The skin on my hands became thick like leather.

Amidst all of this, Kerri and I decided to move in together. It was the start of a new life, and our passions united us. With Kerri's outgoing personality and my creative flair, her inspired dancing and my spirited drumming, we were a dynamic duo. We really knew how to ham it up, too, constantly cracking jokes and engaging people wherever we went. It was like the *Kerri and Dave Funtime Show*. Drumming and dance was at the heart of it all.

While outwardly it appeared to be all blue skies and sunshine, the constant threat of my affliction loomed like a storm that never went away. I put on a heckuva show in those days, playing it off in public like nothing was wrong, even while my spine was busy fusing like molten iron in the forge. But as soon as the curtains closed, Kerri shouldered the weight of my pent-up anger and frustration. Time and again, we'd finish loading our gear after a performance, say some cheery goodbyes to the crowd, and head straight to the hospital for an intravenous dose of whatever they were willing to shoot me up with to make the agony dissipate. Even at the hospital, we'd manage to get the grumpy third-shift nurses laughing. All I needed was an audience and the right amount of morphine. That's how *I* got through it. I'm not sure how Kerri did.

～

I was living in this frenzied, almost desperate world of rhythm and pain when the news came. The grand master of the *djembé*, Famoudou Konaté, was doing a workshop tour of the United States. He'd be within range of where I lived.

When his tour came to Portland, Maine—just a few hours away—I dropped everything and went. It was a three-day affair, with five-hour sessions each day, and I was in heaven the entire time. Famoudou was a sprightly old fellow, looking more like a twenty-year-old than the sixty-five he was. He had a smile that lit up the room and an energy that belied his small stature. He held every participant spellbound, and left no doubt that we were in the presence of a gifted master. Famoudou's teaching was concise, and his abilities as a teacher and storyteller were unparalleled. Through him, the rhythms gained further meaning and context. Though he spoke mostly in French through a translator, musically, I spoke his language. I played his phrases with ease, and Famoudou took notice.

After the first day of the workshop, I introduced myself nervously. I was a skinny white guy in the presence of an African master, and it was humbling. He eyed me up and down, assessing me. When he shook my hand, his expression changed. Instead of letting go, he pulled my hand closer to inspect it, running his fingers over my leathery callouses. He held my gaze for a long moment while my heart raced. With a simple nod, a quiet understanding passed between us. This was to be my new teacher.

Before the workshops were concluded, Famoudou spoke to me in broken English.

"You come, Guinée. My house. Conakry. Work-shop."

That was all he needed to say. As it turned out, he offered month-long immersion workshops each year at his home in Conakry. After what I had been through in Ghana, a month was nothing.

Kerri and my family were understandably nervous about it, but whatever concerns they had fell on deaf ears. I was going, and nothing could stop me.

The following December, my visa, vaccinations, and a personal letter of invitation from Famoudou to placate the Guinean embassy were all in place. My travel bag contained a sketchbook, music notebooks, a recording device, and enough Percocet to sedate a herd of elephants.

I was ready to embark on the next leg of my musical journey into the heart of Africa. I had no way of knowing where it would take me this time, but I was a willing passenger into the unknown.

Conakry, the capital of Guinée, is home to more than two million people—and growing. There is an exodus of sorts coming from the rural countryside, as young men and women leave behind the relative security of their villages in hope of a better life in Conakry. What they find instead is an inferno of poverty. The unemployment rate hovers around ninety-eight percent, and competition for basic living resources is fierce. Tension between the government and a hungry population often reaches a crescendo. Massive public demonstrations are commonplace, and often result in deadly conflicts with the police.

It is here in the tempestuous city of Conakry that I stayed at Famoudou's home. Despite the poverty all around us, a treasure trove of ancient cultural traditions opened up under Famoudou's tutelage. The people I met moved with pride and grace, and showered goodwill upon those who arrived with open minds and hearts. And magic rippled beneath the surface of it all like an underground spring.

The courtyard at Famoudou's place was a perpetual hub of activity. During the day, locals mingled with the twenty-odd international students staying at Famoudou's three-story guesthouse (the only multi-story building in the suburb of Simbaya). Craft vendors set up shop just outside, selling handmade jewelry, clothing, and replicas of sacred African masks. Malinké, Susu, and Peuhl musicians offered private lessons to eager students. Unemployed men loitered patiently, hoping to earn some money in exchange for services, or issued outright requests for handouts. Unmarried Guinéen men and women alike sometimes managed to woo wide-eyed tourists. Their charm and sensuous beauty were their assets in this regard. If successful, securing a white husband or wife would guarantee an improved social status, and promise an end to the poverty that gnawed at them daily.

The weeks at Famoudou's passed quickly. I filled my sketchbook and notebooks with drawings and music. Classes went on for six hours a day. The rest of the time was filled with festivals, excursions into the city, and social outings. In addition to studying the drums, I encountered a little-known wooden flute called *tambin*, or Fula flute. I took a few lessons to get me started.

One month at Famoudou's was not enough for me—not by a long shot. Pandora's box had been opened, and its depths were inexhaustible. Teachers like Famoudou are rare. In Guinée, his knowledge and wisdom flowed from the cultural reservoir that was its source. I wanted more.

When I returned home, I immersed myself in the French language for the next year. It was clear that Guinée was the source of the music I was hungry to learn, and I didn't want language to be an obstacle. My students at home were eager to learn the new music I had acquired, and their financial support made a return trip seem not only feasible, but sensible. This was my job now, and I needed to be prepared.

By the following winter, my language skills had improved greatly. I was ready for whatever Africa could throw my way, and I returned to Famoudou's house in Conakry for three months. It was then that I met Lanciné Condé, the master of the traditional flute known as *tambin*.

On a hot February afternoon in Conakry, quiet settled over Famoudou's normally bustling courtyard. The heat that day was too much, and almost everyone had retired to the shelter of their homes to wait it out.

I was in my room, half-heartedly playing one of the flutes I had recently acquired. The first time I heard the *tambin*, it was like the voice of Africa herself taking flight upon the wind. I was instantly enchanted, and had to know more. But teachers of the *tambin* are difficult to find. This particular woodwind—a side-blown, or transverse flute—is notoriously difficult to play, despite only having three holes. Many never give it a chance, and those who do often give up on it. Though this had been part of its special appeal to me, in truth, I was currently struggling with it.

Just then, there was a knock on my door.

"David? You are there?"

I got up and opened the door. A young woman greeted me politely.

"*Bonjour, et desolée de te déranger.* Someone wants to see you. He has heard that you learn to play *tambin*. He has several flutes to show you."

I didn't hesitate to meet this stranger. Though I had practiced daily during the past year, without a teacher, my progress was slow. But now, it appeared, a teacher had come looking for *me*.

Lanciné made an impression on me right away. He was confident yet relaxed. I gauged that he was my elder by only a few years, but his face had that weathered look that comes from hard work in the sun. His eyes revealed a light that struck me as both wise and mischievous. And while many of the other Conakry guys came across as boastful of their musical prowess, Lanciné was nonchalant. His French wasn't great, but neither was mine.

We didn't need to talk much. He casually pulled out two wooden flutes, and silently handed one to me. He made a gesture that said, "Go ahead, let's see what you can do."

I was on the spot. The heat was dissipating, and a small crowd gathered around us. The flutes were a curiosity, and the growing audience wanted to see what would unfold. I mustered up my courage and played the song I knew best, a traditional melody called *Sofa* which heralds the great warriors of old. When I finished, Lanciné smiled and nodded his approval. He brought his flute to his lips, and inhaled deeply. The dazzling sounds he produced took the crowd aback. This was no ordinary musician. We were clearly in the presence of a virtuoso, a true master who had no need for boastful words.

We scheduled our first lesson. It went so well that we worked together every day for the remaining months I stayed at Famoudou's. His laughter and kind, patient manner accompanied our lessons. But as our apprenticeship grew into friendship, his stories slowly revealed a life that had been fraught with hardship.

∿

"As a boy, I spent my childhood as a shepherd," Lanciné told me one day. "I was entrusted with the care of a small flock of sheep and a few head of cattle."

Lanciné told me how he rose early each morning to water his flock at the river, and then led them over forest trails to an open field where they pastured. Offset from the center of that field, a giant kapok tree grows. Perched on its roots, Lanciné surveyed his flock for entire days and often into the night.

"It was there in *la brousse*," he said, "that I played my flute. And it was there that I become a musician."

Most musicians here have *un maître*, a master with whom they apprentice. But Lanciné never mentioned his teacher. I found this curious.

"Lanciné, who was your *maître*?" I asked. "You never speak about him."

To this he simply raised his arms to the sky. "Allah gave me this music."

He had no teacher, no *maître*. But his story went deeper than that.

"I was seven years old when I received my first flute," he went on. "In the fields, I listened to birdsong and the wind in the trees. I played my flute along with these sounds." His expression became distant as he spoke. "It was like a magic spell would come over me when I played. The music just came."

Such were the humble beginnings of his musical "apprenticeship."

"At night, I often stayed with the herd. From there, the sound of drumming in the village reached me. There were great festivals in those times! I listened to the rhythms and songs. I learned them all from afar."

Lanciné explained how the music remained clear in his head. Alone in the field, he worked out the finer points of the rhythms and melodies. Additionally, on trips to the nearby town of Kouroussa, he heard both traditional and modern music crackling through tiny radios. When he returned to his herd, he took out his flute and recreated what he had heard over the airwaves.

"One day when I was older," he said, "I surprised everyone by showing up at a big festival. One of the older men playing a *dunun* drum stepped away for a moment. I grabbed his sticks, and started to play. No one understood how I could play the rhythms so well. They had never once seen me play a drum—and until then, I hadn't. They thought a magic spell allowed me to do this."

His mysterious abilities earned him a reputation. But his family discouraged him from pursuing music. According to the traditional Mandé caste system, it is only through birthright that one can pursue certain activities. Lanciné's father, a stern man named El-hadj Sékou Condé, was an adherent of the traditions. The Condé clan, quite simply, were not musicians. As such, Lanciné had no business messing around with music.

Lanciné's family made their disdain for his musical pursuits clear. One day, Lanciné's uncle Mamadi found Lanciné playing the flute. The uncle doled out a severe beating. The message was received. From then on, Lanciné only played in secret, alone in the field where his herd grazed, and far from the watchful eyes of his strict family.

Another powerful tradition had a hand in determining Lanciné's fate. This was the all-important process of initiation that every Malinké youth undergoes. For the boys, this initiation occurs at the age of thirteen or so. It culminates with the ritual ordeal of circumcision under the knife of the blacksmith. More than just a superficial transition into adulthood, the ritual cutting releases the wild, untamed energy of youth. It renders one an actual *person*. Without this process, an individual would remain a child forever.

Lanciné remembered his initiation well, and spoke about it often.

"The young initiates, the *bilakoro*, are taken from their families," he explained. "The older men prepare them for the ordeal that they must face. They dance the *Soli*. It is an important moment in every man's life."

The festival of *Soli* lasts several days. The *bilakoro* dance without rest, spurred on by ceaseless drumming. The whole village is present to watch.

"*Soli* music is ancient, and there are many songs," he went on. "Everyone knows the songs well! The rhythms give us courage as we dance. At the end of three days, we are no longer *bilakoro*, but *solima*—those who are ready to be transformed."

On the final eve, the *solima* dance throughout the night. The frenetic drumming urges them toward the final phase of their transformation. At dawn's light, the exhausted *solima* are led into the bush. They line up to face the blacksmith's blade, and anxiously await their turn.

"We are afraid, for we know that not every *solima* survives. But when the blacksmith comes to you, you must not cry out—to do so would bring shame to your whole family." The boys grit their teeth and force their eyes shut as the blacksmith cuts. The pain is sharp, and the blood flows.

After the procedure, the boys remain isolated in the bush for several weeks to heal. Their transition into adulthood is ongoing during this time. At last, the boys return to the village, where a grand festival awaits them.

Lanciné remembers the metamorphosis that took place. The drums erupted and he surged forth, dancing proudly in front of the whole community. He had survived. He had not cried out. And he was now a man.

As he grew older, the *Soli* tradition became important to Lanciné for another reason. A local blacksmith named Amadi Diarra—a specialist *circonciseur* for the *Soli* rites—heard about Lanciné's musical abilities. The flute was an important part of the *Soli* music, but skilled flute players were hard to find. Amadi approached Lanciné's family, appealing to them that Lanciné must be allowed to accompany him in the *Soli* proceedings.

In any case, Lanciné was old enough to make his own decisions. He jumped at the chance to work with Amadi, though he was defying both tradition and the will of his father. With Amadi the blacksmith, Lanciné constructed new flutes out of sturdy *tambin* vine that grows alongside the river. He covered them with sheepskin, and decorated them with strips of red cloth to signify the flowing of blood that marks a person's transition into adulthood. The flutes themselves became power objects. With them, Lanciné became a *Soli* specialist, playing the music that gave courage to the young initiates as they transitioned into adulthood.

For Lanciné, playing the flute for the *bilakoro* and *solima* during *Soli* was important work. But just as importantly, Lanciné had transcended the boundaries of birthright and lineage. And another transformation had taken place: he was now a bona fide *musician*. He no longer had to play in secret.

~

For Lanciné, both life and rapidly changing times in Guinée brought more transitions, and with them, heartbreak and despair. At the age of twenty-two, the sudden death of Lanciné's mother shattered him. His family was broken. And, as he soon found, musician's work was hard and paid little. Restless and just starting a family of his own, Lanciné made the difficult decision to leave the village. First and foremost, he had to find paying work.

Lanciné headed to the remote town of Siguiri, in the northeast of Guinée. A new gold mine had recently opened, and it needed workers for its ambitious mining operations. In the mines of Siguiri, Lanciné was soon entangled in a story that goes back a thousand years.

Gold is embedded deep in Siguiri's history—and in its earth. Located at the confluence of the Niger and Tinkisso rivers, Siguiri's sources of gold have been renowned since the third century AD. When Sundiata Keita founded the Mali Empire in 1235, Siguiri was already a major producer. By the fourteenth century, Mali was the largest empire in the world—and it was Siguiri's gold that fueled its growth.

In the glory days of the burgeoning kingdom, the Mali Empire controlled a region in West Africa the size of the United States. Siguiri was the beating heart of the Empire, and Mali was the source of almost half of the world's gold. One of its most renowned *mansa* kings was the prestigious Mansa Musa Keita. The Mansa was the richest man in the world—and possibly the richest man ever to have lived.

Under Mansa Musa's reign, the kingdom stretched from the Atlantic Ocean to modern-day Niger, about two thousand miles. The Mansa's wealth was indescribable, even by today's standards. During the king's pilgrimage to Mecca in 1324, his expenditures were so great that it devalued gold itself worldwide for a half-century after. Some economists and historians estimate that Mansa Musa's wealth, adjusted for inflation, would today be worth some $400 billion—indeed making him the wealthiest man in history.

So much wealth is not so easy to control. Musa's spending of what he deemed infinite riches was nothing short of reckless. It attracted the attention of kingdoms to the north. The growing empire became hard to defend. After the death of Mansa Musa, the empire faced conflicts, and disunity arose. By the mid-seventeenth century, the deterioration of the kingdom was well under way. Independent chiefdoms emerged. Absent of a great leader to organize the expansive territory, the Mali Empire crumbled into dust—though the fabled gold that had given it rise still shimmered beneath Siguiri's surface.

After the fall of the Mali Empire, artisanal gold mining continued to be an important activity for Siguiri locals. Today, the clear waters of the Niger, Tinkisso, and Sankarani rivers still reveal the flash of gold, and are a reminder of the wealth that once sprang from the Earth—and that fueled an empire.

In the Siguiri Basin, *orpaillage*—the process of panning for and washing gold from the river—plays a large role even today. Local goldsmiths in Siguiri are reputed to be the best anywhere. Men and women toil alongside each other on the banks of the Tinkisso to extract specks of gold dust. The process is laborious and grueling. But it is the sustenance of many of Siguiri's people.

The history of the region took a sudden turn in 1992. Under the corrupt régime of then president Lansana Conté, a new national mining code was adopted. It opened the way for serious exploits by foreign companies. Within a few short years, dozens of international companies had set up mines in the Siguiri watershed.

In 1997, a company named AngloGold Ashanti, the third-largest gold-mining company in the world, secured exclusive rights to a thousand square miles just outside Siguiri. With the potential for enormous profits driving the project forward, operations commenced immediately. Under the new contract, a fifteen percent profit stake would fill government coffers. Corruption was rampant. Government officials fattened their pockets.

Land clashes between AngloGold and the locals erupted. The company forced villagers to sign consent forms relinquishing all rights to their ancestral lands. The mines displaced the villagers, who received no compensation. When many resisted, the government sent soldiers to ensure the locals dispersed.

To add insult to injury, artisanal gold mining was banned. It was a stunning blow. Devoid of their traditional work, many people had no choice but to work in the mines. Conditions were dangerous, and the wages pitiful.

Shortly after the Siguiri mine opened, Lanciné found work there. He was broke and hungry.

"It was the worst experience of my life," he explained. "Fourteen-hour days. Oppressive heat." He shook his head while he spoke, as if trying to rid himself of the memory.

In the mines, access to food and water was limited. AngloGold mined unprecedented amounts of gold from the open-pit operation. When the mine sent its first shipments of gold in 1998, the year's extracts totaled over two hundred thousand ounces—over six *tons* of raw gold. Each year, production increased by twenty percent. But for the workers, an entire day's wage was scarcely enough to buy a single meal in Siguiri.

Lanciné had left his tranquil village in the quest for a better life, but arrived in what he described as a living hell. The mining life poses inherent health risks to the workers. Respiratory problems and impaired lung function are chief among these. Lanciné recounted sleepless nights from endless fits of coughing, only to wake early to return to the mine. He was trapped. Too poor to do anything else, he depended on his meager wages just to stay alive. He knew he had to escape.

The end came when a rockfall in the mine barely missed Lanciné. A close friend with whom he worked was killed in the accident. Lanciné finally called it quits. With the equivalent of a few dollars in his pocket, he left the mine, and vowed never to return.

Lanciné's destination this time was the bustling city of Conakry. To get there, he crossed five hundred miles overland from Siguiri. When he arrived, one thing weighed on his mind, and called to him from within his heart: it was the ancient *tambin* flute. Could he find work performing and teaching in Conakry? The old *djembefola* Famoudou Konaté hosted students from around the world. Perhaps some would be interested in learning the flute.

Lanciné walked into Famoudou's courtyard, weathered from experience and dirt poor. He approached a young woman and inquired whether any students were interested in the *tambin*. The woman knew of only one.

The music, Lanciné told me, was a gift from Allah. It was his destiny. When I heard him play that day at Famoudou's house in Conakry, something in my heart said it would be my destiny, too. Lanciné had not needed a *maître* to teach him, but I did. And so, I became his apprentice.

It was this simple flute, with Lanciné as my humble guide, that carried me deeper into the traditions of Africa. Over the next decade, I spent two or three months of almost every winter with Famoudou and Lanciné in Guinée. At Famoudou's house in Conakry, I studied *djembé* and *dunun* drums six hours a day. During lunch breaks and after dinner, I took *tambin* lessons with Lanciné. He taught me the secrets of this flute, and passed down the majority of songs in his repertoire. I became his flute-making apprentice as well, learning to construct the instruments to his high standards of aesthetic beauty and tonal quality.

The highlights of my travels, however, were the long trips to the Hamanah region, situated along the Niger River. Though the world knows it as the Niger, the Malinké locals who have lived along its banks since time immemorial refer to it as the Djoliba.

The first time I waded into and crossed the Djoliba, it might as well have been a baptism in the Jordan River in Al-Maghtas by Christ himself. For these were the headwaters of the music that had become my new religion. It was the birthplace of the *djembé*—and I found myself at its source. It was here I wanted to stay.

The years passed, and I grew as a musician and an artist. Back in the States, my *West African Style Drumming* program thrived. My performance troupe, now called *Landaya Ensemble*, was busy throughout the year, and was making a name for itself. Kerri was my star *sangban* player.

As my abilities as a musician and artist progressed, however, so too did my autoimmune disease. I struggled to manage it. In Africa, I made a promise to myself: I would take the painkillers only at night. The music was sacred, and I didn't dare dilute my experience of it. For a while, this personal agreement held sway in America as well, particularly when I was teaching or performing. I suffered a lot in those days, but as long rhythms occupied my mind, I could take it.

Eventually, Kerri and I talked about getting married, and she waited expectantly for me to come around to it. But I knew if we did, she wouldn't just be marrying me, but my affliction as well. I had no illusions about it, nor did my doctors leave any doubt: on my current trajectory, ankylosing spondylitis would deform and ultimately disable me. This was unacceptable to me, but I saw no way to stop it. How long did I have before the pain became too intolerable to live with? And what choice would I have then?

I didn't know how many good years I had left, but I wanted to soak up whatever experiences I could in the meantime. I had no long-term view, no plan for the future, and certainly no ideas about settling down and starting a family. When I did finally propose to Kerri, I knew I was being dishonest. My life would be a short one. Kerri was already a widow before we could even get married.

For the time being, I knew only that drumming was my life, and it justified the return trips to Guinée each year. And so, my knowledge of traditional Africa grew. The pages of my dusty Hamanah sketchbooks provided the source material for new paintings. It was like those old days in college when I first worked as an "artist anthropologist," and it felt right to me. I had also amassed a collection of music transcriptions that would have made any ethnomusicologist envious. Very soon, I would have to do something with all this research. Maybe I'd even write a book while I still could. The notebooks held an archive of cultural traditions that, I feared, might one day slip into obscurity. That I'd do the same was a predetermined fact.

After almost two decades, the sands in the hourglass were running out. The pain grew in intensity and spread to other parts of my body. My spine and neck became increasingly rigid, and movement was difficult. The constant torment led me ever further down a dangerous road of narcotic drugs that left me shattered and fragmented as a human being. I needed much more than just pain relief now. Ankylosing spondylitis was crushing my very soul, and I couldn't take much more. I scoured medical journals in hopes that a new treatment was in the works, but the true source of my condition eluded even Western medicine. Hope faded away like the last fleck of the sun sinking behind a dark mountain of despair.

Eventually, I broke my promise to myself. I took the pills both night and day, as prescribed: two painkillers every four to six hours, as needed. And I *needed* them all the time.

As I ventured deeper into Guinée's ancestral homeland, traditional Africa infiltrated the core of my being, and my focus shifted. I began to hear the whisper of ancient secrets. Ancestor spirits walked amongst the living. Sorcery was afoot. Curses became real, and I knew with certainty now that I had indeed been cursed all those years ago in Ghana. Western medicine would never save me. Africa wanted something from me, and would not set me free until I found out what it was.

Lanciné and I trudge closer to the forest's edge, and I remember. Though it was music that once drew me to Africa, it is *magic* I am after now.

The sun bears down on us as we walk past giant acajou trees. The heat is oppressive. Threatening clouds continue to form on the horizon. My thoughts turn again to Famoudou.

I shall see you again before the rains come.

Is there yet hope that he will arrive? No, it is folly. Whatever the outcome, my African journey is almost over.

PART II

Famoudou Konaté (far left) c. 2006. Village near Kouroussa, Guinea

8

WALKING

AT THE FOREST'S EDGE, the path is overgrown with vines. We stop before a narrow opening in the undergrowth and push aside the thicket, revealing the way forward. Ahead, the trail presents itself like a passage into another realm. I turn and look behind me to the village for comfort, but I can no longer see the last of the huts. We've reached the outer limits of the village, and there are no dwellings this close to the wild country.

"*Allez*, let's go," I say to Lanciné. I take an abrupt step forward, only to be stopped short by what feels like a gunshot to my hip. I groan through clenched teeth. It reminds me that the ancestors are close, and pain is the language they use to speak to me. They won't let up until I've completed the tasks. I grimace and take another step, but Lanciné puts his hand on my shoulder. I anticipate his words before he even speaks them.

"Daouda, there is no need to suffer so. We can drive *le véhicule* as far as the next village, and then walk from there. We still have far to go once we arrive."

I adjust the straps of my backpack and set the black portfolio case onto the ground. I'm irritated, but in truth, I could use a break. After considering his proposition, I shake my head. The path ahead is rugged —too rugged for the little car, which wasn't designed for this kind of travel.

"Lanciné, we've discussed this *tant de fois*. For the last time, taking the car is out of the question."

He sighs, and shakes his head. Technically, it's still my car, so I get the final say. Beyond just being stubborn, my argument for not taking the car is legit: I'm afraid the wear and tear of repeatedly driving that old jalopy on deeply rutted cow paths will jeopardize my return trip home.

If there is one, I remind myself. That particular detail still remains to be seen, and is, for the moment, largely out of my hands. Nonetheless, I still want to ensure we have a vehicle capable of making the grueling twenty-five-hour drive back to Conakry. It won't be possible to find another car here in the village, and I've spent too much of my dwindling cash on purchasing and repairing this heap of junk anyway. Decrepit as it may be, it now represents the last remaining link to my old life. To *home*.

"Daouda, why did we buy the car, if not to use it? You are being foolish to walk in such pain when we can drive."

"*Foolish?* Huh! No, I just don't want to push our luck, Lanciné. The car is barely holding together now as it is."

Lanciné mutters something in Malinké that I'm sure isn't flattering. I think quickly for other *walking vs. driving* arguments, and I come up with another justification for walking.

"*Voilà*, Lanciné, *écoute*. Too much sitting isn't good for me. The more I sit, the more my joints stiffen up—and the worse the pain becomes. I *have* to keep moving." This is all true, and even my doctors back home would agree with me there. It's probably a sufficient argument now, but I decide to play my trump card anyway. "And plus, walking is good for your blood pressure."

I see the effect on Lanciné's face immediately, and I feel a touch guilty for using his high blood pressure as leverage. Lanciné has a history of it, and I know it scares him. It's his own invisible curse.

I learned this little fact about Lanciné on a prior trip, when I had come to live with the Condé family at their compound in Conakry. Around this time, one of Lanciné's sons named Lancéï fell seriously ill. He had started looking a little under the weather a few days earlier, but like many people here, he wasn't prone to complaining about such things while others were literally starving. No one appeared overly concerned about him.

One morning, Lanciné and I were sipping our coffee beneath a mango tree when the sounds of vomiting jolted us from our reveries. Lancéï staggered from his room, soaked in sweat. He took a few paces, heaved once more, and then collapsed in a heap. A group of family members rushed to his side.

"We have to get him to a doctor!" I exclaimed, always willing to play the part of Captain Obvious.

Lanciné sucked in his breath and nodded, but I knew his concern. Doctor's visits are a luxury we take for granted in the West, but most people in Guinée don't have the money to go, let alone pay for medications. Overloaded, understaffed hospitals can and will refuse life-saving procedures if the family can't pay. But Lancéï clearly needed medical treatment. I offered to pay for whatever Lancéï needed, and insisted on accompanying him to the doctor's office.

We arranged for a taxi and gulped down the dregs of our Nescafé while we waited. The taxi took forever. By the time it arrived, Lancéï's situation had gotten even worse. We carried him to the car, and two of his brothers dangled him from the back seat so poor Lancéï could wrench his guts out on the side of the road. He was the definition of miserable. No matter what health problems I had—and they were numerous—I could be grateful I didn't have what *he* had.

The doctor's office was located on a side street, in a tiny room that contained a desk, a wooden bench, and a bed. We lined up on the bench —me, Lanciné, his eldest son Fodé, and a close family friend named Laye.

The doctor was a skinny, thirty-something African guy wearing round spectacles, who was fluent in Malinké, Fula, Susu, and French. He even spoke some German too, apparently just to make people like me struggling to learn a second language feel even worse. He took a blood sample from Lancéï, who was now prone on the bed, occasionally rolling on his side to hurl noisily into a bucket. Right before our eyes, the young doctor put a sample of Lancéï's blood on a slide and examined it under a microscope. I was strangely fascinated. Imagine, I had to come all the way to Africa to see how this was done! The doctor pushed his specs onto his forehead and peered into the lens. After some scrutiny, he identified the *Salmonella typhi* bacteria, responsible for typhoid. We all took turns looking through the microscope—a few of the guys were totally freaked out by what they saw. I wish I understood all the expressive Malinké uttered around that microscope; I bet there were some real linguistic gems.

The doctor prescribed a course of antibiotics, which we would need to pick up at the local pharmacy. Everyone was relieved, and though Lancéï was still curled up in a ball and moaning, the family was now joking around with the doctor. I guess dealing with an illness like typhoid is a fairly regular occurrence here. For Lancéï, there would be no stay in a hospital room, no flowers and Hallmark "get well soon cards" on the bedside table to cheer him up, no sir. Just a shit-ton of nuclear antibiotics and plenty of water—and hopefully not the same contaminated water that landed him here in the first place.

Lanciné alone still looked fidgety. He said something quietly to the doctor in Malinké. I didn't need a translation; the doctor pulled out a blood pressure cuff and placed it on Lanciné's arm. His blood pressure was really high—a fact of which Lanciné was aware. But apparently, he had stopped taking his hypertension medicine.

"I do not know why this problem has returned," he moaned. "I finished the whole bottle of pills last year. Perhaps they were no good."

"What?" I exclaimed. "You never had the prescription refilled? You gotta keep taking them."

I thought back, and yes, he had recently been complaining of not feeling right during our daily walks into town. These walks were quite different from our peaceful strolls in the village, and included a dicey freeway crossing in which we had to balance on an impossibly narrow, three-foot tall median between six lanes of chaotic traffic, and then sprint across in a high stakes, real-life version of Frogger. That's urban Africa for you. He'd always have to stop and rest after that, and I figured it was just because it was so goddam *harrowing*. But now I understood, and it was obviously concerning.

Until now, I had wrongly assumed that hypertension was a condition specific to us in the West, with our unhealthy diets of cheeseburgers and french fries. Lanciné, though, is a village guy approaching fifty who lives on a simple diet of fish, manioc, and rice. He's a Muslim, so alcohol is out. Tobacco is a rare treat, as cigarettes are sold as singles. And at the risk of sounding insensitive to the reality Lanciné shares with most Guinéens, he doesn't have the luxury of overeating. Daily exercise coupled with intermittent fasting—a health trend in the Western world—are built-in features of life in Africa. So, what's got his blood pressure up?

Maybe it's the stress of extreme poverty and the poor living conditions in Conakry. Who knows? I've also heard that consuming kola nuts is a factor in hypertension here. The fruit of the kola tree are sacred in West Africa, and are used in religious ceremonies and divination. They're also great for energy. Containing natural caffeine, the kola nut was the unsung hero of the original Coca-Cola recipe, along with coca leaves (from which cocaine is derived). I've often seen Lanciné chomping on several kola nuts and washing them down with strong black coffee and three lumps of sugar. Now that's a buzz!

The doctor looked at him sternly. "Lanciné, you will need to stay on medication to treat *la tension élevée*. Permanently."

Lanciné bowed his head. For him, the curse was two-fold: paying for the medication long-term would be problematic. Had my French been up to the task, I would have offered some additional advice about cutting back on his kola nut and high-octane, sugary coffee fix. Instead, I simply offered to pay for the medication.

Fodé and Laye wanted in on the fun of having their blood pressure checked, too. The doctor agreed to go down the row of us on the bench and check our *tension*. Fodé and Laye were textbook examples of what healthy blood pressure should look like. Like a lot of young guys here, they could have passed for Olympic athletes back home in the States.

The doctor came to me. I was nervous, for I was harboring my own shameful little secret: I too had a history of hypertension, but had ditched the Lisinopril prescribed to me a while back. My blood pressure had returned to normal with some diet changes and exercise, and I got cocky about it.

But now the truth was rearing its head: my blood pressure was elevated again, considerably. *Shit damn!* With a roar of surprise and teasing laughter, Lanciné punched me on the shoulder. I think he felt better knowing we were in the same boat. On doctor's orders, we would *both* need to pick up hypertension meds at the pharmacy.

Years later, and hundreds of miles from Conakry, I still find it hard to convince Lanciné that walking daily can actually help lower his blood pressure. It's counterintuitive to him, and I get it. Additionally, walking means something quite different here than it does in the States. Back home, we walk for pleasure, taking a stroll in the park or going for a hike in the woods. We do it to counteract our eternal state of sitting. That concept is foreign here.

To help illustrate, I remember hearing a *griotte* woman sing a mournful song. The *griottes* are the so-called "praise singers" who play such an important role in Malinké culture. The song was called *Taama diya le*, which translates roughly to "walking to the place there," and it laments the reality of poverty. When one is poor, the song goes, one has to walk everywhere—walking here, walking there, to this place and then that place, countless miles of walking. And moreover, I had not failed to notice, this walking is often done while balancing five gallons of water on one's head.

No wonder Lanciné is opposed to the idea of another long walk, when we could be sitting in an actual car—no matter how old and battered that car is. For Lanciné, walking is the very symbol of poverty.

This time, however, I win the argument.

"Daouda, perhaps you are right. We will walk the rest of the way. It will be good for our blood pressure, and we can take our time."

I don't gloat about it. "Thank you, Lanciné. You remember to take your *tension medicament* this morning?" We've been in the habit of reminding each other, since we're both prone to forgetting.

"Yes, Daouda, I am sure of it. You?"

"Yeah," I sigh. What a couple of old farts we are. Real fucking adventurers.

With that resolved, we cross the threshold of the forest, and leave behind the relative safety of the village. Just then, I remember the other little white pills I swallowed not too long ago, which are finally starting to kick in. *Hallelujah, baby!* Or perhaps because I'm in the company of a devout Muslim, I should say, *Alhamdulillah!* In either case, the happy chemical glow spreading through my body means I can enjoy a window of time when movement isn't total agony. Now is the time for walking.

9

PROTECTION FROM WHAT?

EVEN WHEN WE'RE walking on the narrow path, Lanciné doesn't let me out of his sight. Perhaps it's out of concern, or maybe it's something else—but I'm aware of it. Honestly, it's been bothering me for some time now.

Why am I feeling this way? I try to extricate my real emotions from the quagmire of synthetic endorphins swirling in my brain. This I know: Lanciné is here to help me. He is my lifeline in the village. This is his home, after all, and it's his family that tends to my daily needs. I *depend* on him. I am, therefore, *dependent*.

Perhaps there's the rub. I've never liked needing anyone. Hasn't life taught me that it's better to rely on myself? Whether I like it or not, though, I can't complete this quest alone. Famoudou is apparently not coming, and I need Lanciné.

But still.

"*Petit frère,*" he says. "Watch your footing on the trail. The terrain here in *la brousse* is quite rough."

I roll my eyes, but bite my tongue. I'm not a child, for God's sake. Or Allah's sake. Or whoever, I don't know. In any case, I sigh and keep walking. I should just accept that I have a *grand frère*, and that his brotherly concern prompts him to be closer than my own shadow at times. I mean, we've gone through some crazy shit together.

I remember some close calls. There was the time in 2007, when violence erupted during nationwide strikes. Extreme poverty and frustration with an aging dictator had reached a breaking point, and the people took to the streets. A strict curfew was imposed, and the military split over disputes about back pay owed to them. The country tumbled into chaos, and gunfire rang out day and night. Guinée was spiraling toward what we all feared might be civil war—and I was stuck in the middle of a hot zone. Lanciné helped me survive that one, though I fared much better than he did, ultimately escaping the country on a U.S. Air Force cargo jet while he remained. The violence and subsequent pillaging left Conakry—and his home—in a state of shambles. All that Lanciné had built in life was reduced to wreckage.

For years after, I felt continuous guilt about how *that* had ended. It was my privilege that allowed me to escape, and we both knew it. When I returned home, it was to a nice rental house I shared with Kerri in a quaint New England town. At the time, we both had decent jobs. We felt none of the strain of poverty that gnaws at Lanciné, nor did we live in an area where political tensions could actually turn *deadly*. Ours were privileges that Lanciné might never know. Yet that day in Conakry, he had cared enough to see to it personally that I made it onto that plane, even while bullets rained down around us. He knew damn well where that plane was taking me.

Is it the fact that he *cares* about me that is setting me off? I mean, why would a guy like Lanciné care about a pill-popping white guy from America that doesn't fit in anywhere? And yet, day after day, Lanciné maintains his careful watch over me. I can't even go for a simple stroll in the village without him. Why does he care so much?

Well, *shoot*. We've still got a long walk ahead, and I'll be high as a kite for a bit longer, so I might as well take a stab at answering that. Besides the fact that Lanciné really is a nice guy, I suspect there's an element of caring built into his cultural programming that we lack in the West. I once read about an indigenous group—I've since forgotten which one—whose language has no word for "thank you." Sharing and reciprocity are the norm, so there was never any need to develop the concept of "thank you," which implies the deal is done. As in, *Thanks for the bread, see you later, Fred.* As if two stupid little words actually repay the favor—and sometimes, we can't even muster *that.*

In the village mentality, however, even a ragged stranger who ends up on your doorstep *must* be provided for. In comparison, that we in the West can allow so many to go without is simply abominable. Despite our abundance, our cultural programming allows it.

As for Lanciné's caring, I also can't ignore the issue of our quest, a good deal of which centers around ancient traditions and elders. Here, the elders are still doted upon with the respect they've earned during their lifetime. As such, Famoudou's words were law.

And you, Lanciné, shall accompany him to the village. You will see to it that all is done as I have described. The traditions will be respected.

Yes, Lanciné is bound to this quest, same as I, because an elder has mandated it. Does it feel a little less warm to think that he cares because he is obliged to by his culture? Maybe, but it's splitting hairs. It's still a helluva lot warmer than not caring at all, and more dependable than relying solely on human nature.

Hold on a second—Famoudou had also said: *And you will wait for me in the village.* That was also a mandate, wasn't it? That's why our argument a week earlier had both baffled and infuriated me.

"Daouda, Famoudou is not coming," Lanciné had said. "You must accept this. We should return to Conakry at once."

I'm pretty sure smoke came out of my ears. I attempted to shoot fire at him through my mouth and melt his head, but what came out instead was, "Lanciné, if you need to return to Conakry, so be it. I understand. But I am *not* leaving. I will stay here alone if I have to."

His response had been quick and blunt, like a blow to the head. "You will not survive here without me, Daouda. You are an *étranger,* and do not know the ways of the village."

Ah, that word: *étranger.* I can't shake free from that label, no matter where I go. Here, the word is used for international travelers like myself, but it also signifies any stranger to a region. A person who doesn't *belong.* In Malinké, they say *möö gbèdè*—simply, an "other." But more commonly, I am called by the familiar term *tubabu.* This is the word coined centuries ago for the strange white people who arrived in boats. They were the harbingers of the colonial period. To the villagers, these early explorers were curious folk indeed: they paddled the Niger *upstream* at a time of year when no rational person would do so. The Malinké villagers called them *tubabu*. So a loose translation of *tubabu* might be: someone who goes against the current. I guess that describes me pretty well.

I am a stranger in these parts, for sure. Furthermore, I paddle upstream more than I ought, and of course, I'm white. I'll always be a *tubabu*. But Lanciné knows my language skills and familiarity with the area have greatly improved after all this time. I know my way around, in more ways than one. Surely, he could loosen the leash a little?

I'm pulled out of my thoughts.

"Daouda, stay in the middle of the path. You're too close to the edge. And Daouda? Keep your eyes out for animals."

It's all I can do to keep my eyes from rolling.

Well, he's right, though: there are real dangers out here. We're walking on a trail that cuts through the heart of wild territory, what they refer to as *la brousse*, or "the bush." There are no roads here, and no direct access to the nearest town, except for two river crossings. The first requires paddling one of the large dugout canoes called *pirogues*. The other is by hand-pulled barge. But these options are only available during the dry season. Alternatively—if one has all day to do it—one *could* take a vehicle over miles of winding cow paths. These paths cut through several neighboring villages and a series of overgrown fields, leading to a dilapidated railroad trestle suspended a hundred feet over the Niger. The crossing here is fraught with peril, and most people opt for the river crossings.

Those are the choices. Other than that, we are cut off from essential services like medical supplies, and all but the most basic necessities. In the case of injury, snake bite, scorpion sting, or worse, one has few options.

Famoudou once told me a story that served as a reminder of just where I was. When he was a boy, a lion terrorized the village. At first, this lion only took livestock. It arrived at night like a phantom. The villagers found traces of its kill in the morning. The lion got bolder. It attacked in broad daylight. Then, the villagers' greatest fears came true.

The lion took a child.

The village sent out a hunting party to end the lion's reign of terror. Famoudou, perhaps ten at the time, served as a lookout for the hunters. He surveyed from high up in a solitary tree that overlooked a sea of grass. The group of men ventured further and further away searching for the lion.

Long, tense moments passed. Famoudou noticed a stirring in the grass a hundred yards from the men. Was it the wind, or simply a bird that had perched itself there? No, a form moved from within the grass, as quiet as a shadow. Then he saw it: the massive lion appeared briefly, slinking on its belly, drawing itself steadily toward the hunters. Just as quickly, it returned to shadow. Famoudou lost sight of it. He called out to the hunters—but oh! They were now too far away to hear. Moments later, the lion resurfaced, this time half the distance to the men. Famoudou could only watch.

The lion was upon them. Swiftly, it pounced on Famoudou's uncle, who was carrying the sole rifle. The rifle flew out of his hands and he disappeared beneath the lion's massive body. A terrible skirmish ensued as other men flailed to ward off their assailant. Famoudou watched in horror, sure he would be returning to the village alone. In a desperate flurry, the men recovered the rifle. Shots rang out, and the commotion stopped. The lion was dead.

The uncle and several of the men sustained injuries, but no one was killed. The group marched back into the village, battle-scarred but victorious, carrying the massive lion between them.

Famoudou would never forget the event. But that had been long ago. Over time, lions became scarce.

As Lanciné and I walk, the thick bush closes in all around us. I think about this story, and the others I have been told.

"Do not go near the *malin*, the hippopotamus, if you see them," I am frequently warned. "Or if you see what looks like a stick floating in the water, watch out! It could be the *banba*, the crocodile."

During the rainy season, both crocodiles and hippos come this far south in the swelling Niger River. I read once that hippos actually pose a greater threat to humans than any other large land mammal, and can sprint thirty miles an hour when they need to. They are responsible for more than five hundred human deaths in Africa each year. The last place you want to be is between a hippopotamus and the water. It might be the last thing you see.

But this is the peak of the dry season, and both the hippos and crocs have retreated far to the north in Mali.

What does worry me is snakes. I once witnessed villagers killing an enormous python, more than twelve feet in length, that descended from a baobab tree. This particular shady tree is a favorite resting place for many of the villagers. The type of giant snake I saw that day is not venomous, but kills by constricting. They can take down goats and antelope; I do not know if they pursue people, but I can imagine.

When this particular giant slinked out of the tree that day, shouts of panic arose from the women and children perched beneath it. The men wasted no time in clubbing the snake to death. It took a whole group of adult men to lift the body of the giant serpent and haul it away. I watched in fascination as the villagers carried it off.

I was curious, so I asked rather naively if the snake posed a threat to humans.

"No, it's dead," was the only response I got as they marched up the path, hauling the snake's limp body.

Recently, Lanciné's watchfulness has driven me to seek moments of solitude. Most days, in the heat of the afternoon, Lanciné either settles in for a nap or is busy attending to other village affairs. During these times, I pretend to nap. But when Lanciné is either asleep or off doing other things, I sneak away for quiet strolls alone in the bush.

It's not just my exasperation with Lanciné's close guard that compels me on these seemingly foolish promenades into dangerous territory. You see, when you're an *étranger*, and the only *tubabu* in the village, you become something of a celebrity, like it or not. Or perhaps *spectacle* is the better word? I mean, many of the kids here have never seen a *tubabu* before. Although I normally thrive in front of an audience, the thrill of being the center of attention has worn off. The packs of kids who follow me around are like the paparazzi, minus the cameras.

They're harmless, though, and some are even heart-meltingly adorable, vying to hold my hand as we stroll. Nonetheless, the pressures of having both a sworn protector *and* a devoted fan club are considerable. My quiet moments alone are hard won. I'll take my chances with whatever dangers face me in the *la brousse*.

Though I'd like to think I'm some sort of *Crocodile Dundee*—sleeveless and brave, taming wild hippos with a look, or wrestling crocs or something—the truth is far from that. During my walks, the only large animals I ever see are cows. Don't get me wrong, I'm still wary of them. These aren't the brown and white milk cows I used to pet when I was a kid, no sir! These are badass, mean-looking cows. They tower over me, and most have sharp horns. They seem to sense that I'm an *étranger*, and are spooked by me. And they definitely don't understand English because my gentle cooing of *there there, nice cow* has absolutely no effect. Sometimes I see little kids hanging off them fearlessly, but I'm cautious and give them a wide berth anyway. Lanciné needn't worry about me.

I have taken note, however, that these cows roam freely through the village. They bear no visible identification. Who do they belong to? No one seems too concerned. Apparently, the local cows know their way around and don't wander far. Everyone knows whose cow is whose cow.

I'm a little jealous, really. These local cows have more freedom than I'm granted by Lanciné.

Perhaps Lanciné's watchfulness is for my own good. Beyond lions, snakes, or giant cows, there are other concerns that make these dangers seem mundane. These are the *supernatural* concerns. Matters of the occult are taken quite seriously here. The greatest danger in *la brousse* is not the rogue snake or wild animal, but rather the *djinn*, the spirits of the bush. These spirits are often what keep people from venturing out on the path alone. *Especially* after dark.

A while back, a friend in the village named Samba told me about *les esprits de la brousse*.

"These *djinn*, they are there. You do not see them, but sometimes you feel them. You might think it is the breeze that touches you, but when you look, the air is quite still. Not a single leaf is moving. Then you know it is a *djinn* that brushed by you."

I gulped. Samba was born and raised here, and was a respected *donso,* or hunter. He knew the wild territory well. Even by day, he wore magic amulets at his waist to protect him from these spirits.

"There are good *djinn* and bad *djinn,*" he continued. "Some keep watch over us. They see all that happens in the village. But the spirits of the night—*ah!* You do not want to venture out at night. Only bad things come to those who are still out when the sun sinks below the horizon." Samba shook his head slowly and wagged his finger at me.

I am not typically of the mind to succumb to such fears. But this is Africa. The village at night holds a palpable air of mystery, and people speak of a deep magic. Perhaps being surrounded by people who believe it gives the idea power, somehow makes it real. Or maybe it *is* real, and I don't know it. The line blurs. My rational Western mind tries to explain the magic away, but I've seen strange things in Africa that leave me wondering. Africa is beguiling. It's easy to get swept up in the dark rhythms of the night, when masked figures dance by firelight and the incessant drumming fills your senses.

I asked Samba to tell me more. My curiosity, as usual, was getting the best of me.

"*Les esprits de la nuit,* they bring terror," he explained. His tone made me shift uncomfortably in my seat. "Night is the time of dark spells. There are secrets here as old as the Earth, and only initiation into the ancient societies can reveal them. The secret societies were created to protect us from dark forces. At night, when you hear the drums announcing the arrival of *Kòmò* or *Konden,* do not leave your hut! For only those initiated into its secrets are safe from their magic. Death comes to those foolish enough to venture out and look upon the masked figures."

Indeed, it is only the hunters and those initiated into the secret societies who venture into the bush at night. The *donsow* like Samba are skilled in the art of the hunt, but they are specialists of a different sort. They work in the realm of invisibles, and act as mediators between the seen and unseen forces of the natural world. In the bush, the hunters always wear protective amulets or *gris-gris,* like the kind Samba wears now.

"The amulets keep the hunter safe from the spirit of the animal," he tells me. "To kill a wild beast is easy—but the spirit of the animal? That is a completely different matter. It is not the animal itself that poses the greatest danger. It is the animal's *nyama* that is dangerous."

In the Malinké worldview, every element in nature contains a powerful spirit energy called *nyama*. It's a sort of life force, if you will. Metal, fire, wood, earth, clay, even words and music: everything contains *nyama*. Plants and animals are no exception. After killing an animal, hunters purify themselves before re-entering the village, so the *nyama* of the animal doesn't follow them and do harm.

Later that night, a commotion awoke me. Drums started up, and soon the villagers joined in with chanting. I bolted upright on my straw mattress, and my blood suddenly turned cold. I fumbled for my flashlight and switched it on to see if Lanciné was still there. His cot was empty, his blanket crumpled on the floor. Where did he go? Did I dare venture outside, alone? I was warned. So I stayed put, paralyzed with terror. I wondered what was transpiring beyond the thin walls of the mud hut. I needed Lanciné to tell me what to do, and to protect me from my own bumbling curiosity.

Magic…spirits of the night. My mind turned, and I was breathing hard.

The drums outside were beating furiously. I was startled as the door swung open and Lanciné rushed in. In the dim light, his face was gleeful.

"Daouda! Come. Samba has returned from the hunt, and the village is singing his praises!"

Tonight was not an occasion of secret societies and sorcery, although magic was certainly afoot. I dressed quickly as Lanciné extolled his virtues.

"Ah, that Samba! Neither *djinn* nor wild animals could best him, for his *gris-gris* was strong. Even amidst the evil of night, his amulets have protected him. The village shall feast!"

Outside, the villagers were dancing in Samba's honor. He was a magician in his own right, returning from the bush with life-giving meat for the people. It is a form of magic that not just anyone can wield.

I emerged from the hut to the light of a crackling fire. The dark sky above contained more stars than I had ever seen. Samba was dancing like a man possessed as the drums spurred him on. His brown hunter's tunic was covered with amulets, long rows of cowrie shells, leather bands, claws and teeth, and small mirrors that caught the firelight. They all served to enhance his status as one who is well versed in the mysteries of the night, a master of the wild energies of *nyama*.

Lanciné and I walk ever deeper into *la brousse*, and I wonder: is there magic here? And was it truly a curse that beset me all those years ago, when I first came to Africa? I might never know. Maybe I don't even *want* to know. But as the forest closes in around us, I get an ominous feeling that some other force drives me forward now. I've come too far, and turning back isn't an option anymore. Maybe it never was.

In any case, what life do I even have back home? The only future that awaits me there is one of disability and an inescapable cycle of pain and pills. Loneliness and despair will be my bedfellows then.

It would be better to just end my life here in Africa.

These thoughts have been arising more and more, and I'm starting to distrust myself. Despair is an insult to the gift of life, the ultimate betrayal. It's a privilege not everyone can afford.

I am the pain, and the pain is me.

The voice that says the words is foreign and despicable, but I'm growing too weak to defy it anymore. I just want the pain to end.

Accept it, Dave. YOU are pain. To kill the pain, you must—

NO! The thought is horrible, and makes me tremble.

Lanciné walks close by, and I feel his gaze. I suddenly don't want him to leave my side. I don't want to be alone—not here, not in the world.

Yes, I think. *I need him, and that's alright.* He is my protector, and I often don't know from whom or from what.

Maybe I need protection from myself.

10

A GORDIAN KNOT

LANCINÉ and I fall into silence, each lost in our thoughts. My mind is really buzzing from the oxycodone now, and my thoughts jump like fleas trapped in a jar. It's a little dizzying trying to follow them, but also fairly amusing to observe how my mind works. Is there a method to its madness? It's hard to say, but for some reason I'm thinking about knots and folklore. Like a prisoner to an in-flight movie I can't turn off, I give in and watch it play out. The film opens with a page from antiquity, and unfolds along the Sakarya River on the Anatolian peninsula of Western Asia:

According to legend, when a young Alexander the Great brought his armies to the Phrygian capital of Gordium in 333 BC, he was presented with an enigma. At the gates of the city, he found an oxcart yoked to a pole with a knot so intricate it was incomprehensible. A man named Gordias, who was the father of the legendary King Midas, had tied the knot a thousand years earlier, and the oracles had proclaimed that whoever could free the knot would go on to rule all of Asia. But the oxcart and its mysterious puzzle remained unsolved in the city for a millennium, and the lore grew.

By the time Alexander arrived, the First Persian Empire had reduced the once-thriving kingdom of Phrygia to a mere province. At the ancient citadel of Gordium, Alexander and his armies bided their time, awaiting the next move of their Persian opponents. While they waited, the enigma of the knot tantalized Alexander, and an overwhelming desire to solve the ancient riddle seized him.

Alexander stood before the ox-cart and the enigmatic knot, and was perplexed. "If it was made, then it can be unmade," he mused. He knew countless travelers to Gordium before him had failed to decipher it. What happened next is debated by historians. In one account, Alexander declared, "It makes no difference how the knot is loosed!" He raised his sword, and with one mighty blow, cut through the knot. But in the account written by the Macedonian officer Aristobulus, Alexander rethought the problem. The Gordian knot could not be unloosed simply by manipulating the rope, so he instead pulled the pin from the pole to which the yoke was tied, and drew off the yoke. The knot fell free, and a thousand-year riddle was vanquished.

Alexander considered his victory over the Gordian Knot to be a sign. That same night, thunder and lightning shook all of Gordium, and Alexander and his men knew the gods were pleased. Emboldened, he went on to conquer Egypt and great swaths of Asia, thus fulfilling the prophecy of the oracles. Both Alexander and the phrase "cutting the Gordian knot" were immortalized.

Like the impetuous Alexander, I like to think I can reverse engineer and conquer anything. Sacking kingdoms isn't really my thing, but still, I love solving an enigma. If you present me with a musical instrument—let's say, an ancient, three-holed African flute—and casually ask me how it works, I'll have no choice but to reverse engineer it so I can properly answer your question. For me, that means I'll take it apart, study it obsessively, put it back together, and repeat that process two or three more times. By that point, I'll have realized just how Gordian the workings of a flute actually are, so I'll travel to Africa to pepper an unsuspecting master flute maker with questions. When I get home, I'll read everything I can about how air moves through a column to produce specific musical notes. Armed with an adequate knowledge of the relevant physics, I'll teach myself to code so I can write a computer program to calculate equations for effective tube lengths at specific frequencies, as well as for the precise tonehole correction factors based on tube diameter and wall thickness. Then I'll start making my own flutes.

Pretty normal, right?

By the same token, ask me over dinner why Western society seems dead set on maintaining its current trajectory toward self-destruction, and you won't see me for seven months. When you do, you'll quickly realize that I haven't slept most of that time, and probably forgot to eat, too. Then, you'll innocently meet me at the corner pub for a beer, where I subject you to a lengthy discourse on human history from the Pleistocene epoch all the way through the Holocene, elucidating the epistemological shift that occurred during the past millennium. By the time I reach the Anthropocene epoch—the first geological period on Earth ever shaped by human activity—your eyes will have long since glazed over and you'll realize we're the last ones at the pub and dammit, you've got to work in the morning.

You still want to ask me any questions?

How about this one: So, Dave—how come you and Kerri never got married?

Silence.

I've tried to reverse engineer what happened to my relationship with Kerri, but have failed on every attempt. Discerning the physics of sound waves in flutes or laying bare the epistemological errors of Western civilization are one thing, but my own woolly entanglement in matters of the heart? Now *that's* a Gordian knot. Every shot I've taken at unraveling our failed engagement have ended in frustration. Alexander the Great, I'm knot.

So how does a relationship go on *after* a failed attempt at marriage? I suppose routine, comfort, and fear of change all played a role in our continuation down a path that was heading toward a cliff. I mean, we were too far in to turn back or change directions, despite both knowing the danger that lay ahead. The warning signs were visible along the trail; our inability to tie the knot three years after our engagement was surely one. But we kept at it like a couple of warriors because we're fighters and that's what we do. When all you know is love's battlefield, you start each day by gearing up for the next campaign, evaluating your failed strategies, and trying out new ones. Sure, we bore some decent scars from it, but at least we were fighting in the arena of a life we knew. That life certainly had components of a life we actually wanted. It seemed worth fighting for, and so...we *fought*.

"Kerri," I said during one of those fights, "maybe we're just not cut out for the institution of marriage. I mean, maybe that institution is broken. Did you know that forty percent of marriages today end up in divorce? Makes saying 'til death do we part' kind of meaningless, don't you think?"

"Well, that still leaves sixty percent that *do* work." She had a point. Damn.

"But even so, I don't think marriage means what it used to. You and me, we're not even religious. So why do we need some priest to pronounce us man and wife? Shouldn't love be enough?"

I thought my rationale would be appealing, but instead I was dashing Kerri's dreams of marriage against the rocky shores of logic. The brain and the heart rarely play nicely together. She wanted a Prince Charming to sweep her away to our fairytale castle, but I was succeeding only at being Prince Dreary.

"They say the failure rate for second and third marriages is more like sixty to seventy percent," I said. "Marriage just doesn't have the same meaning it did a hundred or a thousand years ago."

"Marriage is a way to demonstrate a commitment to staying together," she countered. "It's important."

The rest of the argument played out like a fast-paced chess match. I've always performed better at these kinds of things when I have infinite time to consider my strategy, but here, I suspected I might lose in record time. It was my move.

"I think two people who love each other enough will stay together. There's other ways of showing that you're committed."

"So, are you committed to me?" Her directness caught me off guard. My knight was under attack.

"I'm still here, aren't I?" It was a poor move, but the rules of the game say you can't take it back once you've played it.

"When you're not running around in Africa."

"I always come home to you."

"And then you're straight off to the art studio. I think you love your muse more than you love me." She folded her arms.

"You are my muse." I looked at her endearingly, hoping she would buy it, but no dice.

"Bullshit. You're just saying that."

Oh, for fuck's sake. "Well, you can't stop me from making art," I said. "It's the only thing that makes me happy these days." I knew before the words left my mouth it was the wrong thing to say.

"Why don't *I* make you happy?"

Even I didn't know the answer to that. My happiness was pinned to the wall and kicking for a thousand reasons, and I never would have placed the burden of it solely on her. But I fired off an angry counterattack anyway.

"Because you hate my muse." I was flustered, and going off script.

"A second ago, you said I *was* your muse. And thanks for confirming I don't make you happy, by the way." I knew the battle was nearing its end, one way or another. The pieces would have to fall.

"Well, maybe you're not committed enough to helping me *make* art!" I shouted, though what I really wanted was for this to be over and to fold her into my arms.

"And maybe you're not committed enough to *me!*" she retorted through choked tears.

With that, it was checkmate. I crumpled.

"Kerri, I'm just scared." Now I was crying, too. "I don't know what my future looks like with this stupid disease. How can I commit to a lifetime together when all I see ahead of me is pain?"

I must have sounded truly pitiful, because her expression softened. After a long silence, she offered a truce. "Maybe we can find a way through it," she said. "Together."

It was reassuring that my painful condition didn't frighten her off. I had envisioned that when this disease got worse, I would go it alone. I didn't want to drag someone else down with me. But maybe I wouldn't have to.

I moved closer to her, and put my arm around her.

"Yeah, I think I'd like that."

In lieu of marriage, we bought a house together. This seemed like an acceptable means of solidifying my commitment, and thankfully, it didn't involve priests and altars. I should have been wary that it involved real estate agents instead. In any case, when we saw the property, with its shimmering field of grass, swimming pond, wooded trails, and old chestnut post-and-beam barn, we both knew it was something we wanted. Here was a place made for homesteading, with ample space for gardens and maybe even some chickens and a goat or two. It would be our very own sanctuary from a callous world. And we could build it *together*.

Luckily for us, the kind folks at the bank were more than willing to help us achieve this dream. We were a couple of kids with no savings, insufficient credit, piles of medical debt, and barely enough income to cover the mortgage, but so what? The bankers *believed* in us, and the American dream too—and that's what counts. They were real sweet, those folks at the bank, and certainly had no incentive to steer us wrong. Though I never really bought into the American dream, a nice warm slice of that particular homemade pie had been placed right in front of me. Why not indulge a little?

When we closed on the house, I was fresh back from a three-month stay in Guinea. I returned from that trip with a full-blown case of malaria, which somehow turned into a triple-whammy scourge that included generous helpings of pneumonia and mononucleosis, too. Travel in Africa has its price. The day we put our signatures on what seemed to be a mountain of papers, I had a fever of 103.5 °F and could barely keep myself upright. I had no idea *what* I was signing, and could only think about going home and moving our bed closer to the bathroom so I didn't have to walk so far.

A month later, I reluctantly climbed out of bed, still weak from mono. It was time to start moving into our new place. My ankylosing spondylitis had also decided to flare up that week, so I powered up on both Percocet and prednisone to keep myself on my feet. Still, a light breeze could easily have knocked me over. I somehow mustered enough strength to get over to the new house and start working. There was lots to be done.

First off, we decided to pull up the old hardwood flooring, which had seen better days. We pried it up to reveal the subfloor, and Kerri put her foot straight through it and almost found herself in the basement. Turned out the house was rotting from the ground up, and the foundation would need to be rebuilt.

"I guess the building inspector missed *that*," Kerri said as we stood over the gaping hole in the kitchen.

"Wasn't that the building inspector recommended by the bank?"

"Yeah. A little fishy, now that I think about it. Should we get a second opinion?"

"Too late. That would be like getting a second doctor's opinion after the first one already removed your spleen. Speaking of which, my spleen hurts."

"That's cuz you still have mono, dude. Why don't you go lie down for a few minutes? I'll call someone about the floor."

The situation with the house didn't get better from there. During our first month of homeownership, we raised the house up on stilts, dug a deep trench around its perimeter, and rebuilt the majority of the foundation. Short on money, we did much of the work ourselves. To replace the house's crumbling sills and joists, we took turns dangling each other upside down by the feet into the basement while the other person cut the rotten joists with a circular saw. It was all grueling for me, but Kerri was an indomitable foreman who seemed to thrive on home renovation.

"Any chance for a day off, boss?" I'd ask. "Back is killing me today."

"Let's push a little more. It's exciting to see it coming together!"

"Oh yeah, just *great*. Hey, you see where I left my prednisone?"

Over the course of the next year, we also installed new sheetrock on the walls and ceilings, dealt with the lack of insulation, plugged the leaks in the roof, and attempted to drain the lake that had formed in the basement. The barn needed new footings and major support work as well. The list kept growing, and so did my pain.

To pay for all this, we both needed to get second jobs. This left us very little time for actual homesteading. Then, a year after we purchased the property in 2007, the housing bubble popped and the subprime mortgage crisis reared its vile head. Work dropped off for both of us, and we struggled to pay the mortgage. Stress compounded the physical pain I was already in, and efforts to renegotiate our loan were futile. The friendly bankers disappeared, probably to some tropical island where they sat in the sun drinking tequila and laughing at those poor kids they suckered into buying their phony American dream.

Five years after buying the place—and despite having dumped an extra seventy grand into it—our house was worth way less than we paid for it, and there was no good way out. Handcuffed by bills, we struggled to save some semblance of the dream we once had. The house now owned *us*, and costly trips to Africa were off the table. In the wake of all this, it became clear that we probably weren't ever going to get married —but neither were we quite ready to give up on love.

In dark moments like these, sometimes the best thing you can do is call an old friend. So I did. I let the landline ring about ten times and was about to hang up, when at last someone answered.

"Hello?" He sounded winded, like he had run inside to get the phone. I pictured him in his workman's overalls, his hands dirty from digging in the soil. It was nice to hear his voice after too many years.

"Erik? It's Dave. Long time, old buddy."

"Hey man! Glad you called. You've been on my mind recently. Everything OK?"

"Aw, ya know, tough times here. But we're OK. How 'bout you and the wife?" The last time I had seen him, he and Jess were at the farm in upstate New York, but I knew they had relocated since then.

"Bit of the same. But you should come see us. Jess and I have a farm along the Hudson River now. Real nice place. We're farming full-time, supplying organic veggies to restaurants in the city. Come and stay with us if you need to get away."

I was a little envious. *Damn*, that Erik was unstoppable. A man with a plan. And still married to his high school sweetheart, who was a real peach.

"That sounds great, Erik. I'd love to see you both. When's good?"

"Anytime. How about next weekend? We've got some planting to finish this week, but should be freed up by then."

"Deal. What's the address? I'll leave Friday after work. On second thought, maybe I'll ditch work and come up sooner. Fuck the dumb shit, right?"

"Totally. Just get your ass here, we'll have some fun. I've got some friends I'd like you to meet."

I was ready for a little fun, what with all the stress, work, and recent doctor's visits. Plus, I was eager to see Erik and Jess, who clearly had some life things figured out. I might pick up some pointers, you know?

When I arrived, I could tell Erik had matured. He was no longer a kid, but rather a man who seemed to have found his path in life. His hard work at the new farm had paid off. He had a serious small-scale farming business going in the Hudson Valley, and he was doing it right.

"What happened to the family farm in upstate New York?" I inquired.

"Too stifling. My parents are retired and living there full-time now, and they're crazy religious. Always some stupid church stuff going on. Finally, I was like, fuck the dumb shit. I had to get out of there. I can call my own shots here."

"Right on. Looks like you guys are doing well here. How are you and Jess?" I was eager to talk about relationships and marriage, since I was currently struggling in that arena.

Erik sighed. "It's not all roses, to tell you the truth. Married life has its challenges. Jess doesn't let me have any fun. It's like that Dylan song, where he says 'This gal I got, she's killin' me alive, makin' me into an old man, and man, I'm not even twenty-five!'"

We both laughed. "Oh, I know, man. Now that we're in our mid-thirties, I guess we have to accept that we're grown-ups now. Mortgages and bills and responsibilities and all that stuff. Maybe it's good for us though—settle down a bit, ya know? And I'm sure Jess is just looking after you. How's it been going with your...?" I tapered off. I was curious about his prior substance abuse challenges, but didn't want to push.

"Fine. I can handle it. Hey, too much talking. Let's have some fun tonight. I'm dying for you to meet some people. Real cool cats. They might be having a party tonight. I need to close up the greenhouses first, but why don't you get settled in and have a walk around the property? Jess is excited to see you too. You might find her over at the herb garden."

When I caught up with Jess, a different reality quickly became apparent. As I approached, I saw that her eyes were red and puffy; had she been crying? She greeted me with a warm hug, then stood back and wiped her eyes, leaving a smudge of wet dirt on her cheek. She turned away quickly, but her sniffles let me know I had caught her in a moment. We exchanged pleasantries while she showed me around the herb garden, which was filled with the aroma of basil and garlic, thyme and rosemary. But I knew something wasn't right, and didn't want to beat around the bush with a friend I'd known for two decades.

"Jess, what's going on?" I asked. "I don't mean to pry, but…"

She let out a big sigh. "Things aren't great, Dave." I waited for her to collect herself. She continued, "I think Erik is using again, but he won't admit it. I've told him if I find out he is, we're through. I'm not putting up with that shit anymore."

I gulped. *"Damn*—I was afraid of that. Are you sure?"

"No, I don't know for certain. But he's hanging out with these friends who are into meth and God knows what else. Sometimes he's gone for a night or two, and he isn't the same when he comes back. I'm just…" She stopped and choked back fresh tears, her voice wavering. "I'm just afraid for him, that's all."

Light dawned on Marblehead. "Uh-oh. He's mentioned some friends a couple times now. Says we're going to see them tonight. Something about a party. Are those the same guys?"

She shot me a look. "Oh, *fuck*—yeah, that's them. He'll take any excuse to hang with them. Dave, look—do us all a favor, and don't go tonight. Those guys are nothing but trouble. I'd stay clear of them, if I were you."

The visit was putting me in the middle of a sticky situation. I had been eager to cut loose and have some fun for a few days, but this sounded like more than I bargained for. That night, I told Erik I wasn't up for a party.

"Let's just hang here and catch up. I'd love to hear more about the farm and everything. And I still haven't told you about all my travels to Africa."

"OK, man, that's fine. I heard from my friends that the party isn't happening anyway. Some other time."

"Yeah, sure. Some other time."

But I knew there wouldn't be another time. And during my first night at the farm, it was clear that a wide chasm had developed between Erik and Jess. It was awkward. It all left me with a bad feeling, and I didn't sleep much. In the morning, I made a lame excuse about getting back to the house to meet with some contractors, and headed home with lots to think about during the drive.

The next year passed in a blur of work, bills, and never-ending pain. Kerri and I struggled to stay afloat, in more ways than one. After six years of trying to make it work, we considered just letting the house go to foreclosure. The idea of losing the house further taxed our already-strained relationship. The homestead had been our substitute for marriage, and now that dream was withering before our eyes. Could our relationship survive the loss?

Needless to say, my yearly trips to Africa became a thing of the past. I was depressed about it, and the house felt like a noose around my neck that I was wriggling to get free from. Plus, I never had any time to make art. They say that if you don't pay homage to the god, the god will abandon you. My muse was currently nowhere to be found, and my life was more tangled than a Gordian knot.

One night, the phone rang. It was Erik. He didn't sound good.

"Jess left me. We're getting a divorce. I could really use a friend, man. Can you come see me? I'm staying with those friends I told you about until I can find my own place."

If Jess had left him, that could only mean one thing. She had been clear about her terms. And I was suspicious about those "friends."

"I...I'd love to, but...I'm really mired in work and life stuff. Raincheck?"

He was quiet for a long moment—long enough for me to feel guilty about not putting things on hold for a friend.

"Alright, Dave—I understand. I'll take a raincheck. But let's not make it too long, OK?"

"OK, Salty Dog, I promise. And please stay in touch—if you need to talk, I'm here."

"I will. Thanks, man. I'll talk to you soon."

"And Erik? Take care of yourself, old friend. Make good choices, OK?"

The line went dead. It was the last time we ever spoke.

11

THE STING OF THE SCORPION

LANCINÉ HAD STOPPED WALKING. It's hotter than hell out, and we are once again exposed to the direct sunlight.

"Daouda, *t'es fatigué*—you are tired. I can see it." I've slowed my pace as the pain in my hips fights to break through the painkillers. Lanciné has noticed.

"I'm OK," I respond. "Let's keep going." We still have a ways to go. Better to push through the pain.

"*N'ba,*" Lanciné says, "*Allah toro dööya.*" May God comfort you.

"*Amiina, amiina,*" I reply. Amen to that, brother man.

Lanciné's expression changes. "Ah, Daouda—I almost forgot. Lamine says the healer's preparation will be ready tonight."

"*What?* You spoke with Lamine? When?" Lamine is a close friend of Lanciné's, and our trusty driver and mechanic. He's also the son of the village marabout, or holy man, and one of our key liaisons in the next village. Given that Lanciné is ever by my side, I'm surprised I didn't know that he spoke with him. But then again, Lanciné is frequently on his cell phone, which still gets service here and there. I often have no idea who he's talking to when he speaks in Malinké. As a result, I'm left in the dark about what's going on. Vital information swirls around me, but I'm not privy to it. It's a consequence of leaving so much in the hands of others. My fate is theirs to control.

But the subject of the healer is important to me, and Lanciné knows it. He hesitates before responding. Is he hiding something? No, he wouldn't. But there's something different in—

"Lamine called earlier this morning," he tells me. "I looked for you, but couldn't find you. He spoke with the healer, who finished collecting the herbs yesterday. He's made the preparation, but it needs to sit for a day. You still have the money, yes?"

I gulp. The money is trivial, but I'm nervous about the preparation. I pushed Lanciné for weeks to take me to the village healer, but I hadn't known what I'd encounter when the time came. The visit had been confusing, and I'm still trying to decipher what transpired.

"Do you know what specific plants he used? Will he tell me how he prepared the medicine? And where the plants grow, and—"

"He is very knowledgeable, this man. Everybody trusts his abilities." He's circumventing my question. Or perhaps he doesn't understand why I'm asking. Our conversations are often like this, an amusing display of linguistic gymnastics that must leap across cultural barriers. Me always asking *what* and *why* and *how*, and Lanciné shaking his head at my baffling tendency to ask so many questions.

"Well, do you think it will work?" I persist, though the question is pointless. I'm just looking for some assurance.

"If Allah wants for it to work, then it will work. *Insh'allah.*"

I've gotten used to hearing that Arabic phrase, which translates to something like "God willing." It holds such a finality. A conversation closer. How do you respond to it? For example, I'll ask someone if I'll see them tomorrow. I like to plan, you know? The response: *Insh'allah.* Even tomorrow is unclear. It's in the hands of a great power. So why plan? Or I could ask, "Do you think it will rain later and cool things off?" *Insh'allah*—if God wills it! How about: "Will our decrepit little car make it all the way to the village?" *Insh'allah! Insh'allah!*

I get it: life is uncertain. But when it comes to my plight of healing, *Insh'allah* is too slippery. And I'm still wrangling with a world that has *nyama* and *djinn* and ancestor spirits. It's disorienting. Back home, I'd grown accustomed to the illusion of certainty. *My* world had weather forecasts and scientists and little white pills that did what the bottle said it did, time and again. But here, I'm faced with mysteries too great to comprehend. I lack control. Worse, it's forcing me to see my old illusions for what they are: a pretend life raft that I cling to like a drowning man. Here, I have no raft. And *that's* a hard pill to swallow.

"OK," I push, "so we'll go see the healer this evening?" I shouldn't have bothered asking.

"*Insh'allah.*"

I chuckle to myself. I hope we can visit the healer later, although I'll need to prepare better questions about the plants. And I'll need to make sure Lanciné doesn't go rogue in his freewheeling translations again.

Plant medicine has become a topic of much interest to me these days. Western medicine has fallen short of my needs, and it's been costing me a pretty penny besides. The medical industry in the West has little interest in cures that aren't profitable. If it can't be made into a pill, patented, and sold for a high price, it's shoved aside. The plant world, however, has generously offered its healing services to humans since forever, and doesn't charge a dime. Plants, the true pharmaceutical geniuses of the world, defy the medical industry's profitability requirement.

For the medical world, the problem is that single extracts of plant components are often not as effective as the whole plant. *Artemisia annua* is a perfect example. This super-plant contains dozens of active components which work together to produce powerful healing effects. The whole plant, when made into a tincture or a tea, cures even the worst cases of malaria without side effects, and there's no evidence that the malaria parasite can become resistant to it over time. Artemisia is easy to grow, making it a cheap and accessible remedy for one of the world's largest health problems.

Instead of seeing the potential to save lives, however, the pharmaceutical industry saw the potential for profits. They formulated a drug from Artemisia's main component, *artemisinin*. This monotherapy, however, proved to be less effective against malaria due to its low bioavailability; turns out, it needed the synergistic effects of the whole plant. So to improve the effectiveness of the isolated *artemisinin*, scientists combined it with other chemically derived antimalarials, such as *amodiaquine* or *mefloquine*.

Early clinical trials of this "Artemisinin Combined Therapy" (ACT) drug were promising. The World Health Organization (WHO) endorsed it as its recommended front-line therapy for malaria in countries hit hardest. But it still wasn't as effective as the whole plant, and Big Pharma needed to ensure that ACT's profitability wasn't threatened by freely available (and more effective) folk treatments. They lobbied the WHO. Under their pressure, the WHO issued a statement on their website that reads in part: *WHO does not recommend the use of Artemisia annua plant material, in any form, including tea, for the treatment or the prevention of malaria.* The document provided a slew of misinformation about the plant.

The WHO's statement had its effect. It dissuaded governments and health officials from promoting life-saving herbal remedies of Artemisia. Though Artemisia has been used safely against malaria in China for a thousand years, it is now illegal in many countries. Big Pharma won. According to MarketWatch, profits from sales of the antimalarial drug ACT are expected to reach $697.9 million by 2025.

It turns out there are significant problems with ACT. For starters, it's expensive to produce, which makes it unaffordable in regions hit hardest by malaria, which also happen to be some of the poorest. But just as importantly, the *plasmodium* parasite that causes malaria becomes easily resistant to the ACT drug. In effect, this creates strains of "super malaria" that cannot be treated by conventional means. Evidence suggests that in places where ACT is heavily used, malaria is actually on the rise. In African villages where Artemisia tea is consumed, however, malaria cases are dropping rapidly.

I'm sure whole-plant cures exist for many other ailments—maybe even mine. From tropical diseases like malaria and typhoid to common ailments like arthritis and hypertension, perhaps cures already exist in the biological labs of our rainforests and backyards, just waiting to be found.

In regard to my condition, I'm taking matters into my own hands.

I've seen how the pharmaceutical industry operates, and I'm not holding out for their goodwill. Too bad there's not a pill for altruism. Maybe the Big Pharma execs should smoke more weed.

Of course, to find my own cure, I've needed to overcome a few of my shortcomings. In the beginning, this included a complete lack of experience in botanical study, as well as a worldview in a wild state of flux. I'm an artist, after all, not a scientist. But when it comes to research, I apply the same standard of impeccability that I apply to my art. I hope my years of digging through medical journals and poring through books on the botany of West Africa will start to pay off.

What healing herbs might be hiding all around me in *la brousse?* In the village, people have an intimate connection with the local flora. I suspect there is a wealth of knowledge here, but language barriers are a challenge for which I depend on Lanciné. He's a much better flute player than he is a translator. But still, I have high hopes that my recent inquiry with the healer will reveal a treatment for my condition. Will serendipity favor me? Will my desperate prayers be answered?

Insh'allah.

I guess I'm not so different.

Though the true nature of my quest is slightly more esoteric—it involves ancestors, sorcery, and the like—finding a medicinal cure is never far from my thoughts. It all seems pretty far-fetched, I know, but I'm a desperate man. You can call it serendipity, luck, or God's will, but that's exactly the territory I'm headed for, without much of a compass. Just some prayers and the words of an old shaman to guide me.

Though my byway to the hinterland of healing passes through the outer realm of probability, there must be some trace of hope driving me forward. Do redemption and healing lie at the end of this quest? Well, stranger things have happened. I remember an article I came across once in a *National Geographic* magazine. The article jumped out at me, as I rarely see the words "ankylosing spondylitis" in print. The story was about the venoms of poisonous creatures, and their potential as medicines. At the time, I was on about a half-dozen medications that were great at *causing* problems but lousy at *fixing* the one that mattered. I was curious about new and unique research, so I read on. I was shocked to read the story of a traveler in Mexico who suffered from ankylosing spondylitis. Like me, his case was bad. At times, it left him unable to walk.

While swimming one day, the article recounted, the man was stung by a scorpion. He was rushed to a nearby hospital. The doctors identified the scorpion as *Centruroides sculpturatus*, or the bark scorpion—one of the most venomous species in North America. If not treated right away, stings from the bark scorpion can cause paralysis or death. Luckily for this man, an antivenom was available, and he was given the injection. Within a day or two, the man recovered. Much to his surprise, when the pain from the scorpion sting subsided, so did the pain from ankylosing spondylitis. It never returned. Apparently, the venom from the scorpion put his chronic illness into remission. The man swore that if ever his condition returned, he would gladly let himself be stung by a scorpion again.

I thought about that story often. There are, of course, scorpions in West Africa, though I'm not sure about the variety. I often daydream about it. In my little reveries, I'm sitting there minding my own business when one of those little buggers comes along and stings me on the ass or something—and I'm cured forever. Oh, the possibility! The idea makes me wild with fantasies of health and vitality. *If only.*

After reading that article, I vowed to keep an eye out for scorpions. In truth, I went *looking* for them. What would I do if I found one? I mean seriously. Who the hell daydreams of being stung by a *scorpion*? Would this be my fate one day?

Insh'allah, baby!

There had, in fact, been an incident where I came close. We were at Famoudou's house in Conakry, getting ready for our morning drum class. The young woman sitting *right next to me* cried out, then leapt from her chair and howled uncontrollably. I looked down and spotted the small scorpion which had crept into her sandal. It stung her on a most sensitive area—the tender underside of her foot. Clearly, the pain was intense, because the young woman passed out. There was a flurry of activity. A group of African men rushed over, and they acted quickly. I was unable to intervene, though the words hung in my mouth: "Me too! I want to get stung too!"

Too late. My chance at putting an end to my interminable pain was thoroughly dashed with the dull thud of a rock landing on the scorpion's tiny body.

Both the young woman and the dead scorpion were whisked away, and I was heartbroken. Why hadn't the scorpion chosen me? I wondered if there is a word that means the opposite of *Insh'allah*. A single word that could say, *No, David, God does NOT will this for you, you must suffer this terrible affliction forever. And furthermore, it will NOT bloody well rain today either, it will be fucking HOT all day—so get over it.*

That would be quite the word.

~

As for the visit to the healer, I have to trust it will happen when the time is right. I just wish Lanciné knew what it means to me, and understood the sordid path of "medicine" I've walked all these years.

From the Western perspective, my pain is related to inflammation. The word *inflammation* comes from the Latin *inflammationem*, which means "a setting on fire." In terms of the body, however, it's simply the immune system's response to an injury or infection. In general, inflammation is a good thing. It's a sign that our bodies are fighting the good fight on our behalf. But when the body's inflammatory response appears to do more harm than good, and "mistakenly" damages healthy cells, conventional medicine calls foul. We assume the immune system is malfunctioning, and dub it an *auto-immune* disorder. And that's what I have.

My doctors and I went to battle. First, it was a seek-and-destroy mission against inflammation, the soldier of the immune system. When we couldn't contain the inflammation, we assaulted the immune system itself. It was civil war. Doctors sat like generals behind their desks, deploying chemical troops into the front lines of what turned into an epic battle. In the end, the only winners were the pharmaceutical companies, who were getting richer every day from the likes of me.

First, my doctors served me a plentiful bounty of opioid painkillers with a cornucopia of anti-inflammatory drugs like acetaminophen, ibuprofen, or naproxen. For my voracious pain, those were an appetizer. Kid stuff. With frequent use, these non-steroidal anti-inflammatory drugs, or NSAIDs, compromise the lining of the gut. This is the all-important barrier keeping pathogens from leaking into the rest of our body. When the lining of the gut goes, more inflammation follows. The enemy was crafty.

The pain got worse. A stronger class of drugs called COX-2 inhibitors were called to the battlefield. Vioxx was the first to arrive on the scene, and it was a real showstopper. But when patients on Vioxx began dying from heart attacks and strokes, a related drug called Celebrex took its place. This caused my stomach to bleed, and I was left with an ulcer.

My doctors had more tricks up their sleeves. They added in a category of medicines known as "disease-modifying antirheumatic drugs," most notably methotrexate. This worked wonders for a time. But then I noticed clumps of my hair falling out in the shower. I freaked out. My immune system was toying with me—or I with it?

Like military strategists who would not be outdone by a cunning guerrilla adversary, my doctors called on expensive specialists to join the fight. Their offices buzzed and hummed with all the chaos of a war room on the eve of an assault. Afterwards colorful medical pamphlets littered my kitchen table, each advertising the next greatest drug to hit the market. To start with, doctors prescribed long-term courses of corticosteroids such as prednisone. That's when the action really started! I received injections of cortisone in my butt, followed by months of prednisone and Percocet. I was high-flying and pain-free. Who cares if I never slept? Man, I got a lot of shit done. I went up, and I went down. Night was day, left was right, and my internal compass went haywire. Jacked up on this combo, my anger would erupt like an ancient volcano god awoken from his slumber. Everything and everyone was an affront to my inner prednisone demon. I'm sure I damaged some relationships during this time.

Kerri took the brunt of it. After we bought the house together, the war came to her doorstep and she had no choice but to join the crusade or be swallowed up by it. Man, what resilience she showed, as she battled to save hearth and home. When I was too battered to go on, she was there to dress my wounds and put the sword back in my hand. But even with all these medications, the pain sometimes exceeded the limits of human tolerance. Off we'd go to the emergency room. These trips resulted in morphine injections followed by intravenous drips of the anti-inflammatory Toradol. It sounded like the name of a Greek god. *Toradol the Mighty! Toradol the Invincible!* Man, the stuff was strong. Who knows what the hell it was doing to me. These were wild times.

As the years passed, I became a human lab experiment, and I was paying for it out-of-pocket. In those days, ankylosing spondylitis was one of those conditions that made you one hundred percent uninsurable. The Kenyan-American God of Universal Healthcare named Obama had not yet surged up to hurl thunderbolts at the insurance industry. So I was stuck with about $25,000 of medical debt—and growing. I awaited the coming of Obama like a prophecy. When he arrived, I watched the ensuing battle over healthcare like one would have watched the Titans and Olympians duke it out in Thessaly.

Not that insurance helped me. Soon, I was introduced to the wonder drug Etanercept, marketed as Enbrel. Insurance companies didn't cover it because it was too expensive. Enbrel is a real dandy of Western medicine, a prime example of how badly we misunderstand this disease. Remarkably, Enbrel is made from genetically engineered Chinese hamster ovary cells, and infused with DNA to produce specific proteins. It suppresses the immune system outright, making one susceptible to a host of other illnesses. Sure, it lowered my inflammation levels, but I caught every strain of flu known to man, and risked getting lymphoma.

Once a week, usually while locked in the bathroom and crying, I injected living, mutated hamster cells into my own body. Each dose cost $1,400. My blood pressure skyrocketed to 200 over 95 and nearly killed me on several occasions. Though I forced myself to the battlefield each day, I knew deep down I was losing the war.

Despite their fancy degrees and research funding, the white-coats and Big Pharma had it all wrong. Or maybe they knew damn well what caused my condition, but there was no money in curing it. In any case, their approach was flawed. It's what we might call an epistemological error. When one has a faulty view of the world, no amount of science or technology will make things right. A smart fellow once said, *you can't solve a problem with the same way of thinking that created it.* I'm only beginning to learn this.

Over time, my worldview broadened. I turned my attention to natural, "alternative" treatments. Hell, after injecting mutated hamster ovary cells, no idea sounded too bizarre. I was willing to try anything. But real healing would require me to expand my own view of the world. My own epistemology needed recalibration.

In hindsight, it took me too long to let go of my blind faith in Western medicine. But when I did, new avenues appeared. These avenues were not actually new, but reincarnations of ancient knowledge. Though the world is changing, and cultures are vanishing from the planet at an alarming rate, perhaps not all has been lost.

As the years went by, I followed the trail. I learned to listen to my heart. Though my quest for healing had begun as a war, it turned into a spiritual pilgrimage. In my wayfaring, I had new guides. Healers. I hadn't sought them out, but my journey put me directly in their path.

There is a saying: *when the student is ready, the teacher will appear.* After a decade of suffering, perhaps I'm finally ready.

Lanciné and I fight our way through the ever-thickening forest, and I can only pray that my sojourn to the depths of Africa will be enough to finally end this curse. Will it be a scorpion's venomous sting, the powers of sorcery, or some ancient healing wisdom that cures me? Or will I discover a simple plant like Artemisia in *la brousse* that proves to be the palliative I've dreamt of?

As we walk on through the glaring heat, my fear is that only demons await me where we're headed.

12

SOLEIL DE PLOMB

MY EYES STING from salty sweat, and my shirt clings to me like cellophane.

"Eh *Allah*, it's hot," I remark, as if saying so will somehow change that fact. I remember the figurative expression in French, and say it aloud: *"Il fait un soleil de plomb."* Which is to say, the sun feels like it's made of lead.

"What?" Lanciné asks. Maybe he didn't hear me. I repeat the phrase.

"Daouda, I do not know what this means. How can the sun be made of lead?"

"Uh, I don't know. It's just an expression. You know, because the sun feels heavy. You don't use that phrase here?"

"No, Daouda, we do not say that here. In Malinké, we say, *funtanin kasiya kosöbè:* the air is so hot, it is like steam. This is the month we call *taraba*, which means the time of the big heat."

"Oh. In English, we call it March. And it's freezing cold where I live. Or, where I used to live, anyway." I'm not actually sure where I live anymore.

He tries to pronounce it, but it comes out like *Marrrrt*. "What does this word mean in your language? That it is cold?"

"No." I think for a moment. "I believe it comes from the name of a god—the Roman god of war, *Mars*, I think. But I have no idea why it's named that way."

Lanciné just nods. It's mindless chatter, and it helps take my mind off more pressing things. Like shamans and quests. The thought makes me shiver, despite the steamy air.

"*Taraba*," I say, just to keep myself in the present moment. "Big heat."

"Yes, that is it. Big heat. We do not have a god of war like you *tubabu*, although we have many great warriors among our ancestors. Like Almamy Samory Touré, who fought against French colonialism until his dying days. And we do not have a sun made of lead." He laughs. "No, when we are hot, we say, *tara bada n mina*—the heat captures me."

Seems fitting: it has captured me, too, and holds me in its grip. There's no way to escape it.

We keep walking, and I'm aware of the discomfort in my hips and spine. I am ever its prisoner. I close my eyes for a moment, and tilt my head toward the sky. Unbidden, an image of the shaman flashes across my mind.

The ancestors are never far away. They will hold your feet to the fire until you have accomplished all that you need to.

I blink hard to make the memory go away, but now it too has captured me. As the sun's weight bears down on me, I know I can't escape what I came here to do, and can't turn my back on the path that led me here.

For years after my first trip to Ghana, Amaa's parting words lingered in my mind: *You will find a wise medicine person in your land of America. Or perhaps, a healer will find you.*

A healer had in fact found me, though I was slow to recognize it. While Kerri and I struggled to keep our home after the housing market crash, a friend named Julie was pursuing a study of indigenous healing traditions. Her husband was a drum student of mine—a really good one—and I guess Julie and I were destined to meet. I probably wouldn't be here if we hadn't.

Julie was about my mom's age, and had a gentle demeanor that arose from a quiet wisdom. Her primary teacher was a man named Eliot Cowan, who had studied Chinese Five-Element Acupuncture with the renowned Professor J.R. Worsley in England. Later, Cowan pursued shamanic training with a Huichol Indian named Don Jose Rios in the Sierra Madre mountains of Mexico. After completing a twelve-year apprenticeship, the Huichol people recognized Eliot as a *Tsaurirrikame*, or elder medicine man. With the guidance of his Huichol mentors, Eliot brought these two ancient traditions together in a practice he called *Plant Spirit Medicine*. His goal was to revitalize age-old healing practices long forgotten in the West.

Julie was dedicated to her studies with Eliot, and unwavering in her path. This was her life's work, her calling. Her hard work and commitment paid off, and over time, she became one of Eliot's most talented students, and a healer in her own right. As part of her comprehensive training, Julie needed patients to practice on, and she knew I was desperate for healing. I figured it couldn't hurt to try, since it was no weirder than injecting Chinese hamster ovary cells, and decidedly less painful. I agreed to be one of her first patients.

During weekly visits, Julie used local plants to begin a process of restoring balance between my body and spirit, mind and emotions. Though her techniques were foreign to me, the underlying philosophy was similar to what I had learned about indigenous healing in Africa: all illnesses stem from an imbalance, and only by finding the root of that imbalance can the illness be cured.

I enjoyed my visits with Julie, though I knew little about the actual nature of her work, which might as well have been voodoo. Nonetheless, her treatments had a balancing, calming effect on me, so why not? Over the years, Julie became somewhat of a spiritual adviser to me. She listened patiently, and was never short on wise counsel. Win-win, as they say.

My deepening friendship with Julie also opened up new avenues that forced me to reckon with powers I didn't understand.

"Dave," she said one day, "I know a Huichol shaman who is traveling in America right now. She's renowned for her abilities, and is coming to the northeast. I've offered to put her up for a few nights. Why don't you meet with her? I could set it up for you."

I couldn't think of any reasons why not, save my Western pragmatism that still left me a bit of a skeptic. But close-mindedness seemed like a lousy reason to decline the offer, given my terrible anguish.

"Yeah, sure, Julie—I'll give it a shot."

"Good. I think you'll like her." She chuckled to herself. "Just be forewarned, she's a feisty one." She let out a laugh, and I could only guess why. Maybe she knew what I was in for.

As Lanciné and I march closer to our destination beneath *un soleil de plomb*, I remember that first encounter with the shaman. It was an introduction to certain indigenous concepts that are challenging to the Western worldview. But despite my skepticism, I was ever curious about the traditions of native peoples, particularly when it came to healing. I was prepared to try anything that might ease my suffering. I would have followed the path wherever it led.

Where it took me was to the spiritual views of the Huichol people. The Huichol are a small indigenous group in the Sierra Madre Mountains of Mexico, near Ixtlan. The Wixáritari, as they refer to themselves, are the last tribe in North America to have fully maintained their pre-Columbian traditions. No small feat, given the propensity of the white European to decimate, subvert, or convert every culture that stands in its path. According to carbon dating of ashes from their sacred fireplaces, the Huichol have dwelled in that region for at least fifteen thousand years, and have maintained their culture into modern times.

The Huichol worldview, as I came to find out, is quite complex, and features a pantheon of deities that represent the natural forces of the universe. *Tatewari*, or "Grandfather Fire," is principal among the deities. *Tayau*, the Sun God, and *Kauyumaki*, the Sacred Deer, also play important roles in Huichol cosmology. There are dozens more.

For the Huichol, all the Earth is alive with spirit, sacred and inviolable. Similar to the concept of *nyama* in West Africa, everything under the sun contains a life force, or spirit. The Huichol live in constant conversation with nature, and the shaman, or *marakane*, functions as an intermediary to this living spirit world. In annual pilgrimages to the sacred land of *Wirikuta*, the shaman harvests the sacred peyote cactus.

Peyote grants the *marakane* access to the realm where both ancestors and deities reside, and transports the spiritual pilgrim to the source of all life, where true healing is possible. Here, dreams and visions intertwine with the ongoing dance of life. It is not for the uninitiated.

When Julie first introduced me to the old shaman, I came only with a painful condition and my sorrow. I had no notion of what she might actually do to help. But she came with a sophisticated understanding of a world alive with spirit, and a vision of healing I may never fully grasp.

I remember when we sat together at the sacred fire that first night. When I arrived, the old woman knew nothing about me, nor I of her. I merely explained that I had an autoimmune disease and severe pain. Though I didn't say as much, I was looking for a quick fix, a miracle perhaps. But finding the source of healing is not so easy. I would soon have my work cut out for me.

The flames from the shaman's fire flickered in the darkness. The moon had risen earlier, but was now partially concealed by silver clouds. I sat rather awkwardly before her, shirtless in the cold autumn air. After a precursory examination of my back, she fanned sage smoke on me with a large bundle of feathers. Now she sat before the fire, praying. A lit cigar dangled from her wiry fingers, and an old fedora rested at an angle on her head.

She raised her eyes from the fire.

"This plant, it is like a deity," the old woman said. "And it has become rather cross with you. You must appease it."

I didn't have a response to her cryptic remark, so I said nothing. Smoke whirled around us hypnotically. A few crickets chirped nearby, and the last of the season's cicadas hummed.

"It has a powerful spirit, this plant. It is strong medicine." She stared at me from across the fire.

I half-nodded, not even vaguely understanding where she was going with this. My throat was dry and scratchy from the smoke. "I might need you to explain," I croaked.

"You have to understand," she said, "every plant has a spirit. Even rocks and mountains, they have a spirit too. Nature is alive with spirit. And plants are medicine. It is their spirit that heals. By the same token, they can do harm when misused. And this particular plant? It is powerful."

Where we were heading was still about as clear to me as fog over a lake. I awaited more, but she was quiet.

She bowed her head and prayed before Tatewari, Grandfather Fire. After a long silence, she finally revealed, "The plant of which I speak is Marijuana." She said the word with reverence, like it was a proper noun. "It is a powerful plant spirit, a deity. And you have offended it."

I was a little shocked, and more than a little disturbed to hear I had offended a deity. We had not spoken of marijuana, nor had she asked about it. I wasn't sure how it was relevant to my pain. I stared at her blankly.

I certainly had my heyday with marijuana when I was younger. But to me, it was just weed, dope, ganja, or if I was feeling particularly formal, cannabis. Definitely not Marijuana with a capital M, like I was talking about a *god* or something. Whatever I called it, my usage of it became less frequent over time, what with the cocktail of weird pharmaceuticals I was on. But even as my pain progressed, the buzz around medical marijuana grew, and it became more acceptable as an alternative medicine. Dispensaries popped up everywhere. Many people swore by it for pain, so why not look into it? I obtained a heaping bag of the greenest, kindest buds I could find, and eagerly rolled spliffs that would have made Bob Marley proud. I'd ease back onto the living room sofa, dutifully put on some reggae, and wait for some blessed relief. But oddly, it had the exact *opposite* effect. My pain would always be worse. At first, I thought it was a fluke. I persisted. Always with the same result: more pain. Hmm.

"You use Marijuana, sonny?" asked the shaman.

Confession time. "Uh...well...sometimes. But not so much lately. It always seems to make my pain worse, so..."

She nodded. "And do you not think this is odd? A plant which relieves pain for so many, but causes more pain for you?"

I didn't know what to say. I had to admit, it *was* pretty weird.

"You see, plants have to be respected. And you have done something to anger this plant spirit. I do not know your relationship with this plant, or what you may have done. But you must make amends."

"How do I do that?" I asked, though I wasn't sure I wanted the answer.

"In the same way you would in any relationship when you have made a mistake: you must apologize. You must make it an offering, and ask for its pardon."

I breathed out heavily. This wasn't what I had expected, but what did I know? This was an inquiry with a *shaman*, not my rheumatologist. It was new territory, and I had come here to learn something new.

She leaned toward me in the dying firelight and laid out exactly what I must do.

"You will make a small shrine, somewhere in the woods where it won't be disturbed. You must hang a feather over it. In the shrine, place two bowls. Fill one with corn and the other with tobacco. These are both sacred plants. You must visit the shrine daily and see to it the bowls are always full. You will start this immediately, and must continue doing so until the first thunderstorm of spring."

She paused to let it sink in, and then added, "You must do all this with the *utmost* of sincerity, always humble and apologetic. Your intentions will determine your success—or failure."

It was a prescription for restoring balance, but it was only the beginning.

"Let me make this very clear for you, sonny." She pointed her cigar at me and looked me in the eye. "This plant, Marijuana, is strong medicine. But it is not for you. You must never use this plant again. Can you agree to that? Can you promise that?"

Never again was a tall order, and she saw my hesitation. She insisted. She wanted my word, and wanted me to say it out loud. At that moment, I had to decide whether I would take this seriously. Deep down, I must have wanted the balance at the heart of her prescription.

"Yes, I can agree to that," I said, startled to hear the words come out of my mouth.

"Good," she replied. For her, that particular matter was settled, but I suspected there was more. She returned her gaze to the fire. After a while, she opened her eyes and said, "There is another plant, however, that you must actively seek out. It is calling to you for some reason, and you must find it. Its name is Artemisia. You must get to know this plant. Spend some time with it. Even put some beneath your pillow when you sleep. Then, in dreaming, you may come to know what it is that she asks of you."

"Artemisia?" I asked. "You mean, like, mugwort?" There are many plants in the genus *Artemisia*, including the one that cures malaria. In Greek mythology, Artemis is the goddess of the hunt, the wilderness, and wild animals.

"Yes, that is the one. When you find a patch of Artemisia growing, you must ask its permission before you take any. Give it an offering of tobacco. Have a small taste of its leaves, and then you may harvest it. Keep some in your house—especially beneath where you lay your head at night."

She made me repeat her instructions, and nodded, satisfied.

With that, our visit was done. It was late at night, and I had work to do.

The next morning, I did as she said. I built a shrine in the woods behind the house. From a low branch, I hung a red-tailed hawk feather above the shrine. I filled two wooden bowls with corn and tobacco. And for the duration of the long winter, I tended to this shrine daily.

Soon, my little shrine was buried beneath two feet of snow. I carefully shoveled it out each morning, and kept those bowls filled. Surprisingly, it was no chore. Rather, this daily ritual became the best part of my day. Alone at daybreak in the crisp winter air, I found precious moments of peace.

I eventually found the plant called Artemisia, too. It grows throughout southern New England, so I had to travel south from the mountains where I lived to find it. I dried some leaves and placed them in a sachet beneath my pillow. At night, dreams came, the likes of which I had never experienced. They were crystal clear upon waking, and resonated with meaning. Through the depths of winter, these dreams infused my days with a purpose that was otherworldly yet strangely familiar.

Winter held its icy grip for a small eternity. But one day, in the early hours of an April morning, I awoke to a loud crack of thunder and the pitter-patter of rain on the roof. I knew I was done, and could take the shrine down. The long months of practicing this daily ritual had changed me, and provided me with a connection to something deeper, however vague my understanding of it was. It was the beginning of a path toward harmony—but just the beginning.

My ordeal with ankylosing spondylitis was far from over, however, and the pain intensified like the heat from a lead sun. As the foundations of my life began to crumble beneath its weight, doubt and skepticism plagued me. Whether it was a curse that had captured me or some spiritual imbalance still eluding me, finding the source seemed like a task beyond hope.

There were two things I knew: I couldn't do it alone. And it wouldn't be the last time I encountered the old shaman.

13

A HOUSE ON FIRE

THE ORANGE GLOW of the bonfire pierces the dark of a moonless night, causing long shadows to leap like phantom dancers. The sound of drums is almost deafening, and their calculated dissonance is jarring enough to give me an uneasy feeling. Strange things are afoot in the village tonight.

The heat of the immense fire at my back is quickly becoming uncomfortable, but I'm focused on the silhouettes of the drummers before me. I try to take comfort in the anonymity of shadows, for I know my presence at this sacred event goes against custom. According to the old tradition, only those initiated into the secret societies would ever witness it.

I scan the small crowd around me for familiar faces. I see Lanciné among the trio of *dunun* players who pound the skins of their barrel-shaped drums with heavy sticks. His face is absent of the joy that typically accompanies him at festivals. Nearby, a *djembé* crackles like heat lightning, and I recognize the playing immediately. The phrases are eloquent and precise, and I've spent countless hours studying their sophisticated rhythmic lexicon. I'm shocked by the realization that it is Famoudou himself who orchestrates the event. He skillfully pushes the ensemble to a crescendo as sparks from the roaring fire tumble around us. The flames are dangerously close.

The time has come. From out of the blackness of *la brousse*, a frightful masked figure emerges. Its form is immense, and flickering light plays off shards of broken glass adhered to its ghastly form. Horns protrude from its head, and large fangs complete the image of a monster both sacred and terrifying. I know at once the mask is Kòmò, the figure-head of the most feared of all the Malinké secret societies. A reckoning must be at hand, for it is Kòmò who casts judgment on those who bring disorder to the community. His punishments are severe and unforgiving. The crowd of dark faces around me are none other than Kòmò's initiates.

My back is drenched in sweat from the nearby fire, and I squirm to ease my growing discomfort. Suddenly, Kòmò surges into the center of drummers, whirls like a dervish, and plants himself right in front of me. My heart almost stops beating, though the drums do not. The rhythm sounds wicked now, and his proximity is unnerving. Kòmò looms before me, impossibly tall, and his gruesome face is all too clear in the fire's glow. I want it all to stop, and wish to be taken away from this macabre event. But with Kòmò before me and the inferno behind me, there is no way out.

Famoudou steps forward into the pale light, and stands beside Kòmò. His hands are fast and decisive on his drum. In the firelight, Famoudou's face is transformed, as if the event has returned him to a youthful version of himself. Our eyes lock for a moment, and his gaze is deadly serious. It is then I realize all eyes are on me. With growing horror, I understand that the reckoning today is mine. Kòmò takes a step closer, imposing and dreadful. He slowly raises his arm and points a spindly finger behind me. I know I must look, but I'm terrified by what I will see.

Cautiously, I turn, for I know I must face the judgment at hand. And then I see the source of the fire: it is my own home, engulfed in flames. My heart races. How can this be? What bizarre magic or trick of the mind has conjured this impossibility? The blaze reaches a hundred feet above the roof, and the sight of it leaves me trembling. I cry out, but no sound comes from my mouth. I struggle to comprehend the wreckage before me, the burning mass of what was once my life. And then my horror is complete as I see Kerri standing at the front doorstep, framed by menacing tongues of fire, deadly cinders falling all around her. Her face is contorted in grief and anguish, but she cannot pull herself away from our burning home. My feet are frozen in place, my desperate attempts at screams silent. Kòmò seizes me in an iron grip, and a horrible pain rips through my spine. I crumple to the ground and darkness consumes me.

I awoke from the dream soaked in sweat, as if the heat from the fire had been real. It was not yet dusk, and Kerri still slept beside me. I was glad I hadn't woken her with my nightmare. I slid my hand beneath my pillow, and touched the sachet of dried Artemisia, the potent bearer of dreams. Until recently, those dreams had been infused with beauty and subtle meaning, but as of late they had turned dark, their symbolism too potent for comfort. The terrible Kòmò mask, which I saw during my last trip to Africa, had been plaguing my dreams the past several nights.

Though the sun wouldn't rise for some time, sleep would not come to me. My mind turned, ever grappling with our reality. After six years of struggling to make things work at the house, Kerri and I were reaching the end of our rope. Negotiations with the bank had failed. It was 2012, and every third house in our neighborhood bore a foreclosure sign in the front yard, the insignia of the housing crisis. Kerri and I were drowning in debt, and we might soon be joining their ranks. I feared the ordeal of seeing our dreams burned to the ground would tear us apart.

I climbed out of bed, wincing from pain but careful not to wake Kerri, and headed to my studio to sit and think. Recently, I had transformed the small space into a flute-building workshop, and my easel and art supplies were heaped in a pile against the wall. Multiple muses can't fit into one life at the same time, it seemed. For the time being, it was the flutes that consumed what little free time I had for creative projects. But at least it was something, and making the flutes according to Lanciné's guidance was all that connected me to Africa these days. Five years had passed since my last trip, and Africa was starting to recede into memory—and along with it, my identity. Endless pain, work that was never enough, and bills I might never pay were what defined me now.

I pushed aside the pile of half-built flutes, sat in my creaky old chair, and put my feet up. Hanging on the wall above me was the last painting I did, which was now several years ago. I sighed at *that* thought. The painting depicted a festival in the village, with Famoudou at the front of a crowd playing his *djembé*. It was a fine painting—my best work, really —and it made me recall those days in college when I first mixed art and anthropology. I wondered where the old painting of Elmina Castle was now. Who did I sell that painting to, so long ago? I couldn't even remember, but I hoped it was to a friend. Maybe I'd get to see it again someday. Hell, maybe I'd make *art* again someday.

I pondered all that had transpired since Kerri and I stood before the whitewashed walls of that infamous castle in Ghana a decade earlier. The years were slipping away, tumbling down a chute with little resistance. Our thirties were almost gone, and Kerri and I still hadn't married, and had no kids. Gone were our carefree days of adventure and discovery. Our future was anything but certain, and the clock was ticking as my condition worsened every day. I didn't know how much more I could take.

I glanced at the time. 3:30 a.m. The pain was already searing. I had needed two Percocet just to get me into bed last night, but those had long worn off. Amidst the clutter of my workshop table, I spied the little plastic container. I picked it up and gave it a shake, listened for the familiar rattle, and was alarmed to hear I was running a bit low. *Oh, what the fuck.* Kerri wouldn't be up for hours, and I was in pain. I could call the doctor later today and make arrangements for more. I gobbled a couple down, and waited. On an empty stomach, it wouldn't be long until I got some relief.

Meanwhile, thoughts of Kòmò the reckoner and a house on fire filled my head. I could practically feel the heat at my back from the growing inferno in my life. And later today, Kerri and I had an appointment to keep with a different sort of reckoner.

∾

We were mostly quiet during the hour-long drive, each wrangling with our emotions. When we arrived at our destination, we lingered in the car for a few moments before reluctantly stepping out. Our lawyer's home office was nestled into the woods in a small Vermont town, just over the border from New Hampshire. We had searched for just the right guy, and had settled on Michael, a nature-loving, open-minded fellow who saw the injustices of the system and fought for the little guy. His easy, relaxed approach had made us feel at home in disorienting territory. He seemed both relatable and knowledgeable.

We knocked at the door and Michael greeted us.

"Come in, you guys. Make yourselves at home. Can I offer you some tea or coffee?"

"Sure, I'll take a coffee." I hadn't slept much, and fatigue was setting in.

"Just water for me," Kerri said. "Thank you."

Michael went to fetch the drinks while Kerri and I seated ourselves in front of his desk. I reached for her hand.

"It's going to be OK," I said, though I wasn't exactly sure how.

"I know. I'm glad we're here. I'm still scared, though. I don't want to lose everything we've worked for..." She choked back a few tears, and I squeezed her hand a little harder. God, we'd been through so much.

Michael returned with the hot coffee and water, and sat before us. His office was rustic and homey, and smelled like pine.

"Well, let's get started. I've gone through your numbers, and..." He furrowed his brow and paused a moment, seeing our worried gazes. Perhaps he was trying to find the words that might soften the blow. He exhaled deeply.

"Look, you guys, it's not what you want to hear, but I'll get right to the point. I know you've been fighting hard to keep up with your payments, but right now, foreclosure is your best option. You have to understand, the bank is playing by their rules. They expect you to succumb to guilt and fork over whatever money you have left, and then they'll take your house anyway. And when they do, they'll collect the insurance for the full value of the house—insurance you've been paying on their behalf—and then they'll sell it at market price anyway. It's a double dip, and they're going to make a pile of cash on it. That's the way it works. Please don't waste a single moment feeling bad about not paying them."

He had our full attention.

"But you can play by their rules, too. Don't make it personal. I suggest you stop paying them entirely. Seriously, don't give them another dime. We can string this out as long as we can, and give you guys a fighting chance to get back on your feet."

I looked at Kerri, whose eyes were watering again. I knew losing the house would crush her, but Michael was offering a way back to a life we could manage.

"So, what do we need to do?" she asked after a long silence. "How do we pull this off?"

"Well, I know it's gonna be a hard pill to swallow," he replied, "but I suggest a double bankruptcy. Since you're not married, you can file singly, one at a time. We wait until the last possible moment to file the first one, and the moment you do, they have to cease the foreclosure proceedings for six months. After which, we'll file the second bank-ruptcy to buy you another six months. That gives you more than a full year to live in your house for free, save up all you can, and find a new place to live. When they finally foreclose—and they will—you'll be in better shape to start a new life."

It *was* a hard pill to swallow, but hey, I had gotten good at swal-lowing pills—between eight and ten a day, by my reckoning. This at least seemed like a pill that might offer some long-term relief. I wished my doctors would propose something like that.

"And plus," he continued, "all that medical debt you're swimming in? That'll be gone too. Wiped clean."

It was a glimmer of light in an otherwise bleak sky. Without that debt, I'd have time again. Time for art, for friends, to reclaim some semblance of a life I actually wanted. It wouldn't erase my pain, but it might ease the stress that compounded it. I didn't need to hear much more to know this was our only way out. Kerri had more questions.

"What about my college loans?" Kerri asked. "Are those going to be wiped clean too?"

"Huh!" Michael guffawed, but quickly regained his composure and feigned a cough. "I'm sorry, Kerri, but unfortunately, no. Until the day comes when we get an elected government smart enough to see that student debt forgiveness would be a huge benefit for our country, you're stuck with it. Which is to say, you're probably stuck with it forever."

Kerri slumped into her chair. This wasn't going her way at all.

After some further discussion, Michael wished us fortitude with our decision, and bid us farewell.

"You know how to reach me," he said. "I'm here to help. Call anytime."

Kerri cried most of the way home.

"We've worked so hard on this house," she said through tears. "The foundation, the floors, the new roof, the barn—and we're just gonna admit defeat and walk away from all of it?"

I hung my head, knowing it was a fight we weren't going to win. There would be casualties, and I felt responsible for the whole thing. If only I didn't have this disease. If only I had been smarter, more capable. I was losing faith in myself and my ability to survive in this world as a creative person.

"Yes, Kerri. I think we've lost this battle." I cringed at the words. The house was supposed to be a sanctuary for our dreams, but instead, it was crushing them. We had considered every option, and they were all losing propositions. "I just don't know what else we can do, Kerri. But when this is over, we can start fresh. Me and you. *Together*."

The last bit put me on precarious footing. We had spoken more than once in the past months about the possibility of going our separate ways if we lost the house. Until now, the house had served as the glue that kept us from drifting apart. I didn't actually know if the next chapter of our lives would be written together, but I wasn't about to leave her side after all she'd seen me through.

After long days of deliberation, we agreed to do as Michael had suggested. He helped take the sting out of the otherwise painful process, and for that, we were grateful. With the sizable mortgage payment off our plates, stress abated for a time, but the year passed all too quickly. Kerri and I drifted further apart. When the time came to pack up our belongings and start moving out, the tears began to fall anew. Though she would never say it, I knew deep down I had failed her. And losing our home made me feel I had fallen short at the most fundamental level: as a *man*.

It was while I was packing boxes in the bedroom that I came across the book in her nightstand drawer. *Too Good to Leave, Too Bad to Stay: A Step-by-Step Guide to Help You Decide Whether to Stay In or Get Out of Your Relationship.* The subtitle made me wince. I wondered how many steps there were, and which one she was on. The house was burning in more ways than one.

The last day at the old farmhouse arrived with the swiftness of the executioner's blade. The tears fell like rain as the bank agent pounded the nails into the foreclosure sign. We felt each one drive into our hearts. We drove away watching the house and barn get smaller, along with the life we had worked so hard to build. The surrounding fields remained unplanted and unharvested, like so many other dreams.

After we lost the house, we tried to salvage the life we had, to move on. We found a rental in the next town over. It was a fresh start—at least that's how I saw it. I was liberated from the burden of the old house. Gone was the stress of bills piling up and costly repairs to make. I missed the ol' homestead, but I couldn't waste time dwelling in the past. I had to redeem myself, and I had work to do.

At the new place, I had more time, and with that, I had ideas. I was chomping at the bit to make art, and do something with it to help us out of our financial mess. I set up an art studio. Every morning, my newfound inspiration launched me out of bed like rocket fuel. I was finally going to write and illustrate a *book*. About *Africa*.

Kerri was languishing in the loss of the house, but I was coming alive. Even my pain subsided for a time. I managed to put the pills aside, which brought further clarity and energy. The monochromatic shades of my emotions brightened to delightful new hues. Being off the pills was like awakening on a spring morning to find the gray of winter replaced by bright greens and yellows, all shimmering beneath a cobalt sky.

Over the long winter, I put myself to the task of creating a book that portrayed Africa's richness. I made maps and drawings. New paintings adorned my easels. I photographed all this new artwork with artifacts I had collected, and meticulously created collages that resembled manuscripts unearthed from the sands of the Sahara. To accompany this visual feast, I wrote everything I knew about the traditions of those living along the *Djoliba*, the Niger River. For good measure, I transcribed a dozen traditional rhythms to assist students of West African drumming, and included them in the book.

I was on fire. On each page, the Africa I knew and loved came alive again. Her rhythms, majesty, and mystery lifted me up. I had a sense of purpose I hadn't felt in a long time, and completed the book in less than six months.

I put the finishing touches on the final painting, and stared at it on the easel for a long time. The old blacksmith's eyes were dark, yet so knowing. Sako Gbè's presence filled the room. It was Sako, a renowned sorcerer, who was the esteemed leader of the feared Kòmò society. He epitomized the essence of the mysterious and ancient, and his mystique enthralled me. I trembled at the thought, but I knew I would use his image for the book's cover.

With that, the book was complete. I called it *Djoliba Crossing*, hearkening to my first crossing of that river and into a whole new world. Holding the first printed copy of my new book was my proudest moment. It was my treasure chest of memories, and I needed only reopen it to behold the riches within. It had all been real.

I thought back to my college days and my old girlfriend Camille, who had since made a name for herself in the art world. Maybe I'd make something of myself after all. I was eager to prove to Kerri I could do something with my talents that would actually benefit us. My art needed to earn its keep around here, lest it be the subject of further condemnation. I was treading on thin ice as it was.

Alas, I live in a modern world that cares little for archaic treasures, and for whom the stories of the old cultures mean little. I suppose I shouldn't have been surprised that the book went nowhere. Like many modern works of creative expression, it was quickly buried in an icy cultural blizzard of meaningless entertainment and two-second news blips. Its ultimate failure confirmed for me that the modern world had little place for the likes of me amidst its frenzied search for disposable thrills. At any rate, I had to admit I had been horribly naïve to think my niche book about West African culture would somehow become a breakaway hit in the mainstream publishing world. What a fool.

Not a year after, my pain climbed to astronomical levels and my self-esteem plummeted to rock bottom. Pills became my sanctuary from both emotional and physical distress once again. Finances got tight, since I had spent what little savings I had on printing books. I doubted Kerri would stay with me now, and I couldn't blame her. I was the most gifted failure you might ever meet, and it was disparaging that a guy like me with all these talents couldn't find a way to succeed in the world. *I* was the house on fire, and anyone foolish enough to get close to me was bound to get caught in the flames.

During my weekly visits with Julie, I bemoaned the book's lack of success.

"Julie, *why*? I mean, I felt called to make this book. Was it really for *no* reason? God, I just want to know what the point was. I just want to know *why*."

"From the shaman's point of view," she replied, "the question 'why' is pointless, Dave. Some things are unknowable. You made the book because you had to make the book, that is all. You enjoyed creating it, didn't you? There may still be some other reason, but we just can't see it yet. Or maybe not. Trust in the wisdom of the universe, and let it go. Move on to the next thing."

I saw the wisdom in letting go, and maybe even knew my sanity depended on it. Though it hurt, I vowed to tuck it away and get on with my life. God knows, I had other work to do.

I relegated the book to the dusty attic of forgotten treasures, but I couldn't bury it deeply enough, for it still gnawed at me. Perhaps the book still contained some small quantity of magic. Like an artifact waiting to be unearthed, it would eventually be the catalyst that propelled me further into the dark secrets of Africa—and closer, I hoped, to my redemption. I needed healing, and I needed it badly.

14

THE SOUND OF SIRENS

LANCINÉ AND I MARCH ONWARD, and the forest canopy opens up briefly to expose the sky. Although the sun is relentless above us, ominous dark clouds are building on the horizon. They add to the sense of foreboding growing in my heart. It's too early in the season for rain, but the seasons have become as unpredictable as the lightning bolts of pain that shoot through me as we walk.

"Lanciné, it looks like rain ahead," I say.

He stops and assesses. "No, Daouda, I am not so sure. The clouds will build like this for many weeks. They are only taunting us. We will be gone from the village before the rains come. Remember, we have an agreement."

The unnecessary reminder makes me bristle. We've come so far, but my future remains as uncertain as the coming of the rains. Both the sun and the book I carry on my back feel heavy as lead.

Africa came knocking at my door again just a year after Kerri and I lost the house. I probably should have politely turned her away. Between dealing with a relationship verging on collapse and a body that wasn't faring much better, I had pretty much all I could handle. But like all sirens, Africa knew the right ways to seduce me. Despite the danger I knew lay ahead, I was like a hapless sailor, blinded by her song to the inevitable shipwreck on the rocky shore.

The trip came about through a close friend and *djembefola* from Guinée named Sayon. To say that Sayon was a good drummer would be an understatement. Raised in a small village in the Faranah region of Guinée, he received his first *djembé* as a gift from his father at seven years old, and apprenticed with a master in his village. When he moved to Conakry as a young man, his burgeoning talents garnered the attention of none other than the grand master himself, Famoudou Konaté. Famoudou took Sayon under his wing and made him his protégé. Over the decades that followed, Sayon honed his skills to razor precision. Coupled with his deep knowledge of the traditions, he earned a reputation as one of the premier *djembefolas* in the region.

I met Sayon in Conakry around the same time I met Lanciné, and we became friends right away. I can say without reservation that Sayon was the most positive and happy person I'd ever met, and it was impossible not to be swept up in his joy. As they say, enthusiasm can be contagious. Conakry is also where Sayon met and wooed his wife Lev, an American dance student I knew from back home. Their eventual marriage was fortuitous for many reasons. Not the least of these was that it afforded Sayon the opportunity to embark on a new life in the States, which carried positive implications for his entire village. And it was lucky for me, too—when Sayon took up residence and sought work in a Vermont town just an hour from me, it was only natural that he joined our six-piece performance troupe, then called *Landaya Ensemble*.

Soon, our newly restructured group, *Sayon Camara and Landaya*, became a rhythmic force to be reckoned with. Our concerts and cultural presentations were charged with new energy and enthusiasm. On the stages of small festivals and local concert halls, I traded *djembé* solos with our dynamic new frontman. Kerri and our dedicated crew in Landaya backed us, pounding out traditional rhythms on the *dunun* drums. For Sayon, it was thrilling to move to a new country in midlife and slide right into a competent band that already knew his music, not to mention get paid something like real money. For me, Sayon was the missing piece to an unfinished puzzle, and Landaya was one of the few puzzles in my life that still made any sense.

During our time together, Sayon and I spoke often about his ambitions to introduce his culture to American audiences.

"David," he said during one such conversation, pronouncing my name *Dah-veed*, "I want that you help me. We bring students to *mon village*. We make workshop together in Africa."

I liked the idea, of course, but was wary about taking on a big project after my recent fiascos with the house and the book.

"Geez, Sayon, I'd love to help, but I just don't think I have time to organize a student trip, let alone travel to Africa myself. Money problems, you know?"

"*Oui*, I know well. Money always very difficult. But we no go for long time. One month only. You stay with you teacher Lanciné in Conakry, you no pay big money. We make village trip together. Lanciné, he come too. Food no expensive in village."

Well, it *is* pretty inexpensive to stay in the village, if you do it right. The only big cost is getting there, and plane tickets to Guinée were pretty cheap at the time, given the political turmoil and uprisings of the past several years. Still, getting *myself* there and back safely was one thing. But a trip to a tumultuous third-world country with a group of inexperienced travelers? That was another.

"Hmm, I dunno, Sayon. Organizing an Africa trip for a whole bunch of *tubabus* is a whole lotta work. I'm not sure I can take it on."

Sayon had realistic expectations for his first such endeavor, though, and wanted to reassure me we wouldn't be getting in over our heads.

"We start small-small. No big-big," he said, and I couldn't help but smile at his phrase. "Five, maybe six student. We say to Landaya group, 'Landaya, you come Guinée.' Maybe one, two person more."

Traveling with my dear friends and bandmates in Landaya *did* sound appealing. These were folks who had started off as my students years ago, and through hard work and determination, had become quite capable drummers. A group trip to Africa under Sayon's tutelage would enrich their playing and provide us with new inspiration for our concerts. Now *that* was something I could get on board with. Hell, I could even write the whole thing off as a business expense.

"Well," I said, softening to the idea and trying it on for size, "I suppose if you and Lev can pull together the logistics, *maybe* I can assist once we're there? I know both cultures, and could be a bridge. If students happy, Sayon happy, you know?"

"*Oui*, Sayon very happy! It no be big work for you. You will have many free time." In a sing-songy voice, he added, "You play music with Lanciné, you visit Famoudou..." He was really singing my song now. Now that he was all warmed up, he got right to the tune's irresistible hook. "I think you must bring book, you show to Famoudou. You make gift to village for book. This very good opportunity for Dah-veed. It bring good luck."

That last refrain stopped me cold. Presenting the book to my mentor, Famoudou, along with the customary gifts of reciprocity, was an act that was both culturally expected and long overdue. I really should have sought his blessing before I even started the book, but life was already too complicated. I often wondered if I had brought about my own bad luck by not adhering to custom.

"Well, Sayon, that does sound good. I really *ought* to show Famoudou the book..." I trailed off as my brain sternly reminded me of what I'd be getting into with an Africa trip, and all the responsibilities I'd be leaving behind. Without missing a beat, my old friend Erik's voice joined in the final rousing chorus:

Fuck the dumb shit! Life is short!

Even Tetteh from Ghana had a line in this song:

Do some-thing before you die!

The siren song of Africa was too much. A groan escaped me as my poor brain realized that my heart had already boarded the plane. Any further attempts at logic were useless.

"Alright, Sayon," I declared. "What the hell. I'm in! Let's make it happen."

Sayon was elated. "Ohh, thank you, Dah-*veed* ! I very happy. I *love* Landaya group. We will make very good music together in Africa!"

Momentum for the trip picked up rapidly without much effort on my part. Sayon and Lev wasted no time in making preparations to host a student group in Sayon's village, located in the Faranah region of Guinée—an area where I hadn't spent much time yet. The source of the

Niger River is in this region, in a village known as Tembakounda in the Djallon Mountains. We'd pass right through it on our way to Sayon's home further north. My excitement grew.

My crew in Landaya, as it turned out, were wholly on board with the trip, equally swept up in Sayon's unbridled joy. They were all ready to drop everything for a month and take off for Africa, with only one notable holdout: my star *sangban* player, Kerri.

She approached me one day to talk, and I knew something was up.

"Dave, this is hard for me to say," she started, her eyes about to overflow with tears. I braced myself. "Performing with Landaya has become too much for me. I'm leaving the group."

I was a bit stunned, but couldn't say I hadn't seen it coming. *Life* was a bit much these days, and we were both eager to take some things off our plates. But she was a founding member of a group that had weathered almost a decade. I mean, it's not like we were the Rolling fucking Stones or anything, but ten years is a good run for any band. And for Kerri and I, Landaya had always been something that was *ours*. *Together*. But times were changing, and nothing lasts forever. I knew I had to let her go. It would be a weight off both of us.

"I understand, Kerri," I said. "If leaving the group relieves some pressure for you, then do what you need to do. You'll be missed, for sure. But your happiness comes first."

We embraced for a long while, both aware it was the end of an era for us. Our individual pursuits for happiness made us like two ragged explorers lost in the desert without water. Our search for sustenance in an otherwise barren landscape was leading us away from each other.

Kerri wasn't done with what she had to say.

"Dave, I..." She faltered for a moment, and I looked at her reassuringly. She heaved a breath, then said, "I don't want you to go back to Africa. There's too much to do here at the new house. Winter is setting in, and I don't want to be here alone."

"Kerri," I grunted, my warm emotions quickly turning to exasperation, "Come on. I *have* to go. Sayon and everyone in Landaya are counting on me. And this may be my only opportunity to seek Famoudou's blessings for the book. He's no spring chicken, you know?

He's gotta be pushing eighty by now, in a country where the life expectancy isn't even *sixty*."

Kerri sighed. She knew once I had my heart set on something, little would stop me. We argued, but like a boulder at the foot of a mountain, I wasn't going to budge.

"Fine," she said at last, in a voice that made it clear it wasn't. "If you really have to go, so be it. Just don't expect me to wait around for you forever. I'm tired of being alone." She stormed off in tears, leaving me fuming and bewildered.

The wheels of multiple gears were turning, though they grated in opposition to each other. I was stuck between them, and they were grinding my soul to a coarse powder. I didn't know what life I wanted, but I was being forced to choose.

As the bitter cold of winter set in and the first snowflakes fell, my pain rose to excruciating levels. My body felt like an antique car with way too many miles on it. I knew my traveling days wouldn't last forever. Though I suspected I was pushing my luck in multiple realms, I made my decision. When I departed for the warmth of Africa, I knew seeking Famoudou's blessings and returning to his village were not optional for me, and that it might well be my last trip. But sirens were sounding, warning me that the path I was choosing was fraught with new peril. I could only wonder if Kerri would still be there when I returned.

15

TOUCHING THE SACRED

WHEN I ARRIVED at Famoudou Konaté's house in Conakry, a group of elders were sitting beneath the tree in his private courtyard. It was a place I knew well. I had spent many winters right here, under the tutelage of the master. But now, all was quiet. There were no students, no crowds gathered. Years had passed, and Famoudou was aging. He rarely held workshops anymore.

Lanciné, Sayon, and I sat among the distinguished group. I looked at the wizened faces of the elders, and tried to make myself appear smaller. The book was still hidden in my backpack, but as the greetings concluded, all eyes turned to me.

"Where is this book?" Famoudou asked. "Bring it forth now. I am eager to see it."

The small assembly was silent as I reached into my bag with trembling hands, heart racing. I had never imagined how it would actually feel to sit before a group of respected elders in Africa and place my heart before them.

I passed the book to Lanciné, who handed it to Sayon, who placed it before my mentor.

Famoudou picked up the book and glanced at the image of Sako Gbé, the old blacksmith, on the cover. He set it down just as quickly.

"This man, he has died."

The words came as a blow. I hadn't known. I bowed my head, and sat quietly, waiting for Famoudou to continue. Was he angry with me?

The elders too were quiet, waiting for Famoudou to speak. I squirmed beneath the weight of their gazes. Lanciné and Sayon sat confidently beside me. That at least was comforting. We had just spent three weeks in Sayon's village outside Faranah, and the trip had brought us closer. I saw these guys as nothing less than brothers now.

Time came to a standstill, and the silence was unbearable. Famoudou's words carried weight. If he condemned the book, I would be devastated.

Famoudou picked up the book again. He creased his forehead as he examined the painting on the cover.

"This man, he has died," Famoudou repeated. He returned the book to his lap. "But through your book, he now lives forever."

The air lightened, and I breathed a sigh of relief. Famoudou flipped through the pages, and the lines on his forehead relaxed. Soon, a smile appeared on his face.

"Ah! The *baratii*. You have depicted them well."

He was looking at the drawings of the men who dance the *dununba*. The drawings depicted them with the axes and leather whips they hold while dancing to prove their strength.

"And *Mamaya!*" He let out a laugh as he took in my illustration of the dancers in their white robes. "Yes, this is how it is danced in the village."

Famoudou slowly turned the pages, and remarked at each piece of artwork. The images showed people from his village who were well known to him. At each page, he spoke their names aloud.

"Moussa Keïta…Nansady Babila…and here is Djouba Fodéya! And Djelilouma Kouyaté…" On and on he went. I beamed.

Here and there, he paused. Some people had since passed away. Village life is tenuous. Illnesses like malaria, yellow fever, and typhoid take people suddenly. Even small wounds became life-threatening. From one day to the next, the community changed. Famoudou was pleased I had paid tribute to these people. Their memories would live on, too.

As Famoudou turned each page, the other elders crowded around to see. Their faces too lit up with joy. As he read, Famoudou brought up the possibility of making a return trip to the village, together, to present a token of gratitude and respect. The idea of a road trip across Guinée with the grand master of the *djembé* himself was thrilling—if we could pull it off. I was three weeks into what was supposed to be a month-long stay. But for this, I wouldn't hesitate to extend the trip.

Still, I was nervous. In the final pages of the book, there were drawings of sacred masks. I wasn't sure how Famoudou would react to seeing these printed in a book.

For an outsider like me, the significance of fetish masks has always been difficult to grasp. When removed from the context of their associated music, dances, and religious rites, they are mere objects. Beautiful and mysterious perhaps, but objects just the same. In the context of their traditions, however, these masks are nothing short of magic. They have the power to bring the metaphysical into physical form; that is to say, they are a tangible representation of the universe's unknowable and unseen powers. When the masks dance, they invoke both ancestor spirits and the gods themselves.

The symbolic imagery of the masks is striking. They are often covered with shells, horns, dried blood, grass, dirt, small mirrors, and more. These objects all contain their own *nyama*, and collectively add to the mask's power. Both beautiful and grotesque, the masks conform to a visual aesthetic that evokes wonder and mystery. They are art infused with magic, sculptural pieces that carry great meaning.

Understanding the masks requires a lifetime of context. A village child hears from birth the songs and narratives that accompany these masks, forming a web of meaning that is inseparable from life. Saturated in such meaning, the masks invoke both wonder and fear, and always respect. For those born into the culture, the idea that sacred masks become dancing gods is as real as rain.

During my time in the villages, I saw many of these masks, and was witness to a number of their festivals. Some are public affairs, and it disturbed no one that an outsider was present. Others, however, are so sacred that the presence of a foreigner was unthinkable. Some masks cannot be looked upon by the uninitiated. Even uttering their names is taboo, for their secrets must be kept. During such occasions, I hid myself away, and listened from afar to the sound of drums.

Even in remote regions where such traditions have persisted, however, times are changing. The rising tide of Islamic influences and the reach of the modern world have resulted in a breakdown of traditions, which is perhaps why I saw certain sacred masks. As a young visitor in a foreign land, I was both fascinated and repulsed by them. They cast a spell on me, though I was naïve to their power.

When I made the book, I recalled my experiences of Africa's mysterious side. I drew the masks. What compelled me to do so? Sheer fascination. Insatiable curiosity, perhaps. Or maybe it was because many of these masks are exhibited as "art" in museums around the world. I didn't see any harm in drawing them.

I spent hours rendering the *nyama*-charged details of each mask, drawing from both memory and my village sketchbooks. While I worked, I listened to my field recordings of the rhythms played for each mask. These were powerful art-making sessions. As rhythms filled my head, I was transported back to Africa, and the hours disappeared like wisps of smoke from a candle. The masks appeared on paper like I was summoning them from the realm of the ancestors themselves. Their potent symbolism left me trembling, both the spell-maker and the recipient of those spells. I was *conjuring* the masks, *willing* them to reveal themselves before me. But like an apprentice stumbling upon the magic chest of the wizard, I knew not what I was opening.

Art is magic, as any Malinké mask-sculptor knows well. There is *nyama* in art. In the village, initiated blacksmiths carve these masks. Doing so invokes ancestral spirits and the forces of nature, and brings form to that which has no form. Through their initiation, the blacksmith sculptors are protected from the dangerous forces released in their very making.

To the Western mind, this may sound like hocus-pocus. But to those steeped in the traditions of the sacred masks, drawing them was dangerous business. I was uninitiated, and thus unprotected from their *nyama*.

Some of the finished drawings frightened me, so I never shared them. This was much different from the artwork I had produced for the Elmina book so many years ago. But I dared include several mask drawings in *Djoliba Crossing*, along with transcriptions of their sacred music. In doing so, I was unwittingly dancing the line between anthropologist and something quite else.

~

I recall an incident from an earlier trip when I was traveling with Famoudou and several other students.

In the courtyard where we stayed, there was a tree. From it, a most curious object was suspended by rope: a single antelope horn. Whoever hung it there had affixed to it rings of cowrie shells and various other items. They then smeared it with dried blood, and sprayed chewed-up bits of kola nuts across its surface. Various other ingredients were placed inside it, and the horn was sealed off.

It was not a friendly-looking object, and did not invite user participation. I stayed clear of it.

That was not the case for another young traveler, whose curiosity got the better of him. Rather innocently, he wandered over to get a better look. Before he could be stopped, he reached up and touched the object.

Famoudou and several other men sprang to their feet. A flurry of commotion ensued. They tried to stop him, but it was too late. The boy held the object in his hand.

"You *fool!*" cursed Famoudou. "You do not know what you have done." He muttered something under his breath and hurried away. The outburst shocked me. Famoudou was typically very mild-mannered and tolerant.

Famoudou returned several moments later and gently removed the object from the tree, careful to handle it by the rope. He wrapped it in a small blanket and disappeared once again. When he returned, he reprimanded the boy.

"You must never touch such *gris-gris* objects. They are dangerous. Handling them can bring great misfortune." Famoudou was dead serious. "We must consult a healer, and find the appropriate means to cleanse you of its *nyama*. For your sake, I hope we can do so before it is too late."

In some ways, *nyama* is like an electric current that courses through everything. Touching a live electrical wire, for example, can cause its current to flow into us and give us a nasty shock (or worse). And now, I saw that *nyama* can be transferred in such a way as well.

The next day, Famoudou arranged a visit to a local sorcerer. I guess he figured it would be a good education for the foreigners, because several of us were invited along.

The sorcerer's hut was humble and crudely built, with a cramped, dirty interior. The only light came through a narrow doorway. The sorcerer was old, and sat bare-chested along the far wall. Around him, bones, skulls, beaks, and feathers littered the floor. Jars of powders and leaves sat on dusty shelves. These were the ingredients with which he made various amulets and medicines.

Famoudou explained the situation, and unwrapped the *gris-gris* object. The old sorcerer considered it for a long time. He then produced some kola nuts, and cast them to the earthen floor like dice. When they split apart, some halves fell face up, and some face down. The old man used the result to divine the remedy.

The boy needed a specific anti-potion, and quick. But the old sorcerer did not have all the ingredients on hand, so it was up to the boy to find them by whatever means possible. I do not remember all the ingredients—many of them were plant ingredients that could be gathered in the bush. But one item stood out clearly: a lock of fur from a lion.

Under Famoudou's urging, he took the matter seriously. He was able to collect the ingredients, mostly from the forest and marketplaces. He even procured the lock of fur, which I had imagined was going to be a deal-breaker. With all the objects in hand, he returned to the old sorcerer alone to finish the task. I did not hear any more about the incident, and I do not know his fate.

∼

Famoudou flipped to the last pages of my book, and let out a short gasp. He had arrived at the drawing of Kòmò, the ancient and terrible being who counters the darkest forces in the universe. Kòmò, who judges the deeds of the wicked and doles out punishments with severity. In Famoudou's time, Kòmò was never to be looked upon. To do so meant certain death.

I was with Famoudou the night Kòmò emerged from the darkness, its horns and fangs protruding menacingly from its mask. Famoudou had turned away from its hideous visage as the drummers played its arcane rhythms. Afterward, he refused to talk about it.

What folly compelled me to render its terrible likeness on paper? I do not know. In the depths of my pain and despair, I was attracted to it like a moth to the flame.

Famoudou's expression turned serious, all too reminiscent of the look I saw after the incident with the boy and the *gris-gris* object. He closed the book and again examined the cover. The image of Sako Gbè stared out at us. He had been a blacksmith sorcerer of great renown, and was the leader of the Kòmò association in the village until his death.

Famoudou folded his hands across his lap, then brought them to his face. He turned to me.

"Now we *must* return to the village."

I was an outsider here, a white man. I had ventured too close to the traditions, and touched something sacred. But what was done, was done. There was a price to be paid.

Though my pain was debilitating from weeks of travel, Famoudou and I agreed to make one last voyage to the village—right away. I made calls to change my return flight, and readied myself for the grueling trip back to the interior Hamanah region, some twenty hours away. What had started as an idea for a casual road trip now took on the gravity of a sacred mission.

But political tensions in Guinée were high that year. Military road-blocks made passage difficult. Roads were in disrepair. Though we tried, Famoudou and I were eventually forced to turn around, and never made it to the village. I had no choice but to return home.

Before I left Guinée, Famoudou and I decided upon a sum of money that he would later disperse in the village on my behalf. It felt trivial to me, but it was the best I could do. Famoudou, at least, was satisfied that the temporary offering might forestall any grave misfortune.

"Of all the people who have come to study with me," Famoudou reassured me, "only you have returned. The village respects my word. If I am happy with the book, the village will be happy. You need only my blessing. And I give that to you now."

Famoudou's blessing was a relief, but I was unresolved nonetheless. My chance at real redemption had eluded me, and knew I would have to return someday.

I departed from Guinée terribly disappointed, and was greeted in the States by a brutally cold winter, and a hearth that was equally chilly. Though Kerri was still there in form, her heart was shuttered away in an icy fortress of resentment. I had been away too long, and she wasn't going to let me forget. Nor would the escalating pain from ankylosing spondylitis, which threatened to solidify the joints of my spine into a frozen scepter that would never thaw.

16

A TICKING CLOCK

"DAOUDA, we're going to rest here. The heat has captured me, and I need to pause a moment." He points to a grove of trees that offers some shade, and fans himself a little too dramatically. He's being kind, and giving me an excuse to get some relief from the incessant throbbing in my joints. I'll take the break, though I won't admit I need it.

"Sure, Lanciné. If you need to rest, that's fine with me."

The faint trace of a smile appears on his face. "Yes, Daouda, that would be good."

Daouda. I like it when he calls me by that name, the one given to me in Africa. It means "David" in Arabic, but it's become more like an alternate identity. It helps me escape the past.

I drop my pack to the ground and examine the tree's roots for a spot to sit. The shade is a welcome relief. As Lanciné and I talk lightly about this and that, I appreciate the time to just be present with an old friend beneath a shady tree somewhere in Africa. The rest of the world might as well not even exist.

The forest around us hums and buzzes. I'm dwarfed by the trees towering above me. My insignificance is evident.

Perhaps in the end, none of this will have mattered. I am like a grain of sand that will be swept away in the Sahara.

A soft breeze rustles the leaves and I close my eyes. I could stay in this moment forever. Back home, the modern world races around in its perpetual, meaningless frenzy. I don't care. I don't belong to that world now. Maybe I never will again.

But I can't escape the past, nor can I stop the memories from arising.

Just six months earlier, I was waiting in a hospital room in America. The room was sterile and white, windowless and hostile. Couldn't they at least have added a few plants? A skylight that let in a glimmer of blue sky? I wanted to be outside, barefoot with my feet in the dirt. In the mountains perhaps, by a stream cascading over rocks. *Anywhere* but here, actually. Could I slip out the door? I'd been waiting a while. Earlier that morning, I had considered canceling the appointment, but—

The door opened abruptly. *Shit. No way out now.* The doctor greeted me and shook my hand. He held my charts and X-rays under his arm, and promptly set them on his desk without looking at them. A frown appeared on his face, and he straightened his white coat. He'd been following my case for a decade and a half, since my return from Ghana in 2001.

"It's progressing too rapidly," he said matter-of-factly. It didn't surprise me. The pain told me that every day. But what he said next came as a shock.

"Our next course of action is to operate. To permanently fuse the spine. It's not safe for you to be walking around like this—if you had a fall or an accident, you could break your spine. It's become too brittle."

I stared at him, suddenly not sure whether I trusted him. This past year, I had worked so hard. I'd lost weight, started working out, and changed my diet.

"Plus, you've lost too much weight," he said, "Are you OK?"

I thought I looked OK, all things considered. I'd always been good at hiding my condition. But no words came out of my mouth.

"At your age, it's difficult to regain muscle once you've lost it," he informed me.

At my age! When had I become elderly? I was forty, not eighty. I shot him an incredulous look, but said nothing. I wasn't going to make this easy for him.

"Listen," he said with a sigh, "I highly recommend you consider this. This disease isn't going anywhere. The surgery is the only long-term solution we've got. It'll help ease the pain. More importantly, it will keep you safe. But there are risks with the surgery, of course, and you should understand the possible outcomes—"

I stopped him there. "Outcomes! Like *what?*"

"Well, your mobility will be limited, for one. You might need help doing certain day-to-day things. Bending over to lace your shoes, lifting things, and so on. You'll certainly need to reconsider traveling. And you'll likely need to stop performing with that heavy drum strapped to your shoulders, and—"

He stopped himself as my face went as pale as a ghost. He was terrifying me and he knew it. His shoulders drooped, and he let out another sigh.

"Look, Dave. I've known you a long time. I've seen this disease progress, and I know how much you've suffered. But you have to ask yourself now, what kind of life do you want from here on out? The fragility of your spine is a real concern that could put your life at risk. It might be time to try something different, you know? To go a different route. And it's *definitely* time to consider different treatment options. You can't just keep taking pain pills for the rest of your life."

I glared at him like a stubborn teenager. I hated what he was telling me, but I was admittedly at the end of my rope. He was probably right, but there was no way I was ready to swallow the bitter pill he was offering me, not without a fight. I mean, a life where I couldn't perform, hike, travel, or even tie my goddamn shoes? *That* was a life I didn't want. If this was my best alternative, I would prefer to die. I imagined taking one last, arduous hike into the mountains, never to return. Or maybe I'd finally give myself to Africa, and die quietly in some remote village. But were these my only alternatives? Was there really no other path to healing than what the doctor was proposing?

"Look," he said again, sensing he was getting nowhere, "I want you to talk to a member of our team. She can provide you with more information. You can take some time to decide. Sleep on it a bit. We don't have to rush into this, but I want you to consider it."

He wrote down a room number on a small piece of paper, and shook my hand one more time before leaving me to my thoughts. My mind raced, making one last desperate attempt to reverse engineer the situation. If my life hadn't been a Gordian knot before this, well, it certainly was *now*.

I glanced at the paper and read the room number. Back down to floor one. I inched myself off the bench to avoid another spasm, and took the stairs to the first floor just to prove to myself, however painfully, that I still could.

I arrived at the room, which strangely resembled my grandmother's living room. Everything was too neatly arranged, too proper. But here, it felt contrived. A middle-aged lady talked at me about things I was sure were not meant for me. Her speech was rehearsed. She used words like "disabled" and told me there would be services available to assist with life, post-procedure. I said nothing. I wanted to run, to flee this situation, to wake up from this troublesome dream. My life was going horribly wrong.

We scheduled a follow-up visit in one month. I had precious little time to consider having my spine surgically fused, and my life indelibly altered. As in, *forever*. If I had the surgery, there would be no going back to the life I once had. No more drumming, no more Africa.

The drive home took about an hour. If it's true that time flies when you're having fun, then perhaps the converse also applies: it drags its sorry little ass when you're miserable. That way, you can really drench yourself in the bitter dregs of it, like a dry sponge soaking up warm dog piss from a linoleum floor. The hour-long drive felt like days.

It wasn't just the doctor's visit, but the convergence of recent events that left me sobbing. I occasionally pounded the steering wheel as if all of this were its fault. *Fuck you! This can't be my life! This isn't the way it was supposed to go!*

Worst of all, I was coming home to an empty house. I hadn't even started to comprehend *that* reality. It had only been two weeks. As I drove, I struggled to piece together a dizzying string of events that were still all-too fresh.

Following my return from Africa, Kerri and I were forced to move once again, after discovering that the couple we were renting from had been cashing our rent checks from the Outer Banks of North Carolina, but not paying the mortgage. To our surprise, a bank agent arrived to foreclose on the house, and was equally surprised to find renters occupying it. I guess everyone had different ways of dealing with the housing crisis. There was little we could do but start refilling our moving boxes, still freshly stacked in the garage, and load them onto a truck.

The weight of the past years was crushing us. In yet another rental house, we attempted to resuscitate our relationship, but the fight was gone from us. We were warriors of love who had fought one too many battles. Despite attending counseling sessions and trying to negotiate our way into a new life, our relationship never returned to what it once was. We had lost too much, and gained too little. We became strangers to each other.

In the new place, I once again tried to connect with my artistic muse, thinking that finding some semblance of personal happiness would make me more tolerable as a partner. For a time, I found sanctuary in my art, but it was a guilty pleasure. The hours spent in the studio were hours not spent with Kerri.

Summer turned to fall, and then to winter. The pain sought me out like a vengeful phantom, and haunted me interminably. I writhed on the couch while Kerri angrily cooked dinner. She was understandably frustrated. She needed a partner, but my condition consumed me, and I took refuge only in my art. Empty bottles of Percocet littered the floor of my studio like little gravestones, marking the slow death of my emotions. I withdrew ever deeper. Eventually, I stopped even making art. Darkness closed in, and my world returned to gray.

I hated the pain, really despised it. But it was *in me*. My anger had no outward object, so I turned it inward. The words "I am *in* pain" became "I *am* pain." My identity got tangled up with it. I began to hate myself. The worse my pain got, the more focused that hate became. *I hate you, I hate you, I fucking hate you!* I would scream at my pain-self. Hate was the only emotion strong enough to cut through the haze of painkillers.

Kerri could take no more, and we agreed to separate that summer. I was dead weight, and I could no longer ask her to shoulder the burden.

I needed to fight this battle alone. We both wept openly as we loaded her stuff onto the truck one last time. She had endured so much, but I had nothing left to give.

Alone in a near-empty house, I mourned the loss. Sixteen years together had brought us more than our fair share of hardships, but we had shared adventures, too. Africa had beguiled us both. She saw me through the best and worst of it. I guess if you took the sum total of all those years, and divided by the square root of something-or-other, I could see arriving at *Too Good to Leave, Too Bad to Stay*. Maybe the book had helped her do the math. Miraculously, we parted as friends.

But now I was left with *this*. The *curse*.

I understood with certainty as I drove home from the doctor's office that I'd be facing a life of disability *alone*. I would grow old and poor by myself, and the years would increasingly deform me. The imperfections I had tried to hide for so long would become chiseled irreversibly into physical form for all to see. Who would want me then?

The weeks that followed the doctor's visit passed in a blur. The house was eerily quiet, and the orange and red leaves of autumn were the only contrast to the gray sky. Winter was near. The pain was always worse in winter.

The gears of a great clock were ticking, and loudly. Surgery…*tick*… disability…*TOCK!* Every day that passed was a day closer to a life I didn't want.

Unless I can find some way to end the curse.

In the deep silence of an autumn night, I sat beneath the stars and pondered my life. Every spasm in my back brought a correspondent ache to my heart, and spread to my soul. The disease had become unmanageable. My spine might crumble at any moment. The threat of surgery loomed before me. I was fragile, and utterly alone in the world.

Nearby, a barred owl broke the silence, calling for its mate. I waited for the second owl's response. Long moments passed and I feared for the owl. Maybe it too found itself alone in the world.

I turned my situation around. Thoughts rose like waves in the tumul-tuous ocean of my mind, and pounded the shores of my being. Narcotic painkillers were leading me further away from myself. My anger had turned to self-loathing. Music, art, and Africa were becoming strangers to me.

It might be time to try something different, you know? To go a different route. The doctor's words echoed in my mind. Yes, something different. But what? Was surgery really the only solution?

Over the years, I had tried everything. Medicines, physical therapy, diet changes, natural treatments, and more—what else could I try? My head hurt from thinking. The problem was too great. Maybe there was no good way out of this.

I wondered about Erik, whom I had again lost touch with. I hoped he was faring better in the aftermath of his failed marriage. Had he turned back to substances to cope? I felt for the familiar rattle of pills in my pocket. It was all too easy.

After a time, my mind went quiet. I had no thoughts left to think. In their place, the quiet space of eternity slipped in, both unbearably deso-late and heartbreakingly beautiful. In the stillness, I heard a quiet voice within me.

Go easy on yourself. You can get through this.

The barred owl hooted. I waited for the response. None came.

The voice inside me spoke again, asking gently, *What do you need, old friend?*

It was a break from the normally persistent storm of self-abuse. Well, I knew what I *didn't* want—but what *did* I want? I wasn't sure I knew the answer anymore.

The night lingered. The owl continued to call for its mate, and the constellations shifted above me.

What do you need? The voice persisted.

I sighed. For starters, I wanted time to slow right the fuck down. It was alarming how the years had raced by unchecked. Time had lost its friction, and slid past me too easily. When did that start? My thirties were a blur. I had clearly established routines. Day in and day out, these routines allowed for an automated existence. Another work day, another weekend. Another trip to the doctor. Another birthday, another Christmas, another spring and summer and fall and winter again. Time accelerated. Now, I couldn't find the brakes.

There was a curious exception. In Africa, amidst strange landscapes and experiences that were always new, time moved impossibly, delightfully slow. Single days were their own quasi-existence. Recounting the events, I would often ask myself, "Had that *just* been this morning? It seems like forever ago!"

It's similar to the endless summer days of childhood. Riding a bike through the neighborhood, exploring a patch of woods here, discovering that little stream there. Then came lunch and a leisurely nap. A swim in the lake. Then back to exploring. A feeling of playful discovery accompanied it all. When the day finally came to an end, I was exhausted and pleased. My day's discoveries played back on the screen of my eyelids as I drifted into contented sleep.

I wanted time to move like *that* again. As a child, time hadn't mattered. It was the things I did that counted. I needed to find a way, be it by some magic or force of will, to slow down time. To reclaim my life, my purpose for being. Did some slipstream exist that could allow me to become the version of me I really wanted? To make my time on Earth count? Our time here is finite. It's the only thing we truly own. What we make of that time is all that matters. If we're not careful, we let it slip away.

Do some-thing before you die.

Tetteh's song from all those years ago resurfaced. I had to reclaim my life. I had to seize whatever time I had left and make the most of it.

What do you really need most? the inner voice asked. This time, I knew the response.

I need to feel good about myself again, I replied. *I need to accept who I am, and accept my pain. I need to learn to love myself again. I just don't know how anymore. I need help.*

Warm tears rolled down my cheeks. For the first time since I was a child, I prayed. I don't even know to whom. "God" had become a notion tainted by the bitter taste of religion. I had long ago gone rogue, as they say, and contented myself to find my gods in nature, in the glory of creation, in mountains and trees and in the songs of babbling brooks. Was there a deeper, ancient wisdom who I could ask for guidance? I sure didn't know. But if there were divinities out there that listened, or a Great Spirit that overlooked the desperate lives of humans, I implored them for the courage and wisdom to know what to do next.

From above me, the owl called out. Almost immediately, the response came from across the way. The two owls called back and forth to each other as I slumped to the earth, my body shuddering from exhausted sobs. I was still there when the morning star appeared and dawn's first light filled the sky.

The sun rose and fell in a stream of indistinguishable days. I was still a broken man.

I need help.

Where does one turn for such matters? When you have a broken bone that needs to be set, you go to a doctor. But when your *soul* is broken, who do you see?

My faith in Western medicine was failing. I had only my experiences to draw on. I thought back to my first trip to Ghana, and Amaa's parting words: *You will find a wise medicine person in your land of America. Or perhaps, a healer will find you.*

And then I knew: I had to return to the shaman. The thought filled me with a strange dread. I resisted the idea at first, but was it so crazy? I mean, what did I have to lose? She might be traveling in America—if she wasn't currently on one of her sacred pilgrimages to *Wirikuta*, the place where the world was created. I could at least call her. Perhaps she would know what to do.

It took me three days to muster up the courage to dial her number. She answered the landline after a few rings.

"Hello, this is Dave, a close friend of Julie," I said, not sure she'd remember me. "I came to see you a few years back about—"

"I know who you are, sonny," she interjected. "I've been expecting your call for three days now. What took you so long? Come see me at once."

The phone call only lasted a minute. She told me where to find her. Once again, the mysterious wheels of fate were turning.

17

SHAMAN TROUBLE

THE SHAMAN'S face appeared stark and grave in the dim light. Her lips were pursed, her eyes hidden beneath the brim of her old fedora. Her shadow darted and danced before me in the light of the flickering orange flames. I glanced at her nervously, trying to avoid her piercing gaze.

We were alone. The night was moonless. A nearby river murmured faintly over rocks. The autumn rain had subsided, but a cold breeze shook fresh raindrops from the canopy that enfolded us in darkness.

I had come a long way to see her. Now that I was here, the feeling was surreal. How long had it been since my last visit with the shaman? Two or three years, I estimated.

"How has your pain been?" she asked.

"It's been bad." I told her everything. We spoke for a long while before falling into silence.

Wood smoke swirled around us. Leaves of white sage burned atop the fire, making the smoke fragrant and sweet. In her weathered hands, the woman held a sheath of feathers, bundled together like a wand. She used them to fan smoke on me, purifying and cleansing me. She closed her eyes and prayed for what might as well have been an eternity.

I fidgeted uncomfortably, waiting for her to speak.

"Show me the book," she said at last.

I was taken aback, as I hadn't mentioned I had written a book. I always kept a copy in my backpack, though, and I pulled it out now. On its cover, the image of Sako Gbè appeared ominous. Though I painted the image, Sako was strangely unfamiliar now.

I handed the book to her. She examined it, her expression unchanging.

"This man, he has crossed over," she muttered.

"Yes, he died several years ago. He was a respected elder in his village. Reputed to be a sorcerer, in their tradition."

She nodded, and returned to her silent prayers. She was in private consultation with…who? What spirit entities did she engage with? I did not know.

After a long period of silence, she turned to me. "You are in a bit of trouble. And it is very serious."

I gulped hard. The past few years had brought me a lot of this unwanted trouble. From the depths of memory, Amaa's words rang out in my mind.

You have been cursed.

The woman peered right through me as she spoke. "The ancestors are not to be fooled with. It would have been much better for you if this man was still alive."

I stammered. "I…I'm told his wife is still living, in the village." The words tumbled out of my mouth. I didn't know if it was important.

"That may be of some help to you."

The breeze picked up, spraying droplets of rain. The late November air made me cold and desolate. Winter would be setting in soon.

She turned the book over in her hands, leafing through the pages. I glimpsed my precious drawings inside. I wanted to be proud of them, but now I was struggling.

She handed the book back to me.

"I am not from Africa," she said. "This is not my village, nor my culture. But traditional cultures are the same in many ways. For us, the ancestors are never far away. Your work in Africa has brought you very close to them. Many people travel to places like Africa but remain on the surface. But you—you have penetrated the surface. The ancestors have noticed."

I wasn't sure if I should feel gratified by this. In truth, it made me more scared. I suddenly wished I could go back in time and change everything. I wished I had never set foot in Africa.

"You have gotten their attention—and whether that is a good or bad thing remains to be seen." She leaned back, and returned her gaze to the fire.

Long moments passed. I remained utterly still. Though my mind was spinning with questions, I was unable to speak.

At last, she leaned forward. "The ancestors speak to us in many ways. Some people have dreams. Some are called to do their work, to interpret their messages for the living. This is the role of the shaman. It is the same world over, in the cultures that have not forgotten. But sometimes, the only way the ancestors can get our attention is by giving us an illness." She looked at me sternly. "This is what has happened to you. And until you find out what they want—and remedy the situation—your illness will only get worse."

The old woman pulled out a handmade cigar, and lit it from the fire. For the Huichol, tobacco is a sacred plant, and smoking is a way of communicating with the element of fire. I once attended a fire ceremony when a shaman smoked more than a dozen of these big cigars, and went into a trance. Alone with this old woman by the fire, I wondered what was about to happen.

"For whatever reason, you have attracted their attention. In turn, *they* have been trying to get *your* attention—for a long time now."

My expression went blank. I didn't understand any of this. Seeing my vacant stare, she sighed.

"I have to explain to you because you are from the European tradition. The white people have forgotten the ways, the *old* traditions. In traditional cultures, when a person becomes sick, they go to see a healer, a shaman, who helps interpret the illness. In this way, the ancestors speak to us, through the shaman." She was giving me an overview of *Shamanism 101*. I felt like a dunce.

I thought back to my trip to Ghana more than a dozen years ago. There, they spoke to me about spiritual illnesses. What was the word they used? It was the *sisa hela*, the "shade" or ancestor illness, that drew their attention.

The old woman sat back in her chair, puffing on the long cigar.

"You must return to Africa, and go to this village," she stated, nodding slowly. "You know this to be true."

The words hit me hard. It had been two years since I tried to return with Famoudou. I wanted to return and pay homage to the people, but I had failed to do so. Pain took over my life. My body now felt too old, too tired for travel. The thought of going back now only filled me with dread.

The shaman continued, "Your relationship with Africa is no longer that of an outsider—you are in the fold now, on the inside. And as such, you are beholden to the customs of the people. You have caught the attention of these ancestors, and now they want you to do something." She tapped her cigar, and the smoke circled her face. The firelight played on the deep lines of her skin.

"Surely, this is related to your book," she went on. "Did you have permission to write this book? Did the people there *ask* you to do this?"

The question was rhetorical. I stammered again. I didn't know I had *needed* permission. My heart told me it was something I *had* to do. I had wanted so badly to make all those drawings and paintings, to depict the masks and rituals, to write down their music. I had wanted to re-experience it all, and to share with the world the wonder I felt there.

I said as much to the shaman. "Lots of people write books about Africa. Why aren't *they* in trouble? Why is this falling on *me*?"

She glared at me. "Because the ancestors recognize you as someone who should have known better. They do not know you have forgotten, or that you are ignorant of the traditions. And frankly, they don't *care* that you are ignorant. They will hold you accountable because you *should* have known."

I could only shake my head. This was too much for me to comprehend.

"If you do not do this, the pain they will inflict on you will only grow worse. They will hold your feet to the fire until you have accomplished all that you need to. You *must* go back."

She paused to stoke the fire. Sparks leapt up, dancing like fireflies and then disappearing into the darkness. I wanted to run away, to hide from this. But something inside me urged me to be courageous, to face my fears of the unknown.

"The people there, they will help you," she said. "They will know what to do. Seek out the elders." She pointed the cigar at me. "You know who they are."

Famoudou. He was an elder, and steeped in the old traditions. We had remained close. I could talk to him. Would he understand? Or would he think I was just another foolish white person, talking a whole lot of nonsense? I had shown him the book. We had tried to work out a plan to return to the village. For his part, he was satisfied.

There was Lanciné too, of course. I had written about his village. Perhaps he would be willing to help. But help with *what*, exactly? What was I supposed to tell them, anyway?

The old woman read my thoughts. "You will explain to them your illness. Tell them you need to find a healer, and that you need to make amends in the village. Tell them you want to honor the traditions of their ancestors. They will pray for you, and they will tell you what to do. You do not need to worry about the details. Just find the elders, and let them take matters in their hands. You will watch things unfold before your eyes. You will see."

She drew on her cigar and squinted her eyes in thought. "And remember," she added, "nothing happens by chance. Pay close attention. Even the most unlikely of people may have a part to play."

A new reality began to creep in. *Am I really going to do this?* It seemed crazy. Where was my life going? I had nothing right now. My relationship with Kerri was over, and I had only the prospect of debilitating surgery ahead of me. Perhaps I had nothing to lose. And who knows? Maybe my physical healing was intertwined with my greater purpose in life, and this was the path I needed to take.

The shaman was scrutinizing me, and I suspected she was reading my thoughts again. My discomfort grew.

"Listen," she said. "The world today is a much different place. A great crisis is consuming the planet. In the old times, the cycle of death and rebirth always brought a soul back to its same people. If you were a Huichol person, for example, you were reborn a Huichol. One progresses through their spiritual journey this way. It is the natural way of the spirit."

The old woman exhaled. "But it is not like that anymore. The world is in great need of healing. It needs the wisdom of the old cultures. And so now, souls cross the lines. A Huichol soul might not be reborn as a Huichol person, but instead as a white person, in order to bring healing to the white culture. And you—why have you been so drawn to this village in Africa? Are you not a white man, born in America? Yet, the traditions call to you. There is healing in them. You may have some part to play in the healing of the white culture. If it is so, the elders will tell you."

I thought back to my first crossing of the Niger River. As I entered the village that first time, the drums roared above the canopy. I felt such deep emotions. What were they? It was a feeling of coming home. But no, I was enamored with the thrill of someplace so different and new. I loved Africa. That was all.

She again pointed her cigar at me, her eyes fixed on mine. "You have had this illness for a long time. It has been calling you to your true path, but you do not know how to listen. Perhaps the pain will *always* be there to remind you. It is time you start listening."

We sat in silence for a long time. My thoughts swirled in a painful mess of confusion. I saw my past journeys to West Africa stretching out behind me. I retraced my footsteps, and the path led to this moment.

The night drew on. The fire was dying out, its light fading. I was cold and tired. At last, the old woman broke the long silence.

"So, it is settled then!" she exclaimed, slapping my knee. I was not settled at all. "You will make your preparations, and return as soon as you are able. Do not rush this. There is no way of telling how long you will need to be there. Whatever the elders ask of you, you must do." At this, she leaned back and cackled uproariously. "Ha! They may ask you to stay there forever! And if that is the case, you must accept it."

She inhaled from the stub of her cigar, and billowed out a cloud of smoke.

"Well then, my friend, it looks like you're going back to Africa! Ha ha ha!" The shaman's shoulders shook with laughter. "Have a nice trip, sonny!"

She was still laughing as I slinked away from her fire. I was most certainly *not* laughing. I was deeply afraid.

~

That night, sleep did not come. My mind was burning, my soul tormented.

When the morning light appeared, I was dazed from sleeplessness. But I had made my decision: as crazy as it sounded, I would go back.

I rang Lanciné on the phone later that morning. He was in Conakry. I told him everything. To my astonishment, he was completely unfazed. Like it was all simple day-to-day stuff, he said he would make some calls. He assured me things would be ready for me when I arrived.

For me, all that remained were the preparations.

I purchased plane tickets and applied for my visa. A single-entry visa to Guinée was usually good for a maximum of six months. But when the visa arrived in the mail, I found they had granted me a *two-year* visa. I hadn't applied for that. My longest stay in Guinée until this point had been three months. Three very challenging months.

There is no way of telling how long you will need to be there. They may ask you to stay there forever! And if that is the case, you must accept it.

I packed for a stay of indeterminate length, preparing for both the heat of the dry season and the cool rainy season. I emptied my savings account. After purchasing the plane tickets, I had a paltry $1,800 dollars left to my name. Luckily, a little money can be stretched a long way in Guinée. For safety's sake, I borrowed some extra money from Julie and her husband, who were willing to help support my endeavor.

I thought carefully about pain management. While I was open to the possibility that some weird magic was afoot, I wasn't going without backup. For the past few weeks, I'd been circumventing my doctors and substituting oxycodone with a powerful tea made from a strange powdered leaf from Southeast Asia, known to botanists as *Mitragyna speciosa*. Called *kratom* on the streets of Indonesia, this plant has effects similar to opiates, but doesn't actually bind to the opioid receptors in the brain. In theory, this makes it less addictive, so I thought I'd give it a try. As I found out, it was an effective pain reliever. I packed a veritable shitload of this weird stuff in my bag and hoped it would make it through customs. As an added precaution, a casual visit to my doctor left me with a hefty three-month supply of Percocet.

Of course, I'd need some reading material for the long flight. I perused my bookshelves, and stumbled across an old one by the ethnobotanist Wade Davis: *The Passage of Darkness*. Davis had solved the mystery of the Haitian zombie phenomenon, discovering a native concoction of medicinal plants and fish neurotoxins that induced an appearance of death so convincing it even fooled Western doctors. In doing so, Davis immersed himself deep within a culture of *vodoun* that had its roots in West Africa. I remembered enjoying the book, and a treatise on ancient healing and the occult seemed fitting. I tossed it in my bag.

The night before I departed, I examined my luggage. Something was missing, and I knew what it was. The next morning, with only a couple of hours before my flight left, I dashed off to the art supply store. I stocked up on pencils and various papers, along with a portable drawing board. As an afterthought, I purchased a small black portfolio case to transport whatever art I might create.

I was ready.

On a cold January morning, Kerri saw me off at the airport. It was a nice gesture, I thought. Or maybe she wanted to be sure I got on the plane. In either case, when we parted ways, our goodbyes had a finality to them.

As I approached the boarding gate, I turned to look at her one last time. Tears streamed down her face, and it broke my heart. I forced myself to turn away, and took the last step through the gate and away from the life we had known together, maybe forever. I wanted her to be free of me. In my absence, she could embark on a new life. I hoped she would meet someone who could provide for her better than I had, and find the happiness she so deserved.

I boarded the plane and settled into my seat, and rummaged through my bag for my water bottle. It was then I noticed Kerri had slipped a card into my backpack. I opened it cautiously. Inside was a hand-written note.

To my best friend. May you find the source of true healing in Africa. Love always, Kerri.

Then, I almost choked on my water. She had included a picture of a scorpion.

My plane taxied down the runway, and I had no idea what fate awaited me in Africa. This time, I didn't know if I'd be coming back.

PART III

Lanciné Condé, 2016

18

THE MUSE AWAKENS

WHEN I OPEN MY EYES, I realize I've been lost in memory for some time. Above me, trees rise like ancient pillars, the elders of the forest. Though Lanciné and I have indulged in a decent rest from our walk, my spine burns like a red-hot ember. The painkillers have worn off, but I don't dare take more. My head needs to be clear for whatever comes next. We are drawing near.

I glance up to see Lanciné already standing, his small bag over his shoulder.

"*An nye wa,*" he urges me. "Let's go."

We resume our walk, but my pace is no faster than a crawl. I can't hide my suffering anymore. Each step tests my resolve, but I must endure it. One way or another, this will soon be over.

Under my breath, I whisper the name of the blacksmith's sorceress wife, "*Mousso Gbè.*"

She must be close, for I feel her presence now. It both pulls me forward and fills me with dread. The book I carry on my back feels like a terrible burden, a reminder that I've drawn too much attention to myself through meddling in sacred matters. From beyond the grave, Sako Gbè wants something from me.

~

When my plane touched down in Conakry three months earlier, my visit with the shaman was still fresh in my head. She had been unwavering, and it terrified me. The implications of her words made my blood turn cold.

Sometimes, the only way the ancestors can get our attention is by giving us an illness, she had said. *They have been trying to get your attention—for a long time now.*

My mind and heart had long been engaged in a battle royale between doubt and fear, hope and disbelief. Now, I had to choose. The idea that ancestor spirits were calling to me through disease was difficult to reconcile with my old worldview. But what if there was so much more to this world than what could be proved by scientific inquiry alone? What if the shaman—and all the old cultures—were right?

To heed the cautions of the mind is prudent, but to ignore the pleas of the heart is perilous. My life was falling apart, and I needed to do *something* to ease my misery. Maybe I couldn't avoid surgery forever, but I would never forgive myself if I didn't try.

At any rate, it was too late to change my mind now. I disembarked the plane in the sweltering heat of a Conakry night, bolstering my courage and my failing faith in myself. I hoped I wasn't crazy.

Seek out the elders. You know who they are.

Of course, this could only mean Famoudou. I needn't do this alone. I hoped he would understand.

Lanciné met me outside the airport. It was late, about 2 a.m. local time. We exchanged the customary greetings.

"*Iniké, iniké, mon ami!*" he exclaimed. His enthusiasm and kindness put me at ease.

"Ah! *Mon grand frère, ça va?*" I replied, calling him my big brother in a gesture of respect.

"Yes, all goes well. Everyone is eager to see you again. You have stayed away too long."

I had reason, but I was sure to get an earful about it anyway. *When you are away in America, you are so lost to us,* a friend here once told me. The irony was that I was so lost to myself, too. That was more difficult to explain.

We took a taxi to Lanciné's compound in Kipé, a suburb of Conakry. All was quiet. A mango tree stood at the center of the small courtyard, with a monkey chained to it. *When did Lanciné get a monkey?* I wondered. As I passed by, the monkey grabbed at me with a shriek, drawing a sharp rebuke from Lanciné. Beyond the tree, several connected dwellings surrounded the courtyard. These housed Lanciné's extended family, perhaps two dozen people who slept side by side on the floors.

Embarrassment filled me as we unloaded my mountainous belongings. I had more possessions with me than most people here would acquire in their lifetime. My discomfort grew when I realized Lanciné had arranged for me to have a private room with an actual mattress. This room usually housed several of his boys, but they had generously vacated to allow me some privacy and comfort. Lanciné had even hung a mosquito net over the mattress, a luxury most people couldn't afford. I thanked Lanciné earnestly for all this. Utterly spent from the long night of traveling, I retired to my quarters.

I fell into a fitful sleep, and wandered in strange dreamscapes that echoed my apprehensions.

What am I doing here? Have I made the right decision?

Only time would tell. When I awoke too early, it was to the unmistakable sounds of tropical birdsong, the clanking of pots, the rhythmic pounding of millet. Wood smoke wafted into my room. Outside my door, Africa was awakening.

I spent the next days getting reacquainted with Africa on a whole new level. This would be home now, and I didn't know for how long. A flurry of visitors beset me, and I struggled to recall the all-important greetings in Malinké. My language skills were rusty.

Greetings are an important part of Malinké customs. They are not superfluous, as they often are in the West, but important social rituals that must be done correctly, every day. Glossing over them risks disrespect. The longer it's been since you've seen someone, the longer the greetings go on. And for me, it had been a while. So with every new visitor, rapid-fire turns of phrases needed to be repeated, and each new visitor would invariably throw new ones at me. When I couldn't respond—or worse, replied with the incorrect phrase—the whole court-yard erupted in laughter. To make matters more complicated, the greet-ings are different depending on the person's relative age to you. Greeting an elder is not the same as greeting a peer, and different again for someone who is your junior. And lastly, all these greetings vary depending on the time of day.

With all this complexity at hand, I made a game of learning the phrases. Everywhere I went, I shouted greetings in Malinké:

N'na, good morning! How is your health? May God give you long life!

Good afternoon, karamöö! How goes it in your village? God bless the Condé clan!

As my skills improved, I picked up a few phrases I could use for comic effect:

Good morning, ködö! Were there four legs or two in your bed last night?

When asked the same question amidst embarrassed giggles—talking openly about nocturnal activities was taboo—I'd answer completely deadpan, "*Wöörö.*" Their expressions would turn to shock. Six legs were too many.

I was anxious about the tasks ahead of me, but Lanciné reminded me that events move in their own way here. I was on Africa time now. What was the rush? I might be here forever.

Just find the elders, and let them take matters in their hands. You will watch things unfold before your eyes. You will see.

I waited, and kept a keen eye out for this mysterious unfolding of events. During long days of readying myself for the unknown, we'd pull two chairs into the shade. Lanciné would open up his case of flutes and pull out two. This was a great way to pass the time, and why not continue my apprenticeship?

Lanciné always chose the song. Without a word, he'd start playing and didn't stop until I figured out the phrases and played along. The moment I caught on, he changed the melody and ripped into more elab-orate phrases. That's how teaching worked here. Explanations were short or nonexistent. My persistent questions only irritated my normally patient teacher. So I played.

When we weren't doing that, there were the *dembadons*. These going-away parties for a new bride-to-be are very common in Conakry. The *dembadon* festivals were also how Lanciné made a living. Lanciné's *dembadon* performance troupe consisted of his sons and a few other drummers, along with dancers and a couple of *griotte* singers from the village. Two or three times a week (but not during the rainy season, or during the month of Ramadan), Lanciné's group played at these pre-wedding celebrations.

They were raucous affairs, these *dembadons*. They drew from the same musical source as the village music I studied with Famoudou, but here in Conakry, they seemed jacked up on steroids. The rhythms were fast and loud. The *griotte* dames possessed vocal cords capable of cutting steel bars, and they'd sing through microphones connected to blown speakers. It was painfully loud, but that was the Conakry *dembadon* vibe. I often sat in on these sessions, which was a great honor. It was loads of fun, even if I worried my ears might start bleeding from the extreme volume.

It was the duty of the partygoers to chip in for the musicians. If it was a good night, they'd throw money into a huge platter placed before the drummers, or better yet, stick cash directly to the foreheads of the sweat-drenched musicians. The better the music and dancing—the more it moved people in spirit, and whipped them into a frenzy—the more money they contributed. At the end of the evening, piles of loose bills were gathered from the courtyard, meticulously counted, and split between all the drummers, dancers, and *griottes*.

At the end of one particularly successful *dembadon*, everyone noted that I had played especially well. The drummers handed me five thousand Guinée francs, and everyone laughed. It was less than a dollar, but here it was enough for a modest meal. I blushed a little, but inwardly I beamed with pride. It was my first paying gig in Africa. Maybe this was the start of a new life.

When I wasn't playing during the *dembadons*, I found time to start drawing again. I was tentative at first, since I was rusty and unsure what people would think. But my confidence returned, and soon I was producing decent sketches. When people saw themselves and their friends portrayed in my sketchbooks, it always caused a stir of laughter and astonishment. It seemed like a good thing, so I kept at it. In no small way, it was a return to my old self—and I wanted more of it.

~

Amidst all this fun, I had work to do. My heart didn't let me forget I was here on a mission. It pulled at me daily, and at night my dreams swept me away into spirit lands filled with perplexing imagery.

I'd often awaken in the darkness to strange surroundings that reminded me of my equally strange purpose here. Unfamiliar noises arose from outside my window, from the ceiling—or worse, from just beyond the thin mosquito netting. Cockroaches skittered on the floor. Occasionally, a bat got in through the window. An owl lived in the ceiling, and it created a racket when it returned at night with a freshly caught meal. Unable to return to sleep, my thoughts would turn anxiously.

At other times, pain came on so strong that it was my own cries that woke me. I'd lie there writhing in agony until dawn's light when I could unbolt the iron door Lanciné insisted I keep locked at night. It swung open on creaking hinges, and I'd sit beneath the mango tree gritting my teeth, constantly harassed by the monkey, until Lanciné and his family had risen.

I was determined to stay away from the little white pills unless absolutely necessary. But to make my alternative pain-relieving tea, I had to wait for the women to start a fire, bring out a cauldron, and draw water from the well. By the time they did this, the pain was unbearable. Throughout the day, I'd run out of hot water and become everyone's biggest pain in the ass. At my self-conscious requests, the women would restart the fire and fetch more water. I hated being dependent on them, but they simply would *not* let me do it myself. I was their guest.

I explained my predicament to Lanciné, and showed him the *médicament à base de plantes* I was making into a tea for pain management. A trip to the market was in order.

"Daouda, we can buy an electric thermos. The government turns on the electricity for our neighborhood three days a week now. When *le courant* comes on and you see the light bulbs illuminate, you can heat up enough water to last you the whole day."

I liked this idea. So off we went into the sweltering armpit of Conakry, the market known as *Marché Madina*.

Like all trips to this sprawling market, it turned into a hot and bothersome all-day affair. Lanciné, the grand master of bartering, haggled over dozens of Chinese-imported electric water heaters. Lanciné wanted the absolute best for me, and he wanted it at a good price. After many hours, we ended up purchasing one that was mighty powerful. Whenever I plugged it in, the lights dimmed throughout the entire neighborhood. You could have powered a small rocket with this thing. But I was grateful to have this control back in my hands—and with my pain a constant, I drank *kratom* tea day and night.

Since my arrival, I couldn't stop thinking about having an actual art studio. Now that I was getting settled at Lanciné's place, we agreed I should pay rent. This was home now, and it was time to set up shop. And what's more, my artistic muse was awakening, and I could feel her tugging at my heart. I was eager to do some larger drawings in my free time, but lacked a surface to work on.

As we drove home from the market in a taxi, my new electric kettle in hand, we passed the shop of a local furniture maker. I glimpsed a wooden table by the roadside, sitting in the sun. It called to me. I had no doubt it was my new drawing table.

"*Arrête! Arrête!*" I yelled to the driver. *Pull over!*

Lanciné looked at me quizzically, and the driver swerved to the curb. I pointed to the desk, and Lanciné nodded in comprehension.

We got out to inspect it. It was handmade and rustic, but decent quality. It even had a few drawers where I could store some supplies.

"It is a very nice piece of furniture, Daouda," Lanciné remarked. Like all things I purchased here, he understood full well that when I left someday, it would become his. Some of Lanciné's kids and grandkids were of school age, and I had seen them sprawled on the ground trying to write in their composition books. It would be the first desk anyone at his house had owned.

We spoke to the woodworker. The stain was still drying, so the desk wouldn't be ready until tomorrow. The price was non-negotiable, which made things easier. Lanciné didn't put up a fight. I pulled out a pile of bills from my backpack and paid for it.

We stood there admiring it for a moment, until a large bug scurried out from one of the drawers and skittered across the surface of the desk. I was momentarily concerned.

"Ah, it is nothing!" the woodworker assured me, laughing heartily. "*C'est l'Afrique!* There are bugs everywhere." He slapped me on the back. "Come back tomorrow. I will have it ready for you."

The next day, we returned to fetch my new desk. I realized I would need some lamps too, as presently I had only candles and my headlamp for lighting. As it turned out, a desk lamp is a novelty here, and was challenging to find. It required a return trip to the inner bowels of *Marché Madina*, and more bartering. During the excursion, my pain flared up, and I guzzled more tea. I was high-flying while Lanciné worked tirelessly to find me the right lamps. This was a whole lot of effort to accommodate *un étranger*, a *tubabu* with curious needs. But we left the market with two little lamps that could be clamped to my desk.

We returned to Lanciné's place sweaty and exhausted, but I got straight to work on setting everything up. By the end of the day, I had a humble art studio in West Africa.

On days when we had electricity, I worked in the evenings and early mornings, fervently making drawings of people from the day's festivals. Their images came alive on paper, and their expressions and emotions played out before me with that same curious magic I knew as a child. And I was never alone. My muse had reawakened, and I was obliged to pay her homage.

While I worked, something else nagged at me. I couldn't delay the inevitable.

Find the elders, and let them take matters in their hands.

It was with this in mind that Lanciné and I set out to find Famoudou. But as it turned out, the old man's whereabouts were hard to determine these days. With no students to look after, he came and went at his whim, sometimes for days at a time. He rarely used his phone. His family assured us he was still in Conakry, though at seventy-five, he had become more vocal about his growing distaste for the noisy city and its changing culture. Many of those closest to him wondered when he would return to the village for good.

Each day, Lanciné and I crossed the city and headed into the dusty hills of Simbaya to find him, but to no avail. Every attempt left my deteriorating body screaming at me, along with the desperate voice inside me that reminded me what was at stake.

If you do not do this, the pain they will inflict on you will only grow worse.

Africa was testing my resolve, and I suspected it was only the beginning of my trials.

19

THE OLD MASTER'S PLAN

There's a saying in Malinké:

Kèebaa sìgirino sé mén jé, dindin lòorino mèe wò jé nòo. An old man who is sitting can still see things a young man who is standing cannot.

It took us five all-day attempts to find Famoudou, but when we finally did, the old man was sitting alone on a short wooden stool in his courtyard, like he had never left. His round spectacles rested on his nose, and he leaned over, intently focused on carving some blocks of wood.

It was a stark contrast to the memories I had of this place. Gone were the sounds of drums and the chatter of students. Time had moved on.

Upon seeing the courtyard again, nostalgia filled me. To my left was the small building that had once stored huge piles of *dunun* drums and *djembés*. In those days, fresh goat or calf skins hung from the walls, ready for more drums. I remember the pungent smell of the skins, flies buzzing around them incessantly. Famoudou or some of his sons would soak and then stretch them over intricately carved wooden shells. Raw elements of wood and skin were thus fashioned into musical instruments that carried both beauty and power.

In front of me was the area where Famoudou had held our classes.

But gone were the circle of chairs and rows of *dunun* drums. In those days, a younger Famoudou had led us, breaking down the rhythmic components. With him, we developed a vocabulary for our solo phrases. He showed how the solos corresponded to the movements of the dancers, and he was a master at demonstrating the conversation that took place. During those sessions, I filled notebooks and studied them until the language of the drums became my own.

Those were easier times. Though I had not been without pain, my youthful fervor propelled me through it. Now, Africa had called me back to her once again, but on different terms.

Our footsteps echoed in the courtyard as we approached. Like our last visit, both Lanciné and Sayon accompanied me. They were both my big brothers here. They understood the culture and traditions, and could help me navigate this strange new world. Since Sayon's French was better than both Lanciné's and mine, he would help tell my story.

Famoudou was deep in concentration, and didn't notice us at first. Sayon was the first to speak.

"*Iniké*, master. You have visitors."

Famoudou raised his eyes. His jaw dropped when he saw me.

"Heh? *C'est pas possible!*" he exclaimed. He stood to greet us, not fully believing that I stood before him. More than two years had passed since our last visit. Time had left its marks upon both of us. He was now an old man, and I was no longer the boy he had trained years ago. My illness was evident now in the stoop of my posture.

We embraced, and greeted each other in the old customs.

"*Iniké, n dencé,*" he said. "*Tana tè?*" Greetings, all is well? He had called me *dencé*, but it was a word I didn't know. Lanciné and Sayon exchanged a glance.

I responded in my best Malinké. "*N'ba, tana sii tè. Alatando.*" Yes, all goes well. God be praised.

Although, as he'd soon find out, not everything was going that well.

Lanciné and Sayon offered him the traditional greetings too. They conversed in Malinké, and I stood back and admired these three human beings, all master musicians. They had all imparted so much to me. I was humbled to stand among them.

The depth of emotions that arose from seeing Famoudou was unexpected. He was my teacher, of course, and a mentor. At times, he had been an advisor, counseling me on issues no one else in the world could have. Navigating social interactions in Malinké culture was not easy for an outsider, and Famoudou's insights were invaluable. I looked up to him tremendously. As the years went by, something like a friendship grew between us, though *friend* was not quite the word. Famoudou was nearly twice my age, and came from a culture that separated us in distinct ways. How would I characterize our relationship? I suppose he was more like an uncle, or—

"*N dencé*—my son," he said, placing his hand on my shoulder. "*Mon fils*, you have returned."

I was momentarily stunned. *Mon fils*. He had never called me that before.

"So, you have come back to Guinée," he said. "And you stay with your *maître* Lanciné, and continue learning the *tambin*?"

"Yes, Famoudou—I have come back, and I'm staying with Lanciné. Our work with the flute continues. Except Lanciné is often impatient with me," I joked, punching Lanciné on the shoulder. "He thinks I haven't been working as hard as I should when I'm away. And I'm afraid he's right—I've forgotten much."

"Maybe so, but you are lucky to have him as a teacher, and he is lucky to have you as a student. It is difficult for the *fulefolas* to find students. Learning the flute is hard work, and not many even try." Then he inquired, "And how is your wife?"

He was referring to Kerri. It had always been easier to tell people we were married, instead of explaining the banalities of domestic partnership in America. We both thought we would eventually marry anyway.

"Kerri is doing well," I said, concealing the truth. "She sends her warmest greetings. She will be happy to know you are well."

I hadn't told Lanciné or Sayon the truth yet either. The news of our split would have upset them. They never could see why we didn't have a big family, which was desirable here in Africa. My tirade of lame excuses fell on deaf ears. It didn't matter now, because it was over. That fact was still sinking in, and I wasn't yet in a place to discuss it. Grief would have to be deferred. Other matters were more pressing.

"Famoudou," I broke in, eager to change the subject. "I have come for your guidance. I have unfinished work to do." I faltered for a moment. My emotions welled up rapidly, and I feared tears would spill from my eyes. "Oh, Famoudou. There is so much I must tell you! I need your help…" I tapered off, my words failing me.

Famoudou put his hand on my shoulder. "*Allez!* Come now! We shall discuss everything. Sit with an old man awhile. My lunch is just arriving."

One of Famoudou's daughters emerged from the house with a steaming platter of rice and a bowl of manioc stew. Famoudou looked at the three of us. "Have you eaten? We have plenty. We shall eat together, and discuss what needs to be discussed."

The four of us sat down to eat. I remained quiet while my friends conversed in Malinké. My thoughts turned restlessly. I was scared to tell Famoudou why I was here.

While we ate, we were joined by a young *djembefola* named Mori, who was an apprentice of Famoudou's. He was several years younger than me, and we had once been friendly. But at some point, his view of me changed. Perhaps it was my book, or my work teaching the *djembé* in the U.S., or maybe it was my close relationship with Famoudou. Regardless, I had the clear impression Mori didn't like me—and now he was here. I was suddenly even more uncomfortable, and my resolve faltered. With the present company, we would be discussing my health, my journey here, and, in short, my very future.

I searched for courage, and wondered if I should delay the conversation until he was gone. But then I heard the shaman's voice. *Nothing happens by chance…Even the most unlikely of people may have a part to play.*

I glanced at Mori, and our eyes met. For better or worse, he was going to be part of the discussion.

When we finished eating, Sayon began the conversation. For the next hour, Famoudou, Lanciné, Sayon, and Mori spoke in Malinké. The exchange was dizzying to me. Sayon paused here and there to translate, but the conversation mainly happened without me. From time to time, they turned to me with questions. The words spilled from me awkwardly.

Yes, the illness has gotten much worse.

If nothing changes, I will need an operation, to fuse my spine. I will be disabled.

The old woman is what you would call a sorcerer, a spiritual healer in your culture, with the gift of divination.

She spoke about the ancestors…my book…and the old blacksmith Sako Gbè…

The discussion went on, and I grasped for familiar Malinké words. At last, Mori broke into French. It was obvious he wanted me to hear what he had to say.

"He is a white man! He takes our culture without our permission, and puts it into his book. And what recompense do we receive? What payment has he given?" He was angry, and I understood.

Famoudou was quick to speak up on my behalf. Mori was unaware of my last visit, during which I had presented Famoudou with money for the village. I had failed to make it to the village in person, but I had now returned to make it right.

If I am happy with the book, Famoudou had said then, *the village will be happy. You need only my blessing.*

Mori, however, needed more convincing.

In my mind, the book had been a failure—it had barely broken even. But still, my earnings hadn't been nothing. More than nothing is still *something*, and that *something* is more than what most people here have. This was the point of contention for Mori. That *something* should have been shared. This is the way it works in the village. But I'm an outsider, not from this culture. So, where did that leave me?

Famoudou held a trump card that was about to change everything—for both Mori and me. He spoke to Mori in Malinké, gesturing toward me frequently. Then he turned to me and spoke in French.

"David is my adopted son." He looked me in the eye before going on. "*Mon fils adopté!* You will make a trip to the village with my instructions. As my son, you will be welcomed there as family."

Famoudou knew the power his words held. They had their effect: Mori's expression changed dramatically. He nodded silently, accepting what Famoudou said.

For my part, it appeared I had just been adopted. Famoudou's words had their effect on me, too. I knew this bound me to the village, and to its traditions. I was compelled now more than ever to uphold my mission and see it through to whatever end.

With that, the old master set out his plan for me. I diligently wrote down his instructions as an uneasy feeling arose in the pit of my stomach. I looked at the daunting list of tasks and related names and places, and had no idea what challenges I would face along the way.

At least I wouldn't be doing it alone.

"I will send word to the village," Famoudou said, "and to my brother who lives there still. They will ensure all is ready for you when you arrive. You will await their word, and you must be ready when it comes."

The shaman's words rang in my head.

Just find the elders...you will watch things unfold before your eyes. You will see.

He turned to Lanciné and said firmly, "And you, Lanciné, shall accompany him to the village. You will see to it that all is done as I have described. The traditions must be respected."

Lanciné nodded in comprehension. He now had his own mandate, and we were bound together on this mission.

Famoudou redirected his attention to me. "And as for Mousso Gbè—the wife of Sako the blacksmith—we do not know how she will react, nor what power she still possesses. You shall await my arrival in the village before you even consider approaching her."

The thought made me shudder. I had almost forgotten about the old sorceress. Famoudou's stern look did nothing to abate my fears.

A hush fell over the group, and my mind raced to comprehend what had just transpired. Famoudou rose abruptly.

"Heh! An old man needs his rest. I am not so young as I once was."

The conversation was closed. He dismissed himself, and it was our cue to be on our way.

Before shuffling away and retiring to his house, Famoudou said to me, "My son, I shall see you again before the rains come. You will wait for me in the village. And you will show the book to *no one* until I am with you."

20

THE SECRET OF AIRPLANES

IN LIGHT of the plan set out before us by an aging *djembefola*, Lanciné and I had preparations to make. The journey would entail driving three hundred miles through rugged terrain to a roadless village, where we would remain indefinitely. First and foremost, we needed a vehicle to get us there.

Under more normal circumstances, we could have hired a bush taxi to transport us. But a taxi to the remote town of Kouroussa would be expensive. From Kouroussa, we'd be heading off the map to Lanciné's village on the Niger River, which was a walkable distance to Famoudou's village. Hiring a bush taxi for such an overland trip would also mean paying for the chauffeur's travel expenses, including meals and lodging—and the same for the mechanic that would certainly have to accompany us, since service stations were non-existent en route. Traveling overland without a mechanic is either reckless or naïve, and while I might have been the former, I liked to think I wasn't the latter. This wasn't my first rodeo, as they say.

In addition, we would have to consider the cost of gas. Remarkably, this wasn't included in the price of the taxi on such trips. We'd also need to transport back-up reserves, since there would be few opportunities to refuel on the road. I did the math in my head—it all added up pretty quick. Given these considerations, I thought my best option was purchasing my own vehicle. After my mission was complete, I could give the car to Lanciné and his family. It would be a tremendous gift. Here in Guinée, few families own a car.

Needless to say, Lanciné liked this idea, so we set out to find a suitable vehicle. My funds were limited, and given the unimpressive selection of used cars in Conakry, we were left to decide between a paltry selection of finalists. We narrowed our choices using an inexact fusion of mechanical considerations and sheer gut intuition. Since neither of us were too savvy when it came to automobiles, we relied heavily on the latter. I dare say we even took into consideration certain matters of the occult. Divination is a handy tool if you know the right people. And this was Africa, after all.

The most promising vehicle we considered was over thirty years old, a patched-together Renault literally held together by rope and tape. It was quite the specimen, perhaps more like an artifact. The Renault was deep cobalt blue with a hatchback. Those were its most admirable qualities. As for its less desirable traits, it would need a new motor and four new tires, and ultimately much more. The majority of cars here are like this—European-make vehicles that were scrapped decades ago, but somehow still deemed fit for use in Africa. Inspections, emissions control, safety standards, and other apparent frivolities don't exist here. In the case of this particular hunk of metal, the floor sported holes big enough to see the countryside passing between your feet. I have since learned that this is not the ideal vantage point for seeing the rural landscape of West Africa.

Travel in the remote areas of Guinée is a dicey affair, and we needed to feel confident in our choice. We'd be trusting our lives to this car, after all. That said, our standards were pretty low, based on prior experiences. We had both traveled overland in vehicles far more dangerous. One had even caught on fire.

Lanciné and I stood before the little blue Renault, considering whether to purchase it.

"You think it'll run?" I asked.

The man selling the car was eager to demonstrate. He jumped in and reached beneath the wheel to press some wires together. The Renault chugged to life, spewing black smoke from its tailpipe. Apparently, the key didn't work, so it would need to be hot-wired each time. This didn't faze anyone.

"*Voilà*," the guy said, turning the car off as quickly as he had started it. "It is a fine vehicle. You will see. I am sure you will be very pleased."

Lanciné had an air of utter disgust like he was smelling spoiled fruit. I knew Lanciné well enough to understand exactly what he was up to: he wanted this car, but when it comes to haggling over a price, there is nobody on Earth as ruthlessly shrewd as Lanciné. I had learned from our recent experiences in the markets to sit back and let the master work his magic on my behalf. At times, he drove shopkeepers to the point of demoralization. Getting the absolute best price is a point of pride for Lanciné, a man who grew up in one of the poorest nations in the world.

Buying the Renault was no exception. Though the seller was initially gleeful at seeing a white American as his buyer, that glee waned rapidly. I stepped back to watch it unfold. The exchange in Malinké was too fast for me to keep up, so I had to rely on body language to interpret the scene. After ten minutes of abuse, the seller turned his back to us. It looked like Lanciné had gone too far this time, and killed the sale.

Lanciné turned to me, and gestured toward the man. "Daouda, *allez* —give him the money." I was shocked. We were buying the car.

"How much?" I asked.

"Two million, seven hundred thousand Guinée francs." I scrambled to do the calculations. The exchange rate was something like 7,850 francs to $1 USD. So, what the hell was two-point-seven million divided by seven thousand and fucking whatever? *C'mon, think!* Operating in multiple foreign languages was already taxing me. I was absolutely cooking in the midday sun. I glanced at the Renault one more time.

What sources of intuition or varied logic prompted Lanciné to choose the little blue Renault? He had surely seen much worse. Or perhaps it was because in West Africa, the prevailing worldview maintains that every element in nature contains *nyama*. And what is a car but a complex collection of elements? This *nyama* business was not my area of expertise. But something about the little Renault spoke to Lanciné.

I shrugged. Maybe I was tempting fate. I reached into my bag and counted out millions of Guinée francs in increments of five thousand. I handed over a mountain of cash. The little blue Renault was now mine. Or as Lanciné would soon start correcting me, *ours*.

After purchasing the car, the discussion turned to the topic of a driver. Neither of us felt comfortable driving on the treacherous roads of rural Guinée. We'd need a skilled driver, and preferably someone who could make repairs as well. We chose a young friend of Lanciné's named Lamine. He was good with cars and had reputedly driven across the whole of Guinée without stopping except to refuel—a remarkable feat of both stamina and skill. He would be a worthy asset. What's more, Lamine came from the same village as Famoudou, and his father was a well-known *marabout*, or Muslim holy man. I think this fact earned him extra points with Lanciné. Maybe he knew we would need Allah on our side.

But still, there was the task of refurbishing the blue Renault. We delegated the task to Lamine, and checked in on his progress every day or two. Typically, this resulted in me parting ways with more cash. We headed into town to find used car parts, since it was impossible to find new parts in Conakry. During these excursions, I started feeling like a real local—I mean, picking through heaps of used car parts in the junk-yards of third-world Africa? Not necessarily a touristy thing to do. But I loved it. There was a certain thrill about the whole adventure before me —though my fears were still undeniable. I suppose that added to the thrill.

The repairs consumed a lot of time, but I was beginning to accept that nothing happens fast in Africa, and hell, I wasn't going anywhere else. We spent a solid week shopping around for a good deal on a used motor and acceptable tires. We then spent two additional weeks over-seeing various repairs. When at long last the Renault was ready, we washed it and stepped back to admire our newly refurbished piece of machinery. Its blue coat glistened in the sun. Lamine had meticulously adorned it with racing stripes and a tinted adhesive sheet on the wind-shield. Friends and family members stopped by to admire it. I had to admit, it looked decent. The Renault now seemed worthy of an overland journey into the heart of Africa.

Feeling rather smug about our accomplishments, we got right down to business. The journey would be dangerous. Supplies and medical facilities in the village were non-existent. We had, thus, considerable arrangements to make, and strategies to plot out. I trusted Lanciné's experience, and followed his lead. Which is to say, for the next two weeks we hung out and sipped coffee at the local café while awaiting word from the village. We played a lot of flute. *Dembadon* festivals occupied the rest of our time. In the evenings, I made a lot of art. I suppose I should have been more worried about our lack of preparations, but as instructed by an obviously competent shaman, I put things in the hands of elders and waited for them to unfold.

To ease any lingering apprehensions, I occasionally consulted the notes I had taken at Famoudou's. Were we missing anything? It was easy to get caught up in Africa time and let it slip away.

"Lanciné," I said one morning over coffee, "my notes say we need a sheep—*un mouton*. And quite a few chickens. You have any thoughts about that?"

Lanciné considered it a moment. "We can buy the chickens in the village, no problem. But a sheep will be too expensive there. We should buy *le mouton* in Conakry before we leave. Much better price here."

My funds were getting stretched, so I appreciated Lanciné's frugality. But it also raised a red flag. If we bought a sheep in Conakry, we'd have to transport it all the way to the village. That meant twenty-odd hours of driving—if nothing went wrong. I imagined the trip with a live sheep in the back seat of the little Renault. Where would we all sit? Jesus, it was such a small car.

"Sooo...we buy a sheep here and drive with it *all the way* to the village?" By stating the obvious question, I was sure Lanciné would see his logistical error.

"Yes. This is no problem. We can buy a very good sheep here. Much better than in the village. We do not want a skinny *mouton*. We want a fat, healthy one! So we will buy it here in Conakry, and get a good price. In the village, *il coûte les yeux et la tête.*"

I laughed at the expression, *it costs your eyes and your head.* But I was still sheepish about the prospect. I'd seen plenty of these beasts in Guinée, particularly during the festival of Tabaski—the "Festival of Sheep," or *Aïd el-Adha* in Arabic. These sheep weren't the soft, curly-haired ones you'd count at night to fall asleep, no sir. The sheep I saw in Africa were large with coarse fur, had big curly horns, and were a bit unruly when unhappy. Which they always seemed to be. I couldn't imagine one of these fellows curled up in my lap while we drove over roads with crater-sized potholes. The drive *sans mouton* was torturous enough.

"Lanciné," I persisted. "I don't mind paying extra for a sheep once we arrive. Surely, we can find a good one there? I've seen lots of fat sheep *au village*." I knew next to nothing about buying sheep. But still, what was a few extra dollars?

Lanciné looked at me incredulously. "Daouda, always you are too eager to throw your money around. Here in Africa, we do not have that luxury. A sheep is a very expensive thing for us. In the village, *un mouton* costs one million, two hundred thousand Guinée francs. In Conakry, you can buy *un mouton* for only nine hundred thousand. That is a big difference."

I did the math. A sheep in the village cost a hundred and twenty bucks. Buying one in Conakry would save me about thirty dollars. That seemed like a fair trade-off for not driving twenty hours with a pissed-off sheep. I thought about how easily I could blow thirty bucks back home. A couple of drinks at the pub with friends. A night out at the movies. It cost thirty dollars to fill my gas tank, and I did that several times a month. Though I'd have been ashamed to admit it to Lanciné, I probably spent thirty dollars a week on lattes at the local coffee shop back home. *God, what a privileged little shit I am.*

A painful memory arose. It was the time some American pals and I treated our Guinéen friends to lunch in downtown Conakry. I thought it'd be a nice thing to do. And plus, after several months of eating manioc and bony little river fish, I'd been dreaming of a nice juicy chicken with french fries.

We came to a restaurant across from the *Marché Niger* called *Le Damier*, which served French cuisine with an African flair. Not to mention they were a *pâtissier chocolatier*, a chocolate confectioner. Their in-house chocolates and pastries were out of this world. It would be an indulgent treat, I knew, but fun to take the village guys there.

Upon entering the upscale restaurant, Lanciné and company were visibly uncomfortable. The maître d' seated the nine of us upstairs, and passed menus around. Though most of the village guys couldn't read, they knew numbers. I hoped they weren't looking at the prices. It was expensive, much like what you'd pay in America for a nice meal out.

I beamed with pride when the feast arrived, along with icy-cold sodas and bottles of *Perrier*. Lanciné sat next to me, and he had a plate of french fries with his *boulette de poisson et couscous d'igname*—fish dumpling with yam couscous. A bottle of ketchup sat before him. He was eyeballing it, but not reaching for it.

"Go ahead," I said, gesturing toward the bottle. "You like tomato ketchup? Have some on your *pommes frites*."

He hesitated. "How much does it cost?"

"The ketchup?" I chuckled between mouthfuls of chicken. "Nothing. It comes with the meal. Really—have at it."

"The ketchup, *c'est gratuit?* It is *free*?" He found it hard to believe. I reassured him it was true. His eyes lit up. Maybe it was too good to be true, or maybe he didn't want it to go to waste, all that ketchup in a bottle. Either way, he emptied the entire bottle onto his plate, and ate it with a spoon.

When we finished the meal, the waiter came with the bill. We went downstairs to pay. The restaurant had strategically placed the register next to the pastry displays. How could we resist? We added dessert to the bill and bagged it up for later.

We tried to pay discreetly. But the cash register had an enormous digital display that faced outward, with bright numbers. The woman behind the register tallied it up, and everyone watched as the number climbed. A hundred thousand here, a hundred thousand there, it kept going up. The total came to around 700,000 Guinée Francs—just under ninety dollars for the nine of us.

On the ride back, my village friends were silent. It was awkward. Finally, my friend Mamady broke the silence.

"David—please, you mustn't tell *anyone* we came here with you."

"*Pourquoi*—why?" I asked. I guess I'm the grand master of *naïveté* after all.

His voice quavered. "It would bring great shame to all of us. Our friends, our family, they would never let us forget it. The money you have spent on one meal was enough to feed our entire village for a month."

Well, it had been a memorable experience, that's for sure. Just not in the way I had hoped. I felt like an idiot. The waste and selfish individualism that is the norm in my country was never more apparent. I had learned a hard lesson, and it is one I carry with me.

The lesson was rearing its head once more.

Retournons à nos moutons!—let's get back to our sheep. Saving thirty dollars on the purchase of one sheep was important to Lanciné. Frugality is a point of pride to him, a moral obligation even, hence his shrewd bartering in the markets. As Lanciné reminded me, a fifty-kilogram bag of locally grown rice—about a hundred and ten pounds—costs two hundred fifty thousand Guinée Francs. Yup, around thirty dollars. That much rice can feed a lot of hungry folks. Therein was the crux of the matter: spending the extra thirty dollars for convenience' sake was unforgivable when so many people went hungry every day.

I gave in. We'd buy a sheep in Conakry, and I'd deal with it in the car. If I was going to do this crazy quest of healing, I would do it the African way. After some discussion, we decided to spend the thirty dollars we'd save on a fifty-kilo bag of rice to donate to the village.

Lanciné was pleased. The sheep? Not so much.

Meanwhile, Africa time crawled along like a three-legged gecko. (Yes, I've seen these. Life in Africa is hard for everyone.) My painful condition plagued me day and night, and my suspicions grew. Could there be more to it than a malfunctioning immune system? The question pulled my spiritual assumptions onto the playing field. Add to this the reality of being single after sixteen years, and I felt bewildered and quite alone in the world, drifting and searching for something tangible to hang my hat on. My only securities were music and art—and a faltering hope that this journey would lead me to healing.

The days moved in an entrancing rhythmic dance of slow time. Minutes were like eighth notes, the hours like quarter notes, and days themselves like one last whole note on the ancient wooden flutes. If there was a soundtrack to this slow dance of time, it was the flutes themselves.

Lanciné and I tackled my flute lessons in earnest. He had much to teach me, and I wanted to dig deeper into the songs. The music became a window into the Malinké worldview, and challenged my own fragile vision of the world. I grappled daily with the notions of reality, healing, and my future.

Lanciné taught me dozens of new songs that shed light on the traditions of Africa. These were songs that spoke of the Malinké heroes, like Sundiata Keita, the Lion King of Mali. I never tired of hearing Sundiata's stories. The songs about Fakoli, the war hero and hunter, were particularly challenging for me, in more ways than one. Fakoli was reputed to be a leader of the *Kòmò* secret society, and I wanted to know more.

The songs for the *Soli* initiation rites were a large part of Lanciné's repertoire, and we touched on them all. I learned the music that accompanies the mask dances, too. There was music for *Balanen*, the porcupine and village bogeyman, and songs for *Konden*, the lion who tests the courage of the *bilakoro* before their initiation. Deeper we went, and we played the music for the red panther named *Soliwulen*, a formidable sorcerer who drives evil spirits from the village. I had seen these masks in the village. Their commanding dances left me mesmerized and bewitched. Learning their music was like dipping into a part of their magic.

Lanciné mostly tolerated my persistent questions. Even so, some topics were too difficult to explain *en français*. For Lanciné, French is a fourth language, and he struggled to translate Malinké words for which there is no French equivalent. And some topics were secret. When we touched upon these, he would smile and wag his finger at me.

"Ah, Daouda! You ask too many questions. Let it be. It is time now to move on."

And so we would. Some mysteries would remain mysteries.

One day, we were working on a song that was part of the ancient Sundiata Epic. I asked him to explain the significance of the lyrics, which started off with the words *Nyama, nyama, nyama*.

"Ah, Daouda, it is complicated. There are different interpretations of this song. For some, *nyama* refers here to the lineage of Sundiata, which is like a field of grass. While anyone can enter into the grass, the grass itself will bow to no one." He reflected for a moment, choosing his words. "But the word *nyama*, it also means filth, or garbage."

I was puzzled. "Come again?"

"Yes, *nyama*, it is in all life, and is potent and sacred. But *nyama* is also the byproduct of all action—the waste." For emphasis, he pointed to a small garbage can.

I had to think about this. So, *nyama* encompasses both the sacred and profane, but what does that actually mean? I was about to ask him to elaborate on this dichotomy. But right at that moment, his attention turned sharply to an airplane that flew low overhead. He leapt out of his chair to follow its trajectory, ignoring me.

In Conakry, Lanciné lived not far from the airport. Planes took off and landed regularly, and he had memorized the exact schedule. When a plane flew overhead, he'd stop all activity to carefully observe it. And now, the plane had Lanciné transfixed.

When the plane passed from view at last, Lanciné turned and looked at me. His expression changed.

"*Daouda!*" he exclaimed, waving his finger at me. "You white people, you are very clever! You have the secret of the airplanes, and yet you do not share it with us Africans. You refuse to let us in on your secret. You fly all around the world while we toil on the earth below you."

He approached me suddenly, his eyes ablaze.

"*Allez, dis-moi!*" he ordered. "Tell me the secret!"

"What—? Lanciné!" I half laughed. I didn't know what to say.

"Go on, Daouda! I tell you a great many things. Now you must share the secret of the airplanes with me. Then you and I will be on the same level, and I will fly wherever I please. You know the secret—now *tell me!*"

"Lanciné!" I retorted. "I'm sorry. No, I do not have the secret. I don't know how to make or fly an airplane." Like practically everyone in America, I had studied some basic physics. But the concepts of flight were just words to me. I could have stammered on about things like *drag* and *lift* and *thrust* fairly nonsensically. It would be useless information. But my face must have revealed I was considering it.

"Ha! You are lying to me!" he accused. "I can see it in your eyes!"

"I am *not* lying!" I burst out.

"You are, *too!* Reveal the secret!"

We were both laughing now, and I decided to take sport in it.

"Fine. Lanciné, you have played me well. I shall tell you the secret of the airplanes. But it is a very big secret. In exchange, you must first reveal the secrets of *Konden* the lion and of *Soliwulen* the panther. Do we have an agreement?"

"Ahhh *Daouda!*" He shook his head violently and waved his finger at me. "Heh! You have put me in a difficult position. How do I know you will reveal the secret of the airplanes?"

I shrugged my shoulders. "I guess you'll just have to trust me." I was grinning now that I had the upper hand.

Lanciné shook his head, chuckling lightly. "Nooo, Daouda—some secrets must remain. You will keep your secret of the airplanes, and I will keep mine."

I sighed dramatically. "Yes, I suppose that is best."

He sat down next to me, and we fell into a comfortable silence. Our worlds were so different, his and mine. My world had airplanes and smartphones. We even put people into outer space. But *his* world contained magic and sorcery, and people danced comfortably with the unknowable. I wondered if we would ever bridge those worlds, if it was even possible.

After a while, he picked up his flute and handed the other to me. We resumed playing without a further word.

As the melodies of our flutes joined the slow waltz of an afternoon in Africa, I knew what we *did* have was friendship, and a shared love for music. For the moment, those were all the bridges I needed.

21

VISITORS IN MY ROOM

WHILE I STAYED PUT and awaited word from the village elders, Conakry hummed and buzzed around me. The city's motion was tireless as it chased the twenty-first century, which threatened to leave Conakry buried in its wake. In contrast, my days slogged by like time was pulling a giant plow behind it. My anxieties about the impending journey were constant, and I turned to art for both comfort and escape.

Lanciné's place was starting to feel like home, and I spent a decadent amount of time in my new studio. While I worked, I entertained the idea that I might become a permanent resident of Africa. To my surprise, the thought didn't horrify me. But what did was the ticking time bomb of my deteriorating spine, which counted down closer to zero with each passing day. Art was the last thread that still connected me to sanity—and art is no sanity at all.

By now, it was well known what I was doing here. Like in any small community, gossip here traveled faster than a herd of gazelles with a lion in pursuit. Though my presence was no cause for alarm, it did create a buzz of chatter, and I didn't need to be fluent in Malinké to know I was the topic of much conversation. As I sat in my studio drawing for hours on end, residents peeked through my open doorway and scattered like flies when I glanced up. Over time, the visitors grew bolder, and I saw no reason not to invite them in. Soon, curious onlookers filled my studio and watched over my shoulder as images appeared on paper. It was my own form of magic, and they were transfixed by my little show.

The curiosity was mutual. During breaks from long drawing sessions, I'd pull a chair outside and watch in fascination as Africa went about its daily business of survival. In the afternoons, the courtyard was mostly occupied by women, since the men were typically out searching for work. In Conakry, I observed, the traditional division of labor that kept village life running smoothly had broken down. Here, the work customarily performed by adult village men didn't exist. Many were thus left to search endlessly for scarce jobs, or worse, to pass their days in idle desperation. The women, however, never stopped working, and their activities were almost always accompanied by singing and laughter. I envied the simplicity of their lives.

One young woman took a particular interest in me. Had I been less preoccupied with the journey ahead of me, I might have recognized sooner that her long glances and coquettish smiles were something other than normal curiosity. She spoke no French, so our exchanges were mostly wordless. Nonetheless, these visits became increasingly frequent, and she often stood in my doorway, silently observing me as I worked. Her presence was comforting, and she flashed a smile whenever I looked up. This would go on for ten minutes or more, until a scolding voice called from across the courtyard.

"*Aminata!*"

Without a word, she'd scurry away and return to her chores. But I had learned her name.

In the evenings, I was often joined by two of Lanciné's sons, Lancéï and Mamoudou, who were around eighteen and twenty-two respectively. They were good company and spoke excellent French, so we passed pleasant hours chatting away while I worked. They proved to be useful art critics, as well.

"This portrait is turning out good, David," Lancéï said one night. "It looks just like her, but…" He studied my drawing with a cocked head and squinted eyes. "Hmm. But the nose, is it too long?"

I leaned back. *Shit*. He was right. Sometimes I got too close to the drawing and forgot to step away from it, which is when those kinds of errors became apparent. But every drawing was an opportunity to practice and learn, so despite the imperfections, it was satisfying work. After sufficient critiquing and subsequent reworking of each drawing, I slid them into the black portfolio case along with all the other completed pieces. The collection grew daily, and so did my skills.

Sometimes the boys would come with friends.

"David," Mamoudou said one evening, "We are sorry to disturb you, but our friends would like to see your artwork. Would you mind showing them?"

I didn't mind at all. Lanciné had joined us too, and I was proud to display my work. I retrieved the drawings from the case and spread them out on the floor in an informal exhibition. A dozen graphite faces stared back at us, their expressions frozen in a moment that would now last forever.

"Ahhh, Daouda!" Lanciné exclaimed. "What sorcery is this? Have you captured these poor people's souls?" He inspected the drawings individually, holding the paper at different angles to scrutinize them. "*Nooo*, Daouda, these are really good—too good! I do not know how you do this. But I am afraid that you have become *un diable*—a devil!"

He was half joking, but the awareness that my artwork might be seen as witchcraft concerned me. I thought back to my work depicting the sacred masks, and was reminded of the magic inherent in art-making. I glanced at my backpack, which hid a single copy of my book bearing the image of a deceased sorcerer. I shuddered to imagine what his widow Mousso Gbè might think. I would have to tread carefully.

Famoudou's parting words echoed in my mind. *You will show the book to no one until I am with you.*

Whether I was a devil capturing souls in my artwork, or I was channeling a muse that was to me more like an angel, there was no doubt that my art was beginning to flourish. In any case, mine was an opportunistic muse, and since I had been instructed to wait until village elders devised a plan, I had time. I worked feverishly, often late into the night, and when the first light of day streamed through my window, I was pulled back to my desk and picked up where I left off.

All the while, I prayed to whatever gods were listening that this work would be allowed to continue, and that it would be sanctified. I knew my spine was crumbling, but I was grateful I still had my hands. If I ever ended up crippled, I prayed I could at least continue to make art. And most of all, I prayed this whole journey would one day make sense to me.

~

Despite my momentary freedom to indulge in art, I encountered a few snags. For one, I discovered a problem with the wooden desk we had bought. The problem always became worse at night. It started with just one or two, which I could easily ignore. But then more came. And they multiplied.

The desk, it turned out, was infested. Some particular variety of African insect had laid eggs in a rotten section of the wood. And now they were hatching.

The insects resembled small cockroaches, reddish-brown with thick outer bodies. As their numbers proliferated, I grew to hate them. At first, they appeared at my feet, but soon they were shimmying across my drawings. My suspicions grew. I aimed the beam of my headlight to the desk's underside, and saw the source. Swarms of bugs slipped in and out of cracks in the wood. The desk itself was alive with them. In the quiet of night, the sound of the bugs crawling from their nest made my stomach turn. And it was just the beginning.

I awoke the next morning before dawn to an incessant tapping mixed with what sounded like somebody sucking their teeth. I looked out in the pale light beyond my mosquito net. To my absolute dismay, the floor was pulsing and swarming with bugs. Kind of like that scene from the first *Indiana Jones* movie with the snakes, but instead with bugs. And I hate bugs.

"Bugs," I said to myself, rolling back over on my mattress. "Why did it have to be *bugs*…"

If there had been a canister of gasoline with a spray nozzle and a flaming torch at my disposal, I would not have hesitated. Alas, being no Indiana Jones myself, all I had in my room was an electric thermos capable of smelting iron. That would do me no good, but I reached for the cord and plugged it in anyway. Maybe my *kratom* leaf tea would make this nightmare end. I made myself an extra-strong batch from within the safety of my bug net, and waited for the warm buzz to come over me. When the liquid courage kicked in at last, I reached for my sandals and made a break for the door. Layers of bugs crackled beneath my feet and I fought to keep yesterday's dinner down.

Outside, the women were gathering firewood and preparing breakfast. Lanciné sat nearby, stirring instant coffee into his mug. I played it cool.

"*Ini sööma*, Daouda—good morning," he said politely, "*Tana ma sii?*"

The literal translation to the question *tana ma sii* is, "did you sleep without evil?"

"*Tana sii té*," I responded. Yeah man, no evil here, none whatsoever. "Is there more water for coffee?"

He shouted something in Malinké to whoever was in the house. One of his daughters came out with a mug full of steaming water. I scooped some Nescafé, and reached across the table for the can of sweetened condensed milk.

"What's the plan for today?" I asked. "More *dembadon?*"

"No *dembadon* today. Lamine will be stopping by with the vehicle. He says he is almost finished, and that the new motor is running fine. This morning he will outfit it with new hubcaps."

"Ah, *c'est super!*" I said. If we were down to hubcaps, we had to be close. "That Lamine, he is *très malin*—very clever. I trust we will have an easy journey with him as our driver."

"Mmm." Lanciné stretched and yawned, looking bored. "The day is hot already."

"Yeah," I agreed. My head was now buzzing from all the tea. "Oh Lanciné—I wanted to tell you. There is a little problem with the desk in my room." I was not one to shy away from understatements.

"Oh? Does it not suit you? I think it is a fine desk, no?"

"Yes, yes—it is a fine desk. It has only one small problem. After breakfast, I will show you. You will see."

We ate a leisurely breakfast of eggs fried in enough palm oil to clog even the healthiest of arteries. When we finished, I led him to my room and swung the door open. He stood in the doorway for a long moment, mouth agape, eyes wide. Bugs poured out of the desk and tumbled onto the floor. It was macabre, bordering on apocalyptic.

"Yes, Daouda. I think this is not so good."

So then, it was a duel of understatements. I would not be outmatched.

"It's a little inconvenient is all. I could probably manage. Unless you think..."

"*Non, c'est grave!* It is *serious.*" He quickly added, "I'll get the boys."

I don't like to play the "helpless *étranger*" card often—but when I do, it's in choice moments like these.

"Excellent idea," I agreed. "Let's get the boys."

When Lanciné's eldest sons arrived, they pulled the desk into the sun and promptly emptied several canisters of military-grade insecticide into every nook and cranny. The residual fumes were overpowering, and I sincerely worried they might bring ecological collapse to the region. I imagined the headline: *White Guy's Infested Art Studio Triggers Large-scale Environmental Catastrophe in Africa.*

Lamine arrived a short time later with the vehicle, and I promptly forgot all about the bugs. The Renault was looking good—real good. Lamine had freshly washed and waxed it, and when he hot-wired it into life, it purred like a baby lion. Sunlight sparkled on newly polished mirrors. The whitewalls of its new tires were impossibly white, and the tinted windows gave it a 1980s gangsta look. We drove around the streets of Conakry, me riding shotgun with my sunglasses on and my arm hanging out the window. I was feeling alright about it, man. I mean, it could have been all the tea I drank, but then again, we only had to hot-wire the Renault once when it stalled at a busy intersection. My hopes were nearly as high as I was.

When we returned later that evening, I was delighted to find that the boys had already moved the desk back into my room. All evidence of what was just hours earlier a plague of near biblical proportions had been swept away. My art studio was neatly arranged and tidied up, my pencils in perfect rows awaiting my next artwork.

With my heroes properly thanked, I got straight to work on a new drawing amidst lingering insecticide fumes.

～

Even with the bugs worked out of the system, I had other issues to deal with. Existential ones, at that. My insecurities plagued me. I felt terribly small in the world. Whatever new footing I had found through my art was still shaky. And when the pain flared up, I couldn't escape the feeling I was being punished for something. This was the work of either the gods or ancestor spirits—I was now sure of it.

The fire in my spine was incessant, and it was mine to bear alone. Day by day, my reserves of green powder dwindled. The longer we stayed here, the faster it would disappear. What alternative would I be left with? It was unthinkable. I had chosen *kratom* tea as a safer alternative to prescription pain pills, but it was more powerful than I initially thought. I was craving it for more than pain relief. When the tea was gone, I knew I would fall back on the pills. And when they were gone? Was I strong enough for what came *then?*

Each day, my old life receded further into the distance. The things I had back home, the possessions I owned, none of them mattered much now. Surely, Kerri was moving on with her life. I hoped she was. A new life was beginning for me too, though it was hard to imagine where it would lead.

I often wondered, *if I die here in Africa, will anyone back home even know?* How would people here get word to them? They had no contact with my family. I was four thousand miles from home. No, if my life were to end here, it would be quietly. My friends and family would wonder what strange fate had befallen me. This feeling—being so small that I could simply disappear—was the most terrifying of all. At night, when I was utterly alone and the bewitching sounds of Africa descended upon me, my existence seemed wretched and insignificant.

In fear and desperation, I began to pray to the ancestors themselves. I knew not who they were, or even if they were real, but this became my new practice. When I'd awake wracked with pain, or from some nightmare that left me trembling, I would implore them for mercy.

Please, end this curse. I will do whatever you ask of me.

I was like a bereft sailor, and Africa was the sea on which I drifted.

Whatever gods ruled here were not the same gods I knew in my former life. But they were my masters now.

~

One night, I awoke abruptly in absolute darkness. The heat was stifling, the air thick. Nothing stirred. The deep silence was unsettling. Within the gauzy shelter of my mosquito net, I couldn't see an inch in front of me.

What time is it? I wondered. I had stayed up drawing too late, and I was exhausted. So what had awoken me?

My awareness came slowly into focus, and I rolled over in an attempt to get comfortable. A sharp pain ripped through the center of my spine. I turned again to escape it, and touched something unfamiliar beside me.

Oh my god!

There was something in bed with me. I felt its weight on the mattress next to me. It was heavy and cold, clammy to the touch.

My heart raced, and I was suddenly wide awake, fumbling in the dark for my headlamp. What creature had climbed under the mosquito netting while I slept, and what the hell was it? Was it a serpent that had slithered in? Or perhaps one of the lizards that climbed on the walls of the building? I had seen one just the other day that looked different from the rest, shiny black with white eyes. It had been climbing near the open window of my room, and I had pointed it out to Lanciné.

"Yes, that one is very dangerous!" he said. "Do not go near it."

My window had only vertical iron bars across it, spaced about two inches apart. Enough to keep an intruder out, but not a lizard. Had one climbed in during the night?

I recoiled sharply from the object beside me on the mattress. My horror grew. It moved with me. No—it was attached *to* me.

I flailed at it desperately as panic overtook me. It was then that I understood exactly what it was: my own right arm hanging from me, lifeless and cold, utterly without feeling.

I sprang from the mattress and tore open the mosquito netting. Now on my feet, I reached with my other arm for the lamp and hoped there was electricity. There was. Light flooded into the room and I stared at my lame arm. It was a sickly pale white, as lifeless as a corpse.

I cried out in terror. Why was this happening? I shook it desperately, but still could not feel my arm. Long minutes passed and no sensation returned. A thought entered my mind: *I might lose my arm here in Africa.* I instantly felt sick to my stomach, and lurched over to the waste bin and vomited.

Fuck! Fuck! What am I supposed to do?! Surely, this was the result of my deteriorating spine. Some nerve had finally been pinched off while I slept, and blood was no longer circulating there. Then, understanding came like a blow. I would no longer be able to make art. Good God, would they have to amputate my arm, here in a hospital in Africa?

Oh god, oh god! Please don't let me lose my arm!

In tormented defiance, I forced my spine to straighten, and heard several loud cracks, accompanied by an immense bolt of pain. It felt like I had broken something. Or...broken *through* something? I knew from medical explanations that the tendons between my vertebrae were calcifying, turning into bone that would eventually fuse my spine like cement. This can cause certain nerves to become compressed and eventually damaged. I reckoned I had just busted through some of that calcification—but I wasn't sure yet if that was good or bad.

I straightened my spine a bit more, and though the discomfort was intense, I felt a release of pressure. A warm tingle started in my shoulder and spread to my forearm a few moments later. I regained some hope. I shook my uselessly dangling arm, hoping to force more blood that way.

Thirty minutes later, my fingers began to tingle. I wondered how long they could go without blood flow before they became permanently damaged. I looked over at the near-finished drawing on the table and shook my arm all the more furiously at the thought that it might remain unfinished forever.

It was a full hour before feeling fully returned to my arm and fingers. I fell to the mattress, utterly spent, the mosquito net torn from the ceiling and crumpled around me. What was this new curse that had come upon me? Would it happen again?

The image of Sako Gbè appeared in my mind, along with the words of the shaman.

The ancestors are not to be fooled with. It would have been much better for you if this man was still alive.

The disease was progressing, and time was running out.

Until you find out what they want—and remedy the situation—your illness will only get much worse.

Was this truly the work of the ancestors? Were they trying to get my attention?

No—I am only losing my mind, I thought. This was all madness. I had to escape from here, for my sanity's sake. If I went back home, I could forget this whole quest. I could have the surgery and be done with it. The surgeons would cut my back open to access my spine. They would fuse it together with metal rods and screws into a rigid and unmovable staff. I would be disabled for the rest of my life. But the nightmare would be over.

My thoughts tormented me. I couldn't wait here in Conakry any longer. Even if we did get word from the village soon, what further damage to my spine and nerves was I risking here? Could I endure any more of this? No, I had to call it off. In the morning, I would tell Lanciné I was going home. I had made up my mind.

In the meantime, I needed to get some sleep, but even slumber frightened me. What evil would befall me if I dozed off? I remained vigilant during the long night, and forced myself upright each time the numbness in my arm returned.

When morning came, golden rays of sunshine streamed through the iron bars of my window. I made a fist with my right hand, testing it carefully. Satisfied but still dazed, I arose and walked into the courtyard.

Lanciné was awake, drinking his coffee beneath the tree. I took a deep breath and was about to break the news, but Lanciné spoke first.

"Daouda, *ini sööma*—good morning. I am glad you have risen early. We have much to do today. Tomorrow before dawn, we depart for the village. The elders are ready."

The words I had been ready to speak froze in my mouth. My heart confirmed what my head feared, and the reality struck me full force. I was powerless to stop the wheels of fate. We were going to the village.

22

FULLY LOADED

I BOLTED UPRIGHT. It was pitch black out. I reached for my phone to check the time. Almost 3 a.m. The knocking on the metal door that had awoken me resounded again.

"Daouda, wake up," Lanciné said. "It is time."

I rubbed my eyes and struggled to form words in the appropriate language.

"Daouda, are you awake?" he called again.

"Yes, Lanciné," I replied finally. "I'll be out in a minute."

I switched on my headlamp. The electricity was out, so I was glad I finished packing the night before. My clothes were draped over my chair, ready to wear: a pair of old jeans, a favorite light t-shirt, a many-pocketed tan vest, and a thin *shemagh* wrapped around my neck for protection from the dust. I slipped on my sandals, and grabbed my weathered old fedora and sunglasses. I glanced in the dusty mirror, sucked in my gut, and thought I looked like a proper adventurer.

Satisfied, I pushed open the iron door and stepped outside. But I misjudged the first step and put my foot down awkwardly, losing my balance. I landed in a heap of dirt, sending a shock wave through my spine.

And so it began.

I dusted myself off self-consciously and looked around to see if anyone had noticed. Of course, it was 3 a.m., and almost everyone still slept. I took a deep breath of morning air. It was refreshingly cool. The stars were out, and the courtyard shimmered with soft moonlight.

Lanciné emerged with a cup of hot coffee. I was grateful the electricity had still been on the night before, as it allowed me to prepare several thermoses of hot water in advance. I was concerned about the pain during the long ride. At least I would have my *kratom* tea.

I joined Lanciné for coffee in the stillness of pre-dawn, tingling with nervous energy. The thought of embarking on a new adventure made me feel alive, despite my concerns that it was flying in the face of logic. I had packed carefully, but logic apparently wasn't coming with me.

I glanced around at the place we'd be leaving behind. I thought about my little art studio, and all the people I had met here. Would I be coming back here, ever? I didn't know.

They may ask you to stay there forever! And if that is the case, you must accept it.

I took a moment to admire the sheep we had purchased, which was tied to a tree by the gate. *Monsieur Mouton* was fat and healthy, and would make a nice gift to the village. I looked for the Renault, which had been parked outside the night before. It wasn't there now.

"Where is Lamine?" I asked. "And where's the Renault?"

"Lamine returned to his house last night to sleep. He should be here any moment—if he hasn't overslept." He frowned. "Perhaps I should call."

He reached for his cell, an early model Motorola flip phone, and navigated to the address book. I sipped my coffee, relishing the warm mug in my hands and the coolness of morning.

"Daouda, help me find Lamine's number. There are too many phone numbers here."

We scrolled through the list, which contained hundreds of names. Lanciné couldn't read them, so I was often called upon for assistance. *Daouda, find the number of so-and-so,* or *Does this name say Facily Kouyaté?* It wasn't an easy task, as many people share the same names. He'd ask, *Can you find the number for Sekou?* And there would be thirty-odd *Sekous* in the list. The last names were no help either, and it took me forever to understand these weren't always last names, but names of villages indicating where each person was born. It was an endless source of confusion for me. It's a shame I lived a great deal of my life thinking there was actually a guy named Mamady Faranah. That's time I can't get back.

I searched through dozens of *Lamines*, and finally came to one that said *Lamine Kouroussa*. That was it! Even I knew that one—Kouroussa was where we were heading.

"Try this one," I said. If I was wrong, we'd be calling some other Lamine in the middle of the night.

Lanciné called, and it was the right Lamine. Good thing, too. I didn't need a full translation to understand Lamine hadn't yet risen. Lanciné's gruff rebuke included some tasteful linguistic morsels. I jotted a couple down in my notebook, in case I ever needed them myself.

I wuli, i wulu kaya! Wake up, you dog's penis!

Eh Allah, i juwo! Oh my God, you asshole!

I was deeply impressed with Lanciné's tactful diplomacy at such an early hour. I imagined Lamine was moving along right quick now.

Lanciné's anger was justified, as it was vital we get on the road early. Military roadblocks were plentiful on the road from Conakry, but there'd be fewer at this time of day. Roadblocks often meant paying exorbitant bribes, but as I had learned from my last attempt with Famoudou, they could also make for a short trip. Our first obstacle was not the African countryside itself, but just getting out of Conakry.

Lanciné and I brought our supplies to the gate, which included a mountainous pile of mostly unnecessary crap I had packed in my luggage. I cringed when I saw Lanciné had only one tiny suitcase. We were also transporting a hundred-pound bag of rice, a diesel generator, and several five-gallon canisters of gasoline. The sheep watched with mild curiosity, not yet realizing it was joining our circus. It was going to be a tight fit. At least it was just the four of us—me, Lanciné, Lamine, and *Monsieur Mouton*.

We finished hauling our gear over as Lamine, looking under-slept and irritable, pulled up in the Renault. He was not alone. In the back seat was the young woman Aminata who had been paying me visits. I had since learned she was none other than Lamine's sister. Next to her was an older lady I didn't know. In crude terms, one might have said this lady was overweight, but here, they prefer to say "traditionally built." She had this particular tradition down pat.

Anyway, I wondered what they were doing here at this hour. Lanciné and Lamine had a brief conversation while I started loading. The two women remained in the car. I gestured towards them quizzically.

"They come," Lamine said. He was a man of few words, and his French was even worse than mine.

I glanced at Lanciné. "Seriously?"

Lanciné nodded. "Yes. This woman," he said, pointing to the traditionally built lady, "she will only come as far as Kouroussa."

Kouroussa only shaved off about an hour of the entire twenty-hour drive, so she might as well be going the whole way. I pictured being squashed in the back seat with this generously sized lady and was about to object. But another of those valuable life-lessons came to mind. During a crosstown taxi trip a few years ago, a Canadian friend named Robert and I were absolutely pinned between some of the largest ladies I had ever seen in Guinée—perhaps in all of Africa. Since Robert and I were both exceedingly clever, we spoke in English so no one could understand us.

"*God,* these ladies are *fat!*" Robert said. The inappropriateness of it caused me to have an uncontrollable giggle fit. The two of us snickered and guffawed. Robert offered up a few "yo mama's so fat" jokes, and soon we both had tears running down our cheeks. It was all so wrong, like giggling at a funeral.

The taxi stopped to let the nice ladies out. Before walking away, one of the ladies turned to us and said, in perfect English, "Have a very nice day." Our faces turned to stone. What were the chances, the two most traditional ladies on the African continent also spoke English? *Shit.* What a couple of jerks we were.

Now, I looked at the lady in the back of the Renault. I sighed, and said nothing. She was coming.

Lanciné continued, "And Aminata—she will come to the village with us, and there she will remain."

I could understand why Aminata would want to take the trip. She was a village girl who spoke no French at all. Like many village folks who came to Conakry for one reason or another, she despised the city and was anxious for an opportunity to get back home. Over the past few weeks, she and I had actually become pretty friendly, and people had noticed. In fact, her family had jumped quickly to a suggestion. *Perhaps you might consider marrying her? She is a very good cook, and could bear you many children.*

I'll be honest. Being recently single myself, I had watched Aminata saunter across the courtyard on more than one occasion, her soft hips swinging just so. Good lord, her sensuality was almost too much to take. And I was not blind to the seductive glances she cast my way. It was enough to cause a few momentary lapses of common sense, wherein I wondered if getting married and making a whole lot of babies in Africa would be such a bad fate. Her cooking *was* quite good, after all. *Ah, stop it, you fool!* No, no—I needed to be on my best behavior. My life was already complicated enough. I politely declined the marriage suggestion, using my standby excuses that I was already married (a bald-faced lie), and that in America, having multiple wives is frowned upon (quite true).

In any event, Aminata had seen her opportunity. A free ride to the village was an offer she wasn't going to refuse—even if there hadn't *been* an offer. At least not by me. She wasn't budging. I sighed again.

I estimated the total weight in the car. Five passengers. A hundred pounds of rice. The fattest sheep money can buy. A diesel generator. Extra tanks of gas and all our luggage, much of which was heaped on the car's roof and secured with rope. Well over twelve-hundred pounds, I calculated. Too much for the Renault.

Lanciné misread my concern. "Daouda, do not worry—you will be comfortable. Myself and the two women will sit in the back with the sheep. You are the *patron* now. You can have the front seat all to yourself."

The ladies sat with their arms crossed. I knew I wasn't going to win this one. I shrugged my shoulders, said, "*Bienvenue!*" to the ladies, and tossed my hat on the front seat. The two women smiled smugly. Lanciné loaded the sheep, which looked numb with shock. Feeling a bit of the same, I hopped into the passenger's seat and readied myself for take-off. We were fully loaded.

Lamine fumbled beneath the steering wheel for the wires. The

Renault rumbled to life like an old snoring hippo, and the undercarriage scraped against hard stone as we pulled away.

Off we went into the darkness of an African city that still slept. As the road passed beneath us, I silently said goodbye to Conakry. With each mile, the possibility of returning home to have surgery slipped further away. I was betting my life on the words of a shaman, and a lunatic hope in tradition, ancestors, and magic.

23

LOVE IS A SORCERER

THE FIRST HOURS of the voyage passed reasonably well, thanks in part to Lanciné's diplomacy at the roadblocks we met leaving Conakry. We encountered more of these than expected at such an early hour. But Lanciné was calm and cool, even when confronted by burly soldiers with machine guns. I remained quiet except when interrogated, and kept my responses brief. While Lanciné negotiated, I held my breath, worried that the slightest perceived infraction would bring our voyage to a halt. When Lanciné instructed me to do so, I handed over the bribe money, grateful these soldiers didn't have grander imaginations. All told, I only parted with a few hundred thousand Guinea francs, the equivalent of fifty or sixty dollars. But still, it made the interstate tolls back home seem pretty reasonable. And I didn't have to pay those at gunpoint.

Once we were off the Conakry peninsula, the sun revealed a glorious day. For a time, the morning air remained soft and fresh. We passed through verdant rainforest, and the little Renault climbed rolling hills and mountain passes as best it could. Lamine skillfully navigated narrow, winding roads that bordered steep ravines. These stretches of road should have been terrifying, but I was well into my first thermos of tea, and buzzing pretty well. The danger seemed unreal, rather like watching a movie. I was exhilarated just to be on the road again.

We passed through the town of Coyah, the main source of Guinée's spring water. Three hours later, we stopped in Kindia, the nation's fourth-largest city, which felt to me more like a rustic small town. Its dusty streets were lined with wooden vendor stalls and ramshackle tin-roof storefronts. Here, we stopped for breakfast and took our pet sheep for a walk. While we strolled, I conversed with the traditionally built lady, whose name was Fanta. She was well-spoken and polite, and her pleasant manners made me glad she was here. She treated me with perhaps more respect than she ought, given that she was my elder. I thought it curious that she called me *patörön*, or *patron* in French, meaning "boss" or "man of the house."

Along the main route of Kindia, we found a roadside café that served coffee and omelette sandwiches. The five of us seated ourselves at an outdoor table with wooden benches. The café's proprietor brought us instant coffee with a can of sweetened condensed milk. Even this tasted divine to me, like it was the flavor of adventure. As we sipped our drinks from colorful ceramic mugs, I watched the sleepy town of Kindia come to life.

We were well into Malinké and Susu territory now, and I took note that very little French was spoken here. During past trips, I had focused my language studies on *la langue française*, figuring it would eventually be a bridge to learning Malinké. But now, it was little help, particularly as Aminata taught me some phrases over breakfast. She was determined to help me overcome my vernacular deficiencies, but without a common language to assist us, the exercise turned into an amusing game of charades. On any other day, this style of language lesson might have been frustrating. But today, I took pleasure in the flirtatious game.

Aminata began her guessing-game lesson by gesturing with her arms, in a way that appeared to me as if she was collecting rays of sun. The morning sun did feel quite nice, and I assumed she agreed. I offered my guess.

"Sunlight?"

Lanciné translated, and everyone burst out laughing.

Fanta gave me the correct answer. "She says, come eat breakfast. *Na dabö kè.*"

I wasn't even close.

Aminata giggled, and the game started again. She pointed to my sandwich and repeated, "*A diman? A diman? A diman...?*"

A-hah! I thought, *omelette sandwich*. I told Lanciné my guess, and he conveyed it through choked snickers.

Lamine offered the answer this time, and I think he enjoyed seeing my smug confidence turn into mock exasperation.

"She ask if sandwich good—*c'est bon? A diman?*"

I threw my hands up in pretend bewilderment, which brought more laughter. I laughed too, momentarily forgetting the crazy precept for our journey. The moment was delightful, sitting together with new friends at a tiny café a million miles from home. Speckled sunlight filtered through overhead trees, and the fragrant smell of wood smoke evoked unnamed memories. God, it felt good to be traveling again.

As we chatted gaily, I looked across the table at Aminata. Her hair was pulled back under a colorful headdress, and golden rays of sun played on her smooth ebony skin. What would it be like, I wondered, to be married to an African gal and have to cross these language barriers in a much different context? A voice rose inside me, admonishing. *For fuck's sake, Dave! Cut it out with those kinds of thoughts already!*

I shook it off, and carefully studied the bottom of my coffee mug. The last thing in the world I needed was to become somebody else's burden—or to be distracted from my real mission. But as I peered over my coffee cup, Aminata cast a playful glance at me, her lips softening into a smile. The effect was disorienting, and I suddenly realized that the Elmina Castle of my heart was conspicuously unguarded. Where the hell was the gatekeeper? I scrambled to deploy the proper defenses, but the drawbridge was malfunctioning. I would need to make repairs before my fortress was subjected to further attacks.

The proprietor of the café returned and spoke to us in Susu, apparently just to disorient me even more. Everybody else spoke Susu fluently, and he looked at us expectantly. Nobody moved or said a word. After an awkward moment, Fanta turned to me, and spoke softly.

"*Mon patron*—the man is here with the bill."

The real meaning of *patron* became clear. Yes, I was the big boss man, and it was my road trip, so I'd be paying. I looked around at my companions, and thought about the lives they lived here. They had so little, and breakfast at a café in Kindia was a small expense for me. I was fortunate to have them with me to ward off the fear and loneliness that otherwise plagued me. I counted out the bills, knowing it was a small exchange for their company and good-natured laughter.

"*Iniké*, Daouda," Lanciné said after I paid. "We all thank you for this."

"No, Lanciné—thank *you* all." I put my hand on my heart, and offered them a smile that I hoped transcended languages.

We rose from our seats and began walking back to the Renault, and I knew I wouldn't be here without them. Nor would I want to. The road ahead would be long, and for the first time in a long while, I didn't want to be alone.

Back on the road, the day heated up quickly. As we left the forest region and entered dry savannah, the road turned to dirt. The potholes grew larger. At times, I got out and directed Lamine as he steered around craters, hugging their ridges. I cringed when the Renault's bottom scraped against hard rock. At other times, we all had to get out to avoid bottoming out completely. It was slow going.

Ahead of us, the road stretched interminably, a long line of unpaved red track reaching to the horizon. The region was only sparsely populated, punctuated here and there by rural settlements. Rustic mud huts appeared on hillsides that overlooked the otherwise flat savannah. I wondered about the people who inhabited those little houses, and what their lives must be like. It appeared exotic and otherworldly to me, but to these people, it was home. I wondered if I would ever feel that way about this place.

Lamine was focused and methodical, and the miles passed slowly beneath us. As we drove, the rest of the passengers were quiet, so I was left to wander in my thoughts, to dream, and to gaze out at Africa as she passed by. Though my spine ached badly, I enjoyed being *en route* to somewhere, anywhere. I was *in* the journey now, and there was something to be said for that. It's not the destination that counts, but rather the journey itself, right? In the grand scheme, perhaps what matters most is the manner in which we travel through life. What happens along the way is largely out of our control, but what we make of it is up to us. We can choose to find some beauty in it, or we can choose not to.

It all sounded good—but the truth is, I was struggling with it. It was easy to forget that my perceptions shape my reality. Whether or not I accepted such concepts as ancestor spirits and spiritual illnesses was irrelevant, to a point. The real question was, could I begin to view this trip as a journey of *healing*, and not a journey of *suffering*? Hell, could I see my *life* as such?

The difference seemed important. Deep down, I wondered if my pain was actually self-inflicted, a product of my self-loathing and buried emotions. If our perceptions are so powerful, then perhaps I had manifested this illness. Perhaps it was a curse of my own making.

I tried to see past my suffering, like seeing through the mist over a lake after a summer rainstorm. I mean, we all suffer from something. Life ain't for sissies. Isn't the First Noble Truth of Buddhism that all life is suffering? It's easy to get stuck on that idea as a wholly negative one. But perhaps what it means is that suffering is the inroad to liberation. What if the only way to be free from our suffering is to first accept and embrace it?

The thought struck me. Was my pain actually a path to something better? I didn't know what that something better might look like. And I wasn't sure I had the guts to accept it when the pain got bad. What I had for those moments was a pocketful of pills. Siddhartha I'm not.

Il faut avoir du courage. One must have courage.

Yes, it takes courage to accept our pain, and even more so to reckon with our true nature. We are impermanent, and it's scary. So we cling to our misperceptions and illusions. Though we might accept change on some levels, we often view our suffering as if it's unchanging. But all things are impermanent. In light of this, it seems the only reasonable approach is to always be ready to let go of how things presently are.

Was I ready to let go of my old perceptions of who I was? At that moment, hardly. I was bound up in my identity. Much of that identity was, in turn, bound to pain. I needed the pain to confirm the illusion of who I was, and so it came full circle. How could I be free from suffering, when I used it as my excuse to swallow more painkillers and numb my deepest existential fears?

It was a revelation to me that I wasn't ready to let go of my suffering. Perhaps I was actually afraid to be healthy. Then, I'd have no more excuses, nothing else to blame for life being too hard.

I sighed, and gazed at the passing landscape.

So, here I am, driving deeper into Africa, searching for healing. But maybe the source of healing is already inside me.

It was the kind of idea that appealed to my artist's heart, though my brain found it frustratingly intangible. But whether I liked it or not, pain was my teacher now. It had led me all the way here. I could either embrace my suffering as the path toward healing, or continue along the road of denial. I didn't yet know which one I would choose.

Find the courage to accept this suffering, my heart said. *There is no past or future. Just now. Be in it.*

For a moment, it all seemed beautiful. The red dusty road beneath us. The little blue Renault, a chariot carrying us into the dreamscape of Africa. Even my pain brought meaning to this moment. I grasped to hold on to this feeling, but like sand through my fingers, the moment passed. But I had glimpsed something, and it was a start.

Somewhere near Mamou we came to a halt, and my musings along with it. The road had been mostly absent of other travelers, but now two vehicles were stopped ahead of us. We got out to see what was going on.

Lanciné spoke to the drivers, and returned.

"What's up?" I asked.

"*La route n'est pas finie d'abord*—the road is not yet finished."

"*What?*" I panicked. I didn't know they were doing road work way out here. "When did they start working on it?" I asked.

Lanciné scratched his head. "1950. No—maybe 1952."

"Jesus Christ. And it's not done yet?"

"The government ran out of money, but they will finish it soon."

"Jesus," I said again, not knowing who else to call on. "Do they need to borrow some money? I've got a couple hundred thousand in my bag."

Lanciné glared at me. The lack of government resources for public works was a sore spot.

Lamine walked ahead to survey, and then spoke in Malinké. Lanciné turned to me.

"Daouda, get back in the car. We will go through anyway."

I glanced at the road ahead—if you could call it that. It looked as if someone had dropped a bomb on it. Or maybe a meteor had hurtled through space and landed in that very spot. I shook my head slowly, but walked back to the car anyway. If anyone knew how to traverse roads like this, it was Lamine. And he was determined to get through.

The manufacturers of Renaults assuredly did *not* have this kind of travel in mind when they designed them. Nonetheless, we veered around the other cars, toward the crater. I mustered up all my faith in *nyama* and ancestor spirits and all sorts of other things I didn't understand—and braced myself. Lamine steered into the crater. For a moment, we hung at its rim and faced nose down toward the bottom. Then, gravity took over. Lamine's foot pressed hard on the brakes, and the car slid into the basin, turning sideways as it did. I gasped as we lurched down, fearing the car would roll. But Lamine gripped the wheel hard, and we shifted our weight to compensate. The Renault held steady.

Several bumpy minutes later, we crossed the depression and began our ascent. Lamine gunned the gas and the tires spun furiously. Black smoke rose from beneath the vehicle, along with the smell of burning rubber. We pitched backward, and Lamine slammed on the brakes. For a moment, we held at the rim—but would go no further. We were going to have to push it up the crater's steep wall.

Lanciné and I got out and walked behind the Renault. It looked dicey. If the car rolled backward, we would have to dive out of the way to avoid being crushed. And I was concerned about exerting such force on my spine.

It's just not safe for you to be walking around like this—if you had a fall or an accident, you could break your spine.

Lamine hit the gas. I scrambled for a better position, digging my feet into the earth. The tires spun clouds of dirt and pebbles at us, and Lanciné and I leaned into the Renault, straining with all our might. We were getting absolutely sprayed with dirt. If we stopped, the car would roll back on us. We dug in and pushed, grunting loudly.

The front tires found traction on solid ground at last, and the Renault lurched ahead and crested safely. Both Lanciné and I fell forward and landed in a heap. I turned to him, and our eyes locked for a moment. We both burst out laughing.

"Daouda, you are *dangba*—a dirty mess!"

I laughed. The word *dangba* was used to describe the unkempt beggars in the streets of Conakry, of which there are many.

"You're not looking so good yourself, *mon ami*," I said, spitting dirt. Lanciné's black hair was red with African earth.

We returned to the car and climbed in. Lamine was nonchalant, like it had been nothing. He casually pushed a cassette tape into the Renault's player. He hit play, and I recognized the voice of Mory Kanté, one of Guinée's most famous singers and *kora* players. Lively music streamed through dusty speakers as Lamine stepped on the gas. We were rolling, and once the wind was blowing through my hair again, I felt reinvigorated. I took a moment to revel in the adventure, and I could only wonder what lay ahead.

Whatever comes, I thought, *I will accept it. All of it. Even the suffering.*

We rambled down the road in our dust-coated Renault, and Mory Kanté sang through our speakers:

When I'm walking, I think of my true love
Seated in my car, I think of my true love
Do you see darling, love is a sorcerer…
Destiny unites those who love each other…

I settled into my thoughts once again.

Love…sorcery…destiny. With a twinge of sadness and regret, I wondered what Kerri was up to. I pushed the thought away. Surely, she was moving on without me. Maybe she had already found someone else. *I don't care*, I told myself. I was in *Africa* now, having a grand adventure. Maybe it would be my last, I didn't know. But if it was, I would go out with a bang. Come what may, I would give myself to this adventure, and not look back.

Kanté crooned, *Do you see darling...love is a sorcerer...*

I caught a glimpse of Aminata in the back seat. She was turned to the side, gazing out the window, lovely and lost in her own thoughts. What reveries filled her head? What dreams did she have? I would probably never know. And just then, she caught me looking at her, and she smiled shyly. I smiled back, slightly embarrassed, and quickly returned my gaze to the horizon. The road stretched out before me like an arrow pointing toward the village. It beckoned me.

You must return to Africa, and to this village...you know this to be true.

The village was still a long way off, and we had many hours to go. I poured myself a strong cup of tea and settled in for the long drive, content for the moment to daydream about a new life in Africa.

24

THE PASSAGE OF DARKNESS

THE ROAD from Mamou toward Dabola turned monotonous and wearisome. My thoughts drifted as I came in and out of sleep. Halfway in dream state, a question began taunting me.

What is the cure?

It was a loaded question. Of course, my doctors had told me repeatedly that there was no cure for ankylosing spondylitis. But clearly, if I was still asking, I didn't fully believe them. They just didn't *know* what the cure was. That's a big difference.

About halfway between Mamou and Dabola, we crossed the Bafing River, and the question lingered like the scent of sheep and body odor in a small Renault. To relieve myself of both the stale air and the maddeningly elusive answer, I rolled down the window and gazed at the flowing waters of the river. Further north, the Bafing met the Bakoye River in Bafoulabé, Mali, where the two rivers gave birth to the mighty Senegal River. These rivers flow across borders and meander through mountainous regions where dozens of native languages are spoken. The waters are the lifeblood of those who dwell on their banks, providing fish and an enriched soil basin for farming.

Where was the source of the Bafing River? I didn't know the answer to that question either, so I waxed poetic instead. *Does a river ever truly begin or end? Or is it just an ever-changing manifestation of elements that at this moment, we call the Bafing River?* A river yields and acquiesces, changing its course in response to the terrain through which it flows. But at the same time, it carves stone and earth, transforming the very landscape beneath it. My illness was like a river that flowed through my life. Somewhere deep inside me, a perfect storm of physical, emotional, and spiritual elements had manifested into what we call illness. It was transforming my body, and my life. But where did it begin, and could I change its course?

To find the cure, you must find the source.

With that thought at the forefront of my mind, we stopped for lunch at a roadside food stand. Happy to be out of both the car and my head, I struck up a conversation with a local man named Boubacar. We exchanged stories, and he mentioned he was part of a reforestation project along the banks of the Bafing.

"Where is the Bafing's source?" I asked. I figured if anyone knew, it might be this guy.

"The actual source of the Bafing River is difficult to determine," he replied, "for it is hidden deep in the mountains of the Foutah Djallon region."

Boubacar was well spoken, and his refined French told me he had gone to school. He went on.

"In the Foutah Djallon, one finds the source of many great rivers. I was born in the village of Bafing, and we are the guardians of the Bafing River. That is why we started the reforestation project."

I nodded, then asked, "What initiated the project? I mean, it seems like such a pristine wilderness." The Foutah Djallon was sometimes referred to as the Tibet of West Africa. Its largely inaccessible mountains gave shelter to spiritual traditions that have endured for millennia. I was puzzled about the need for reforestation there.

"In recent years," he said, "both large-scale mining and irresponsible forest cutting are taking place even here. The trees hold the soil in place. Without them, the banks crumble and the soil erodes into the river. We are witnessing the desertification of the region. So, we plant native fruit trees to prevent further erosion, as well as to provide food self-sufficiency for the people here."

I was impressed with Boubacar's knowledge, and we chatted a bit more about the greater significance of the project.

"There's a greater purpose that drives our activities," he said. "You see, the Foutah Djallon's forests are the West African lungs of the planet, much like the rainforests in the Amazon. It is an important region, and is sacred to the people who live in its mountains. But the world barely knows it exists. It is urgent that we in Bafing plant trees to aid in *la compensation carbone,* carbon offsetting. It is what we can do for the greater good of the planet."

The information struck me. Here, in a remote part of West Africa with scant resources, local villagers were engaged in a project to offset the problems of the modern world. Though the world knew nothing of them, the village was doing its part for the planet. They were aware that local activities affect not just downstream communities, but the planet itself.

"I think your ancestors would be pleased," I remarked. "I'm curious what part your traditional views play in your effort?"

Boubacar's face lit up. Maybe he didn't expect this manner of talk from a *tubabu.*

"Yes, I hope the ancestors are pleased! They have entrusted us with the safekeeping of our natural resources. It is our duty to live by the guidance and example the old ones provide us. Our ancestral heritage is our source, and we are part of its eternal river. One day, we too will become ancestors. So you see, we begin and end at the source. We must never forget that."

Back on the road again, the rural countryside spread before us. As we traveled deeper into it, I felt transported back through time. Rolling hills stretched for miles in shimmering sienna waves, with only the occasional hut punctuating an otherwise desolate landscape. Overhead, vultures circled in search of their next meal. If not for the road and the little blue Renault that carried me over it, the scenes appeared like snapshots from hundreds, if not thousands, of years ago.

The Renault was my time machine, transporting me to another lifetime. My old life in America was receding into memory. Only my crumbling spine linked me to that life—and that fiery serpent was a constant reminder of why I was here.

We begin and end at the source, Boubacar had said. As we rumbled down this passageway of time, the question returned.

What is the source of my illness? Is there a cure?

My journey to find said cure—if there was one—had started long ago with what I knew: Western allopathic medicine. It's a marvelous system of repairing the body, but not without its shortcomings. Medical doctors approached my problem from the soulless viewpoint that all of nature is a machine, and our bodies were no exception. As if I was a car that wasn't running properly, they attempted to find the exact part that had broken. They focused on ever-smaller components of the immune system, which, in their view, was malfunctioning. When it couldn't be fixed, they suppressed it with chemicals. When that failed, they figured they'd just fuse things into place.

Their goal was not necessarily to find a cure, but rather to slow the progression of the disease, at whatever cost to the rest of my bodily systems. In the best-case scenario, my life would end before ankylosing spondylitis deformed me, pushing my spine ever forward until I could no longer stand upright. I had seen pictures of worst-case scenarios. It wasn't pretty. And according to my doctors, I had it bad.

I sensed that my doctors were overlooking something. Perhaps their mechanistic view of the world was flawed, and they were missing the bigger picture. For my part, I was willing to entertain the possibility that there was a medical explanation *and* a spiritual explanation. But I was far from being an expert on the latter, so I began my inquiry with the former.

What if my immune system *was* in fact doing its job correctly? The search then became quite different. What might trigger my body to react this way? Could it be something so simple as a foreign pathogen? The idea resonated with me.

During the early years of my condition, it was hard to find much information about it. Ankylosing spondylitis was, at that time, still relatively unknown. Since I frequently had to explain it to doctors in the ER, they obviously weren't going to have the answers. I broadened my search, and eventually heard about a doctor in England who had discovered a potential link. He had theories about AS, and was exploring alternative treatments. The link he found was between a gene called HLA-B27, and the bacteria *Klebsiella*. A pathogen. Could it be?

By the time Dr. Alan Ebringer published his book on the subject in 2013—the same year I published *Djoliba Crossing*—I was a decade into my journey of pain. Ebringer's theories were gaining ground, but only in the community of people who actually suffered from AS. These were people who, like me, were desperate for relief. In the U.S., Ebringer's ideas were on the fringe. His simplistic answers challenged the medical *status quo*, and my doctors shrugged it off as nonsense. So I pursued Ebringer's research alone, and conducted my own experiments.

Ebringer based his findings on the concept of "molecular mimicry." This is the idea that certain bacterial antigens can closely resemble certain tissues in our bodies. He suggested that because Klebsiella antigens resemble tissues containing the HLA-B27 gene, the body might be tricked into thinking they are one and the same—and attack both. This, he proposed, was how the disease AS started.

For the first time, my enemy had a name: Klebsiella. Once again, I prepared for battle.

My first approach was antibiotics. But I quickly found out Klebsiella is crafty, able to intelligently morph itself at will and form a resistance to virtually all antibiotics. It shares its learned resistance information with other bacteria, so that by the time *those* bacteria encounter an antibiotic, they are already resistant to it. And Klebsiella can teach itself to become resistant to antibiotics you haven't even tried yet.

None of that stopped me from trying. If I found the right antibiotic, I thought, maybe I could just wipe out the Klebsiella and it would all be over. I found a handful of promising choices. My doctors, however, were reluctant to prescribe antibiotics just to slake my curiosity. Ankylosing spondylitis was *not* an infection, they insisted. To perform my experiment, I would need to trick them.

I found a particular antibiotic called doxycycline that might have some effect on Klebsiella. It was also a viable antimalarial. And guess what? I have a nasty habit of frequenting places where malaria is rampant. So on my next doctor's visit, I insisted I would be taking Doxy as my preferred malaria prophylaxis. And so, my little experiment began.

At first, it worked. On the first trip that I took Doxy, my pain got better—much better. Alas, this approach was doomed to fail. Since travel in Africa also makes one prone to a host of other infections, my gut was soon a hot mess. For months after my return, I suffered from digestive problems. That wily Klebsiella character figured out what I was up to. Soon, the Doxy offered no relief at all—and in fact, only made my problem worse.

The experiment was a lesson in the dangerous pitfalls of antibiotics. Klebsiella would eventually become resistant to them all, which is increasingly a problem for everyone. The World Health Organization released a statement in 2014 to this effect: because of worldwide antibiotic overuse, Klebsiella was now resistant to nearly *all* antibiotic drugs, making it a particularly dangerous superbug. What's worse, research showed that Klebsiella honed its superpowers on the playing field of factory meat farms where antibiotics are routinely used on animals intended for market. So meat products like chicken and beef have become host to superbugs like Klebsiella that are *already* resistant to antibiotics before they even make their way into your gut.

Across the puddle, Dr. Ebringer already understood antibiotics weren't the answer. Ebringer's approach was more straightforward, albeit not easy: he proposed starving the Klebsiella. This meant cutting it off from its favorite food, namely starch. That's a pretty broad category. Starches are the most common carbohydrate in the human diet, and found in practically *everything* I like to eat. Nonetheless, I tried to remove them all from my diet. I said goodbye to bread and pasta, for starters, then potatoes and rice, and finally, crackers and chips of all kind. Sugars were out, too, even those in fruits. Oh, and dairy products proved problematic as well. That left me with...hmm, not much to choose from. The aisles of grocery stores were now overflowing with products that might as well have borne a skull and crossbones on their labels.

For several years, I experimented on and off with this approach, now dubbed the *London AS Diet*. I had varying degrees of success. Over long months of frustrating trial-and-error, my results were hard to quantify.

It was a high-stakes independent study. With each dietary misstep, my pain amplified. All the while, X-rays revealed that my spine was still fusing rapidly.

For me, the jury on diet was still out, although it was my most promising lead. The only certainties were despair and heartbreak—and now I was hungry, too. As the pain spread, I traveled alone down a road of seemingly endless suffering.

Klebsiella never left my thoughts, though—nor my gut. I had my own bogeyman now, invisible but powerful. It might as well have been an evil spirit.

∼

I drifted in and out of sleep as we drew closer to Dabola. Tired of thinking about medical stuff, my thoughts eventually turned to Ghana. It was there that I had first encountered *vodoun*, the oldest religion on Earth. Its roots were right here in West Africa, and I was driving deeper into it. A fine time to ponder spiritual illnesses.

As the afternoon light began to wane, I remembered the book in my bag, *The Passage of Darkness* by Wade Davis. I wouldn't have much daylight left, so perhaps I could do some reading before it got too dark. I fumbled in the bag at my feet and pulled the book out. As I flipped through the pages, I noticed certain passages were highlighted. Had I done that? I had read the book years earlier, but had forgotten that I may have made notes. The highlighted sections were all related to traditional approaches to healing. I scanned them with growing curiosity.

The Vodounist defines health as a coherent state of equilibrium between the physical and spiritual components of the individual.

Of course, health is a state of wholeness. Health is *holy*. But in Western medicine, we focus on disease and its eradication, and not on health as a balance between all systems—even the spiritual and emotional. The difference in approach here was significant. I continued reading.

Much more serious are the troubles that arise when the harmony of an individual's spiritual components is broken. In this case, it is the source of the disorder, not its particular manifestations, that must be treated.

Here was yet another mention of the *source*, and it made me feel like the universe was hitting me over the head with it. Was there an origin to my imbalance, or, like the Bafing River, was its source hidden away? For my condition, a pathogen had been found, but surely, there had to be more to it than that. Were my spiritual components also broken?

As a form of treatment, Vodoun medicine does not ignore the existence of pathogens; it simply comments that the pathogens are present in the environment at all times and asks why certain individuals succumb when others do not.

So a pathogen like Klebsiella could still be a culprit, along with certain genetic predispositions. On the medical level, these conditions must exist for the disease to occur. The traditional vodounist apparently doesn't ignore this. But those predispositions don't guarantee a condition like AS. Why did I succumb, all those years ago in Ghana? The bigger question *why* is irrelevant to Western medicine—but not to those of the traditional healer.

Restoring the patient's health…first through divination, the healer must determine whether the illness has a natural or supernatural origin…

Yes, in Ghana, they spoke to me of this. I had brushed it off as superstition, but maybe there was something to it.

Supernatural illnesses…are caused by malevolent spiritual forces, often sorcery, and they can only be treated by the healer…

I remembered Amaa saying I had been cursed. *You must see a healer. Or perhaps, a healer will find you.*

Then, I recalled the shaman, her eyes closed by the firelight in prayer. *You are in a bit of trouble,* she had said. *And it is very serious.*

I flipped through the pages to a final passage.

It is the intervention on the spiritual level that ultimately determines the patient's fate…and perhaps most important, by a sacrifice so that the patient may return to the earth a gift of life's vital energy.

Sacrifice? My blood suddenly went cold. Why had I been so naïve? I looked behind me at the sheep lying across Lanciné's lap. I thought it was a gift for the village. But it was suddenly all-too clear what Famoudou intended.

Oh…my…God. I am in WAY over my head.

I had come back to Africa to seek healing in the traditional way, and now, it appeared, I was in deep.

We begin and end at the source. We must never forget that.

The ancestors felt close now. The car rumbled down the road, ever closer to the village. There was no turning back.

～

The dirt track beneath us grew bumpier with each dusty mile. Roads like this ate cars for breakfast, and were still hungry for more. Occasionally, we saw rusted frames of automobiles morphing into the landscape like old dinosaur bones. Service stations were non-existent for a hundred miles in any direction.

Several times, we got flat tires. At some point, all of our new hubcaps were shaken loose and left to litter the roadside, like so many other artifacts of voyagers past. The Renault, burdened by so much weight, broke down repeatedly. As I stood in the vast savannah watching Lamine make repairs to a bent axle, I wished I had been a mechanic and not a musician. I felt useless, and could only watch the vultures circle overhead. But somehow, Lamine forced the little Renault back onto the road. Away we went.

With all the breakdowns, we didn't make good time. The sun was setting, and travel at night was a bad idea. In the darkness, potholes or craters that could irreparably damage the car would be difficult to avoid. Washouts, sinkholes, and even ravines appeared from nowhere.

As the day faded, Lanciné and Lamine discussed our options.

"What's our plan?" I asked.

"We are not very far now from Dabola," Lanciné replied. "We will try to make it before dark. We will rest there."

Even I knew the road to the small town was notoriously bad. I was skeptical of our chances of making it there before dark, and doubted we'd find anything open when we arrived.

"Do you think we'll find a place to stay at this hour?"

Lanciné shrugged. "We have to try. Lamine says he knows of a place —a hotel that was used by the mining companies. He isn't sure if it still exists."

That didn't sound reassuring. We had been traveling for sixteen hours without much of a break, and Lamine's fatigue was evident. As he increased the Renault's speed, I gripped my seat ever tighter.

When the sun went down, we had still not reached Dabola. Darkness covered the land like a cloak, rendering obstacles invisible. Even the boundaries of the road vanished. Were we even still on it? The headlights were caked with dust and practically useless. Finally, one rattled loose and went out. None of us spoke our fears.

Through the passage of darkness…

It was now full dark. No moon appeared to light our way. The first stars dotted the horizon, and then appeared in vast multitudes. On another occasion, I might have gazed upon this beauty with awe. But now, it appeared as if we were traveling into the gaping mouth of the sky itself.

Lamine raced onward, perhaps with his own fears of the night. He began to disregard the potholes, which made the Renault rattle tremendously. Meanwhile, my spine radiated with fire. The flames darted out from all directions, causing full-body spasms with each jarring pothole.

I reached for my thermos of *kratom* tea. It was nearly empty, but I managed to get a full mug. I held the mug for a moment, calculating how many hours had passed since my last dose. The effects of the plant were far from pleasant if I spaced the doses too closely. While not an opioid *per se*, its effects were remarkably similar—as were its dangers. I aimed to keep my doses between four or five hours apart.

I glanced at my phone. Only three hours since my last dose. *Shit.* The pain was skyrocketing. I considered it for a moment. I hadn't eaten anything since lunch, so the tea would kick in fast. But I wanted relief, badly.

The shaman's words rang in my mind. *It has a powerful spirit, this plant. It is the plant's spirit that heals—but by the same token, it can do harm when misused.*

She had been speaking of marijuana, but I wondered what she would say about *this* plant's spirit. I considered putting the tea back, but the pain rose up like a demon within me.

I gulped the tea down, and it was a heavy dose. As I emptied the mug, I wondered if I was using this plant appropriately. Was it yet another plant spirit to offend? It was all so confusing.

As we approached Dabola in the darkness, the tea kicked in—and strong. My back loosened up a bit, and soon, my head was buzzing. I tried to focus my attention on the road, but all I saw were swirling clouds of dust.

The nausea hit suddenly, along with a wave of dizziness. My heart raced, and my forehead became clammy. The car lurched forward, and so did my stomach. I tried not to groan.

A road sign emerged out of the billowing clouds of dust. Our headlight caught it briefly. It contained just one word: *DABOLA*.

Aminata started singing from the back seat. We had reached the edge of town.

25

DABOLA AND BEYOND

THE STREETS of Dabola were deserted. Wisps of wood smoke lingered in the air, and dying embers from roadside cook fires glowed faintly. Besides that, all was dark. The electricity was out, and everything appeared closed. Though we had reached Dabola, our oasis was apparently dry. And we were nearly out of gas.

We drove the main road through town, our one headlight barely piercing the darkness. Lamine was exhausted and struggling against sleep, and Lanciné was becoming short-tempered. He and Lamine argued in Malinké. Aminata and Fanta chimed in too, and a heated conversation ensued. I could only sit and listen to the foreign syllables and watch it unfold. The pit in my stomach grew.

Lamine turned onto a street leading away from the town's center. In the darkness, he was only guessing. Shortly thereafter, a road sign indicated we were heading toward Faranah, which was south of here—our destination in Kouroussa, however, was straight east. The three back-seat drivers voiced their opinions. The sheep was now baying too, as if interjecting its own disapproval. To my ears, it was a pandemonium of sounds. My head spun, and it was all I could do to hold on to my lunch. I readied myself, if need be, to instruct Lamine to pull over quickly.

We came to a narrow bridge and stopped just short of it. The bridge was decrepit and badly in need of repair. In the dim light, it was hard to gauge whether it was even safe to cross. Lanciné hopped out to survey more closely, and we all followed suit.

The night air was cool but did little to ease my growing nausea. I examined the little Renault, burdened with weight, and then looked back at the bridge. I had my doubts.

We walked a bit further. The area was thickly forested, and large bats swooped above us, silent as ghosts. From atop the bridge, the sounds of night enclosed us, chirping and rustling in a symphony of stealthy movement. Below us, I could hear the babbling of flowing water. It was the Tinkisso River, and from the sound, I judged we were maybe twenty-five feet above it. From Dabola, the Tinkisso flows north and eventually joins the Niger River in Siguiri, where Lanciné had worked in the mines all those years ago.

"I know this bridge," Lanciné said, as if caught in a memory. "It has been here since my youth. Even before l'indépendance."

Guinée gained its independence from French colonial rule in 1958. That made the bridge at least sixty years old, a relic of colonialism. Ordinarily, this would have been kind of cool, but this wasn't a sight-seeing event—we had to cross this thing. The crumbling stone wings of the bridge were rigged to nearby trees with rope, and the weight of the bridge was now pulling the trees over.

"And I suppose it hasn't been repaired since then?" I asked. "Money problems?"

"This is the way it is in Guinée. The government has money, but the people never see improvements. The roads and bridges are all falling apart. When this bridge gives out, Dabola will be disconnected from Faranah and Kissidougou in the east. Isolated. Yet mountains of bauxite and gold are shuttled out of here on trains beneath our very eyes. It is only the government who gets rich. People are angry."

In recent years, Dabola locals clashed frequently with the police. These incidents often turned bloody. Not that you'd ever hear about it on the world news. Guinée is a place the modern world has forgotten— or never knew about in the first place.

I rubbed my eyes. The bridge could let go at any moment.

"Is this our only way through?" I asked.

"Lamine says there is a place we can stay. An old hotel, not far from here. He knows the family of the proprietor. But going around the bridge will take us too far out of the way—and we're almost out of gas."

I sighed. Running out of gas out here would be bad—real bad. We needed to conserve what little we had left, and hope the electricity returned in the morning. The pumps at the sole gas station in Dabola would only run if the power came back. If not, we could be stuck here until it did. There was no saying how long that would be.

Lanciné folded his arms across his chest. "Daouda, I am afraid we have no other choice. We must cross the bridge."

"Eh, *Allah*. I was afraid of that."

Our planning hadn't accounted for a stay in Dabola, and I had no guidebook—not that it would have done me much good. This wasn't exactly a tourist region. Dabola had grown up around the mining railroad that went from Conakry to Kankan. The mining of bauxite, the primary ore used to make aluminum, is a major force here—Guinée is the world's third-largest producer of bauxite. But the revenue from Guinée's massive exports has done little to better the lives of its citizens. Like at the gold mines, local communities here were displaced without compensation when the mines were established. And whatever minimal infrastructure existed now primarily served foreign mining investments. The locals got the leftovers.

I listened to the flowing waters of the Tinkisso River below. The river powered the hydroelectric dam in nearby Bissikrima. Electricity generated there was directed mostly to the mines, but the surrounding communities did benefit from it—sometimes. The dry season was apparently not one of those times, which explained the pervasive darkness in town.

As for us, we were now up a very dark creek without a paddle—or a map. And not much gas.

Lanciné was getting impatient.

"*Wongai*—let's go. There is no use standing here. The bridge will hold."

A sudden wave of nausea flooded over me, and I struggled to steady myself.

"Lanciné, I think I'm going to be ill." I groaned. "Just so you know." I needed him to be my big brother. I felt homesick. In the past, Kerri would have been there for me to console me, to put her arm around me. But that life was gone. I had no one to care for me, nor I for them.

"Ah!" Lanciné exclaimed, seeing my forlorn expression. "Daouda, *i döja*—have courage." He put his hand on my shoulder. "I think it was the eggs you ate this morning. Always, when you eat eggs, you get sick. I have seen this in you before."

I wasn't so sure. Back home, I ate eggs all the time. But my body was revolting against something. Was it the grilled meat at the roadside vendor near Mamou? Perhaps it had been spoiled. I imagined the colony of Klebsiella now feasting away, causing my immune system to freak out. And the tea, of course, was still coursing through me. The pain in my spine was searing despite it. Maybe I had indeed angered the plant's spirit.

"*Petit frère*, from now on, I will make sure the village women do not make eggs for you. Eggs no good for *un étranger !*" He laughed, slapping me on the back. "Come, my *tubabu*. You will be fine in the morning."

We walked toward the car and cajoled the sheep away from the low shrubs it was chomping. I watched the poor fellow as Lanciné pushed it into the car against its will. A twinge of sadness came over me. I was actually growing a little fond of *Monsieur Mouton*.

By a sacrifice…the patient may return to the earth a gift of life's vital energy.

At the moment, what I wanted to return to the Earth was the gift of my *lunch*. I didn't imagine that counted for anything. I had a bad feeling about the sheep—and the bridge ahead of us. I got back into the car and hoped we were making a sound decision.

Sacrifice. Sorcery. Plant spirits, and the Ancestors. It was all too much.

Lamine inched the Renault onto the bridge.

Think light thoughts, think light thoughts… My mind was heavy as lead.

Halfway across, the bridge groaned. I held my breath, feeling like a passenger on an airplane that was going down. Maybe these were my last moments. I suddenly wanted to reach for Aminata, to feel her warmth, to squeeze her hand in mine. Just to have someone in this world whose hand I *could* hold.

A loud popping noise emanated from the bridge.

Bam!

The bridge's supports were straining. Our weight was too much. But we were halfway across now, and could only continue forward.

CRACK!

Lamine's usually steely nerves gave out. He panicked and punched the gas hard. We accelerated rapidly and hurtled across the bridge. My stomach flip-flopped like I was on a rollercoaster. Moments later, the Renault launched off the far end of the bridge and became airborne. When we landed, the crash was deafening. The front tire blew, and we came to a dead stop.

I opened the door as fast as I could, swung my legs out, and promptly vomited on my sandals.

⁓

While I hurled my lunch, Lanciné and Lamine hurled expletives. For students of the Malinké language, I include these here for educational purposes, with apologies to my more sensitive readers:

Gnamokodé! Bastard child of a bastard!

I bolo ko! Go get circumcised!

N'fa foro! My father's penis!

I bilakoro! You unripened boy who has not yet been circumcised!

I kaya kili! You dick-balls!

Et Allah, Walahéééé! In the name of the all powerful!

They stood inspecting the punctured tire. Things had gone from bad to worse. On the bright side, we weren't swimming in the river, and I was feeling a little better. I walked over to assess the damage. The tire would need replacing, but the rim wasn't damaged that badly. If we were careful—and in fact didn't have far to go—we could risk driving on it. It was the morning that worried me. Where would we end up?

Ten minutes down the road, we came to a side street. Lamine recognized it. We turned, and the Renault crawled down the narrow dirt road.

A building appeared out of the darkness.

We stopped and got out to have a look. It was a hotel, all right—or at least had been. The main building was flanked by what appeared to be guest houses. Judging from its dilapidated condition, this place hadn't been in operation in quite some time.

"*Eh, Allah*—it's not open, is it?" I asked. "I mean, like, not even operational?"

Lamine said something to Lanciné in Malinké. Apparently, speaking French was too taxing to him at this late hour.

"Lamine will go to the main house," Lanciné translated. "He says someone in the family still lives here. He will ask if there is a room we can stay in."

I pulled my phone from my pocket. A few minutes after midnight. We had left Conakry at 3:30 a.m. on what was now yesterday. The trip had drained my strength, and my stomach still wasn't entirely settled. A grumble escaped from above my belt.

Lamine disappeared around the corner. The rest of us lingered in the darkness, peering into the grime-caked windows of what was once an African-style hotel. The doors were padlocked. Through the windows, the rooms appeared like they had been ransacked. Cobwebs filled every corner.

It was a long time before Lamine returned, but when he did, he was with a young man in a robe, who had clearly been awakened from sleep. He held a mass of keys in his hand.

"Lamine says it took some convincing, but the man has agreed to let us stay," Lanciné informed me.

The man spoke in rapid Malinké, and the four of us who could understand nodded their heads while I stood there feeling out of place.

"The hotel went out of business some years ago, when the proprietor passed away," Lanciné said, relaying the information as the man fumbled for the right key. "No one in the family had any intention of taking over the business, so it fell into disrepair. The rooms haven't been used—or cleaned—in years. But at least it's a place to stay."

At this point, I didn't care when it had last been cleaned. All I wanted was to sleep, and I hoped my stomach didn't burst. We grabbed a few of our belongings from the car while Lamine tied the sheep to a tree. Without any cheer, the young man led us to our room. When the door swung open, I shone my headlamp inside and looked around. The cobwebs were thick, and spiders hung in every corner. My light caught silvery strands of webs that spanned entire doorways. *Some of these spider webs are big enough to trap an antelope,* I thought. I imagined getting caught in one as I stumbled to find the bathroom in the night, and the web's builder descending upon me. My thoughts were as dreary as the hotel itself.

Two dank mattresses leaned against the wall. We pulled them down, and they crashed to the floor in a cloud of dust that left us coughing. The pungent smell of mildew hung in the air. Lanciné brushed away the spider webs from a window, and with a hard shove, managed to open it. Fresh air gradually filtered in.

The five of us looked at each other, and at the two narrow mattresses. Lanciné preferred to sleep on the hard ground anyway; he had never taken to sleeping on beds or mattresses. Lamine headed back to the car to sleep there. Fanta, Aminata, and I were left to decide between the two mattresses. I froze, not sure how this should play out. Of course, I should be the gentleman, and offer them the mattresses, right? I could sleep on the hard floor as well. On the other hand, I was the *patron*, the big boss man of the expedition. As such, was I not entitled to the last shreds of comfort? But then an urge came over me to hold Aminata beside me—no, no, innocently, I mean, to sleep beside her, and that was all. The moment made me lonely and forlorn. The thought of being near her brought me comfort. Some awkward glances passed between the three of us.

Do you see darling, Love is a sorcerer...

Aminata blinked at me demurely.

That was when it hit again. The nausea came on fast, and I ran for the door, making it outside just in time to hurl in the dirt. Stronger sorcery than Love was at work that night, and I would find no comfort. Instead, I spent a lonely night outside the abandoned hotel, helpless to do anything as my stomach turned inside out.

Meanwhile, my comrades slept soundly in the ruins of the hotel. In the absolute darkness of an old mining town without electricity, the stars shone brightly above me. I didn't roam far on this moonless night, fearing every noise and suspecting sorcery at every snap of a branch.

Some hours later, the waves of nausea finally subsided, and I returned to the room. Aminata and Fanta slept on a single mattress. The remaining one awaited me.

I wasted no time hunkering down. Before pulling a light blanket over myself, I remembered I had some herbal remedies with me for third-world travel sickness. An herbalist back home had recommended them, but I had forgotten about them until this moment. I pulled them out. The two bottles read *Olive Leaf Extract* and *Virginia Snakeroot*. I downed a couple of droppers of each. As I put them back in my bag, I caught sight of something else I had forgotten: it was the small sachet of Artemisia. I placed it beneath my head and was soon swept away to the realm of strange dreamscapes.

The light is iridescent, and I stand on the banks of a mighty river. The swiftly moving current is dangerously strong. Beyond the far shore, black smoke rises hundreds of feet. The forest is ablaze. Orange flames dart above the trees, close enough to feel the heat.

Beneath the burning forest, Aminata stands waist deep in the water. The water swirls around her, and I fear it could sweep her away at any moment.

She is calling to me, and holds something in her cupped hands. Her lips move as she repeats a single word, but I can't hear over the roar of rushing water. She beckons me to cross, to come closer. It seems dangerous, but some force pulls me to her. Flames from the blaze behind the river seem ready to engulf her.

I step into the water and I fight against the current to make my way to her. She is laughing now, repeating the word, arms outstretched. I can hear the word, though I don't know its meaning.

"Kösön! Kösön!" she says gleefully, like it's a game.

I wade deeper. The current is swift, and I struggle to maintain my footing.

"Kösön!" Her hands are cupped in front of her.

I leap into the current and try to swim. I make it a few strokes closer, and what's in her hands becomes visible.

"*Kösön, kösön!*" she cries even louder.

It's a scorpion. *Kösön.* She holds it out, offering me the gift. She knows I want and need the scorpion's painful healing.

I flail desperately in the water, and reach for her hands. The current becomes too strong. As I lose my footing, flames engulf the forest. Darkness consumes me as I'm pulled under, and the river carries me away.

I awoke gasping for air. Bright light flooded into the room, and I surveyed my surroundings. The hotel room was empty. I fumbled for my phone. It was 10 a.m.

I stumbled outside, searching for my companions. Around a bend in the pathway, Lanciné sat on a bench, the electric thermos beside him. I was shocked to see steam rising from the mug in his hands. How had he—?

"Ah, *ini sööma*, Daouda," he said. "You are awake at last. Just in time, too—the electricity is on. Lamine has already been into town, and the tire has been repaired. The gas station was open and we now have plenty of gas. We are ready to depart."

I looked at the Renault. The tire was indeed repaired. Lamine leaned against the car, cool and calm, smoking a cigarette.

I sat beside Lanciné, still a little bewildered. My stomach had regained normalcy. Perhaps the herbs had helped? Whatever it was, the sickness had passed.

Lanciné poured some hot water and passed the Nescafé. I whisked some in, and savored the first sip.

"Hey, no eggs for you today, *d'accord?*" Lanciné said, chuckling.

I rolled my eyes.

Aminata sauntered by, the mesmerizing pendulum of her hips swinging beneath a light sarong. She cast a sideways glance at me, smirking.

Lanciné furrowed his brow quizzically. He was about to say something, but dropped it.

"Daouda, *an nye wa*," he said instead. "Let's go. We have several hours before we reach Kouroussa."

I nodded, savoring the coffee a bit longer. Moments later, we were on our way to the village, in the bright sunlight of a brand-new day.

26

THE STEEP BANKS OF CHANGE

AFTER ENDURING THE SLOW, decaying road out of Dabola, we were delighted when the route to Kouroussa finally turned to pavement again. The dust was less pervasive now, the air fresh and clear. We sailed along with the windows down, letting the wind whip through the car.

Thanks to the improved road conditions, we made good time to Kouroussa. There, we stopped to refuel before the final leg of our journey. We were close now, and little butterflies of anticipation flitted in my stomach.

Memories flooded over me as we strolled around the small downtown. I had spent time here during past trips, and had always enjoyed how modern and ancient elements cavorted against the backdrop of the Niger River. This is the Malinké heartland, the center of the region traditionally known as Hamana. Though many people still refer to it as a village, Kouroussa is the region's only outpost and serves as a commercial hub for dozens of nearby villages. It's a town that teeters on the steep banks of change, but old traditions still prevail.

As we walked, Lanciné was quick to point out the former homestead of celebrated Guinéen author Camara Laye. Kouroussa was his birthplace, and was the village he wrote about in his most well-known book,

L'enfant noir (or *The Black Child*, in the English version). The fascinating coming-of-age tale, set in a pre-colonial Malinké village, had been invaluable to me in understanding life here. Though I'd read it several times before, I purchased a French paperback version from a street vendor in Conakry before we left, and packed it for the trip.

"These are the gates to Laye's family compound," Lanciné informed me. "Just beyond there, you can see the courtyard where he was raised. And over there is the hut where he was born, and the enclosure where his blacksmith father worked the forge."

It was, for me, simply marvelous. I was peering into a window of history that had previously only existed for me in stories. Seeing it now in person made me eager to re-read the book.

Moments later, modern superseded ancient, and worlds collided noisily. We arrived at a Total gas station where a dozen motorcycle taxis idled outside. Outside the station's mart, I indulged in a canister of Pringles and a Coca-Cola in a glass bottle while sitting beneath a towering caïlcédrat tree. A motorcycle loaded with bundles of grass thatching zipped by me. Then, a *griotte* woman carrying two live chickens broke into song when she recognized Lanciné. She praised his lineage by singing a part of his clan's history. For this honor, we pulled out a few crumpled bills, which she stuffed into her robe while flashing a gold-toothed smile. She was still singing as she walked away.

Yes, Kouroussa was an *African* town, a unique mélange of disparate worlds coated with the dust of centuries. It was on the brink of being modern, and probably would have been, if not for the poverty that gnawed at its people. But there was a heart and soul to the place that couldn't be denied. How else does a people survive such oppressive poverty, and live through ruthless dictators like Sekou Touré and Lansana Conte?

I had often thought Kouroussa was a place I could live. What would it be like to immerse myself in this community, set up a studio, and make art here? I imagined working to the sound of brooms whisking and roosters crowing, African music playing from a crackling radio, the smell of wood smoke filling my senses. I could join the rank of artisans who forged their creations from the pain and joy of everyday life. The thought was scintillating.

Of course, I drew my idyllic images from the pre-colonial Kouroussa of Camara Laye's books and my own admittedly limited experiences. But those visions were now replaced by reality. Instead of wood smoke, clouds of black diesel hung in the air. Trucks roared by, and trash littered the roadside where famished beggars pleaded with passersby for their next meal. Motorcyclists wove through the streets in kamikaze fashion, their bikes impossibly laden with goods from the market. When I wandered across the street, an angry *taxi-moto* driver cursed at me in Malinké. I sighed. These were the blemishes of modernity. But still, Kouroussa had its charms. I could get used to it.

It was here in Kouroussa that we parted ways with Fanta. She had arrived at her destination, and was grateful for it. I wondered if I would see her again, or if she would be just another face that disappeared into the anonymity of the African continent. As they say here, *Allah a'alam*—only God knows.

We turned to leave, and I regarded Kouroussa one last time. Something told me I would be back.

Back on the road, and some twenty kilometers past Kouroussa, we began searching the roadside for the dirt path that led into *la brousse*, and to Lanciné's village. There, we would be staying at his family's compound, where he had grown up. His village was adjacent to Famoudou's, connected by a long path through untamed territory. Using Lanciné's place as a home base, we could travel on foot between the two villages to undertake Famoudou's list of tasks.

The path was hard to spot, even for Lanciné. The landscape was ever-changing, and the clearing we sought had become overgrown. After doubling back several times, we finally detected a disturbance in the overgrowth.

"That's it!" Lanciné declared. We slowed to a crawl. "Yes, I see it now. Lamine, turn here." Beneath a wild chaos of tangled branches, a small, unmarked track led into the wilderness.

Lamine guided the Renault into the dense canopy. The air was immediately cooler. Sunlight barely filtered through the thicket, and it took several moments for my eyes to adjust. Above us, birds sang in a cacophony of calls. Several times, cows blocked our path and had to be cajoled to the side. My heart ached with anticipation.

After about a mile, the canopy opened, and the light became blinding again. The path led first to a grassy clearing, and then ended abruptly at a steep embankment. Beneath us flowed the Niger River, the life-giving waters the locals call *Djoliba*. We could drive no further.

Lamine parked the car, and we got out to survey. The river was wide here, perhaps sixty yards across. On either side, the river had carved sharply sloped banks. With the water being low, we found ourselves at a considerable height above the river. But there was no bridge across, no continuation of the road. I was puzzled. On the far bank, a path led back into the bush.

"We must continue," Lanciné said. He walked back to the car.

"Wait, what?" I asked. "You're not proposing we drive—"

"Yes, Daouda, we must go down."

He had lost his mind. Lamine too was unsure, and remained outside the car.

I stared at the steep embankment. Loose stones and sand skittered down from where we stood. I put an exploratory foot out, maintaining my upper foothold on solid ground. I stepped carefully to test it. The earth beneath me lodged free, and without any footing, I landed on my backside and slid downward. A shock wave echoed down my spine as a warning signal. I dug my heels and hands in hard to stop myself, scraping my palms, and grated to a stop a few feet lower. The ground on which I had once stood cascaded downhill at a 120-degree angle, collecting rock as it went, until it reached the river a hundred feet below. It disappeared into the swift current with a splash. I scrambled on hands and knees until I found solid ground again, and stood.

With my geological investigation complete, I walked back to the car. I had proved my point. The lingering throb in my vertebrae reminded me to be cautious.

"It's not safe," I said. "The Renault will never make it down."

"No—it will make it," Lanciné countered. "It must."

I looked at Lanciné with disbelief. I had already taxed my spinal column with our episode pushing the Renault out of the crater, and the prospect of getting the car down the treacherous slope made me deeply worried.

"Lanciné, *must* and *can* are two very different things. Is there no other way?"

"No, Daouda—this is the only way. We must cross here."

His mind was set. Was there any point in arguing? I didn't know the territory, and he was my guide. But I was missing some crucial piece of information. Aiming the Renault toward the river was ludicrous, and it made our bridge crossing look like child's play in comparison. Standing above the eroding bank, I could only envision disaster in the river below.

Lanciné and Lamine stood beside me with their arms folded. Aminata came over with the sheep, and rested her elbow on my shoulder. She laughed when she saw the scene.

"The bargeman will be here shortly," Lanciné said. "We must get the Renault to the river's edge." He pointed across the river.

I shielded my eyes and strained to see what he was pointing to. On the far side, a tangle of vines concealed an old barge. From it, a thick cable emerged, and led to a tree where it was firmly embedded. I hadn't seen it until he pointed it out. The barge, apparently, was hand-pulled. Someone would need to ferry it across to us. Once that happened, we'd still need to angle the car down the steep embankment and somehow land it flat on the barge. It was hard to imagine how we'd pull this stunt off.

I stepped back a few paces. During the rainy season, the water level rose significantly. The high watermarks indicated the river could reach halfway to our level. That would make things a bit simpler, in theory. But at that level, the river would also be a raging torrent. Without the massive cable pulley, the barge would have been swept away long ago.

This was the dry season—February 7th, to be exact. The water wouldn't get much lower than this. And judging from the state of the barge, it wasn't used often.

"I will call the bargeman," Lanciné said. "He is expecting us. I'll tell him we are here."

Lanciné opened his flip phone, and paused.

"Daouda, help me find the number for Djara." I peered at the long list. There were many people named *Djara*; some were Konatés and Condés and others were names of villages I didn't recognize. I spotted one that looked promising: Djara Batelier. I wasn't familiar with the word, but it looked like a combination of the French words for boat, *bateau*, and *atelier*, for a working group. I spoke it aloud.

"Oui, *le batelier*—the bargeman! That is the one." He placed the call. The reality of it struck me: we stood on the banks of the Niger River and used a cell phone to call the village *batelier* who would ferry our Renault across in an old, rusty barge.

The call was brief.

"Djara will come and ferry the barge across. We should be ready when he arrives. We must get the vehicle to the water's edge."

Lanciné calculated the logistics. He was adept at turning a *must* into a *can*.

"*Alors*—Lamine will steer the car down. Daouda, you and I will steady it from the sides. We'll use rope."

Lamine was game. We removed the luggage from the top of the car so we could use the rope that had secured it there. After hastily piling the gear into the empty car, Lanciné rolled to the ground and fastened the rope to the Renault's undercarriage. He and I would hold it from either side and pull as needed, like herding a wild bull, while Lamine alone remained in the car to steer. Aminata stood a safe distance away with the sheep, looking doubtful. I shared her concerns, both for the car and for the safety of my spine. One bad slip, and that would be the end of me.

I was about to say something to get out of doing it, but my pride swelled. I resented the limitations of my condition. Over the years, it had prevented me from doing things I loved. I hated feeling useless—or worse, *helpless*. No, this was a *man's* job, dammit, and I was going to suck it up and be brave. Besides, Aminata was watching me.

While we schemed, two men appeared on the far side of the river. They wore workman's clothes and gloves, and worked quickly to uncover the barge. The cable clanked against the barge's wooden deck as they let the slack out. Soon, the barge was free from the bank.

They made their way across, fighting to maintain their line against the current. As they approached, they pulled hard on the cable that tethered them to the far side. After several more minutes, the barge sailed into the bank below us. The two men poled it into position, straightening it out so the nearest edge of the barge's deck was parallel to the shore. They were ready for us.

We got ourselves into position as Lamine hot-wired the Renault into action. He advanced to the edge, and Lanciné and I followed on either side, maintaining a slight tension on the ropes. Loose sand caved beneath me, and I struggled to maintain a foothold. The Renault was causing a small landslide. Chunks of earth broke free and tumbled into the river below.

Lamine stepped on the gas. The front tires went over the edge, and the carriage hung up. For a moment, the front tires spun uselessly, the front end suspended in air. *Rear-wheel drive would have been nice*, I thought. *Yes, the next time I buy a car in Africa—*

"Daouda, *PULL!*"

Lanciné and I cranked the rope, and the Renault teetered before tipping downward. Lanciné let out a wild whoop and I joined in with my own. The Renault's forward momentum carried it—and us—rapidly toward the water. It was all Lanciné and I could do to keep up, slipping and sliding alongside it.

In a flurry of dust and commotion, the Renault started to get away from us. I lost my footing and went down, yanked along on my back by the Renault. Pressure in my spine mounted. Fusing vertebrae crackled. I strained with all my might on the rope and cried out as a searing pain shot through me. I was about to give up the fight, when the front bumper of the Renault collided with the deck of the barge in a loud clamor. Plastic splintered and glass shattered. The Renault stopped moving. I landed just inches before the water.

I let go of the rope and pulled myself up, wincing with pain. The Renault pointed downward, its nose to the barge. It was too steep an angle for the front tires to make contact, and the Renault was caught on its cracked front bumper. Fragments of blue plastic and glass littered the ground. I imagined my spine might also be in a similar state. Inside the car, Lamine's chest was pressed against the steering wheel, and he hit the gas sporadically. The tires just spun. There was not enough earth beneath it.

One of the men produced a shovel, and got to work scooping dirt beneath the front tires. When he had raised the level sufficiently, Lanciné turned to me.

"Daouda, now we push."

I nodded. The strange thing was, even though both the Renault and my spine were getting trashed, I was actually having a bit of defiant fun. *Fuck this stupid disease!* It was reckless, and I knew it. I stopped caring, and thought someday, if I ever returned—

"Daouda!"

I snapped to attention. Lanciné and I got behind the Renault. Lamine hit the gas, and rocked the car back and forth as we put our weight into it. The bumper groaned. With one last push and a loud *Craaaaannnk!* the front bumper snapped off completely. The Renault jolted onto the deck, bouncing for a moment on tired shocks.

"You see!" Lanciné said to me, laughing. He gave me a hearty slap on my aching back. "I told you we would make it down. Now we are ready to cross. The village awaits!"

Aboard the barge, I was introduced to the two men, Djara and Mamady. The former spoke French, but the latter did not.

"Welcome aboard!" Djara gripped my hand and flashed me a generous smile. "But we are not there yet. With the weight of the car, it will take all of us to pull *le péniche* across." He pointed to the cable that lay beside us on the deck.

I lined up and took my place behind the four other men. The road we had just traveled was already a memory. The river was all around me, and the forest loomed ahead.

We pulled ourselves slowly across the river. The barge's weight was substantial, though my heart felt light. We chatted and laughed gaily as we ferried across. Aminata sang joyously. She was all smiles in the afternoon sunshine, thrilled to be going home.

Lanciné cackled at the sight of me straining at the cable.

"Now, this is a first for me!" he exclaimed. "Never before have I seen a white man do this. Daouda, fetch me your camera. I want to take a picture of you. No one will believe me."

I thought it might be a good souvenir, too. We paused from our heaving, and I pulled my camera from my bag and handed it to Lanciné, explaining which buttons to press. We lined up again on the cable and posed for a picture.

Aminata clapped and giggled. Djara too was amused.

"Daouda," said Djara, "you are now *un batelier!* Perhaps one day you will take over my post here." I pretended to pull the whole barge by myself. Though they were jesting with me, the memory of the shaman's words hit me:

There is no way of telling how long you will need to be there. They may ask you to stay there forever!

We returned to our work, and drew closer to the village. I was pulling myself toward my own destiny—or perhaps destiny was pulling me.

By the time we reached the far bank, fear had slipped back into my heart. What if my pain never went away? What if I never saw my home again? Back across the river, the life I had known lay hidden in another time and place. That old life was gone.

We disembarked as the sun sank lower in the sky. Ahead of us, a path wove into the forest. I stared into the unknown.

The day changes to night, I thought, *and the night changes to day. The river is changed with the rains. Cultures change. Everything is destined for change, impermanent.*

In the waning light, we set off toward the village in the battered Renault. My whole world teetered on the steep banks of change.

27

A RETURN

THE POINTED ROOFTOPS of the first huts appeared against a crimson sky. Above them, a red sun hung like a ripe fruit ready to fall to Earth.

We entered the village in our strange chariot. The old blue Renault was barely holding together, but Lamine steered carefully between huts as chickens and goats scattered. There were no roads, and at times the passages between huts were so narrow that we had to back up and rethink our route.

Bewildered villagers emerged to stare at the strange obtrusion weaving alongside their houses. I felt out of place, self-conscious about arriving in such a manner. In my daydreams, my entry would have been more like that of an intrepid adventurer marching on foot, like the famous explorers I had read about in my younger days. I imagined how Dr. Livingstone, John Hanning Speke, or Sir Richard Burton would have arrived, carrying their gear upon their backs with grandeur and integrity. Instead, a ramshackle hunk of blue plastic and steel carried my declining body toward whatever destiny awaited me in the village.

Lanciné and Lamine, however, were beaming. I soon realized we were not taking the most direct route, and this was intentional. This was our parade, it turned out, and they were obviously showing off with the car. With each hut we passed, we collected a growing crowd of spectators who followed along like a train behind us.

The Renault sputtered to a stop at last in a small courtyard flanked by mud houses. A throng of people overtook us immediately. Villagers young and old peered eagerly into our vehicle to see who or what would emerge. My heart raced as I prepared to make my grand entrance.

I opened the door and climbed out. Children shrieked and scattered frantically, like they had seen a ghost. I must have been a strange sight, with my jeans torn and caked with dirt, and my old fedora now as red as the African earth itself. The *shemagh* still hung around my neck, smelling slightly foul from the accumulated dirt and moisture. Not least of all, I was a *tubabu*. A bona fide *tubabu* was a sight many of these children had never seen. The word itself was synonymous with a sort of bogeyman: *If you do not behave, the tubabu will come and take you away!* This was the story many children heard growing up. It certainly had its basis in the past.

Lamine unlashed our gear from the roof while another man pulled my belongings from the trunk. He barked orders at some teenage boys, and in a flash, all my possessions disappeared into an adjacent hut. Amidst this, strangers shouted out exuberant greetings:

"Alu ni waale!" Greetings to all!

"N ba, i ni waale!" Greetings back to you!

"As-salamu alaykum!" May peace be upon you!

I was soon mobbed by strangers, and couldn't move an inch. For Lanciné and his family, it was a grand reunion, but for me, it was bedlam. Dark strangers with sunken eyes and protruding rib bones tugged at my shirt. Old men with crooked teeth rubbed the skin of my arm to see if it would wipe off and reveal something human underneath. Lanky boys with threadbare t-shirts whisked the hat from my head, and disappeared into the crowd taking turns wearing it.

When the jubilee began to wane at last, benedictions were in order. A toothless old woman of diminutive stature approached us and gave the blessings:

"Allah ye duba i ye." May God bless you.

To which we responded dutifully, *"Amiina."* Amen.

"Allah si jan di i ma." May God give you a long life.

"Amiina."

"*Allah ye i so sila diya.*" May God give you a good road.

"*Amiina.*"

On and on this went, and Lanciné reveled in the homecoming, while I struggled to make sense of it all. When the benedictions were complete, Aminata pushed her way through the crowd and stood before me. She grasped my hands and flashed a big smile.

"*An bè sinin sööma*—see you tomorrow morning."

I nodded, and she and Lamine promptly departed in the Renault. They were eager for their own family reunion.

As darkness fell, the courtyard quieted and the crowd dispersed. Soon, only Lanciné's family remained. They showed us to our hut, and inside, I was pleased to see my mountain of luggage stacked neatly against the wall. My old fedora was placed on a small table, and I noticed that somebody had already wiped the dirt off it.

"Daouda, *bienvenue*," Lanciné said. "This is where you and I shall stay for the remainder of our time here. You see, we have arranged for you to have a bed, and I can take the small cot."

I looked around and took stock of what would be my home now. The round room was sparse and had a hard-packed mud floor. The bed was rather large and held together by a generous wooden frame. I sat on the edge to test it out, and felt the lumpy mattress, which was stuffed with kapok and hay. The bed could have slept an entire family, and probably did, at other times. I wondered who I was displacing now that I was here.

"Thank you Lanciné—but are you sure you would not rather have the bed? Or your family? I really don't need to have—"

"Not another word about it. The bed is for you. You are our guest, and it is our duty to see to it you are comfortable."

I nodded a little uncomfortably. "Thank you," I said again. "The bed is really nice."

Lanciné straightened proudly, and clapped me on the back.

"Come, my *tubabu*, we will have time to unpack in the morning," he said. "But now, it is time for a meal. I'm famished!"

Just outside the hut, his family had placed a wooden bench and two chairs to be our dining area. Once we were seated, some women presented us a steaming bowl of rice and sauce, and Lanciné and I ate with fervor. Afterward, we drank coffee in contented silence, passing a pipe filled with aromatic tobacco and savoring the cool evening air. The first stars appeared in an inky sky, and an immense stillness set upon us. Soon, the sky shimmered with innumerable stars. The whole universe spread out, like a map to the heavens.

Fatigue came over me like a heavy blanket, and it was all I could do to drag myself inside to the oversized bed, still fully clothed. My thoughts turned as the sounds of night drifted into my awareness. I had returned to a land where ancestors watch over, and spirits are never far. In the absolute darkness of the hut, there was little to separate me from the night. I was both exhilarated and terrified of what awaited me here. But exhaustion soon took over, and I fell into a dreamless sleep.

When I awoke, it was not to the light of morning. Instead, it was the sound of drums that roused me. Chanting and wild whoops accompanied the drums. I grabbed my headlamp and switched it on, my heart racing. Lanciné was gone.

The commotion outside grew louder, and moments later, Lanciné rushed into the hut.

"Daouda, wake up! You must come see. It is *n döönin*, my little cousin. He has returned from the hunt. He is dancing now, just outside."

I arose quickly and emerged to a courtyard illuminated by firelight. Nearby, a man danced wildly. In one hand, he hoisted the carcass of a beast as the drums spurred him on. Women sang and clapped, occasionally emitting shrieks of joy.

Lanciné put his hand on my shoulder, and shook me excitedly.

"The people are happy, for they will have meat. And it is a good omen for our arrival. They say we bring them good luck."

I marveled at the scene before me, but despite the excitement, my eyes were glazing over. I couldn't keep from yawning.

Lanciné laughed. "Go now, *mon petit*—get some rest. Tomorrow is a new day, and it will be a fine day to start our new journey. This I know."

"*Insh'allah*," I replied. It was all I could say before returning to the hut and falling fast asleep to the sound of drums.

PART IV

Crossing the Niger River, 2016

28

THE VILLAGE KNOWS BEST

A ROOSTER CROWED. The sound of shuffling feet, unhurried, reached my ears. A broom whisked softly and rhythmically.

Shoop, shoop.

Dreams faded into reality, and I was momentarily disoriented. The veil of sleep was still heavy upon me, and I wanted more of it. But outside, the day was waking. Nearby voices murmured over the hypnotic sweeping.

Shoop, shoop.

I forced one eyelid open a crack. My surroundings were dimly lit. I felt around for my glasses, and found them against my backpack, which lay beside me on the mattress. The world came into focus. Above me was a circular framework of boughs that held grass thatching in place. To my left, light glowed from the edges of a closed wooden door. An empty cot rested a few paces away, blankets folded neatly atop it.

Shoop, shoop.

The muffled voices drew nearer, and I recognized the morning greetings.

I sööma.

N ba, i sööma. Tana ma sii?

N ba. Alhamdulillah.

Awareness hit me smack in the face. Of course, I was back in the village. My heart raced, and images of the prior night's drumming spectacle resurfaced. *Oh, yes!* I had finally reached the village.

Happiness flooded me. Having survived the trip, my old life was further away than ever. Here, I could put a safe distance between me and the memory of my lost home and failed relationship. I had some reconciliation to do with that old life, for sure, but I could take my time here. This was home now.

Eager to start my new life, I attempted to sit up, but a lightning bolt of pain struck me down in a brutal flash. Shockwaves spread through my entire body, and the true nature of my journey came forcibly back into focus.

You have attracted their attention…

Happiness vanished into uncertainty. I tried again to sit up, but the pain was excruciating.

…and until you find out what they want—and remedy the situation—your illness will only get much worse.

Yes, I was back in the village, where the ancestors resided. They were close, and though I could pretend to hide from my old problems, I couldn't hide from *them.*

The pain they will inflict on you will only grow worse. They will hold your feet to the fire until you have accomplished all that you need to.

This time, I hadn't come to immerse myself in music. This was no vacation. I had tasks to undertake—and given my level of pain, they were pressing. But my first major hurdle was just getting out of bed, and even that felt unmanageable.

Have courage.

I braced myself. With one swift movement, I bolted upright. As expected, a grenade exploded within me, and what felt like shrapnel tore through my body. I groaned in anguish but forced myself to remain upright.

The pain was intolerable. I needed tea. Lots of it, and fast.

I looked around the sparse room for the thermos, but it was nowhere to be seen. I struggled to my feet, and limped gingerly away from the bed, like walking on a field of landmines. The door was only a few paces away, and I just needed to make it there without tripping another explosion.

When I reached the door and pulled it open, bright sunlight erupted into the hut. The light hit my eyes like a dozen sharp needles, and sent a burst of new pain into my skull. *What the...? Oh, shit.* The extreme light sensitivity was characteristic of the autoimmune condition *iritis*, a painful inflammation of the iris related to AS. I had suffered through this before. Severe episodes can cause permanent vision loss, and sometimes require an injection of steroids in the eyeball.

I shielded my eyes from the demonic sun rays, and noticed the thermos on the doorstep. I tugged at its handle to test the weight. *Sweet.* Lanciné must have asked the women to heat water over the fire. I was grateful for this small act of mercy.

I grabbed the full thermos and shuffled inside. Rummaging through my bags, I found the packets of green powder, along with a pocket digital scale. The packets bore labels with names like *Vietnam White, Red Borneo, Maeng Da, Green Malaysian* and *Indonesian White*. Each variety had different properties, and I had come to know them all. Some were better at relieving pain, but made you sleepy; others made you feel like you could take on the world. Well, that's what I needed right now. I carefully weighed out a strong dose of *Maeng Da* and dumped the powder into a mug. I topped it off with steaming water, and sat on the bed and waited.

A half hour later, my muscles began to relax, and I stood carefully. The pain was still there, but dulled somewhat, like a layer of soft gauze hung between it and me. My emotions, though clear upon waking, were now muted similarly.

I put on my sunglasses and fedora to protect my aching eyes, and limped out of the hut. Outside in the small courtyard, Lanciné sat in a plastic chair at the wooden bench that served as our table. Steam rose from the mug of coffee in his hands.

"Ah, Daouda, *ini sööma*—good morning." I eased into the empty chair beside him, and he handed me the canister of coffee.

"*N ba, Lanciné,*" I said, testing out my Malinké. "*I sööma. Tana ma sii?*" *Good morning, the night has passed without evil?*

"Ah Daouda!" he laughed, happy I was speaking his language. "*N ba, tana sii tè.*" He tested me with a few more phrases, but quickly lost me.

"Daouda, your Malinké is getting better. You will need it. Very few people speak French here."

"I'll keep working at it. What's the plan for our first day?" I didn't want to waste any time getting started.

Lanciné sipped his coffee, contemplating. "Daouda, today we have many people to greet. It is the custom upon arriving in the village. Before we do anything else, we will make the rounds."

"Will we go to Famoudou's village as well?"

"Yes, later this afternoon. There, we will greet Famoudou's brother, as well as the *marabout* and the head of the *numu* association—the blacksmiths. You have your notebook? We'll need the amounts."

The news that we'd be starting right away was encouraging. First, we'd meet with the village elders and present monetary gifts to various village associations. Though an offering of gifts was good manners for a visitor to the village, the gifts I brought would serve double duty. I had ancestors to appease, too. I went inside and retrieved the notebook. When I returned, a young boy approached with a cloth sack.

"Ah, the boy is back," Lanciné said. "I gave him money to buy bread, but I thought the little *bilakoro* had run off with it."

The boy placed the sack on the bench. I peeked inside. The long loaves of French bread were still warm. In the village, bread was baked fresh each morning in rustic wood-fired ovens. From a smaller plastic bag, the boy produced a round container of Laughing Cow cheese, *La vache qui rit*.

"Daouda, you are ready for breakfast?"

Indeed, I was famished, though I'm sure Dr. Ebringer would have cringed. A breakfast of bread and cheese was hardly on the London AS diet. Not the most nutritious meal, but it was what we had. Supplies were limited, and what's more, Lanciné had placed a ban on eggs since my last incident of all night vomiting. My personal bogeyman, Klebsiella, would feast today. At least I had plenty of tea to numb the pain.

I tore off a warm hunk of bread and opened my notebook to Famoudou's instructions. The hasty scribbles included the phone number of Sori Keita, the man who looked after Famoudou's house in Kouroussa. Famoudou had graciously offered me a room there if village life got rough. He boasted that it usually had electricity, and even had flushing toilets. Imagine the luxury! I had grown accustomed to open pit latrines. It was good to know I had other options. The future was unclear.

Further down in my notes was the important stuff. I had written three numbers, and drawn icons next to each so Lanciné could read it too. The first icon was a sheep. I placed a checkmark next to it, since we had already acquired it. As Lanciné had predicted, it had cost just under a hundred bucks. I glanced up from my notebook, and was pleased to see *Monsieur Mouton* tied to a nearby post, chomping grass. I was as nervous about his fate as I was my own.

The second icon showed a pair of huts with the number 2,400,000 scrawled next to it. Not a bad sum of money, about three hundred bucks. This would go to the organization in charge of community projects in the village. This made me feel a legitimate emotion, even with all the tea circulating in my bloodstream. I genuinely liked the idea of funding village projects, and was particularly satisfied knowing they would decide for themselves *what* projects. I was not the type to impose my own ideals or ideologies. The village knew best what they did and didn't need, and it certainly wasn't Western-style schooling, useless books, or my feeble religious viewpoints.

The third icon was an axe with a long wooden handle. This referred to the blacksmiths, the *numuw* in Malinké. I'd be giving them a cool million. Their former leader was none other than Sako Gbè, who graced the cover of my book. Famoudou deemed it wise to present the *numuw* with a generous gift before anyone was shown an image of the deceased sorcerer, let alone one who had been the head of their most revered association. I was pleased with this decision, and hoped the blacksmiths would be too. I didn't need any more curses.

All in all, the cash gifts weren't staggering sums. But proportionate to my dwindling finances, they were pretty generous. Suffice to say, I'm no Bill Gates. It was about a third of all the money I had left in the world.

I handed the book to Lanciné so I could focus my attention on the more pressing issue of dipping my French bread into my coffee.

Lanciné reviewed the numbers, and nodded enthusiastically.

"*Oui*, Daouda, *c'est bon*—Famoudou has given you good counsel. *Très,*

très bon! I think the village will be happy with this first step. We can discuss the other steps afterward."

Yes, the other steps, I thought. This was only the beginning.

"*Merci*, Lanciné," I said. "Thank you for your help with all of this. I couldn't do this without you."

"With pleasure," he said. He reached beneath his chair and pulled out his bundle of flutes. "But we mustn't forget your apprenticeship! We have a few moments before we greet the village, and there is always time for music here. *Wongai*, let's play!"

Lanciné's cheerfulness set me at ease. I needed to relax, and embrace all that was to come. I picked up a flute, aligned my fingers with the three holes, and felt the soft texture of the wood. I took a moment to admire Lanciné's craftsmanship before raising it to my lips. I took a deep breath as Lanciné raised his flute.

The melodies of our two flutes soared into the village, a sound both ecstatic and timeless. Before long, a crowd of people gathered to hear us play. I beamed proudly as the notes sprang forth from my fingers. Women clapped and sang, and children gawked and laughed at the sight of a *tubabu* playing their music on their traditional flute. I looked at all these new faces, strangers taking a break from their work for the simple pleasure of joining in song. There was joy in their eyes, *real* emotion.

From somewhere inside me, beneath *kratom's* narcotic veil, something like happiness tried to bubble forth. For a few moments, I felt it, and it was real.

I knew not what lay ahead. I could only do my best, and pray that my offerings here would make a difference—if not for me, then at least for them.

29

WHAT'S IN A NAME?

FAR FROM THE hustle and bustle of Conakry, and even further from the rubble of my former life in America, a new phase of my journey began. Now that I had reached the village, it was time to address the tasks laid out for me by Famoudou. But first, I had to get my bearings, both literally and figuratively.

It had been years since my last visit, and the winding maze of huts was confusing. The village sprawled in many directions. Without a clear idea of its limits and boundaries, it was easy to get lost. So with Lanc-iné's hut as the center point, I ventured outward in increasingly larger circles, memorizing landmarks along each path. Over time, I formed a map in my mind of the village's layout.

Similarly, I was determined to explore my inner landscape. As Austrian poet Rainer Maria Rilke once wrote, "The only journey is the one within." I knew I had to figure out how to navigate the psycholog-ical maze of my life. Where does one acquire a map for a journey into the wilds of their own psyche? I supposed the only way was just to begin. So with pain as the center point, I ventured into unfamiliar terri-tory, and often found myself going in circles. But I would form a map.

As I wandered through these two parallel realms, the village itself became a sort of magic reflecting pool. In it, I caught glimpses of myself that were not easy to look at. The reflection was too honest, too revealing to be comfortable. But I could not unsee it. Deep concerns grew inside me like ripples in the water.

The first ripple appeared as Lanciné and I made the rounds, leisurely greeting people. The slow, deliberate pace of village life was a stark contrast to the frenetic activity of my old life. Each person we met gave us their full attention. No one was too busy for us. And hardly anyone seemed too worried about anything. My life, by contrast, was marked by constant stress and a perpetual deficit of time. Always too busy, my relationships suffered. It was a bad trade-off. Despite my diligent efforts to work longer and more productive days, I was getting nowhere. I was miserable.

Another ripple appeared on the surface.

Have I wasted the last decade of my life?

The thought was striking. My life had gotten way out of balance. In pain and numb from pills, I withdrew from my friends. My music projects were going nowhere. Ditto for the book. I did very little with my art. *Why?* I spent my time promoting my projects and trying to get on top of bills, but less time actually creating. Chasing someone else's idea of success was so unsatisfying.

The ripples extended outward.

Do I even know what I want anymore? What would I define as a successful life?

On the surface of the reflecting pool, I saw vague answers. I wanted my life to be simpler, and more meaningful. To have more friends who inspire and challenge me. To work less, play more. Create. Have ample time for a satisfying long-term relationship. To be physically fit again. Ah, if only I wasn't in such pain…

Ah, yes, the *pain*. It always came back to that old scapegoat. It was all too easy to blame it for all my problems.

As the ripples drew outward, new ones formed within the pool. A new concern began to grow.

Has my substance use gotten out of control?

Until that moment, I would have said I was managing it just fine, that I didn't have a problem, and that it was all justified. But whether it was the pills or the tea, it was all the same. I was hiding behind them. I craved them even when the pain was low. And the years had slipped by in a somniferous blur, gone forever.

Far from the routines and trappings of my old life, my reflection became clearer. I gazed long and hard at the image that was forming. And what I felt was shame. Yes, I felt absolutely *shameful* at losing myself in those substances. Though pain was my excuse, I knew full well I was abusing them.

I don't even know who I am without these drugs. I want to be free of them, but I don't know how to stop. I don't know if I can.

In full sight of myself, the problem was naked and exposed. I couldn't deny it anymore. I had an addiction.

My little discovery about myself was a tad shocking. I mean, *addiction* is something that other people had, not me. Wasn't I somehow smarter than that? Maybe I was misreading the situation and overreacting. But no, the thought nagged at me. It wasn't going away, and I couldn't shrug it off by saying "fuck the dumb shit" anymore. This wasn't dumb shit. This was serious.

My thoughts turned to Erik, and his struggle with substances. Though it had started for us both as youthful experimentation and self-discovery—reckless as it may have been—Erik's subsequent struggles with drugs had clearly shown me this was a dangerous line to walk. But surely, I had thought, *I* would never fall into the same trap.

I sighed, and wondered with some sadness how he was managing these days. A pang of guilt hit me. In his darkest times, he needed a friend, and I wasn't there for him. I hoped he was getting on with his life okay, and I made myself promise I would reach out to him when this was all over.

Meanwhile, I needed to turn my awareness outward. I had work to do here, and a quest to pursue.

Lanciné and I promenaded through the village, meeting and greeting scores of people. I couldn't help but try to imagine their lives. What personal struggles did *they* have? Surely, even here one must confront their inner demons, and battle their fears and attachments. Is that not our common struggle?

With each house we visited, I studied the faces of the people we met, searching for their stories. I thought how wonderful it would be to draw them. To engage in that process of *seeing* more deeply that art makes possible. Perhaps in discovering their stories, I might discover something of my own. The idea stayed with me. Maybe here, too, I would find time to make art.

While I was busy confronting uncomfortable truths about myself, Lanciné was relaxed and clearly happy to be home. His enthusiasm and good cheer helped pull me out of what felt like a hopeless pit of despair. As we strolled, he gladly helped me navigate the village, and shed light on social customs. I used the opportunity to learn as much as I could about village life and Malinké culture. My ceaseless questions didn't bother Lanciné much. These short question-and-answer sessions were interspersed with countless greetings. Our frequent stops, I soon found out, were not haphazard.

"First and foremost," he explained, "when one arrives in the village, it is the custom to perform the traditional greetings. There are many people to greet! It can take several days to complete this. But one must not set about other business before making the appropriate greetings— to do so would be rude. And we must make our visits in a certain order. We do not want to be disrespectful."

Without this explanation, it was easy to assume we were wandering around saying hello at random. Worse, in my haste to get to my "Famou-do list," I risked offending nearly everyone. This would have boded poorly for my mission, since showing respect was at the heart of every task. Luckily, Lanciné was very conscious of the traditions, right down to the order in which we went to each house. As we walked, he kept a mental checklist of whom we had and had not yet greeted.

"Ah, Daouda! It is difficult to explain to an *étranger*. But we determine this order by the historical arrival of each family in the village. You see, a long time ago, the first families arrived here and settled in what is now the heart of the village, what we call the *so*. This is where the founders once lived, and today their descendants still dwell here. The families of the *fondateurs* are who we will greet first."

We arrived at the huts of the "first families," and proceeded to each individually. If they weren't already outside working, we stood at the curtain that covered the doorway and called in.

"*A ni tele!* Good afternoon!"

"*An nye bonna!*" they responded. "We are here! *I ma don?* Are you not coming in?"

We took off our shoes and entered, and the salutations would fly. I stood there smiling like the village idiot as they fired off machine-gun rounds of Malinké phrases. Each phrase was interspersed with an exuberant "Uh *huh!*" or "*N ba!*" At last, they turned to me and peppered me with questions. I wasted no time in either mangling the responses, or pronouncing a phrase perfectly only to discover I had answered the wrong question. My perplexed reactions were hilarious to them. Sometimes these people laughed so hard that tears ran down their cheeks, and I couldn't help but join in, despite not knowing exactly what we were laughing about. But at least I was trying, and it was good to let my guard down and laugh at myself a bit. *I might need to do more of that*, I thought. Lanciné patiently corrected my mistakes, and I jotted down new phrases in my notebook for later study.

Onward we went, house after house.

"Next, we visit the *marabouts* of the founders. The *marabouts* are the sages and scholars of the Quran, who provide counsel."

We made our greetings, and walked on.

"And now we must pay a visit to the *griot* families, who keep our clan's histories, and whose guidance in everyday affairs is crucial…"

The sun was high in the sky, and we had visited perhaps two dozen homes. My feet were tired, not to mention my back.

"…and now we must visit the artisans, whose work is invaluable to all community life here. They are called the *nyamakala*, for they are specialists in *nyama*. We must pay them respect for the important work they do. Working with *nyama* is dangerous business! First, there are the blacksmiths, who make tools for farming…and the leather workers… and the potters, and the basketmakers…"

It was hard work, this business of greeting. I was dizzy with foreign words and phrases, new faces and names. All the while, I tried to grasp the layout of the village. To me, it was still a maze. Lanciné tried to clarify things a bit.

"Beyond the *so*, where the families of the village founders live, is the *fudunyolu*. This is where the allies of the founders settled, long ago."

I nodded in vague comprehension.

"Outside the *fudunyolu*, there are the *kabila*, the little neighborhoods. Within those are the *bolondas*—you see here, they're separated by stick fences. The *bolondas* are where families of the same clan live. And within those *bolondas* are the concessions, what we call *lu*. These are small parcels of land granted to individual families, who pass them down, one generation to the next. These concessions are where the extended family lives in their own group of huts." I nodded. I had seen these, each with a courtyard, and many with a small garden plot where families grew their food. It was within one of these *lu* where we were staying.

"In the center of the village, we have the *bara*. This courtyard is where community activities take place. You see there, at the center is the *arbre à palabres*, the palaver tree. It is beneath that tree that important discussions take place. It is a sacred place, and the tree too is sacred. Beyond the *bara*, do you see the path that leads away from the village? It leads to the sacred grove. The spirits of the ancestors reside there. And beyond that is *la brousse*—the wild country. You must never walk there alone—particularly at night."

We had ventured a long way during this explanation, and were now quite far from where we started. Lanciné was satisfied with his overview of the village.

"So you see, Daouda," he said, spreading his arms wide, "it is all very easy to understand. You will know your way around in no time! Now, it is *you* who shall lead us back to our hut. It is almost lunchtime, and I am hungry. *An nye wa!* Show me the way!"

I stared blankly ahead of me, and took two steps forward, but then... no, that wasn't right. I looked to my right. There was that crooked tree, the cow still grazing, and the hut with the green door, and the path alongside it. Was that the way? No. I turned around, and this time I saw Lanciné's face in a smirk.

"Come, my *tubabu*! Don't worry, you will learn. Look—it is this way."

He pointed toward a courtyard with a stick fence, and then, yes, I saw the path, and it looked familiar.

By the time we returned to Lanciné's family *lu*, within their particular *bolonda* that was, obviously, within the *kabila* that was far from the *fudunyolu* and further yet from the *bara*, I was quite lost again. But it didn't matter because a bowl of rice and sauce awaited us on the wooden bench in front of our hut. I was famished, and couldn't wait to eat.

I stirred the bowl of red sauce, and my spoon hit something solid. Up from the soup came the sharply clawed foot of some unknown beast. Long talons protruded from a fist still clenched in its final, dying grasp on life. I dropped the spoon into the soup.

"Ah, Daouda!" Lanciné laughed. "What good fortune. Today, we share in the meat of Samba's kill. *Bon appetit!*"

After our lunch of boiled mystery meat, we retreated to the relative cool of the hut for some respite from heat and walking. My spine was on fire, and I momentarily deliberated just coping with it. I was between a rock and a hard place, I tell you. Should I start cutting back? Probably. But the pain was unrelenting. With a snarl from my conscience, I downed another strong portion of my narcotic-like tea. I'd have to kick the can up the road. Anyway, the tea hit me pretty fast. When the warm glow returned, my conscience returned to its slumber like a sedated lion. I would henceforth need to tiptoe around it.

We lounged in the shade for a while, and I spent a little time unpacking my things and making myself at home in the hut. It was cozy and sparse, and I liked its minimalism. Simple and rustic suited me.

At midday, we headed out for a few more greetings. Then, it was on to Famoudou's village. I was anxious about returning there for the first time in many years. Before we departed, I grabbed my notebook and carefully counted the bundles of money. My first task was just ahead of me.

We departed in the late afternoon by way of the village's dusty main route. Along the way, we passed a small shack with a thatch-covered porch. I was startled when a man called out to me by name. I had met over fifty people this morning. I gave him a little wave, not sure if I should remember him.

"Hello, Daouda! Ah, what's this? You do not remember me?" He rose and took a few steps off the porch. Now I recognized him: it was the bargeman from our river crossing a day earlier. It already seemed like an eternity ago.

"Oh! Hello, Djara," I said, and apologized for not recognizing him. It turned out he was also the proprietor of the local supplies store, and we stood at his storefront. Inside, shelves were stocked with various dried goods, along with coffee, condensed milk, chocolate biscuits, and most importantly, safe bottled water from the Coyah springs in Guinée. I would not be taking my chances drinking the local water.

I paid for a couple of bottles, and Djara tested me on my Malinké. I had learned some good phrases on our morning rounds, and he was impressed.

"Daouda, you are almost Malinké now! Soon, you will be one of us." Somewhat in jest, he asked, "*I jamun*—what is your clan name?"

I shook my head, not sure how to respond.

"*I Konaté?*" Are you a Konaté? "*I Coulibaly?*"

Lanciné was watching to see how it would play out.

"Hmm...*i Keïta?*" he asked. "*I Camara?*"

I took a chance and blurted out, "*N Condé!*"

Djara showed his enthusiastic approval, and Lanciné beamed. It had been in playful fun, but I had identified myself as part of the Condé clan, like Lanciné.

"Yes, Daouda," Lanciné proclaimed, "you are a Condé now. *Daouda Condé*. It is a suitable name for you. From now on, that is what we shall call you."

I tried it on for size. Yes, I liked it. I stood up a little taller.

As we left Djara's storefront, he called out loudly for everyone to hear:

"*An bè köla*, Daouda Condé—see you soon!"

So it was that I became known by a new name, if only in a small village thousands of miles from home. A name is only symbolic, but perhaps there was some power in it. It was an opportunity to shape a new identity. A blank canvas for the person I wished I could be. Not a different me, but the *best* version of me.

As we embarked on the trail through *la brousse* to Famoudou's village, I knew Africa was shaping me once again. There was no point in resisting.

30

A COUNCIL OF ELDERS

THAT AFTERNOON, I crossed into Famoudou's village for the first time in seven years. A wave of emotions toppled over me, filling the dry shores of my being with rivulets of nostalgia. I recalled the feeling I had when I first arrived here more than a decade ago, that irrational sense of coming home to a place I'd never been before. Now, the smells of sweet wood smoke and fragrant grass triggered an inexplicable euphoria. Countless synapses in my brain fired at once, connecting scents with memories, and evoking deeper emotions that had no basis in recollection. The déjà vu was overwhelming. An image arose of standing in this place a thousand years ago, or maybe even ten thousand, at the dawn of the Holocene Epoch when the milder climate invited a new era of human culture to flourish. Humanity emerged from Africa, after all, and to stand here could only trigger some deeply buried recognition of our shared origins. Or maybe it was because—

"Daouda, ça va? You OK?" Lanciné's voice snapped me out of my reverie. "You look like you've seen a djinn." Apparently, I had stopped walking, and hadn't even noticed.

"Oui, Lanciné, ça va. I'm OK. Just…lots of emotions coming back here, that's all. It's been a while."

"I understand, Daouda. For those of us who have been away,

returning to the village makes us feel like this. And when we are away too long, we miss the village terribly."

I nodded as we resumed walking, then asked, "Lanciné, do you ever regret leaving?" The question just popped out, and I hoped it wasn't too personal. "I mean, do you ever wish you could come back here and stay full-time?"

Lanciné sighed. "I think about this all the time, Daouda. But in the village, many of us go hungry. In the dry season, droughts come and the harvest fails. And when the rains do arrive, they fall so hard that life becomes very difficult for the long months the rains endure. Many people get sick. And the seasons have become unpredictable in recent decades, and no one knows why."

I wanted to say something about global climate change, and the irony that indigenous people and the world's poorest are the ones affected most. I thought better of bringing it up, for now. Lanciné had more to say.

"Plus, Daouda, in the village, there are few opportunities for a better life. If I want to send my children to school, buy medications for my family, or build a more durable roof, I need money. A musician can earn no money here. So, like many people, I went to the city."

"Life doesn't seem any easier there," I blurted out, and immediately felt guilty for saying so.

"You are right, Daouda. Life is hard everywhere in Africa. We can't all be so lucky to live in America. But at least in Conakry, I can earn *some* money. My eldest son Fodé is now the first in our family to go to school, and he is learning a great many things. He knows how to use computers and has gotten a job working for the government. The money he earns helps our family live. We are very fortunate in this regard."

"Do you like living in the city?"

"Of course not," he answered without hesitation. "No one who was born in the village prefers the city, but many of us have no choice. I miss the village every day I am in Conakry. But still, I am grateful for what we have."

Though his gratitude struck me, something in the tone of Lanciné's voice didn't have me fully convinced.

"But if you could live in the village and still earn an income, would you?"

"Daouda, of course! That is a stupid question." Lanciné humphed indignantly. "And you ask this like it's a simple matter. But answer me this: how exactly would I do *that?*" He stopped walking, and looked me in the eye. I realized his question wasn't rhetorical.

I considered carefully how to respond. My questions had been hypothetical, and came mostly from curiosity. I didn't want to offer him false hope. And plus, I still wasn't even sure how long *I'd* be living here, or how I'd get by in the long term. My own money would eventually run out. Would I then be in the same boat as Lanciné and his family? I had only vague ideas of how one would earn an income here, and I was hardly an entrepreneur. No, I was an artist who hadn't even figured out how to earn a real income in America—let alone in a tiny village in Africa.

"I don't know, Lanciné." I said, my shoulders drooping. "I wish I had the answer to that. But maybe someday, we can find a way for you to do this. Perhaps we can help each other."

"I would like that very much, Daouda. *Insh'allah.*" He held my gaze for a moment.

"Yes, Lanciné. *Insh'allah.* If Allah wills it."

We resumed walking, and shortly, we reached a part of the village brimming with people hustling about their daily business. Surviving in a subsistence economy, I knew, was hard work. My idealism told me it might also be inherently satisfying, but then again, we often want what we don't have. My life lacked the meaning, balance, and sustainability provided by village traditions. The village lacked resources like electricity, health services, and dependable clean water. Could you have both sides of the coin without sacrificing the other? I dared to dream.

As we walked, I recognized many of the huts and ateliers. Though the hand of progress had changed much, it was still the village I had grown to love during numerous stays. On the surface, the differences were easy to identify: a new road here, an electrical line there. The schoolhouse that had been under construction for so long was finally completed. But beyond what was visible, a subtle shift in my perceptions had occurred. I saw it through different eyes now, for I had changed too. Now, I came not as a student, but as a sojourner into matters of healing and heart. For the first time, I carried no drums, and had no recorder with me to capture rhythms for later study. And just as significantly, I was here without Famoudou—though it was his counsel that still guided me.

Now it was Lanciné, a man well acquainted with adversity, who led me on my journey of healing. Along dusty paths, I saw familiar faces, transformed by years and hardships. Women looked up from their work at the mortar as we passed, and children at play stopped to stare. Men carrying bundles of wood on their backs paused to glance at me from the corners of their eyes. I knew many recognized me. But time and circumstances had left their mark on me, too.

The years came sharply into focus. The chasm between the past and present versions of me was never more evident. Once, a fire had burned inside me. It propelled me to seek meaning and adventure, to live boldly and to feel deeply. But heartbreak, failure, and interminable physical anguish quelled the flame. I retreated to the safety of my heart's fortress, and remained there in isolation, ignorant of both my privilege and the love that surrounded me. How many pills had I swallowed to deaden my physical and emotional distress? Embroiled in pain and confusion, too many years had passed like this. The soul's flame needed love to endure, but I had deprived mine. Could I ever find my way back to love and healing?

Il faut avoir du courage, I sighed, only half-believing I had any real courage left. Maybe the saying should add, *And all the hope you can find.* Courage without hope is only a flash of light that cannot endure.

Perhaps some of that youthful fire still glowed inside me. If so, then surely it was hope that tended the hearth and kept the fire alive. What else could have driven me forward, even now, but hope? What drives any of us forward through hardship or poverty, failure or loss? Yes, hope is the root from which courage grows, though my hope was bound to a spiritual quest I didn't fully understand, and in forces I wasn't sure I believed in. But it was hope nonetheless.

~

We drew closer to our first meeting with the village elders, and I held on to hope like it was my own invisible amulet.

While we walked, I silently rehearsed the words and phrases I'd need to explain my predicament. The old shaman had instructed me to state the facts. *The elders will know what to do.* I needn't worry about the exact details. But language was still a challenge. I'd need to articulate challenging concepts in a foreign tongue—and hope they still hit their mark when Lanciné then translated them into Malinké.

Some words were easy: *back* and *pain* were *le dos* and *la douleur* respectively. *Spine* was pretty straightforward too: *la colonne vertébrale*. The verb *to fuse* is *fusionner*. If I put it all together, I could offer a decent explanation of how the individual *vertèbre* of my *colonne vertébrale* were *fusionnant* together slowly and painfully. It sounded a bit like voodoo when I thought about it. Since medical procedures play zero part in village life, I wasn't sure if the idea of a scary surgery, *une intervention chirurgicale*, would translate. But the notion of being *très malade* and wanting to avoid being *handicapé* seemed like it could translate anywhere.

The explanations would get trickier when venturing into concepts foreign to me. Mentioning I had consulted a traditional healer—someone akin to *une sorcière* in their culture—had been uncomfortable for me when I spoke to Famoudou a month ago. It didn't feel like it would be any easier this time. Likewise, I had felt awkward talking about *les ancêtres*, the ancestors. I wondered if it would raise eyebrows here in the village, particularly when I mentioned *which* ancestors. Everyone remembered the old blacksmith, Sako Gbè.

Finally, how would I explain a curse? Any illness can be a *malédiction*, for they are always unwelcome. But as I had discovered during prior trips to Africa, the boundary between a curse and an illness is vague.

Like Pandora opening the mythical box, I was opening doors I wasn't sure I should be opening. The big gamble I had taken by coming here at all—thus foregoing surgery and further medical care—was that my spiritual state could influence my physical health. Furthermore, I had staked my whole future on the long shot that certain ancestral agents could push that health in one direction or another as a means of aligning me to my true spiritual path. In my Western upbringing, this stuff was fanciful at best, ludicrous at worst. The old me would have relegated it to the department of superstition, but the new me was desperately cobbling together a new understanding of the world as I went. Could a single worldview simultaneously contain ancestor spirits, *les esprits de la brousse*, and scientific reasoning? I still had doubts. I suspected the door I was opening led only to a dark hall where belief and superstition danced around each other like estranged lovers. But my hand was on the doorknob, ready to turn it and peer inside.

I had given much thought to this interplay between superstition and belief during sleepless nights in Conakry. From an outside perspective, superstitions give irrational significance to mundane events or objects. They arise from the unknown. Initially, this includes pretty much everything, until we make our world more known through observing, formulating hypotheses, testing them repeatedly, and hopefully arriving at suitable explanations. Despite our efforts, we aren't always right. Future generations will marvel at how little we knew—that is, *if* we managed to survive that long on a planet we overheated through our misunderstanding of how the world works. And we think we're so smart.

Though we may arrive at drastically different conclusions, every culture has its own way of explaining our existence. Science and religion both strive to do this, albeit in different ways. Both require a curious blend of assumptions and observations, of faith and facts. It's surprising what we are willing to accept on word alone. In my culture, we have a story of a man who was born from immaculate conception, who died and rose from the dead, walked out of his tomb and then ascended into the sky. I grew up with the notion of the Holy Spirit, and of saints who performed healing miracles. We blend our faith with data in an infinitely unique concoction that suits us individually. And while this mix of the empirical and the esoteric may appear in wildly different amounts for everyone, we each amass whatever knowledge we can to help make the world seem safer and more predictable. This predictability might be in regard to the behavior of an atom, or of the gods under a given set of conditions. In either case, as we progressively explain the world away, our reality must shift constantly to adjust to new information. What is deemed rational or irrational, then, is completely subjective—and as our beliefs evolve, is ultimately a moving target.

When predictability goes MIA, what do we fall back on? When our situations or fortunes change unexpectedly, or when tragedy strikes, what words do we use? Fate. God's will. Shit luck. A blessing or a curse. When speaking of ourselves, we say these are our Beliefs, and we hold them sacred. When speaking of those whose views differ from our own, we write them off as superstitions, though we may be ignorant to the evidence that gave rise to them.

To help illustrate, I like to use what I call the "Bacteria and Bogeymen Principle." To the naked eye, both are invisible. I cannot, at this moment, see the bacteria that I otherwise assume to be crawling around me, presumably inhabiting my body by the billions. My schooling has informed me they are there, and my travels in Africa have reinforced the concept on the numerous occasions I've puked my guts out on the side of the road. Bacteria are real to me.

I once tried explaining the concept of microscopic bacteria to some folks in the village when they questioned why I ate with a spoon instead of my hands. I described to them the phenomenon of bacteria, using all the science I could muster. Satisfied with myself, I declared that I was afraid these bacteria would make me sick. The villagers unanimously agreed I was being...*superstitious!*

"Prove it!" they all demanded. At that moment, however, I could not. My words did indeed sound as if I was speaking about magic. I was describing invisible beings that were ever-present and who had the power to cause illness.

Likewise, when those same people spoke to me of ancestor spirits and *djinn*, my Western mind demanded, "Prove it!" At that moment, they could not. But the invisible spirits of their dead ancestors were ever-present, and held sway over the events of their lives. Those spirits were real to them, as was the evidence that proved it to them daily. In the end, we both lacked an experience that legitimized the other's beliefs, so we dubbed each other as superstitious.

With the distorting lens of ethnocentrism removed, however, that superstition may be the result of a well-formed view of the universe, learned since birth, and reinforced by experience. These experiences are coupled with an expectation that the world does and will continue to behave in certain ways. Expectations are powerful. Even in a scientific lab setting, a researcher's expectations can influence the outcomes of the experiment. Which is to say, if a researcher expects or even hopes to find a certain result, the likelihood of finding that result increases. Doubt, then, is an equally potent force. When experiences and expectations come together in just the right way, reality becomes a delightfully slippery affair. The concepts of curses, ancestor spirits, or genies of the bush can become real indeed.

Just moments away from my first meeting with a council of village elders, I was still wrestling with what I believed and what I did not. For better or worse, I came with my own concoction of beliefs and expectations, garnished with a generous topping of desperation, and sprinkled with hope. This murky soup was stewing on the flames of a last-ditch attempt to end two decades of suffering by whatever means possible.

Would I find the right words to explain why I had come, and be able to bridge two disparate worldviews? And furthermore, would the elders believe me, and prescribe a path to healing? My future depended on it, and I was about to find out.

We came to a small courtyard, and stopped. I knew the place instantly, for it was the extended compound of Famoudou's family. I had stayed here many times, slept in the rooms, and eaten my meals right out front. Just beyond was the path to the river, where I had spent many afternoons bathing and frolicking with friends. But now, we would go no further. We had arrived at the house of Famoudou's brother.

The people there, they will help you. They will know what to do.

Outside, several women were pounding millet. Lanciné spoke to them, and one of them went inside to announce our presence, while another brought out some wooden chairs. I was relieved to sit, for my spine was enraged after the long walk.

An elderly woman emerged from the shadows of the house, carrying a basket. I recognized her immediately. My heart skipped a beat.

"Malo!" I cried out. It was Famoudou's *döömoso*, his little sister.

She turned and stared at me, then dropped her basket and put her hands to her face. She rushed toward me gleefully. We embraced, and she held my face in her leathery hands, smiling profoundly. We exchanged the traditional greetings, and she inspected me closely like a grandmother would do to her grandson. My eyes welled up with tears.

Several old men emerged from the house, including Famoudou's *ködö*, his elder brother Fakourou. Four elder men I didn't know accompanied him. I greeted them with the respect due to members of their generation. Lanciné too showed them deference, bowing his head and holding his right arm with his left hand as he shook theirs, as is the custom of respect.

The council of elders was assembled, and Lanciné made the introductions. The village *imam*, or holy man, was present. This was none other than Lamine and Aminata's father, a man known as El Hadji, a title of respect given to one who has made the pilgrimage to Mecca. He greeted me enthusiastically, and spoke French quite well, which was reassuring. Also present was the current leader of the blacksmith's association, along with two elders who oversaw village affairs.

Fakourou sat at the head of our small assembly, for it was he who had called together this distinguished group of men. Per Famoudou's instructions, he would oversee my tasks in the village until Famoudou himself arrived.

After a lengthy discussion in Malinké, all eyes turned to me. The moment arrived, and I gulped nervously, sweat dripping from my forehead.

Fakourou spoke first, and Lanciné translated.

"You are the adopted son of Famoudou, and are welcome here. Many people here remember you, and it is well that you have not forgotten us. Now, tell us in your own words why you have come, so we may know your intentions."

I took a deep breath. Famoudou had been clear that I should not speak of my book until his arrival. I would choose my words carefully. The words of the shaman came to my mind.

Tell them you want to honor the traditions of their ancestors. They will pray for you, and they will tell you what to do.

I began to speak, and trusted that the words would come.

"Over the years, the people of this village have always welcomed me and treated me with kindness. I am grateful for this. I feel a kinship to the people here. Though our cultures and languages may be different, we are children of the same Earth. I have learned much from you, and you have been generous in the sharing of your traditions."

The men murmured among themselves, and I waited for their signal before I went on.

"Many years ago, I first came here as Famoudou's student. Over time, the music of your people became the language we share. I have carried this music with me into the world so that it may find new life. I strive to do this with the utmost respect for your traditions, though I have much yet to learn. My work with your traditional music has provided me much satisfaction, as well as a means to earn a humble living. For this too, I am grateful. In keeping with the traditions, I wish to repay the village."

I had their attention, though I couldn't read their expressions, which remained stoic. I breathed out nervously. Addressing this distinguished group and speaking about my illness was difficult. I faltered, suddenly backtracking in my mind to see if there was a safer route than what I had planned to say. Seeing my apprehension, El Hadji leaned toward me, and placed his hand on my shoulder.

"Go on, Daouda. We are listening."

I nodded, grateful for the reassurance. I could only speak the truth—or whatever semblance of it I understood.

"Years ago, I fell ill to a disease the medicine of my people cannot cure. I have struggled with the pain from this disease for too long, and it worsens daily. If nothing is done, the disease will destroy my spinal column." I choked up then, the full weight of all I had endured striking me as I uttered the words aloud. I couldn't let these men see me cry. I bit my lip, and fought hard to go on.

"Recently, I consulted a healer, a woman who is akin to the sorcerer-healers in your tradition. She advised me to return here, and to seek your counsel in spiritual matters with which I am not well versed. I wish to make an offering to the ancestors of your village, and make amends for any infractions I may have inadvertently made while working with your sacred traditions. I have traveled from afar to do this, and with your blessings, I pray the ancestors may look upon my actions here favorably, and ease my suffering."

I concluded by offering a brief explanation of my illness, and the challenges I was facing. When I finished, I sat back in my chair, my whole body tingling. I had said all I could say, and knew whatever happened next was beyond my control.

The men spoke among themselves for a long while, and my thoughts drifted. The moment was dreamlike, but the pain radiating from my spine reminded me it was real—too real. At long last, Fakourou leaned forward to speak, and I braced myself for the possibility of condemnation.

"We are pleased by your return. You have done well in honoring the traditions, and have received wise counsel, for the ancestors are powerful. *Allahu Akbar*—God is greater than everything. We will help you seek an accord with the ancestors of the village, and we will pray that your offerings here will be accepted."

I breathed a sigh of relief. "Thank you. I am grateful for your kind words."

Lanciné gestured that it was time to distribute the gifts for the village. It was the first step in an act of reciprocity, a symbol of my recognition of the gifts the village had imparted to me over the years. As I reached for my backpack, my hand touched my book, and I felt an overwhelming urge to show it to them now. It was right there in my hand. I needed only to withdraw it.

You will show the book to no one until I am with you, Famoudou had said. I had to trust his guidance, and so I kept the book hidden.

Instead, I took out three bundles of money, each containing a slip of paper onto which I had redrawn my icons, so it was clear where each would be going. I handed them to Lanciné. He distributed them, explaining in Malinké what each was for. As he did so, one part of a karmic weight lifted. I had waited many years and traveled thousands of miles to make this gift in person. I hoped it would be acceptable.

When the gifts had been distributed accordingly, Fakourou spoke for the group.

"Daouda, *barika*. Thank you. And *Allah barika*—thanks be to God. We are pleased with your gifts, and we shall put them to good use in the village."

El Hadji and the other men nodded in agreement. My heart felt a little lighter.

"As for the second part of your request," Fakourou continued, "you shall return in one week's time. And when you do, together we will make an offering. We will pray for you as a son of this village, so that your suffering may be eased. And we will pray that the ancestors will continue to look after us all."

With the first part of my task complete, and the next step laid out before me, I eased back in my chair and tried to absorb the significance of the moment. As we lingered in the shade, I looked at the men around me, their faces weathered with deep lines. They were keepers of one of the world's old traditions, and I was humbled to sit in their presence.

Beyond the little courtyard, the village was mostly quiet, lost in its own trancelike march of time. Sunlight glowed through foliage that swayed ever so lightly, producing dancing jewels of light that reminded me of hope.

~

When the sun's light turned golden and lost some of its heat, Lanciné and I departed. On our way out, Lanciné shook me by the shoulder, grinning broadly. He used no words, but his eyes said it all. The elders were pleased. But I knew it was only the first step.

Along the route, we greeted a few more families. Afterward, we stopped at the concession of Lamine's family to greet them. By the time we arrived, El Hadji had already returned, and sat outside by a fire. His children and grandchildren swarmed around him, and he bounced the littlest on his knee. Nearby, Aminata was cooking over an open fire, and she greeted us warmly.

"*Iniké,* Daouda!" she said with a mischievous grin. "*Na damunin ké.*" She stared at me expectantly. I had no idea what she was saying. She laughed, and the family watched amusedly.

"Daouda, *na damunin ké!*"

I was still baffled. She could say it as many times as she wanted, I still wasn't going to get it.

"*Na damunin ké!*" She rolled her eyes in mock exasperation, then made the gesture of putting food to her mouth. In slow French, she said, "Come...eat...dinner!"

Aminata served up a glorious platter of food. Fresh fish and red sauce topped heaps of steaming rice. My mouth watered at the sight. Perhaps we'd stay a while. Lanciné was ready to eat, too.

We gathered around the platter in a circle, and ate hungrily, using only our hands as is customary. The bacteria could do what they wanted today. I was satisfied with my work for the time being, and now I would enjoy the moment. Scooping food into my mouth, my only thought was, *Why, yes…she is quite a good cook.* The food was delicious. Perhaps I could get used to this life.

Aminata smiled proudly, as if reading my thoughts.

31

THE FLEETING PATHWAYS OF EXILE

THE IMMENSE TREE LOOMED UPWARDS, an ancient monolith that had stood for centuries. Its twisting limbs sought the sky wildly as if to touch its creator, while its roots held an unshakable grip on the earth. I stood beneath the umbrella of its thick foliage, running my hand over bark that resembled an elephant's skin. I marveled at its size; it would take a half-dozen grown adults, arms interlocked around it, to achieve its circumference.

We were at the *bara*, the center of the village—"downtown," as it were. The tree was the focal point, and it stood at the crossroads of several paths that diverged from there. As Lanciné had informed me, this was the village's *arbre à palabres*, or palaver tree. The palaver, from the Portuguese *palavra* meaning "speech," is a veritable social institution in much of Africa, an all-important assembly where collective decisions regarding the community are made. In many villages, a large tree such as this serves as the gathering place for such matters, hence the name, "palaver tree."

Across from the palaver tree was the local café, a favorite hangout where villagers drank small cups of black coffee and chewed kola nuts during breaks from their everyday activities. The rustic café consisted of a supply shack with a shallow porch, where the proprietor brewed coffee over a charcoal stove. Just beyond that was an outdoor seating area—four rows of wooden benches beneath a thatched overhang—which was ample enough to provide shade for a dozen patrons. In the tradition of cafés the world over, men and women gathered here to chat, gossip, or debate the issues of the day. Lanciné sat there now with several friends, doing exactly that. And I was mindlessly admiring a tree.

With my first meeting with the elders behind me, we had time to ease into a new routine, and ease into it, we did. Time cavorted in an almost drunken way, and I lost all concept of the day of week or the date. These details were superfluous to my daily existence now. But while it was easy to get lulled into the trancelike rhythm of days morphing into each other, I couldn't lose all sense of time. My next appointment with destiny lay ahead.

In one week's time, you shall return. And when you do, together, we will make an offering.

The week had slipped by almost unnoticed. Did Fakourou mean exactly one week? Or did he mean it more loosely? I hadn't seen him pull out his day planner and mark it in his calendar, so I had to assume the latter. But how would I know when the day arrived? As I stood beneath the palaver tree, I tried counting how many days had passed since that visit—a surprisingly tricky task. I counted six, but I couldn't be sure, and eventually, my mind drifted elsewhere.

Our daily schedule was unremarkable, yet comfortable enough to wear a groove into the track. Mornings were devoted to my flute apprenticeship. Usually, we held our flute lessons inside the hut, with a small audience of friends and neighbors sitting around us. Other times, we walked past the sacred grove to one of the adjacent fields where nature alone was our audience. For hours, the only passersby were local cows. The setting was so serene that I wished my life could be like this forever.

Be careful what you wish for, I thought, recalling the shaman's words. *They may ask you to stay here forever.*

In the heat of the afternoons, we made a habit of going to the café to relax, socialize, and occasionally do short flute performances. For Lanciné, it was an occasion to be among old friends and neighbors, people he had grown up alongside. Temporarily relieved of his *tubabu* duties, he happily passed the hours in lively conversation. Since I generally couldn't make heads or tails of anything they discussed, I typically contented myself to daydream or read books.

I casually sauntered away from the tree, took my place on the café's benches, and reopened my book. Today, I had my eyes glued to Camara Laye's *L'enfant noir*. Although I had read it before, the scenes came to life in a whole new way while reading it mere miles from Laye's house. Unlike in the States, where the past was often buried in an onslaught of new trends and technologies, here the past was alive. The present hadn't superseded it, but instead politely merged into it. As I read, I had the impression of standing in a river of time, looking both up and downstream. Laye's poetic journey of growth resonated with me, as I grappled with my past and the transformation that was underway.

I arrived at a particularly poignant scene when Laye loses his childhood best friend, Check. In the weeks following his death, Check's ghost visited Laye in the night, and it frightened him. Over time, however, Laye's perception of life and death changed, and his new understanding brought him comfort. It gave me pause for thought, as I had little experience with losing a loved one.

Now whenever I dream of those far off days I can not say exactly what it was I was so frightened of, Laye wrote, *but certainly it's because I no longer think of death like I did then: I think more simply now. I simply think that Check has gone before us on God's pathway, and that all of us will one day walk that path which is no more frightening than the others. The others? Yes, the others, the pathways of life, the ones we set foot on when we are born and which are only the fleeting pathways of our exile...*

The fleeting pathways of our exile! Oh, the thought was tremendous to me. For what are we all, but wayfarers on the highways of life, in temporary exile from our true source? And how we cling to our momentary exile, full of wishes and desires for things to be different. At least, I know I did.

I looked up from the book and caught a glimpse of Lanciné and his friends, laughing and delighting in conversation. I felt a pang of loneliness then, missing my own friends and those carefree days when we'd gather for no other reason than to take pleasure in each other's company. I recalled those afternoons at the ocean with Erik and the gang, catching wave after wave until the sky grew dark and we were too weary to paddle out even one more time. There were mountain treks and road trips too, late nights around the campfire, and endless conversations about our lives and the dreams we all had for them. Those days seemed like they were from another lifetime.

After a few more chapters, I took a break to stretch my legs. Across the way, the tree caught my attention once more. I remembered reading an article once that said most Westerners could identify more corporate logos than trees. I didn't want to be one of those people. I again wandered over to the tree, and stood admiring it before returning to the café.

"Hey Lanciné," I asked, "What kind of tree is that?"

"In my language, we call this tree *bandan*. In French, it is called a *fromager*."

I nodded. The *fromager* is also called a *kapok* tree, and its seeds produce a material somewhat like cotton. The mattress on which I slept at night was likely stuffed with it, along with clumps of hay.

"We say that the *bandan* tree shelters the spirits of the ancestors—and whoever cuts the tree will die three days after. This particular tree is ancient, and has served as our *arbres à palabres* for…I don't know how long, actually. Even the oldest person in the village cannot remember a time when this tree was not here."

"Isn't the *arbre à palabres* always a baobab tree?" I had only stories and books to go on.

"Ah, Daouda! We have many sacred trees here. Yes, there is the giant baobab, or what we call *sida*. And you remember the large trees in Kouroussa, near the house of Camara Laye? Those were the *manguier*, the mango trees we call *mankoronju* in Malinké. The stories say that Samory Touré, the founder of the Wassoulou Empire, gathered his *sofa* warriors right there in Kouroussa beneath those ancient *manguier* trees."

"And those trees are all palaver trees?"

"The baobab, the *fromager*, the *manguier*, the acajou—these can all be palaver trees. And we have other sacred trees as well. Come, we shall take a walk. There is a place I want to show you. It is a place of my youth, and I have not seen it since I was a boy."

We said some goodbyes, gathered our flutes, and set out down a path leading away from the village. Soon, we entered thick forest, and after a few twists and turns, we picked up a narrow trail on which we walked single file. Here and there, vines and branches threatened to block our way. Numerous other trails intersected and darted into a labyrinth of thicket. Lanciné grew quiet, and navigated by memory.

At length, we reached a clearing. An expansive field opened before us. Several large trees stood at the center like sentinels. Cows and sheep grazed nearby.

Lanciné spoke in a whisper. We had come to a place that was sacred to him.

"Daouda…" He cleared his throat. "This is the field of my youth. It is here that I passed my days as a shepherd. Behold," he said, spreading his arms before him, "these are my former flocks. Beneath those trees, the music came to me from Allah himself." He held his hands up to the sky.

I was in awe. He had told me about this place many times. In his stories, it had a mystical quality. But now I saw it before me, and it was real.

We ventured toward the trees. A soft breeze whispered, and the grasses shimmered in unison. I remembered the song which compared Sundiata's lineage to a field of grass.

While anyone can enter into the grass, the grass itself will bow to no one.

A shiver went down my spine. Lanciné walked ahead of me. When I caught up with him, he was weeping openly.

We sat quietly on the roots of the tree. I'm not sure how much time passed, and it didn't matter. I could only imagine what emotions Lanciné was experiencing. In his life, he had known hardship, hunger, and suffering. But here was the place of his humble beginnings. Maybe he was making peace with his past, too.

After a long silence, Lanciné picked up his flute and began to play. The breeze carried the notes across nature's sanctuary, an amphitheater of the ancients. Lanciné's flute added its distinct voice to the chorus of the living. As his song rose and drifted away on the wind, it was clear that we humans are Earth's children, even if we have lost our way. She calls to us in nature, for that is our true home. She needs our songs as she does those of the birds. Lanciné's playing beneath the tree that day was transcendent. I am sure the gods heard, and took notice. I don't imagine I have ever, or will ever again, be witness to such a holy spectacle of music.

When Lanciné finished, he looked at me, and his eyes brimmed over with glassy tears. He gestured with his hand that I should take up my flute too. And so I did, and followed Lanciné down a pathway of melodies as old as time. The two flutes merged into the sounds of the forest, and the resulting music seemed to reach into eternity. We were everywhere and nowhere, the present moment but a single note in the song of the universe. Our desperate lives, too, are but a moment, inconsequential in the grand scheme. Yet we are given the divine gift of experiencing it all as earthly creatures. We are the dream of God, and the dreamers who dream the universe into being. When the fleeting pathway of our earthly exile reaches its end, perhaps we return to the dream as ancestors, everywhere and nowhere, part of a continuum without beginning or end.

Perhaps it has all been a dream, I thought. *A heartbreakingly beautiful dream.*

When the sky was painted in purple hues and the heat of the day bowed down before evening, we made our way back silently. En route, we took a detour down another side path.

"There is one more thing I want to show you, Daouda. It is just beyond here, and you shall see it soon."

We came to an opening where the thicket no longer crowded the forest floor. Before me, another spectacle rose from the ground. The tree was unlike any I had ever seen, and dwarfed even the palaver tree in the village. This tree was perhaps thirty feet in diameter. Its gnarled roots appeared not to reach underground, but rather to climb like a thousand serpents cast to stone. No matter how I craned my neck, the tree's top was hidden from sight.

"In Malinké, we call this tree *doubalen*—a giant ficus. Everyone in the village knows this tree. It is the protector of the village. Its spirit is *benba*, a great-great-grandfather to us."

We stood in reverence. It was a powerful presence, this ancient giant of the forest. Its foliage was teeming with life. Birds darted in and out of nests. Further up, monkeys climbed in the upper branches.

We sat together quietly, and I prayed. Soon, I'd return to Famoudou's village. Fakourou said we would make an offering to the ancestors. Praying beneath this sacred tree felt like a good preparation. The stakes were high. As I sat, I was all too aware of the pain in my spine, which had been growing all day like a storm cloud looming on the horizon.

When the sun no longer filtered through the canopy, we moved on in near darkness. The day had been surreal and peaceful, but I should have recognized it as the calm before the storm. I was not prepared for what came next.

By the time we returned to our hut, it was full dark. Lanciné needed to attend to some family matters, so I remained in the hut, alone. My pain had again risen to almost intolerable levels. I was emotional from the day's events. But that emotion, coupled with the pain, quickly turned to fatigue. The storm was building.

I tried to process the sense of uneasiness arising within me. In the flickering candlelight, I recalled the words of the shaman.

You have had this illness for a long time. It has been calling you to your true path, but you do not know how to listen. Perhaps the pain will always be there to remind you. It is time to start listening.

The storm's first thunder crack arrived, and a bolt of pain shot through me like lightning. An unexpected emotion arose in return: Anger. Then, defiance. My emotions, normally muted from medication, were bubbling to the surface. This time, I didn't want to numb them.

The storm within me erupted as another bolt shot through my spine. It was merciless.

"Fuck this pain!" I screamed, not caring who could hear me. *"Fuck it to hell!"* I slammed my bag onto the floor, and kicked it across the room for good measure. The outburst surprised even me.

They will hold your feet to the fire until you have accomplished all that you need to.

Another lightning bolt struck me. I was under attack, exposed to the storm with no place to hide. I jerked around to find something else to throw. But the motion sent another jolt of electricity through me, and I crumpled to the floor. The lingering pain rumbled like constant rolling thunder. There was no escaping its next strike.

The ancestors are not to be fooled with. It would have been much better for you if this man was still alive.

The image of old Sako Gbè appeared before me like a phantom. His eyes were piercing.

Another bolt struck me with such force that it sucked all the air out of me. I crawled to the side of the bed, gasping, and held on to the bedpost as if it might save me from the pain. The storm was raging now, and tears rained from my eyes in a downpour. The ancestors were showering their brutal wrath upon me, and all I could do was cry useless tears and bear it out.

I searched within me for the glimmer of hope, praying it might reappear and bring some comfort—or at least offer a reason why I shouldn't end my own miserable path of earthly exile right now.

I heard Fakourou's voice in my mind.

We will help you seek an accord with the ancestors of the village, and we will pray that your offerings here will be accepted.

My anger softened momentarily, and my tears formed a puddle on the hut's earthen floor. I had traveled so far to do this, despite all the things I didn't yet understand. I was trying—couldn't they see that? But no, another sharp knife of invisible fury stabbed at my body, like I was a voodoo doll. I simply couldn't take this pain a moment longer. I wanted it to end, and I no longer cared how.

I picked myself up carefully, fumbled for my bag, and searched inside for the bundles of tea. I wasn't sure if a *kratom* overdose could be fatal, or how much I would need to end this ordeal for good. I desperately shook one of the packets, and realized to my dismay that it was empty. Panicked, I shook another packet. It too was empty. One after another, and my worst fears became real. How could this be? I hadn't noticed how quickly I was going through them. My supply was depleted.

I sat on the bed and covered my face with my hands, heaving with sobs. The storm was still mounting in intensity.

Then, something unexpected happened. My phone buzzed in my pocket—an incoming text message. Odd, because I rarely had service here. I pulled the phone from my pocket and read the message. The blood ran out of me as my whole world changed again.

Erik was dead.

I arose without even knowing I was doing so. I fought hard against the torrent of pain that pelted me as I left the hut, and limped into the darkness.

Oh my god. Erik is gone.

I started walking, not knowing where I was going. An onslaught of fresh tears blurred my vision. I passed by huts and concessions, and eventually came to the trail leading away from it all. I followed it knowing only that I had to keep going. Some irrational instinct spurred me onward through the darkness.

I was momentarily startled to realize I had arrived at the sacred grove.

It is said that the spirits of the ancestors reside there. And beyond that is la brousse—*the wild country. You must never walk there alone—particularly at night.*

I was utterly lost in the dark, but I didn't care. My best friend was gone. The text message had been brief. No cause of death had been given, but I didn't need one. I knew full well Erik died from his long battle with drug abuse. In the end, his pathways of exile had led to despair from which there was no return.

I crumpled to the ground, enfolded by darkness. The world spun around me as I writhed in the dirt, overcome with pain and grief. Giant trees rose above, and their branches reached for me like bony fingers. Perhaps ancestor spirits roamed in my presence. I implored these beings for compassion, for hope. But only heartache and uncertainty came.

There in the sacred grove, I sobbed, pounding the forest floor with closed fists as the night cast its spells. At last, exhaustion took over and my shudders subsided. My life energy left me. I hoped I would die.

Strange noises descended from the darkness, and fear came over me.

To die alone and forgotten was my worst fear. Suddenly, I snapped into awareness. Something had brushed against me. I was not alone.

These djinn, they are there. You do not see them, but sometimes you feel them. You might think it is the breeze that touches you, but when you look, the air is quite still.

Around me, nothing stirred. It must have been my imagination. But then, I gasped. A hand touched my shoulder. But it was not the menacing touch of a *djinn*. I looked up through blurry eyes and saw the kind face of Lanciné hovering above me.

Wordlessly, he helped me to my feet. I stood trembling, and he steadied me. We didn't walk until my trembling subsided. His compassion flowed into me, and I knew at that moment I couldn't follow the same path as Erik. There *had* to be some hope—even if it was currently shrouded in pain. With Lanciné's arm around my shoulder, we walked slowly through the dark night. I only wished I could have been there to hold Erik up when he needed me. Some wishes come too late.

When I awoke the next morning, light filtered through the boughs of the thatched roof. A new day had arrived, and I had to find the strength to carry on.

Outside the hut, Lanciné offered me the customary morning greetings, then delivered news that made my heart pound.

"Fakourou has summoned us today. The village is ready, and awaits our arrival."

32

RETURN TO THE EARTH A GIFT OF LIFE

THEY LED *Monsieur Mouton* in by the short rope tied around its neck. When I saw the look of terror in the sheep's eyes, my heart filled with dread. I brought my hands to my face to cover my frightened expression, and found they were shaking.

We were in a part of the village I had never seen before. About forty old men had gathered, mostly wearing flowing *boubou* robes and traditional brimless *kufi* on their heads. They sat on woven grass mats, arranged in a circle on the courtyard's sandy floor.

I sat at one end of the circle, with Lanciné and Lamine on either side of me. Directly across from me, the chief of the village sat regally in a wooden chair. His majestic blue robe and colorful *shemagh* gave him an air of dignity. His entourage of advisors, *marabouts*, and *griots* were seated around him.

El Hadji, the *imam* holy man I had met a week earlier, stood at the center of the circle. Standing beside him was the *naamutigi*, or *naamu-sayer*, whose job was to verify the truth of the words spoken here today.

I regarded the distinguished assembly, and studied their dark, weathered faces. At Fakourou's bequest—and by extension, Famoudou's —they were gathered to take part in a sacred event. And for the first time in all my years traveling here, the ritual I was about to participate in had been arranged on my behalf.

El Hadji began the proceedings in Arabic and Malinké. First, he addressed the assembly, and offered prayers and benedictions. Each phrase he spoke elicited the *naamutigi's* songlike affirmation:

"Naamu!" Agreed, I hear you.

The sun was still rising, and along with it, the physical torment that spread throughout my body like a venomous curse. I hadn't slept much the night before, and felt delirious.

The prayers continued in ever-rising tones. The *naamutigi* matched the *imam's* intensity.

"Naaaaaamu!"

El Hadji invoked Allah, along with names of the deceased. Lanciné translated in a whisper so soft I strained to hear him above El Hadji's incantations.

"He says, 'A foreigner has come to present gifts...the assembly prays they will be acceptable...'"

"Naamuuuuu!"

"They pray for the health and success of this white man who has traveled from afar to pay his respects."

"Walahi!" I swear it!

"They pray that this white man's success will be the success of the village, too."

"Naamuuuuu!"

El Hadji was working up to a fever pitch. The onlookers occasionally bowed their heads or nodded in agreement. He prayed the sacrifice about to take place would be deemed worthy. That the sacred blood spilled today would consecrate the ground of the village.

"Amiina! Amiina!" the crowd responded. *Amen!*

The prayers went on and Lanciné's translations ceased. As the ceremony proceeded, I thought about my long road here. Two decades of pain and suffering. My thoughts turned to Kerri back home, and my family. And Erik, who was gone now, forever.

I'm sorry, my old friend, I thought. *I'm sorry I wasn't there for you.*

I forced my thoughts back to the present moment. There would be a time for grieving, for the loss of a friend, for the loss of my home and my relationship with Kerri, but now was not that time. I had come to reckon with a curse, an insufferable affliction that had plagued me too long. While El Hadji's prayers went on, I prayed quietly that, through some miracle or stroke of magic, I would be rid of this curse. And I prayed that I would find the strength to free myself from the addiction that had rendered me a phantom of my old self—and that I wouldn't walk the same road of despair that Erik had.

It is the intervention on the spiritual level that ultimately determines the patient's fate…and perhaps most important, by a sacrifice so that the patient may return to the earth a gift of life's vital energy.

Matters of the spirit and the heart were at hand. I would soon return to the earth a gift of life, and prayed it would be received well.

The time had come. Two men led the sheep to the center, and Lanciné gestured to me. I stood up cautiously, nervously.

El Hadji's voice continued to rise, the *naamu*-sayer responding fervently.

"Wala-hiiii!"

The men bound the sheep's feet, and turned it on its side.

"Naaaa-muuuuu!"

The sheep bayed as the men held it steady.

Someone placed a knife in my hand. The wooden shaft was smooth, worn from years of use. I knelt beside the sheep, sure the drum beat of my heart was audible to all. The sheep looked up at me, his eyes dark and innocent. I choked back tears. I couldn't shed them now, not with this group of men surrounding me, men who had lived long years and suffered through hard lives, men who knew that the earth gives and it takes. Offerings must sometimes be made.

I'm sorry, I whispered to the sheep, then to myself, *Be brave. Have courage.* There was no backing out now.

All eyes were on me. I pressed the blade against the sheep's throat, but then faltered. I wasn't sure I could do it. El Hadji's chanting echoed as if from far away, though that distance was only an illusion. I was focused intently on the creature before me. I had never taken a life before, and the weight of it bore down on me.

A strong hand gripped my shoulder, and without looking, I knew who it was. Like so many times before, Lanciné was lending me his strength.

I inhaled sharply and plunged the knife into the animal's neck. The blade was sharp, and the cut was clean. A horrible moan and a gagging sound escaped from the sheep as blood gushed from its throat. The pool that formed was shockingly vivid against the parched earth. Little streams of exquisite red flowed between my feet.

I could take no more. The knife fell from my hand and I backed away as the other men took over. The sheep's life ended quickly and mercifully.

Dear God…what have I done. I'm sorry. Please, oh please, accept this offering and end this suffering…

I stumbled backward to my place in the circle, my eyes never leaving the dead sheep. I sat in shock. The prayers resumed for a time, and an open discourse followed, but I was elsewhere. Time melted away. I heard only the sound of voices speaking in rapid Malinké, but I could not comprehend it. The gazes of the assembled men burned into my soul.

The sun was high in the sky by the time the ceremony concluded. The chief and elders all approached me in turn, taking my hand and offering thanks for my gifts to the village. The deep emotion was evident in their eyes. The sacrifice had moved them. The meat, they assured me, would feed many hungry families. No part of the animal would go to waste here. This pleased me, but I was still in shock from the sacrifice. Something had changed inside me and I didn't know what. But what became clear as the elders spoke to me was that certain boundaries between us had just been obliterated. I had earned their respect.

Amidst this, Lanciné turned to me. Tears were welling up in his eyes. He put both hands on my shoulders and looked at me with sincerity.

"Daouda, our hearts are wide open to you. *Allah a nöya ké*—may God make you well. We will continue to pray for you."

I was touched by his words, but could only wonder if the sacrifice would somehow alter my fate? Would the ancestors take notice, and release me from my curse?

Soon, the crowd began to disperse. As Lanciné and I readied to leave, an older man with deep lines on his face approached me. He wore the unmistakable garb of the blacksmiths, a plain tunic with cowry shells at his waist, a *shemagh* at his neck. His eyes were piercing in a strangely familiar way, and I struggled to understand how I recognized him.

He shook my hand, his eyes never leaving mine.

"You do not know me," he said in a thick accent, "but I know you. I am the blacksmith of your *maître*, Famoudou. You were acquainted with a member of my family. The late Sako Gbè was my brother."

The blood ran from my face at the mention of the old sorcerer. How did this man know me, and more importantly, *what* did he know about me? Did he somehow know about my book?

The second part of my journey was complete. Sacrificial blood had been spilled for the ancestors, but my journey was still far from over. The final tasks still remained, and they terrified me. Somewhere in the village, a sorceress named Mousso Gbè awaited me.

33

MARCHING INTO THE UNKNOWN

I STAND ALONE in a great expanse of savannah. The sun is high overhead, and the grasses reach to my waist. All around me is a shimmering sea of amber, and a warm breeze sends rolling waves ahead of me. In the distance, an outcropping of rock appears like a mirage at the crest of a hill, but I cannot see beyond it.

I hold a long, white staff in my right hand. Its perfect roundness seems manufactured and out of place here, but I can lean on it as I walk. It serves me, for the time being. The fingers of my left hand are wrapped loosely around a small object that I must protect. It is an amulet of sorts, but it is precious, fragile, natural. It must arrive safe and unharmed. I am its keeper, for now.

I begin walking, knowing I have a long trek ahead of me. Unsure of how bad the pain will be, I plant the staff ahead of me for support. But as I take my first steps, I notice I have a freedom of movement I haven't known since—when? It's been too long to remember. I straighten my spine, and it too feels loose and flexible. I feel taller now that my spine isn't hunched over, and I gain more confidence with every step. Aware of my newfound mobility and strength, I break into a light jog, expecting to be halted by the familiar stab of pain in my hips—but none comes.

I start to run. It is gleeful, this sensation of moving without restriction, and I wonder if I am in heaven. The grass still stings my legs as I tear through it, but I don't care. I will run until I reach my destination, for nothing can stop me now. I cast the staff aside, knowing I no longer need its support.

Faster and faster I run, and the distance to the hilltop grows shorter with every step. I streak toward it, impossibly light, with a total absence of pain. And then I catch a glimpse of movement in the corner of my eye, and I turn my head sharply, almost stumbling as I do. Someone is running behind me—and quickly gaining on me. I hear the footfalls of the approaching runner, and I don't know if I should run faster or hold up. But then the runner is upon me, overtaking my speed without any apparent effort. I see his face, and my heart almost bursts with joy.

It is Erik.

As he sprints past me, I catch the devilish glint in his eye, daring me, challenging me to outrun him.

"Come on, man!" he yells. "Dig deeper! There's still further to go!"

I grit my teeth, determined, and find the next gear. Together we run, laughing recklessly, the landscape whirring past us in a blur. Erik's face bears an impish grin, and he is hardly breaking a sweat. Then, he surges forward, racing past me easily as I struggle to maintain the pace.

"Salty Dog, wait up!" I yell, but he has gone too far ahead.

When I reach him at last, he is standing on the hillside, cool and collected, looking younger and more radiant than I remember him. I hunch over, gasping for breath, and it is then I notice what is below the hillside. Far beyond, a village is nestled into a valley. Plumes of smoke rise from distant fires. A narrow pathway leads down from the hill and straight to the village.

I suddenly remember what I'm holding in my left hand, and open my fingers carefully. I hope I haven't crushed it during the long sprint. A tickle in my palm tells me it is still alive and moving. I show it to Erik, and he smiles.

"You found your scorpion," he says.

"Yes. But it's not my time yet. I have to bring it to the people."

Erik nods in understanding, and then points to the path ahead of us. "You should go, man. They're waiting for you."

I direct my gaze toward the village, and my mind is burning with questions.

"Will you come with me?" I ask, but when I turn, there is no one there to answer.

～

I awoke from the dream, and the image of Erik faded rapidly. I was still alive and he was still gone, departed forever on distant pathways. As proof of my continued exile, I noted that beneath me was the same clumpy mattress that gave me fits at night. I still wore the same dirty clothing I had fallen asleep in, too exhausted to even undress.

And now, the real moment of truth was at hand.

I turned onto my side slowly, gingerly, hoping not to awaken the beast that lived inside me. Maybe by some miracle, it was gone. Dare I even find out? Yes, I had to know if the sacrifice had worked. If the ancestors were pleased, then surely they would release me from this painful curse.

I only made it halfway to an upright position. My hopes were shattered in one definitive, electric bolt of pain.

～

I'm not sure what I should've expected, really. But on the one hand, I felt betrayed. I had secretly imagined I would awake to find my pain had miraculously vanished. I pictured leaping out of bed and running into the village *bara* proclaiming, "*Alhamdulillah!* Praise be to God! I am cured!"

But when I awoke the morning after the sacrifice, it was to a spine that still burned like the fire of a blacksmith's forge, and vertebrae that felt more fused than ever. Sorrow and dismay were useless sentiments, but very real all the same.

On the other hand, the events of the past day had changed me. The difference was noticeable, though hard to quantify. I mean, these people had *prayed* for me, a stranger from another land who played little part in their daily lives. They had invoked the gods and the spirits of their dead ancestors on my behalf, and it had moved me deeply. Furthermore, the powerful act of returning to the earth a gift of life's vital energy was not lost on me. It was a step toward healing and reconciliation, one that was perhaps long overdue. Although my pain hadn't magically disappeared, my heart felt different, transformed somehow—even if the full extent of that change wasn't evident yet.

What might it mean for the bigger picture of my healing? I didn't have a clue. If mysterious forces were indeed at work, they remained a mystery. The pain persisted. There would be no temporary reprise, no break from it to catch my breath.

Mysteries too great to comprehend, I thought, *and pain too great to bear. Just my luck.*

I heaved a sigh of exasperation, and remembered my dream. The image of Erik looking radiant and strong flashed before me.

Come on man, dig deeper! There's still further to go!

What other choice did I have? I had come too far to consider turning back. Blood had been shed, and now more than ever, I was invested in seeing this to whatever end. I had to keep going.

The most important tasks still remained ahead of me, but they required Famoudou's presence. And until he arrived, I could only bide my time—and deal with the pain as best I could. Because I had exhausted my supply of *kratom* tea, that meant taking the pills. My conscience grumbled at the thought, but there was no telling when Famoudou might get here. The consequences of taking the pills would have to be deferred. The success of the quest was paramount. I couldn't fail.

I arose, wincing in agony, and found the large bottle tucked neatly into the bottom of my bag. I shook it, and heard the satisfying rattle that reminded me there was a hefty three-month supply inside. I gobbled two down with some tepid water, and waited.

When the warmth came over me and the pain diminished, I headed out into the village, numb and soul weary.

~

The lead sun made its arc across the sky, scorching the dry earth. Day by day, the heat grew more oppressive. Plants in the fields withered and drooped, despondent for lack of rain. At night, the air barely cooled. A crescent moon rose over the treetops and hung above the Niger River before retreating to its hidden domain. After too many sleepless nights, I took to sleeping on the floor near the hut's doorway, desperate for what little breeze there might be. When sleep wouldn't come at all, I'd slip outside to sit beneath the heavens. Each night, I saw the moon waxing, growing ever more pregnant, and my anticipation grew with it. I counted the passage of days in the number of pills I had remaining, like a lunatic reverse calendar of my own desperate creation.

I waited. I prayed.

Your relationship with Africa is no longer that of an outsider...you are beholden to the customs of the people.

The sacrifice bound me to this village. I had spilled blood onto its soil. The ancestors had been invoked.

I tried to conjure images of those ancestors. It was their customs to which I was beholden. But who were these men and women who had come before, who had toiled and suffered in Africa, whose lives receded into the river of time? Their legacy lived on in legends and songs. These were a people who had built mighty empires, only to have them crumble into dust. All things are bound to impermanence, yet Africa endures in the spirits of its ancestors. These were a people, too, who had been bought and sold like cattle in a market, and yet whose dignity and traditions persevered. They fought against the tide of colonialism, and when that tidal wave crashed over them, they held on to their identity. Today, the modern world encroaches again, coveting Africa's mineral riches. Buried in its soil are gold, aluminum ore, and diamonds. When strangers come and strip them from the earth, it is Africans who pay the price.

The ancestors have not forgotten their children. The time for healing has come.

Who were these ancestors? I had tread into their realm. As a younger man, I dipped into the well of their traditions, and drank freely from its waters. Perhaps they had indeed noticed. Their traditions are not for the taking. There is a price. Reciprocity is required. And the past must be healed, even if lifetimes must be traversed.

They do not know you have forgotten, that you are ignorant of the traditions. They will hold you accountable, because you should have known.

What was still being asked of me? I beseeched them for answers, and implored them for healing.

They will hold your feet to the fire until you have accomplished all that you need to.

Yes, I still had more work to do. I waited patiently for Famoudou.

The days passed in a hazy, slow march into the unknown, steadily turning into weeks. And still, we received no word from the old man.

34

TO BE ALONE IS THE WORST THING

I AWOKE BEFORE DAWN. Mornings were the coolest time of day, and I had taken to rising before anyone. At daybreak, the heat was tolerable —and it was then that I would go walking, alone.

Lanciné still slept, snoring heavily on the floor. I tiptoed around him and dressed quietly, wincing from pain and stiffness. My joints grated like old rusty hinges. I fished in my vest pocket for the pills, and swallowed two. I pulled the wooden door, careful to not rouse Lanciné, and it creaked open. He stirred for a moment, and I held perfectly still. When his snoring resumed, I slipped out the door.

Outside, cool air greeted me. Stars faded into an azure sky, and a faint trace of salmon hue washed over the sky in the east. The village still slept. I relished the opportunity to be alone with my thoughts. Moments of solitude were hard to come by here. The whole idea of solitude was antithetical to village life.

"To be alone is the worst thing in the world," Lanciné once explained to me. "Isolation is the worst punishment. If you have committed a serious crime in the village, you are banished. In solitude, the exiled villager simply dies of loneliness."

It was a heartbreaking thought, and gave me pause. When I was younger, I had stubbornly asserted that I didn't need anyone. I was self-sufficient in all ways, and proud of it. But age revealed this mode of existence to be a farce, nothing more than a lame practice of shielding my heart from the dangers of intimacy. I used to think the human animal could thrive in isolation, but no—now I knew that was folly. Self-imposed exile was still exile.

Had I forgotten how to love, how to let people into my heart? Did I even love *myself?* I doubted it. I identified myself as pain, and found little to love there.

The tip of the sun broke over the horizon, and painted the village in amber light. I stood for a moment watching the morning come alive. Beams of warm golden light streamed onto my face. It was both beautiful and sad, all this. I wanted to love again, and be loved. I just couldn't remember how.

∽

I headed toward the main path, with no particular direction in mind. I had brought my camera along, hoping to snap some pictures of the village for drawing reference. Someday, if ever I returned, maybe I'd make some new paintings.

Further down the path, I came upon the village mosque. Its narrow spires rose above the village, and its stern architecture was a contrast to the organic shape of the huts beneath it. I snapped a few photos. The disparity was fascinating. Two worlds collided before me. One represented a world in which trees are sacred and *nyama* courses through everything. The past and present intertwine, and ancestors walk among the living. The other dictates abstinence from the trappings of the earthly realm, and surrender to Allah above all else. In doing so, one hopes only to secure their position in the afterlife.

How could these disparate ways of being in the world coexist? Lanciné was somehow the embodiment of both. Each morning, he brought his mat outside to kneel and pray in the Muslim way. Yet he was steeped in the old ways; he was a master, even, of those earthly traditions. What internal conflict, if any, did these two worldviews pose for him? Perhaps, in a perpetual state of poverty and hardship, his future in this life seemed bleak. Surely, the afterlife might be better.

I could only imagine what he thought of me, a Western man who sought healing and redemption in Africa. He viewed America as a promised land that was unavailable to him in life. Though I suffered in my own ways, the relative prosperity from which I came must have seemed like salvation.

"Daouda, even your country's poorest are better off than most of us here in Guinea." I'd heard him express this sentiment on more than one occasion. And I'd seen the heartrending squalor that is life in Conakry. The extent of this city's poverty was hard to imagine until you saw it, and impossible to comprehend unless you lived it. And I hadn't lived it.

Lanciné suspected I thought little of the afterlife, and why would I? To him, my pain was temporary, an illness that would one day go away. And in any case, I could return to my life in the promised land at any moment. Lanciné had no such choice.

The truth, however, was that I had already resigned myself to living out my days in Africa. Poverty didn't scare me. What terrified me was the idea of returning to America alone and still suffering from AS. Would I be trapped in a cycle of pain and addiction, unable to love and be loved? Whatever my existential crime might have been, the punishment of my disease alone would never kill me. In self-exile, I would simply die of loneliness.

Before long, the village started to rouse. Villagers emerged from their huts, and the sound of whisking brooms blended with birdsong. Here, the day did not start in a hurried frenzy. People sauntered outside and sat quietly. They started cook fires, and families joined around them as the water cauldrons heated. There was no scurrying to wolf down microwaved breakfasts, get the kids off to school, and head to work through rush-hour traffic, no sir, not here. Instead, villagers took the time to perform long, slow greetings. Each day was an opportunity to be grateful. If you awoke to find your family, friends, and neighbors still here and *alive* another day, that was something worth appreciating.

I walked past huts, waving shyly and politely saying *i sööma* to each person. I hadn't met many of these people yet. They stared curiously at me as I strolled through their village. When I greeted them in Malinké, they'd often gesture for me to come closer, and so I did. I conversed as best I could. Sometimes, if language permitted, these conversations were an opportunity to glean valuable insights into village life, and into the thoughts and opinions of the villagers themselves. Some had fascinating stories to tell. It got me thinking.

Many would point to the camera around my neck. I'd ask permission to take their picture, and they'd pose for me, tentatively at first. When I showed them their images on the camera's screen, they'd beam and insist I take more. In the morning light, the pictures were beautiful. These photos would make good portrait references, I thought—and I was hankering to get down to that particular business.

When I returned to Lanciné's concession, he was awake and sitting outside.

"Daouda, where have you been?" he asked. "I was worried you ran away again."

I laughed. "No, Lanciné, just out walking for the pleasure of it. Look, I got some good photos." I sat down beside him, and showed him the camera's contents.

"Yes, Daouda, these are very nice! You must take more."

I poured myself some water for coffee, and thought for a moment. I had time to kill now, so why not get to work? My art studio in Conakry had served me well, but I had barely picked up a pencil since arriving in the village.

A boy arrived with loaves of warm bread, and set them before us. I tore off a chunk and chewed it slowly.

"Lanciné, I've been thinking," I said between bites. "We have some time before Famoudou arrives. I'd like to set up an art studio, like I did in Conakry. Famoudou said I could use his house in Kouroussa. Can we look into it?"

Lanciné nodded. "Yes, of course. You have the number for the caretaker?"

I pulled out my notebook and flipped through the pages.

"Yeah, I've got it right here." I had written *Sori Keïta—maison de Famoudou à Kouroussa*. The cell phone number was below.

"Good. We will call him after breakfast, and we shall see what this man Sori has to say."

I brimmed with excitement. Imagine, an art studio in Kouroussa, the birthplace of Camara Laye!

We finished our breakfast in silence as my thoughts consumed me. All I could think about now was making new art. After breakfast, Lanciné placed the call. Sori was already aware that I might call one of these days, and agreed to meet us later that afternoon. The wheels were set in motion.

"Daouda, Sori did mention one thing," Lanciné said after the call.

"Oh? What's that?"

"The electricity at Famoudou's place has not been on for some time now, and there is no indication that it will return anytime soon. We should think about charging our devices, as we'll need them in case of emergency."

Until now, we had been using small solar chargers to keep our devices powered. Each morning, it was our little tradition to climb onto the rooftop of a nearby hut to place our solar-powered chargers onto the roof to cook in the hot sun all day. In the evening, we had only to retrieve them and plug in our phones.

While I had little use for my phone here in the village, I liked to keep it charged just in case. Force of habit, I suppose—hell, I'm an American after all. What was more difficult was keeping my large camera charged. Additionally, to export the photos into a usable form for art reference, I would need my laptop.

"It's a good point, Lanciné. I'd assumed we'd have power in Kouroussa. What do you have in mind?"

Lanciné laughed. "Daouda, have you forgotten?"

"Forgotten what?" I couldn't think of what I was missing.

Lanciné looked a little smug. "All the way here, we transported a diesel generator, and you have forgotten. We should use it now."

Holy shit balls! Indeed, I had totally forgotten about it until this moment. It had seemed like overkill to lug that beast of a machine, but now, I was grateful for it. I could get a full charge on both my camera and my laptop, and be good to go in Kouroussa for a while.

"Lanciné, you're brilliant."

"Yes, quite."

I chuckled heartily, feeling gleeful, if not a bit indulgent. Moments later, we uncovered the generator, which had been stashed behind the hut under a pile of hay, and fired it up. As it roared into life noisily, black smoke spewed forth for a few moments. It sputtered and coughed, and I held my breath, hoping it wouldn't stall. After a few moments, it held.

Villagers came to see what the ruckus was, and of course, Lanciné beamed at having brought electricity to the village. No one seemed to mind that it was louder than a jet plane. I just hoped we wouldn't make it too much of a habit.

Later that morning, Lamine arrived with the little blue Renault, which was looking more battered than ever, with the front bumper and headlights still being repaired. I packed up my art supplies, a small backpack of sundries, and my freshly charged devices. Just before we left, I remembered to grab the little black portfolio case that contained my Conakry drawings.

We were off on another adventure, and my heart was lighter than it had been in months. My muse awaited me in Kouroussa.

~

Not a quarter mile into our journey, Lanciné spoke up. "Daouda, the vehicle is almost out of gas."

"Oh. Well, that's not good." I wondered how he had ascertained that information given that the gas gauge had stopped working. It was all the more reason to err on the side of caution.

"The bigger problem, Daouda, is that Djara the bargeman is not around today, so we will have to take the long way to Kouroussa. We need to stop at the village gas station on our way out."

I shot him a sideways glance. "Wait—there's another way to Kouroussa? And there's a gas station in the *village*?" My small brain could only handle so much new information at once.

"Yes, of course. Nowadays, many people drive motorcycles here. There is a road that goes from here through the villages of Babila, Kato, Fadama, and Baro, before coming to the main route to Kouroussa. And yes, we have a gas station. We are coming up on it now."

We were hardly on what I would have called a road. *Cow path* was more like it. It was, in fact, only a bit further down the same dusty pathway I had walked this morning. But I was fascinated to learn that this path led all the way to these other villages. Baro is the home of a well known *djembefola*, Mansa Camio, and the drumming tradition in his village is strong. If we were heading that way, we'd be traveling along the Niandan River, and Fadama is located on its banks. This village was of interest to me, because Fadama's population consisted primarily of *griot* families, mostly from the Condé clan. Over the centuries, Fadama has been a veritable cultural learning center, dedicated to the dissemination of oral histories through the work of countless *griots*. I was eager to spend time in both these places.

We came to a stop beneath a giant tree with gnarly roots. Several goats and cows mulled about. I looked up at the tree, and was about to open my mouth, but Lanciné read my thoughts.

"It's what we call *dialla* in Malinké. It's an acajou, or Caïlcédrat tree. It is also a sacred palaver tree."

I nodded, and then noticed a rickety wooden cart nearby. It held a half-dozen glass bottles filled with a reddish-brown liquid. Lamine got out and approached it. A motorcycle laden with bundles drove by, kicking up a cloud of red dust.

Lamine picked up two of the bottles from the cart, and a man resting beneath the tree jumped to attention. They spoke a moment, and Lanciné gestured to me.

"Daouda, give the man 20,000 Guinée francs. Ah! Gas is expensive in the village!"

So this was the village gas station. I forked out the bills and paid for the equivalent of two liters of gas. I did the math. About three dollars US. Two liters was only about half a gallon. That made gas here about six bucks a gallon, which was indeed pretty expensive. But hey, we were in a tiny village in the middle of nowhere. For me, the question was not whether it was too expensive, but rather, would a half gallon be enough to get us all the way to Kouroussa? The cart held several more bottles of gas.

"Lanciné, let's not be too conservative. There are more bottles available. I have enough money."

"No, Daouda. That is all we can buy at this time. We cannot deplete the stock, as it would leave other travelers without. It would be wrong of us to hoard it. Once we get to Kouroussa, we can buy enough for the return trip."

It was another small lesson on the village mindset. I would have bought it all greedily and left the shelves empty, just like everyone did at the grocery stores back home before a big snowstorm. Lamine emptied the two bottles into the gas tank, and returned the empties to the shelf. The bottles would be reused, of course.

With that, we were off.

The track led us into the forest, and the Renault rambled over deep ruts. Lamine navigated around free-roaming cows and mammoth potholes. We came to a rusty metal sign with painted letters that read:

Baro —>
Babila —>
Kato —>
Fadama —>
<— Kouroussa

"Hey, Kouroussa is that way," I remarked. "Why are we heading away from it?"

"There is only water that way, and no way to cross it. We will go this way, and in Baro we will come to the main route."

I nodded. All fine with me; I was grateful for the opportunity to take in more of the countryside. My spirit was coming alive from being on the move again.

After a long slog over the wooded path, the forest opened up to large expanses of rocky fields. Sharp crags jutted out of the landscape, at times making it appear impassable. Just when I thought the road would rattle the Renault into pieces, we ascended a hill and came to a railroad trestle at a decent height. We stopped and got out to examine the trestle, which extended over a craggy ravine, perhaps about a hundred yards across. A hundred feet below us, the mouth of the Earth looked ready to consume an entire vehicle in its sharp teeth.

The tracks were clearly no longer in use—not by trains, at any rate. But dozens of rough-hewn boards had been placed loosely over the trestle, parallel to the train tracks. The boards were placed side-by-side to cover roughly a car's width. But these makeshift supports stopped halfway across, revealing the iron skeleton of the old trestle. A fall from this height would result in certain death. I rubbed my chin, waiting for an explanation.

"One of us will walk ahead of the car, and one behind," Lanciné said. "The boards will need to be repositioned as we go. As we cross, we'll take the boards from behind the car and place them in front. In this way, we can cross the whole expanse."

And so it went. Lamine crept along while Lanciné and I balanced on the tracks, careful to watch our footing. It was dicey. Several times, a warped board kicked out beneath the weight of the Renault, and Lamine backed up slowly until we put another in its place. We were literally creating the bridge as we went. After about thirty minutes, we reached the far end, and safely continued on our way. I breathed a sigh of relief.

We passed through several small villages that I assumed were Babila, Kato, and Fadama, and occasionally stopped to greet people. In Baro, we took a break for coffee at the local café, and struck up a conversation with some locals. Baro was the end of our dusty path, and it was here that the main route to Kouroussa was accessible. As we approached the intersection, a giant billboard greeted us.

EBOLA IS REAL.

It was a stark reminder. The Ebola epidemic in Guinea, while mostly under control at that point, was still a concern. Almost three years had passed since the initial outbreak, but new cases were still reported in parts of Guinea. Throughout the crisis, rumors and misinformation about Ebola proliferated almost as fast as the disease. Some thought it was a hoax. Efforts to control the disease were not paired with enough public education, resulting in a unique sort of problem in traditional villages. In one incident, villagers attacked and killed eight health care workers. Without sufficient explanation, the villagers knew only that strange people wearing white hazmat suits were pulling family members from their houses. Days later, those family members were dead. Villagers put two and two together, and assumed the foreign health workers were murdering their loved ones.

Out here, I wondered about the sign's efficacy. Few people read. I asked Lanciné if he knew anyone affected by the crisis.

"Everybody here knows someone killed by Ebola. We lived in terror. For a time, nobody left their houses. We feared our own neighbors. Thanks to Allah, my family was spared."

It was straight out of an apocalyptic horror story. Though there had been an earlier breakout in the Congo in 1976, this particular outbreak began in 2013. A young boy from the Nzérékoré forest region of Guinea was the first case. Scientists believe that bats spread the virus, and the forest region is home to large colonies of Angolan free-tailed bats. Human transmission of the disease occurs easily through bodily fluids —mainly blood, feces, or vomit. Saliva, sweat, tears, breast milk, urine, and semen can also transmit the virus. The average fatality rate was a staggering fifty percent, with rates nearing ninety percent in rural communities lacking access to health facilities. Contracting Ebola was a certain death warrant.

"The disease does not care if you are rich or poor, black or white," Lanciné said. "It erases all social boundaries. One day, epidemics like this will be all-too common. You will see. Even America will not be spared. Maybe then, the world will see we are all equal."

The sad truth is that poor communities always suffer the greatest during such times. Crises like these always pit human nature against altruism. Given the great inequality that already exists in places like America, I cringed to think of what a crisis like Ebola would reveal. At this point, the possibility of a pandemic like Covid-19 wasn't on anyone's mind. But we still had epidemics of our own making.

"In America, we have the opioid epidemic," I offered. "Many people in my country suffer from this." Saying it like this was skirting the truth of my situation. My heart uttered a muffled cry, barely audible over the buzz of opioids streaming through my own body.

"I have not heard of this," Lanciné said. "Is it a deadly illness?"

I sighed. Maybe I didn't want to get into this right now. "Well, something like four hundred thousand people have died from it in the past ten years, and millions of others are sick with it. So yeah, it's a big problem."

"I am surprised I have not heard about it. Is there no cure?"

I humphed, not sure how to answer. I had little time to ponder my response anyway. Halfway to Kouroussa, we ran out of gas.

35

FEELING LUCKY

BY THE TIME we reached the nearest gas station on foot, the heat of the day was at its peak. I drained the last drops of my water bottle into my mouth, and swished it around to bring some relief to my parched tongue.

The station was unimpressive, with a tiny store at one end of a dilapidated lot. Thick iron chains hung across the door. A young woman sat outside, next to the station's solitary pump. She spoke French with a thick accent.

"The pumps are dry," she informed us in an equally dry tone. "The truck will not come until tomorrow. Or maybe the day after." She was sweating profusely, and didn't seem well. "There is another station several kilometers from here. They may still have gas. I do not know."

This was not turning out to be my lucky day. I turned to Lanciné for his thoughts. His face was grim.

"Daouda, you will stay here. Lamine and I will get a ride to the next station."

I would have objected, if not for the rising pain in my hips and back. My limping steps on the walk here had slowed us down considerably.

"Fine. Do you think—"

"*Insh'allah.*" It was futile to ask whether there would be gas at the next station.

Lamine and Lanciné set out on foot. If any cars passed, they might be able to flag down a ride. The heat rising from the pavement blurred their figures as they grew smaller in the distance.

The woman shuffled away to retrieve a second chair. When she returned, she was winded. Beads of sweat covered her forehead. She set the chair down next to hers. I sat warily, not wanting to get too close.

Ebola is real, I thought. *Jesus.* I hoped all she had was a light case of malaria or yellow fever. Ebola made those illnesses seem like child's play.

We exchanged a few pleasantries, but I could tell she wasn't up for much conversation. We fell into silence. My thoughts turned restlessly.

Viruses and bacteria. The planet's oldest forms of life. They've played a crucial role in the evolution of life, shaping the genomes of all species—we simply wouldn't be what we are without them. We tend to regard them as invaders of the human world, but the converse is far truer. It's a viral world, and we are the newcomers to their planet. Epidemics are part of the system by which the planet has always maintained equilibrium. In the modern world, we transport bacteria and viruses readily across countries and even continents. Elements of human "progress" such as planes, trains, and automobiles, coupled with overpopulation, have accelerated the pace at which viruses and bacteria can proliferate. In response to our overgrowth, they'll do what they've always done: enforce the rules of their planet.

Still, to us humans, bacteria and viruses are a bit of a wet blanket. An overgrowth of klebsiella was, at this very moment, causing my pain to soar again. I reached into my pocket and dumped a pair of white pills into my grimy hand. I imagined all manner of invisible critters climbing aboard, taking a free ride into a new host. *Oh, what the hell.* I choked the pills down without any water. They'd do nothing to halt the spread of klebsiella in my body, nor would they halt an epidemic, but at least they'd provide some temporary relief.

So what *does* halt the spread, I wondered? If bacteria like klebsiella have been around since the beginning of time, surely the plant world has developed mechanisms for coping with them. Artemisia, for example, cures malaria, which is caused by the plasmodium parasite. Local cultures in rural China have known about this remedy for centuries. I figured there was probably a natural remedy that would make our bodies less hospitable for klebsiella, and thus lessen the effects of ankylosing spondylitis—we just hadn't found it yet.

I absentmindedly pulled out my phone to check the time. Three o'clock. Lanciné and Lamine had been gone a half-hour already. I noticed I had two bars of reception, and nearly a full battery thanks to Lanciné's generator. Maybe I could pass the time surfing the internet. That was a luxury I hadn't afforded myself in weeks. Maybe I'd learn something new.

I opened the magic eight-ball known as Google, and gave it a spin. I tapped out the words "natural treatment for ankylosing spondylitis" and touched the button for "I'm Feeling Lucky." Oh baby, was I feeling lucky today.

A blog post by an Australian woman popped up. It was dated just a few months earlier. *Recent stuff,* I thought. *Good.*

This poor gal also suffered from AS. I skimmed the article, and my heart almost stopped. She had found a treatment. Her disease was in remission. I blinked, and rubbed my eyes to make sure I read the words right:

Apple cider vinegar.

I laughed out loud, and the feverish young woman stared at me blankly. I read on.

One of my readers, John, left a comment telling me that drinking apple cider vinegar removed all his symptoms of AS. This has been life-changing for me. Vinegar is the best treatment I have found, and after a year on vinegar, I still feel great.

"Hot *damn!*" I exclaimed out loud. "Are you fucking *kidding* me?!" My heart raced. The young woman looked at me as if I had gone mad.

But this was no delusion. Apparently, apple cider vinegar becomes alkaline in the body, and can alter the gut microbiome and thus affect the body's inflammatory response. Unsurprisingly, very little research had been done on it. But as I read the rest of the article, it became evident this woman knew a thing or two. Like me, she had done her research and was familiar with Dr. Ebringer's work on klebsiella and

AS. For her, a strict low-starch diet combined with apple cider vinegar four times a day had done the trick. Dozens of commenters to the blog post confirmed it was working for them, too.

Well, then! This changes pretty much everything.

Clearly, I had to find some of this stuff. Did apples even grow in Guinea? I thought I remembered seeing them in a market once. If they had apples here, then surely they could make vinegar from it?

Just then, a truck approached noisily, and pulled into the gas station. A thick cloud of dust kicked up as it spun to a stop in front of the pumps. Out of the dust emerged Lanciné and Lamine, looking like a pair of haggard warriors. They each held several bottles of gasoline.

Maybe this *was* my lucky day after all.

"Daouda, get in," Lanciné directed me. "This man will take us to the Renault. We will be on our way to your new art studio shortly!"

We made it to Kouroussa by late afternoon. En route, we passed the old homestead of my hero, Camara Laye, and continued onward to the Total station in town for a proper tank of gas. I wasn't fooling around this time. I shelled out almost seventy dollars for a full tank. The attendant was shocked as I handed him a half-million Guinea francs. This was his lucky day, too—few people actually *filled* their tanks here. I gleefully handed him an extra 20,000 as a tip. As we pulled away, I shouted out the window, *"Alhamdulillah! God is fucking great!"*

I was suddenly having a grand time. Kouroussa looked like an oasis after a month in the village. I scoured the landscape for the magical African apple orchards that I just knew must be hidden in plain sight. I saw only mangoes. A few papaya trees.

"Lanciné," I said. "We have to stop at the marketplace. There's something I need."

"Oh?" he replied. "Ah yes, we should buy some supplies. It is getting late. We may need to spend the night in Kouroussa."

I hadn't thought about that. I supposed that once we found Famoudou's house, we could stay the night. *At my new art studio,* I reminded myself.

"Yeah, sure. Let's pick up some food to cook. But do you know where to find apple cider vinegar?"

He looked at me quizzically.

"*Qu'est-ce que c'est?*" he asked. "What's that?"

"*Vinaigre de cidre,*" I repeated, more slowly this time. "*De pomme.*" I was sure he'd understand.

"Never heard of it."

My heart sank. I didn't know how else to explain it.

"Daouda, we can ask around at the market. But I grew up here, and know the markets well. I do not think what you are asking for exists here."

I wasn't giving up hope that easily. We parked the car on a side street and headed into the Kouroussa market on foot. Crowded stalls overflowed with vegetables, herbs, and fruits, but I didn't find a single apple. Lanciné didn't have the translation for *vinaigre de cidre* in Malinké, and most of the vendors didn't speak French.

"Daouda, perhaps we can try in Kindia. It is several hours away, but is a much bigger town than Kouroussa. We may have better luck there. Later this week, we can make the trip."

I was slightly dejected, but had to give up the ghost, for now. To be honest, I was freaking out with the thought that a cure was so close, yet so far away. Kindia was my best hope. But there were other matters to attend to first. After stocking up on snacks, dinner supplies, and coffee for the morning, we placed a call to Famoudou's caretaker, Sori. He was nearby and would meet us at the house with the key. We were only a mile or so away. I hopped into the Renault, tore open a canister of Pringles, and off we went.

When we arrived, the sun was setting. Famoudou's one-story house consisted of a half-dozen rooms, motel-style, with a courtyard at the center. Outside, some of Famoudou's extended family were busy preparing dinner over an open pit fire. They greeted the newcomers cautiously, and Lanciné explained who we were. They eyeballed me with amusement. I was an unlikely guest, and the idea that I'd be staying here to make art was an oddity.

Sori arrived on a motorcycle and pulled out an impressive bundle of keys. Each room had its own entryway, with a large padlock. It took nearly twenty minutes to find the right keys for the two rooms Famoudou had allotted us. One would be my own private room, and the other would be for Lanciné and Lamine.

The sun went down, and darkness fell fast. As expected, the electricity was out, but I was all charged up, in more ways than one. I retrieved a solar lantern and a headlamp from the car, and shone the light in my new room. It was small, and perfectly sparse. Against the wall, a wooden bed frame supported a musty mattress. Above it was a small window with iron bars. A single pace from the bed, a wooden desk and a plastic chair waited expectantly. That was all. It was my new art studio, and it was perfect.

The three of us enjoyed a humble dinner in the open air of the courtyard. I felt rejuvenated. Stars appeared above us, and all of Kouroussa fell quiet. A fire crackled nearby. In the twilight, bats fluttered. We pulled some chairs together and passed a tobacco pipe, relishing the cool air that descended. It had been quite the day, and I found myself once again in new surroundings. New hope lay before me, and I was eager to find out what the future held in store.

I awoke at sunrise, rested and alert. Golden light streamed through the tiny window and fell directly upon the wooden desk, as if the gods themselves were illuminating it for me. I taped a piece of high-quality Bristol vellum paper to my drawing board, and chose some pencils. I sat down to draw, and in contented silence, I invoked the muse of my childhood. As a new day was reborn from the ashes of yesterday, the images appeared before me.

In the three days that followed, I left the room only to eat meals with Lanciné and Lamine, who otherwise contented themselves to head into town with the money I happily provided them. Drawing after drawing came off my board and went into the little black portfolio case. My soul was alive again, and joy streamed into my heart like the rays of sunlight lighting my little art studio in Kouroussa.

On the fourth day, we readied ourselves for a trip to Kindia. I was feeling lucky.

36

BREAKDOWN IN KINDIA

MY BRIEF, flirtatious affair with Luck ended abruptly in Kindia. There was no reason given, no sad love letter to explain our breakup. Just an African town hit by strikes and violence. Marketplaces were closed and shuttered. The chances I'd find *vinaigre de cidre* here were slim to none. I suspected Luck simply ran off with someone better looking than me. Or maybe the gods knew I'd abandon the remaining tasks and return to America if I found my cure. They weren't going to let me off *that* easy.

In any case, the Renault had started to overheat during the two-hour drive. By the time we reached Kindia, the engine was complaining loudly. The problem was beyond Lamine's capabilities. We'd have to find a more capable repairman.

Instead of guzzling down fresh apple cider vinegar and being on my way to pain-free heaven, I found myself baking in the sun at a dirty junkyard. We tracked down a mechanic willing to work on our car, but we needed parts. It was up to us to scour the heaps of junk for the right ones.

Meanwhile, Klebsiella found the pain control dial and turned it up to motherfucking *eleven*. It was screeching. My temper flared out of control. I lashed out at both Lanciné and Lamine. We bickered about pointless things, and Lanciné became disgusted with my disrespectful attitude. Fed up with the situation, I stormed off into Kindia. It was a brash and stupid move that only made me feel more alienated and alone. But I needed to cool down and get my *shit* together, man. My hopes at permanent pain relief had been dashed, the cure dangling just out of reach. It seemed cruel. And in the heat, my thoughts turned desperate and irrational. The ancestors were fucking with me, goddammit, and I was pissed at them for it. I suddenly wanted nothing more to do with this whole African spiritual quest bullshit.

I limped along the streets of Kindia for several hours. I passed buildings that had recently been burned down, and saw cars that had been torched in recent clashes with the police. Some of them were still smoldering, like the anger inside me. I wanted to seize this destruction and turn it on my pain. On myself. Maybe I'd go crazy right here in Kindia, and turn into some raving revolutionary type. I'd go down in a blaze of glory, guns smoking. In disgusted, self-destructive fury, I angrily popped two more pills. *Take that, motherfucker.*

I was gone a long time. I'm sure Lanciné worried about me. In my anger-fueled delusion, I actually wanted him to worry. I didn't know who to be angry with anymore. But as the day continued, I struggled to remember what we had actually argued about. God knows, none of this was his fault. He was trying to help me. Guilt soon overtook my anger. *Man, I am being such a dick.* I pictured Lanciné's kind face as he picked me up from the dirt that night in the sacred grove. He had put his arm around me and walked me back to safety. I remembered, too, how his eyes had welled up with tears after the sacrifice.

Daouda, our hearts are wide open to you. Allah a nöya ké—may God make you well. We will continue to pray for you.

Shit. I knew I needed to go back and apologize—if only I knew where the hell I was. I stopped walking, and looked around. I had no idea what route I had taken. I was lost.

The narcotics were not my friend on the streets of Kindia. On an empty stomach, they kicked in hard and fast. My head was buzzing, my thoughts jumbled. *C'mon, focus!* I was going in circles. And worse, ragged locals were looking at me suspiciously. On the backstreets of a tumultuous African town, I was conspicuously out of place, the only white guy for miles. I easily had a hundred bucks in my pocket, a small fortune here. If ever there was an easy target, I was it.

My anger dissipated, along with the false bravado I felt while storming around Kindia. Fear took its place. I was alone and vulnerable in unfamiliar territory. So I did what any courageous adventurer would do in this situation: I sat down and cried. I raked my own unkempt hair and gnashed my teeth. I apologized to the gods for being such an ungrateful little shit. I lamented not seeing all the good in my life. I thought about my new studio in Kouroussa, and all the art I had recently made. It was *good*, dammit, and kind people had helped me do it while they struggled for their very existence. I envisioned the people I had drawn, and the suffering they endured every day.

By comparison, I had it easy. My family back home loved and cared about me. I'm sure they missed me, too. Each time I headed off on another crazy adventure, they were left to wonder if or when I'd ever return. Kerri had put up with me for so many years, and I never even saw how much she loved me. I knew I was loved and admired by friends, too, though I never could see why. I was imperfect, a failure at everything I did, and I was ashamed of it. I sabotaged any chance of a meaningful relationship. And I knew full well that taking pills day and night were destroying me, but I didn't even love myself enough to stop.

Why was I being so self-destructive? Why would anyone destroy so much good? I didn't know if I could repair the damage I had done. I hoped my loved ones back home would forgive me for taking them for granted. For turning my back on them. For turning my back on *myself*.

I glanced around me through tears of pain and sorrow. *Kindia! Oh, Jesus, I am so far from home.* No angel would rescue me this time. If I was going to make things right, I had to do it myself.

The reality of my situation struck me. A potential natural treatment awaited me, but I was never going to find it here in Africa. No, if I were to put an end to twenty years of pain and suffering, I would have to go home for it. But the only way home was to finish what I had started here.

I picked myself up and brushed the dirt off my jeans. I didn't have a clue where to start, but as the saying goes, a journey of a thousand miles begins with a single step. I placed one foot in front of the other and started walking.

Follow your heart. It was the only thing I knew how to do. I turned down a side street, then another. The buildings became vaguely familiar. I kept going.

When I finally found the old junkyard an hour later, Lanciné and Lamine were sitting in the Renault listening to cassettes of Guinean Afropop. I was stunned to see the car was repaired.

"Daouda, you are late. We were worried." Lanciné's face was stern.

"I know, Lanciné. I'm sorry. And I'm sorry for the way I treated you." It was all I could say. I bowed my head and looked down at my feet, which were barely recognizable beneath the grime.

"It's OK, Daouda. Look, we got you some fresh fruits and vegetables. Mangoes and pineapple. No *vinaigre de cidre*, though. But we got tomatoes and cucumbers, too, and your favorite—avocados. You can eat on the way home. We've got a long way to go."

I thought about that word, *home.*

Yes, I had a long way to go.

37

A VISIT TO THE HEALER

THE SEASONS WERE CHANGING. Billowy clouds formed on the horizon and threatened rain, but none fell. The heat became stifling. The days passed in a torturous march of alternating pain and hope, and my disposition darkened like the clouds that grew on the horizon.

I readied myself for the final stage of my quest, without knowing when it would come. At the end was the promise of a cure, but the obstacles between it and me were frustratingly elusive. Each morning, I asked if there had been any word from Famoudou. The response was always the same. No one had heard a thing.

At night, Sako Gbè and his sorceress wife Mousso haunted my dreams. I had to find her, and I was growing uneasy about it. I became more superstitious with every passing day. The ancestors controlled my fate, but communicating with them was beyond any ability I possessed. I understood with certainty that only Mousso Gbè could help me. I needed her magic. It was she alone who could release me from Africa.

The novelty of village life had worn off, and Africa's seductive rhythms were overpowering me. I knew that if I failed in my quest, Africa would simply absorb me. My life would pass into meaningless anonymity. Somewhere, someday, an unmarked grave in Africa might hold the bones of an inconsequential traveler. There would be no stories recounting my desperate journey here. No one to remember me. Like all things, I would return to dust and fade away.

Lanciné and I pushed forward with our flute apprenticeship, but I no longer knew why. I found little meaning or purpose in the music. Nonetheless, we passed our days in a field on the village outskirts, where we played undisturbed. Despite my despondence, I became proficient at much of the music. At Lanciné's insistence, I kept a notebook of the songs we learned, and the list grew. Each morning, Lanciné asked me to play through the repertoire alone, and after a time, I didn't even need to open the notebook. I knew them all by heart. But it did little to satisfy me.

In the late afternoons, Lanciné and I often played for the villagers. Though I was unsatisfied with my progress, people were pleased, and would comment.

"Daouda, you are Malinké now. Never have I heard a white man play our songs like this before. This is important work that you do!"

I would put on a fine show for them, but after they left, only pain remained. I suspected it might never go away, and in the end it would consume me. Music alone would never save me.

Several times a week, we visited El Hadji and his family. These trips were the only light that broke through my dark disposition. In truth, they filled my stomach with little butterflies because Aminata was there. Her language games were a nice diversion, and her easy laughter delighted me. We teased each other incessantly, and were no longer shy about it. El Hadji took notice.

"Daouda, if you should decide to remain here in the village, my daughter is a fine woman. She needs a husband. You are welcome here in my home."

The thought both exhilarated and terrified me. Was it for this that my quest of healing had brought me back to Africa? Could I find peace with a life here, and live out the rest of my days in the village? There are many crossroads on the fleeting pathways of our exile. It was hard to say which route I would choose. Too much remained to be seen.

When the language games were over, however, Aminata and I had little to say to each other. After a time, we'd fall into long stretches of silence. The language divide was too wide to cross. When the silence between us grew too deep, I turned to Lanciné for help, but he quickly tired of being our translator.

"Daouda, you must improve your Malinké on your own. How is it that you cannot yet speak our language? You are like a child."

His words injured me. I was trying my hardest, and felt I had made some progress.

"How is it that you cannot yet speak mine?" I retorted. "English is such an easy language to learn." I doubted that was true, but I wasn't about to backtrack.

"I have no use for your language, Daouda. English is an ugly language. French is no better. But Malinké is beautiful on the ears, like water flowing over rocks."

It was hard to disagree with the last part. I often found myself carried away in its rhythmic cadence. Malinké filled my dreams now, though the words carried little meaning. I was incredulous that one could master a language as difficult as Malinké in such a short time. Regardless, as we sat around the fire at El Hadji's home, I tried to mimic the words, like a baby learning its mother tongue. Occasionally, I'd unconsciously do this out loud. People would hear me mirroring them, and they'd exclaim amusedly, *"Daouda be diyaamoo Maninkakan!* Daouda is speaking Malinké!" They were taunting me, though, for I was little more than a parrot.

During long afternoons at El Hadji's, the unending stream of nonsensical words fatigued me. One day, amidst an enthusiastic conversation in which I played absolutely no part, I rose abruptly and announced that I'd be off. I wanted to be alone with my thoughts.

"Lanciné, I'll see you at home." I grabbed my backpack and hoped he wouldn't object. I knew the way, and the sun was still high.

Lanciné sprang to his feet. "Daouda, you cannot go alone. It is too dangerous."

"Ha! It is not. You think I am a child, but I am a grown man. I want to walk alone."

"No," he insisted. "I will fetch Lamine, and he will bring the car. Since you are in a hurry to get home, we will drive the path together. Look, I am ready to go now."

"No! I want to walk," I repeated. "I'm going—*alone.*"

I was trying his patience. And it wasn't just this. My erratic moods and constant needs had been wearing on him.

He folded his arms across his chest. "Daouda, I forbid you."

"You *what?* Huh! Lanciné, you cannot forbid me to do anything. I am not your possession. I am a free man."

Lanciné was suspicious. "Why do you insist on being alone? Ah-*hah!* You are trying to run away. Yes, I see your plan now. You will go to Baro or Fadama and you will try to find someone else to care for you."

The thought had never occurred to me. "Lanciné, I am not running away. I just want to walk. Back home, I walk all the time. We do it for the pleasure of it. It's good for your health. All we do here is sit, and I'm tired of sitting."

"Walking is *not* good for the health. Everybody knows this."

"Is too. And you of all people should walk more. When was the last time you took your blood pressure medicine?"

Lanciné said nothing. I suspected he had stopped taking it again.

El Hadji was listening to our argument, and joined in. "I have heard this to be true, Lanciné. Walking helps lower the blood pressure. A doctor once told me this. I, too, have elevated blood pressure, and I walk every day. Doctor's orders. Go on, Lanciné, if he wants to walk, let him walk. Walking is good."

El Hadji's words carried weight.

"You are sure about this?" Lanciné was concerned about his blood pressure, of course. The fear in his eyes told me this curse still weighed on him.

"Yes," El Hadji replied. "Daily walks are quite good for the health."

I gloated a little, but Lanciné only frowned. To him, walking was a chore, and he associated it with poverty. Wealthy people drove; poor people walked. And what's more, it reflected badly on him if people saw me, the *tubabu* in his charge, walking alone in the hot sun.

Lanciné tried another tactic.

"Daouda, in the village, we have traditional medicine for blood pressure. I have recently spoken to the healer, and he has agreed to prepare the medicine for me. From now on, I will take village medicine. You can try some too."

Though I had been close to making my getaway, this stopped me in my tracks.

"You spoke to the healer?" I had been asking him for weeks to take me. "You know how much I want to speak to this man." Lanciné was playing me like a fiddle.

"Yes. I will take you later this afternoon. But by the time we finish, it will be too late to walk home. We will have no choice but to drive."

I grunted. He had me cornered. I couldn't walk home now, because the healer was in *this* village. If I left, I would miss the opportunity. Lanciné was acting like a dealer at a blackjack table—and holding the cards of my health. I suspected the table was rigged, but I didn't know the game well enough.

"You promise?"

"Yes, Daouda. We will go see him *directement* after lunch."

I grunted again and swung my bag to the dirt. It wasn't clear if I had won or lost the argument. When lunch came, I ate rapidly, and tapped my foot impatiently while Lanciné lingered over scraps of bony river fish.

The healer lived on the opposite end of the village from El Hadji. When we were on our way at last, my heart fluttered with anticipation. Hope glimmered, however dimly, but I held on to it. If something as simple as apple cider vinegar could put AS into remission, then surely some African plant existed that could do the same. People here suffered from arthritis too, so they must have a remedy. And since I basically had severe arthritis of the spine, a village herbalist might at least prescribe a remedy to alleviate my pain. Or, perhaps this healer worked in the spiritual realm, and treated the types of imbalances I assumed were at the root of my problems. If that were the case, I'd be keen to glean any new information about arcane topics like ancestors and curses. If it seemed appropriate, I might even inquire what he knew about Mousso Gbè. Thus far, her whereabouts remained a mystery.

Past visits to Africa had taught me that there are two broad categories of healers in the village, what we could describe as *leaf healers* and *spirit healers*. Many Malinké healers work in both domains to some extent, but leaf healers are specialists in the plant world. In the Malinké worldview, plants, like all of nature, are charged with *nyama*. But the medicinal properties of plants are as complex and diverse as the forest itself. Since the difference between a healing medicine and a fatal poison is often only a matter of dosage, a leaf healer must be intimately familiar with the specific *nyama* of each plant. Obtaining a working knowledge of this living pharmacopeia, however, requires a lifelong immersion in a culture that has consumed, observed, and listened to the plant world for thousands of years. Leaf healers are repositories of ancestral healing knowledge—and they're a dying breed.

Spirit healers are a different genre, but essentially work in the same dynamic realm of *nyama*. These are the sorcerers, those initiated into a domain where ancestors walk unseen among the living. The sorcerer communicates with these spirits, and receives guidance on how to work with the wild forces of nature. Their work generally falls into one of three categories: *somaya* is the creation of fetish objects such as masks and amulets; *domaya* involves the reading of cowries and foretelling the future; and *suya* deals with black magic. All three terms refer to sorcery in a broad sense, and at times are interchangeable. But while anyone can technically become a *subaa* (sorcerer) and practice *suya*, the arts of *somaya* and *domaya* require long apprenticeship and extensive training. What they all share is a proficiency with *nyama*—often coercing it into potent amalgamations that allow them to heal, curse, counter evil forces, or even divine the future.

When we arrived, I wasn't sure which kind of healer we were visiting. My expectations were as wild as the plants that overran his untamed courtyard. I had to keep an open mind and my wits about me. Once again, I ventured into unknown territory.

We found the healer outside, hunched on his heels. His hut was simple, even by village standards. In front of it, a kettle boiled over an open fire. Clusters of exotic plants grew in small garden patches. I wandered over to inspect them, and a particularly wild patch caught my eye. It was a robust, leafy green plant that culminated in small yellow flowers shaped like starfish. I wondered if this, or another plant like it, might contain a medicine for my condition.

I greeted the old man in French. He shook his head and laughed. To my chagrin, he didn't speak a word of it. I'd have to rely on Lanciné for translation, and at the moment I wasn't high on expectations about Lanciné's motivation for coming here.

We seated ourselves on the ground in front of the healer. I wasted no time getting to the heart of the matter, and Lanciné translated into Malinké. I picked out little phrases.

"*A kö ye a diminna*—he has a bad back.*" Lanciné traced my spine with his finger to illustrate. Perhaps he was under-explaining it, but he said a lot of other things too. The healer nodded. So far, so good.

I went on, emphasizing that a shaman had sent me here to make amends with the ancestors. I waited expectantly for the corresponding Malinké word for ancestor, *keebaafóloo*. It never came. I suspected Lanciné wasn't translating word for word. Or perhaps the topic of ancestors wasn't this man's realm?

"Lanciné, make sure you tell him about the ancestors," I insisted.

He held his hand up, brushing me off. "I have told him what you said. Now, we will wait for his response."

The healer spoke for a long time, and Lanciné nodded here and there, interjecting occasionally. I repeatedly heard the word for high blood pressure, *tension*. There's no word for it in Malinké, so they both used the French word. I also picked out the Malinké word for malaria, *denbalen*. Apparently, they were discussing Lanciné's health concerns—not mine.

I leaned back, frustrated with my inability to communicate directly. But at last, the healer turned to me for an examination. He pulled off my shirt a bit roughly, and then ran his calloused fingers along my spine. Occasionally he would say "*Uh-huh!*" or "Hmmm, *n see...*" I was uncomfortable and exposed, sitting there shirtless and pale in the healer's open courtyard. Other villagers stopped what they were doing to stare at this spectacle.

The old man spoke again, and Lanciné translated.

"The healer will gather plants for both of us. He has some of these on hand." He gestured to the green plants with yellow flowers I had studied earlier. "But there are others he will need to gather in the bush."

Once he has gathered them, he will boil them, put them into bottles, and leave them in the sun for several days."

I nodded, feeling somewhat satisfied, and we agreed on a price.

"Since Lamine lives close by," Lanciné explained, "I will have him check in with the healer. Lamine can send word when the preparations are ready."

As we prepared to take our leave, I remembered to ask about the old sorceress.

"Lanciné, ask him about Mousso Gbè."

He didn't need to ask. At the mention of her name, the healer's eyes opened wide. He spat out a burst of fast Malinké that contained the word *subaa*, meaning sorcerer, and *suya*, for *sorcellerie*, the art of witchcraft. I gulped. The two men went back and forth for a few moments. I followed their conversation like watching a tennis match from center court. At last, Lanciné nodded and spoke to me.

"He says the woman is still alive. She lives outside the village, but he does not know where. She has not been seen for some time."

The healer narrowed his eyes at me. I thanked him for his time, but he said nothing. He stood and watched me suspiciously until we were out of sight.

By the time we returned to El Hadji's compound, the sun was about to set. The Renault was parked in front of the hut, and I noticed that Lamine had recently washed it. The front bumper was mostly fixed, and I imagined I'd be receiving a bill for this sometime soon.

As we approached, a flurry of commotion and high-pitched shrieks arose from inside the house. Several loud thumps were followed by a violent ruckus.

Aminata ran from the house, screaming.

"*Kösön!*" she cried. The blood drained from my face. A moment later, Lamine emerged, proudly carrying the scorpion in a small jar. I ran over to see. It looked like a miniature dragon.

"It is nothing," he told us. "Just a tiny scorpion." Before I could object, he emptied the jar into the fire, and the dragon's body crackled and was consumed by flames. "Come, we go now. It is getting late."

I put my hands to my face and groaned. *I might never be so frigging lucky.* The gods were clearly taunting me. One tiny sting—was that too much to ask?

We climbed into the Renault, and our tires kicked up a wall of dust as we lumbered off into the bush. I wouldn't get my walk today, but I suppose something like progress had taken place. As we drove away, pain coursed through my body like venom.

Scorpions and sorcerers, I thought. My whole life, it seemed, had come down to this.

38

WHEN THE LEVEE BREAKS

It is hard to relate with certainty the sequence of days now. Perhaps it is because Africa has me in her enchanted spell, or maybe it's because I've started taking the pills night and day. My supplies are dwindling, and the days are indistinguishable, just one uninterrupted line of pain. I sleep very little, troubled by the thought of facing Mousso Gbè. Her dark magic weighs on me. Famoudou's continued absence is disturbing. I worry for his safety.

Now as Lanciné and I walk the path between villages, I think it may be for the last time. The corrosive effect of the past few months has taken its toll. Whatever emotional levee has held me together thus far is crumbling. It's only a matter of time before the levee breaks. I fear the impending flood.

As for Lanciné, I don't know how he puts up with me. I'm constantly irritable, consumed by pain, and prone to erratic mood swings because of the pills. Finding apple cider vinegar in Africa remains a fool's quest. I held on to hope for as long as I could, but now dark thoughts consume me. Lanciné's patience is not without end. He too is nearing his limit. Just a week ago, he suggested the unthinkable.

"Daouda, Famoudou is not coming. You must accept this. We should return to Conakry at once."

We were sitting in a field when he said it, taking a break from our flute lessons. The suggestion infuriated me. I didn't believe him. I suspected he was hiding something from me. For reasons I couldn't see, he had given up on our mission.

And you, Lanciné, shall accompany him to the village. You will see to it that all is done as I have described. The traditions will be respected.

Famoudou's words were law to me. Lanciné was bound to this quest, same as me.

My son, I shall see you again before the rains come.

The clouds were gathering, and the rains were on their way. Perhaps they would be early this year. Lanciné was eager to return before they came, but I had promised to wait. If I left now, and didn't finish what I came to do, then what?

"Lanciné, if you need to return to Conakry, so be it. I understand. But I am *not* leaving. I will stay here alone if I have to."

"You will not survive here without me," he said. "You are an *étranger*, and do not know the ways of the village. Famoudou is not coming. You will perish here, Daouda."

"That would be preferable to leaving. I am *not* giving up."

He sighed, and shook his head slowly. He was right though—if he left, who would take me in? El Hadji? I would need to marry his daughter, but I couldn't speak the language well enough. Plus, I was nearly out of money. I had nothing to offer these people. I would only be a burden to them.

I wanted to cry right then and there, but my pride disallowed it. Instead, I picked up a rock and hurled it as hard as I could, yelling in anguish. The quick movement caused a surge of pain that sent me to the ground. I turned my face from Lanciné, and bit down hard to suppress the tears that tried to escape me.

Lanciné looked at me, bewildered, but not without compassion.

After a long silence, he spoke.

"Daouda, we will stay here one more week." He was resolute, but offered a compromise. "If Famoudou does not arrive, we will go and find Mousso Gbè ourselves. Find her or not, we will return to Conakry. Enough is enough."

I stared at him blankly. We would be defying Famoudou's orders.

But under the circumstances, surely the old man would understand? My heart raced at the thought of seeking the sorceress alone. If we found her, I could be done with this torment. The waiting would be over, and I could return home to the cure that awaited.

Whether we succeeded or not, I sensed our quest was coming to an end.

"One week," I said. "And then you must help me find the old woman. I need you to help me with this. You must promise."

"I promise. But you must promise to return with me to Conakry afterward. *Es-tu d'accord?*"

"Yes, Lanciné. I agree to that." It was settled. I could ask no more of Lanciné. Looking now at my old friend sitting beneath the tree, I felt sorry to have put him through all this. I wished this trip could have been like all the others, carefree and joyful. These were strange times. Life had pushed me to the edge.

Lanciné picked up his flute and began to play. The solemn music echoed through the field. I sat beneath the tree next to him and picked up the melody. My emotions were flooding over. The levee was straining to hold them back.

$\approx$

I spent the final week at the art studio in Kouroussa, drawing like a man possessed. I ate little, and slept only when the light was too dim to work. And now, my little black portfolio case is filled with the only worldly possessions I still care about, more than two dozen completed drawings. I wonder if they will ever see the light of day.

The week Lanciné promised me is up, and still no Famoudou. When we packed up our rooms in Kouroussa, swept the floors, and returned the keys to Sori, I said a somber farewell to my humble art studio, and the dream it had represented. I made good art in that little room, and reconnected with my muse. For this, at least, I am grateful.

We returned to the village last night at dusk, but when night fell, I barely slept. Strange sounds from outside the hut disturbed what little sleep there was. I tossed and turned uncomfortably on the hard ground.

I dreamt about the old blacksmith Sako Gbè, and trembled with fear at facing his sorceress wife.

When morning's light shone brightly, my thoughts were incoherent from lack of sleep. Dreams and reality blurred together. I felt frail and edgy, on the verge of total breakdown. When breakfast arrived, I had no appetite.

While Lanciné attended to his own pre-departure affairs, I pulled a rickety wooden chair behind the hut. These days, I want nothing more than to hide and to be alone. I wished I could escape the destiny before me, and the searing pain inside me.

I am the pain, and the pain is me. It is my curse to bear.

Rhythmic blows of the mortar and pestle resounded throughout the courtyard. A woman broke into song, softly at first, and then she was joined by another.

Eh Daouda lè! Dunin timba, tinya maka, Daouda!

The song was followed by laughter, and I could only wonder what the words meant.

I sat alone with my thoughts of the road that led me here. The memory of the old Huichol shaman arose, her weathered face illuminated by firelight a world away from here. I recalled her words that fateful night I was set on this quest.

If you do not do this, the pain they will inflict on you will only grow worse.

My mind turned to all I had left behind, and all I had lost along the way. Friends and family. My home in the mountains, now empty. Kerri, the love I took for granted. And Erik, the friend I hadn't saved.

Unconsciously, I reached into my pocket for the small plastic container. I listened for the familiar rattle inside. *Good. There are still some left.*

Another bolt of lightning shot through me, and it left me little recourse. I washed two down and waited for the sweet warmth.

When Lanciné found me some time later, he looked tired. His expression was devoid of the joy that normally lit his face.

"Daouda, *il faut y aller.* It's time to go. *Maintenant.*"

I rose reluctantly, and went into the hut to gather my belongings. Lanciné had been inquiring in the village, and had an idea now where we might find the old woman. It was just a lead, and nothing was certain. But still, it was something.

"And what about Famoudou—has there been any word?" I asked.

"I have no news about Famoudou. But time is growing short. You remember we agreed—"

"I know what we agreed, Lanciné."

He nodded, assessing my mood. "Do you have the book?"

"It's in my backpack."

I mustered up all the courage I could find. *Kewó jusôo nánta bennâ le.* One's heart must be courageous.

"*An nye wa,*" Lanciné said. *Let's go.*

I braced myself against the pain, and slung my pack onto my back with a grimace. I felt the weight of the book inside. Before turning to go, I picked up the small black portfolio case. *I have to guard it now. The drawings are all I have left.*

With a deep breath, I walk out of the hut and into the bright sunlight. Lanciné and I march slowly down familiar paths toward a meeting with destiny. There is no turning back now.

Our route takes us around the sacred grove, and we draw nearer to the opening that leads into wild country. The painkillers are kicking in, but the thunder rumbling in my spine and hips outpaces it. I try to hide my limp, as I don't want to raise any more arguments about our mode of transportation—or lack of it. But there is very little I can hide from Lanciné's watchful eyes.

"Daouda, there is no need to suffer so," he says. "We can drive *le véhicule* as far as the next village, and then walk from there. We still have far to go once we arrive."

We argue briefly about it, but in the end, the issue of our blood pressure settles it. Despite the great distance, we will walk.

A lead sun blazes above us, *un soleil de plomb.* Lanciné tells me it is the month called *taraba,* the time of the big heat. But before long, I again glimpse dark clouds in the distance.

"Lanciné, it looks like rain ahead."

"No, Daouda, I am not so sure. The clouds will build like this for many weeks. They are only taunting us. We will be gone before the rains come."

Lanciné and I trudge on, resting only occasionally. We have to push forward. My thoughts turn restlessly, trying to untangle the Gordian knot of my life. The memories of the past decades come into focus, often too painfully. The book weighs on me, for its significance has changed. It was the catalyst that propelled me here, but now, its magic lies in its ability to evoke the spirits of the people depicted within— especially those who have passed on. It drives me forward in a quest I don't fully understand, and burns on my back as we walk toward the dwelling place of Mousso Gbè.

Crossing over now from the forest trail onto dusty cow paths, Lanciné and I make our approach through the back of the village. Millet-stalk fences border the path here and there. Wood smoke reaches us as the first round huts appear on the horizon. The clay structures and thatched roofs seem to be a very part of the landscape, as if the houses had grown right out of the earth. No matter how many times I see it, the sight is still otherworldly to me. I remind myself that Malinké settlements in this region date at least seven thousand years, and perhaps even longer. A chapter from the book of human history is alive and spreading out before me. What is written there is not always clear.

We come to the path leading toward El Hadji's house. But this time, we follow a narrow path leading away from the village, through high grasses guarded by massive acajou trees. Low scrubby brush scratches my arms as we walk through the untamed territory. The path is not used often. Further in, the trail leads into dark forest. Lanciné and I enter it silently.

The ancestors are not to be fooled with. It would have been much better for you if this man was still alive.

The image of the late Sako Gbè appears before me. I can only push onward.

The trail twists and winds, and the forest encloses around me. I wonder what impish spirits reside here.

These djinn, they are there. You might think it is the breeze that touches you, but when you look, the air is quite still.

The forest is as still as a dead man. My skin prickles. Despite the heat, goosebumps cover my arms. Lanciné hastens his step, and I struggle to keep up with his long stride as bolts of electric pain shoot through my hips.

We emerge at last from the dim forest, and come to a part of the village I've never seen. We're a good way from where we started, but soon I hear flowing water. The Djoliba is near. Ahead, a settlement rises out of the landscape, almost indistinguishable from it. The huts are crude and dilapidated. The path leads us straight to them. As we approach, the river becomes visible through a stand of trees. Several women are washing clothes at the river's edge. Lanciné stops in front of the huts.

An old woman emerges, dressed in tattered rags. Her unkempt appearance startles me. Lanciné speaks.

"Mousso Gbè?"

The woman shakes her head. She points a spindly finger toward a disheveled hut at the perimeter of the settlement. Lanciné nods, and walks toward it. My heart beats heavily as I follow him. The hut is badly in need of repair. It makes my heart break, for it is the epitome of poverty, a life of certain sorrow and hunger. And it is the dwelling of the widow Mousso Gbè.

We peer into the dark abode. The hut is empty, and the old woman is nowhere to be seen. We ask the women at the river. One after another, the reply is the same. Mousso has not been here in weeks, and her whereabouts are unknown.

I feel the levee inside me straining. The stark reality hits me. We will never find Mousso, and time has run out. I have failed. The journey here is over.

The levee can hold no more. It breaks at last, and a flood of tears streams down my face.

Without warning, fat droplets of rain plummet from the sky, pelting us. The clouds can no longer hold it back, either. The shower lasts less than a minute, but it is a harbinger of change: the rains are on their way. And soon, I will be too.

39

FACING THE MONSTER

A DREADFUL MONSTER descends upon me in the pitch-dark hut. The beast has the body of a scorpion, but wears an enormous mask covered with amulets and cowry shells. Horns protrude from its hideous head, and it bares its sharp fangs at me. It is Kòmò, the ancient and terrible being who judges the deeds of humans and doles out punishments with severity.

I fight against the beast with all my might, striking at it with my bare fists. It's no good. I am guilty of a crime, and my time of reckoning has come. The monster is too powerful for me. I tumble backward and it falls upon me. Pain rips through my body as it sinks its fangs into my flesh. I let out a terrible cry that I know will be my last.

I awake from the dream breathless and drenched in sweat. All is still in the hut. My spine is on fire, and I have difficulty moving.

Lanciné speaks in the darkness. "Daouda, ça va? You cried out."

"Yes, Lanciné. Just a bad dream. I'm sorry to wake you."

"Ah. Go back to sleep, Daouda. We have much to do tomorrow."

I try to roll over, but the pain is fierce. Images of the monster linger in my head. Sleep does not come. Our departure is upon us, but a sense of foreboding plagues me.

∼

In the morning, we begin our preparations for the return trip. In the midst of packing, Lamine telephones. He must make some final repairs to the battered Renault. It has suffered nearly as much as me these past months. I have my doubts about its ability to carry us back across the countryside. The repairs, it turns out, will delay our departure—perhaps by several days.

Lamine has some other news. The village healer has delivered our herbal preparations. I had forgotten all about it. It feels like too little, too late, but curiosity burns inside me. Lamine will bring them to us in the evening.

The delay in departure also leaves Lanciné and me time to complete my flute training. We are in the midst of several challenging pieces, and it serves as a good diversion for us both.

When we are not occupied with our lessons, I want only to be alone. I slip away for frequent walks, and it bothers Lanciné. His ever-present watch is wearing on me. I know he suspects I will try to run away, and now the thought does cross my mind. I know the way to Baro and Fadama, but I sense running away would be pointless. Even if I did find someone to take me in, a *tubabu's* whereabouts in these villages could only be hidden for so long.

In the late afternoon, Lanciné and I head to a field at the far end of the village to work on our final lessons, away from the prying eyes of the villagers. As we play, I gaze out on the field, and am taken up in the serenity of it. Several cows graze nearby, free to roam as usual. But one is tied to a post. I find it strange.

We take a break from playing, and I ask Lanciné about it.

"That cow is not from here," he replies. "It is an *étranger*, like you. It must be tied up so it does not run away."

A sudden realization strikes me. Anger swells inside me like a sudden tempest.

"Oh, so I am like your cow, Lanciné? That is why you keep such close watch over me? Why don't you just tie me to a post?"

"I would if I could." His words sting me like a poison-tipped arrow.

"Lanciné! I am *not* your possession. Huh! Perhaps I *should* run away. Maybe to Baro or Fadama, like you said."

I'm fuming. I pick up my belongings, ready to storm off.

"Daouda, no! You mustn't run away!" His eyes plead with me. He looks panic-stricken.

"Try and stop me, Lanciné. For too long you have kept me on a short leash. To you, I am no more than that cow over there. I understand now."

My heart is racing hard, and I'm flushed with rage. I'm suddenly aware that I hold the power, and I want to use it to lash out against Lanciné. Just as much, I want to lash out against Africa herself, the muse who has beguiled and tricked me all these years. My anger surges against the ancestors, too. They care nothing for me. This whole quest to appease them has been pointless, and they only ever intended to drive me mad. Perhaps they've finally succeeded.

"Daouda, you do not understand..." He trails off, and his eyes swell with tears. "Please, Daouda. Sit down. I can explain."

Something in his wearied look softens me. *Jesus, I've put this poor man through so much already.*

I bite my lip, and try to cool down. I drop my bag to the earth, but remain standing.

"I'm listening."

He lets out a deep sigh, and turns his head away. The silence in the field becomes deafening. I can see him choosing his words, but he's taking too long. I consider walking away. Before I can, he speaks.

"Daouda, here in Africa, we have so little. We toil in the fields or the mines for next to nothing. We scratch out our existence, and still go hungry. But you—you are all I have. Without you, I could not have returned to the village. And our flute apprenticeship is the only income I have. You asked me once if I would stay in the village if I could earn an income here. Well, here we are. Allah has brought you to me. But when you leave, I will have nothing again."

His words are defeating my anger, taking my momentary power away. I slump to the ground, deflated.

He shakes his head mournfully and goes on. "Everyone in the village knows you are my *tubabu.* They eye you greedily. They want you for themselves, and think that if you lived with them instead, they could have a better life. You do not see their jealous looks, but I do. That is why I watch over you and must prevent you from running away. And it is why we cannot stay here any longer."

Understanding floods over me, but it comes in a jumbled mix of emotions. That I was unaware of this dynamic makes me feel foolish, but it also makes me feel powerless over the injustices of the world that created it. And I'm deeply ashamed I acted this way toward Lanciné. I realize how much I love and admire him, and it startles me to feel it so deeply. He's been my hero for so long now. His courage and joy in the face of hardship are the qualities I lack the most. The only thing I can do is tell him.

"Lanciné, I am your friend. You inspire me every day, and I..." I search for the words in French to express the one sentiment I have so much difficulty saying in any language. "Lanciné, *je tiens à toi profondément*—I care about you deeply. You are my brother. Nothing can change that. I would never abandon you."

I've almost said it. Then, the most significant part rises out of the diffusing fog of emotions. I must first admit it to myself before I can speak it aloud.

"Lanciné, I *need* you." *There, I said it.* The words shake the walls around my heart, and they threaten to crumble. I am not alone in this world, nor do I have to be. Needing others isn't a weakness. We're social, communal creatures, after all. Admitting it feels like a strength.

We exchange a long look. He bows his head low. His walls are down, too.

"Daouda, I don't know how you can say these things. Look at me. I am embarrassed by my poverty. It is shameful."

His words stun me. I think back to my internship in college all those years ago, when I first painted the images of Elmina and its people. I would have traded all the wealth of America for the joy in their eyes. No, it is me who is poor in comparison.

"Lanciné," I say, not sure where my words are heading, "I am here because you possess riches we lack in the West. You have community. An identity. Traditions. When I return to the United States, I will be alone once again, isolated. We may have money and material things in

America, but we suffer from loneliness and heartache of the worst kind. We are disconnected from the earth and from one another by our possessions and the walls we build around them. It is a sickness we do not know how to heal. So we numb ourselves with more and more things, or even drugs and alcohol. Only pain and loneliness will welcome me back to America. But here in your village, there are people who have prayed and cared for me even though I am only a wayward traveler. *That* is why I do not want to leave here. What you have is worth more than all the money in the world to me."

As I speak, a dragon takes shape before me. It is my true sickness, an illness of the heart, and I wonder how I never saw it before. It has spread to the depths of my soul, become manifest in the form of a terrible affliction. I no longer know myself, for my identity is intertwined with pain. All I see is a broken man, punished by the gods for my imperfections. I am an embarrassment, unfit for love—even from myself. But I see now that if I cannot relearn to love myself, then all is lost. The illness will claim me forever, and I will be just another nameless victim of the dragon's insatiable appetite, soon to be forgotten like all the rest.

And what is my addiction but a symptom of this illness? This addiction has the power to destroy me. If there is any hope of healing, I know I must confront this dragon head on, and slay it once and for all.

Lanciné looks at me solemnly. The bridge between us grows shorter. I could just walk across it now. We are two men, walking our own pathways of exile. We're not so different.

"Lanciné," I say, "Life is not fair. I do not know why you suffer in poverty, and why I must return to America in pain. Allah has given us our paths to walk in this life. Who knows? Maybe we chose these lives even before we were born."

Lanciné laughs, incredulous. "Daouda, I cannot imagine choosing this poverty."

"I have a hard time imagining that I chose this pain. But it's what we have. All that remains is what we decide to do with it. It is the only thing we have control over."

A sudden realization comes over me. Maybe my pain isn't a curse from the ancestors at all. Maybe I gave *myself* this curse because I knew I would need it to learn the lessons I came into this life to learn.

The thought almost knocks the wind out of me with the weight of its truth. But then its full power strikes me. If somehow, in the realm before my time on Earth, I agreed to this pain as a means of directing my own spiritual path in life, then perhaps I can also ascertain the reasons—and thus the path I must take to cure it. If this is true, then my spiritual healing needn't be such a helpless quest, subjected to the whims of powers I can't understand nor control. Perhaps it is in my hands, and has been all along.

A light breeze ruffles the dry leaves above me, and the surrounding field is glowing. My eyes and heart are wide open.

I move closer to Lanciné, and pick up one of his flutes. I feel its shape in my hands, and admire Lanciné's craftsmanship. It is a beautiful instrument, and a true work of art. The ringlets of cowrie shells adorning it are meticulously placed in the molded black beeswax. The flute's wooden body is covered with a sheepskin sheath, which adds to its earthy, raw aesthetic. It is alive with beauty, a true symbol of the culture that birthed it. As I hold it in my hand and marvel at its various natural decorations, I think that I've never really grasped the concept of *nyama* until now.

Lanciné closes my fingers around it with his own.

"Daouda, I want you to have this flute. It is my gift to you. It is yours now."

"Lanciné! No, I cannot take this. That gift is too great." I'm humbled that he would even offer.

"It is not for you to refuse," he says. "Our apprenticeship is coming to an end. You are a guardian of the tradition now. The flute never belonged to me. It is Allah who gave it to me, and now it is yours. I will discuss it no more." He picks up the other flute. "Come now, we play together. Our time is growing short."

The music streams forth, and it is sacred. As we play, my gaze returns to the field, and wanders beyond the boundaries of the village, to the sky and beyond. In two days, I will be gone from here. I can only wonder if I will ever return.

~

That evening, Lamine arrives with the herbal preparations, as promised. He delivers two large bottles, one for Lanciné, and one for me. My remedy consists of a liter of green sludge. Lamine recites the prescription as given by the healer. I am to use the concoction both internally and externally.

Inside the hut, I lay down on the mattress and take off my shirt. Lamine pours the leafy green slime over my back and works it in. It is cooling, and makes my skin tingle. I lie on the bed for an hour as it sinks into my pores. I think maybe it brings some relief, but the pain is already too high. One dose of the stuff probably isn't going to fix me. I wish I had more time.

After a while, Lamine takes a small hand towel and wipes the residue from my back. I twist and turn my shoulders to try things out.

"How do you feel, Daouda?"

"OK, I guess. A little looser. Am I supposed to drink the stuff too?" I'm a little afraid.

"Yes. There is plenty left, and you should drink a small cup twice a day. And what is remaining, we can put on your back again."

I try to convey skepticism with my look, but Lamine still offers me the bottle. Would it be crazy to drink some unknown concoction in a remote African village? I'd nagged Lanciné for weeks to take me to the healer, but now that the potion is in front of me, it seems risky.

"I'm not sure if I want to drink it," I say. "How do I know it won't make me sick?"

Lamine laughs. "Do not worry. Look, I will drink some myself." He takes a swig from the bottle, and wipes his mouth with the back of his hand. "See? No need to worry."

I turn to Lanciné, and he nods reassuringly. *Oh, what the hell.* I've come all this way to find healing in Africa, and it would be pointless not to try it. I put the bottle to my lips and tilt it back. The texture makes me gag. The flavor is of fermented, decaying leaves. My throat tingles as I swallow it.

Lanciné holds his bottle. His medicine is orange, and has roots and twigs floating in it. The color is a little like turmeric. I remember the plant that grew outside the healer's house, the one with yellow flowers shaped like starfish. I want to remember the image of the plant, so I can look it up someday.

"What's yours do?" I ask.

"The root of this plant is good for many things. We use it to tan hides, but it also prevents malaria. It treats bad infections. And it is also good for high blood pressure. From now on, I will take this every day." He takes a drink, and hands it to me. "Here, try it."

Gaining some confidence, I gulp some down. The taste is bitter, but not too bad.

"It prevents malaria too? That's amazing." I've had malaria twice in my life, and it's good to know there's a village remedy. I take another mouthful, and hand it back. I can only wonder what plants I have just consumed.

Lamine departs, and Lanciné and I are left in the quiet. A little later, some friends stop by to visit, as they know we are preparing to depart. Soon, guests fill the hut. Though I'm tired, I stay up to enjoy the company of people who were complete strangers a few months ago. They're studying me, but I've gotten used to it. I'm still a curiosity here, and probably always will be.

My pile of bags surrounds me, and I have to move them twice to make room for the visitors. They're filled with clothing and gadgets, many of which I never even used. I consider what's in there, and the burden of useless possessions that we Westerners willingly accumulate. Our abundance is a curse, and I want to be lighter.

I get up abruptly and start unpacking.

"Daouda? What are you doing?"

I don't reply. Instead, I pull out various shirts and hold them up to our guests to gauge the size. If it looks like it fits, I hand it to them. I do the same with all the trousers I have. Next come the shoes. It's a grand giveaway, and our friends are gleeful with their new acquisitions. At last, I come to my pile of gadgets. There are headphones and bluetooth speakers that will connect to their cellphones, and I give them all away. I'm feeling lighter by the moment, and giddy with it all. When it's done, I'm left only with the clothes on my back, my art supplies, and a few odds and ends. Satisfied, I sit back on the bed. My bags are now lean and manageable. I want my new life to be like this, uncomplicated and uncluttered by things. It's a start.

The guests linger into the night, but fatigue finally takes over. I can keep my eyes open no longer. Contented, I fall fast asleep amidst a crowded room of kind souls.

When I awake, it's already morning. The hut is empty, and I'm struck with loneliness. I wish our friends would return with their lively conversation and laughter. But the time has come to leave the village. My final day has arrived.

40

A SAD FAREWELL

WE WALK SLOWLY, for there is no hurry now. I no longer want to be alone. Rather, I want to savor my remaining time here, and my friendship with Lanciné. As is the tradition here among brothers and close friends, we lock hands as we walk. We do not speak, but we know what comes next. The long return journey to Conakry is before us, and beyond that, I must return to America. A dragon awaits me, and it's high time I face it.

We make our way to El Hadji's house. There, Lamine is busy working on the Renault. He is close to finished now. With luck, we'll depart in the morning, but I secretly wish for some complication that will delay his work. We greet him, and he raises a hand in salute before returning his attention to the car.

Aminata greets us when we arrive. She is sad, but we both know my life is not here. Not all paths can be taken. Some other future awaits us both.

"Daouda, *na teleman damun*—come eat lunch." There are no language games today, but she has prepared a going away feast for us.

We eat mostly in silence. The impending departure has me feeling blue, and I poke at my food half-heartedly. El Hadji offers some encouraging words, and says he will continue to pray for me. After lunch, I thank him for all his kindness and hospitality, and present him with the traditional gift of kola nuts.

"El Hadji, *barika*—thank you."

"*Barika ala ye*. It is Allah to whom we owe thanks. Our hearts will be sad when you leave. You must never forget us. *I döja*—have courage."

"*Iniké kosabé*. I will not forget you and your family."

Aminata and I stroll away from the house for a short walk. We walk shoulder to shoulder, and she teases me. I miss her already. She will be staying in the village, where she belongs. Her life is here.

When we return a short time later, Lanciné is ready to make the walk home. I say a heartfelt goodbye to Aminata.

"*An bè sööma, Daouda Condé!*" she says with watery eyes. It literally means *see you tomorrow*, but we both know it will not be tomorrow. In the village, saying goodbye for long is too sad. Life is uncertain. We're both aware we may never see each other again.

As Lanciné and I head for the path, it all feels oddly like a dream that isn't supposed to end this way. I wish I could wake up from it and find that it all turned out differently. I wish some miracle would keep me here, even just a bit longer.

We walk onward.

When we return, I half-heartedly finish packing. Afterward, Lanciné and I head back to the field where he spent his youth as a shepherd. He wants to see it one last time. While we're there, Lanciné asks me to take out my recorder. He has one final gift for me.

"Daouda, we must make a recording of all the songs. Two flutes together. When you are far away in America, you will have it to study from. And when you hear it, you will not forget about me."

I agree this is a good idea, and pull out my recorder. I press record, and the music flows from us in one long stream. We play dozens of songs, and it feels effortless now. Here in the great field, the music feels tinged with all the heartache and joy that Africa can hold. When we are finished, we sit and listen to the recording as a gentle breeze sweeps through the field. Lanciné is satisfied.

We linger for a short time, then make our way past the giant ficus tree, the guardian of the village. I pay my respects one last time, and say a prayer for the people of the village. I pray that if I ever return, it will be under different circumstances. I pray that next time, it will be *I* who can help *them*.

When evening comes, I sit on the edge of the bed and stare at what's left of my bags. I can't shake the feeling that I'm not done here.

Lanciné and I sit outside after dinner, quietly passing a pipe as the stars fill the sky. It is a spectacle to behold, a glittering map of the universe. I think about the adventure behind me now. I came here with gifts for the village according to my means, and made a sacrifice. I hope it will be deemed worthy. Though I fell short in my mission, I know I am richer for the experience.

Lanciné tries his best to cheer me up. I'm grateful for all he has done, and for all he has taught me. I'll leave him with a generous gift that will make his life easier, for a time at least. The wad of hundred-dollar bills is tucked inside my bag, ready to hand him when we reach Conakry. It's the least I can do.

Night falls, and the village grows quiet again. I say one last prayer, and offer my gratitude to the ancestors of the village, and to whatever gods look down upon us. I must persevere. I must find hope to keep me going, and courage to do what comes next.

Lanciné's phone buzzes. It's late. He picks it up suspiciously, and glances at the number. He sits up straight as he flips it open.

"Allô? Oui? Oui, d'accord!" His voice grows with excitement. *"D'accord, merci! Merci! Iniké kosabé!"* He's laughing as he hangs up.

"What is it? Who was that?"

He turns to me and puts his hands on either side of my face.

"It was Lamine. He says that Famoudou has just returned. He is here now, in the village. We will go see him in the morning."

41

RESPECTING TRADITIONS

THE SUN HAS NOT YET RISEN. The light from my headlamp swings from dirt to trees as I search for the path. My feet know the way now, but my eyes want reassurance. I have to trust.

I arrive at the sacred grove, enter, and extinguish my light. The air is cooler in the grove, and a light breeze rattles dry branches. A few paces in, I set my backpack down. It holds only one item.

I sit and close my eyes. This morning will be for prayer. Here in the grove, the ancestors are close. They will hear me, and I will not be afraid. I have come to speak to them directly. I need their help.

I murmur the words in a low voice. I address them by name, and tell them mine. They know who I am, for they've seen me walking the paths of their village for months now. They have seen me suffer, and they have seen my attempts at healing the wounds of my past.

I ask the ancestors for guidance. I want to respect their traditions, but I have forgotten how. I want to remember. I ask them to release me from my pain, to show me the path to true healing. It is not only for myself that I ask this. The whole world suffers. Darkness is falling over humanity, and we have lost our way.

Silence falls over me, and peace comes. The feeling is unfamiliar to me. Around me, I sense the presence of those ancestors who came before me, those souls who, in life, also came here to sit and pray. In death, they have become powerful. But I know they look after those whose intentions are true.

When I open my eyes, the forest is no longer dark. The sun is rising, and I must be on my way. I pick up my backpack and make my way to the path. I have an old friend to see.

~

When I arrive at Famoudou's courtyard alone, the sun paints the village in an orange hue. The old man is sitting in a chair just outside his house. A second chair is beside him. As I approach, he looks up. A smile lights his face, and my heart bursts with joy. He rises, and we embrace. Tears well in my eyes as he rocks me back and forth in his arms.

"*I sööma*, my son. It is good to see you again."

"*N ba, i sööma*, Papa. And you as well."

He stands back and holds me by the shoulders to inspect me.

"You have lost weight! Is your *maître* Lanciné not feeding you?"

"He is taking care of me just fine. But there is not much to the little river fish we eat. And I cannot bring myself to eat another bite of manioc leaf stew."

He laughs heartily. "Village food is difficult for the *tubabu*. Come, *mon fils. Na dabö kè*—come take your breakfast with me. I have porridge and bread, and the water for coffee is almost ready. My daughter will bring it all soon."

As the village awakens around us, I ask him about his voyage, and I'm pleased to hear it passed without much trouble. His car is apparently much nicer than mine. I tell him about all our misadventures getting here, and he laughs.

"I was concerned about that little car when you left Conakry. I am surprised it made it here at all. And the return trip? Are you not concerned?"

"Oh, I'm concerned all right. But Lamine is quite handy. We'll be OK." I'm not quite so sure of this, but that concern is far from my thoughts now. I speak what is on my mind. "Papa, I have carried out your instructions. But there is one task remaining. I have shown the book to no one. You said I should await your arrival."

"Yes, I have heard the village is happy with the respect you have shown them. You are in their good grace. We shall attend to the remaining tasks after breakfast."

One of Famoudou's daughters brings breakfast, and we share the meal, chatting about this and that. He is concerned about the state of the village. Access to modern medicines has decreased infant mortality, and that's certainly a good thing. The birth rate is outpacing the death rate for the first time, perhaps ever. But if the population grows too fast, it will mean food shortages.

The gifts of the modern world, it seems, are both a blessing and a curse. He tells me that increased Western-style education brings disdain for the old ways. Young, educated villagers leave their homes to seek work that doesn't exist in the city. Without knowledge of their traditions, they become like lost ships. The resulting poverty in Conakry is crushing. The promises of the West are empty for the new generations of Africans, and that betrayal breeds only anger—and in the hotbed of Conakry, violence erupts more frequently.

We sit in silence for a time, and I ponder all he has said. A return to the traditional way of life could actually ease the poverty. The population needs to be balanced with the capacity of the land, and the earth must be respected. Maybe there is a happy medium. The village should be free to choose the components of the modern world that suit them, while still honoring the traditions of their ancestors.

When we are finished eating, he points to my backpack. Other traditions still need to be respected today.

"Do you have the book? Bring it forth. I want to see it again."

I retrieve the book and place it in his hands. He opens it and flips through the pages, admiring the images and murmuring the names of the people he sees.

"It really is a beautiful book," he says. "But we must make a list of names. There are many people depicted here, and I do not want to leave anyone out. Write the names for me, and we will summon them all to my courtyard."

I retrieve my notebook. As he rattles off names, the page fills quickly. I don't know how to spell all the names, but I read them back to him to be sure:

Famoudou Konaté. Mansa Fondé. Koulako Bori Dama. Djouba Fodéya. Nanuma Keïta. Wadaba Mamady Kourouma. Nansady Babila. Faramadou Keïta. Moussa Keïta. Sayon Camara. Nansady Keïta. Kalamo Diawara. Bandjou Keïta. Sako Gbè. Sano Keïta. Doubalé Möba. Mamaya danseurs. Fanta Kouyaté, griotte. Djelilouma Kouyaté. Sitan Keïta. Djelimousso Saran Diabaté. Mama Keïta. Tadi Moudou Keïta. Solo Keïta. Ténan Fila Mamady Keïta. Bolonfola de Koumana. Bérété Dunu. Kaba Konaté. Kana Duma. Lanseï Kanté de Conakry. Sekou Keïta, chasseur. Kanko Keïta. Binto Coulibaly, féfö. Soliwulen de Koumana. Kòmò association de Koumana.

And finally, he adds one more: *Mousso Gbè.* An uneasy feeling arises in the pit of my stomach. I wonder if she truly is still alive. And if she is, will she come to us? Both scenarios terrify me. But I must have courage. What will be, will be.

As I read, he considers each name. He dictates numbers, and I write them beside the names.

When we are through, we tally it up. The total comes to 3,160,000 Guinea franc. Famoudou is satisfied. I do the math. Besides the money I have set aside for Lanciné, it's about all I have left. It will leave me scarce little for the return trip.

"And where is your *grand frère* this morning?"

"Lanciné was still sleeping when I left. I am sure he is up by now, and wondering where I am."

"We will call him. When he arrives, we will assemble the people, along with the village elders. We will present your book, and you will make your gifts to each person."

I sit now in the center of the courtyard. Famoudou is seated next to me, and Lanciné stands behind me. I am nervous, but my courage is buoyed by the presence of these two men, my village family.

The assembly has gathered, along with family members and friends who want to witness the event. The little courtyard is near capacity.

El Hadji steps to the center of the congregation and begins to pray.

His *naamutigi* is beside him to verify his speech. The voices of the crowd respond in unison to El Hadji's prayers.

Amiina! Amiina! Allah tando. Thanks be to God.

When the prayers are over, Famoudou lifts the book for all to see. He speaks to the crowd in Malinké, and a low murmur rises from the assembly. At last, he passes the book around, and it changes hands rapidly as villagers descend to peer at its pages. My emotions rise to the surface. I remember those quiet mornings far away when I first rendered the images. It was a lifetime ago, but a bridge has now formed between the past and the present.

Famoudou gestures to me. It is time. I have the notebook, and one by one we call out the names. Each person approaches me, and we look into each other's eyes. I place the money in their hands, and I say, "*Barika*—thank you." The moment is profound for me, and I can see that they are moved too. One after another, I look upon these people who live simply and have so little. My gifts are humble, but will help in some small way. For me, the gift of their blessing is the greatest gift of all. Another weight is slowly lifting.

At last, we reach the end of the list. Famoudou speaks out.

"And where is Mousso Gbè, the widow of Sako the blacksmith? I have summoned her to this assembly. Is she not present? Let her show herself if she is!"

A low murmur sweeps through the assembly. Then, at the far end of the courtyard, the crowd parts, and a hush falls over the congregation. A woman emerges, and steps slowly to the center.

It is Mousso Gbè.

42

THE SORCERER'S WIFE

I RISE TO MY FEET, as if some power is controlling me. My hands are shaking.

Mousso Gbè and I stand facing each other across the small courtyard.

Our eyes meet, and I prepare myself for what will surely come next. What judgment will she cast on me, a white man who crossed too close to their secrets? Fear binds me in place. There is nowhere for me to turn and run, for my reckoning is now at hand. I remember the image of the Kòmò monster descending upon me. The sorceress will channel its power. The dark magic of the secret societies and her late husband will flow through her. She will reveal me for what I am, and the whole community will see.

Mousso takes several steps closer, and unconsciously, powerlessly, I walk toward her. I must be brave. We now stand at just a pace away, and I meet her gaze, taking her in. She is not young, but she is younger than I had imagined her. Her eyes are bright, the lines in her face soft.

And then, I'm taken aback. I notice she is trembling. She too is scared. This is unexpected. Her lip quivers, and I feel like I must say something, but I have no words. Before me now, she is a person, like any other. She is frail, and a widow. Her clothing is tattered. She looks malnourished. I strain to decipher the emotion I see in her eyes, and it pulls me into her world. A magic spell of empathy is cast over me, and I am overcome with feelings of hunger, loneliness, and sorrow that do not belong to me. The emotions are hers, flowing into me, and they are overwhelming. My heart feels like it will sever.

My hands do the bidding of a force greater than me. I unconsciously raise the book, and reveal to her the image of her deceased husband. Her eyes immediately well up with tears. She raises her hands to her face, and then begins to sob uncontrollably. Still under the spell of empathy, I feel all the love she holds in her heart for this man, and all the pain his departure from this world has caused her. Sako Gbè was a kind man above all, and she loved him dearly. She misses him terribly.

I realize how badly I misjudged her. I was afraid of this moment above all else. But now she is here, and she is only a person. She has suffered in her life, too.

The crowd watches silently. Time stands utterly still.

I don't know what else to do. I step forward and embrace her, and she puts her arms around me in return. I feel how light her body is. She is practically a skeleton. We hold each other, two strangers connected unexpectedly by bonds of human emotion. I feel immense love for her. Her body shakes with sobs against mine. Tears flow freely from us both, washing away both time and suffering. I understand now that love is the source of all healing. I've deprived myself of it for too long, and I had to come all this way to find it. The sorceress Mousso Gbè has opened my heart again.

The last walls of my heart's Elmina fortress come crashing down, and love rushes in, searching for the prisoner trapped inside. The dam bursts wide open and there is nothing I can do but let the emotions fill me. And then it occurs to me. If I can feel such depth of love for this stranger, then perhaps I too am worthy of receiving that love. Maybe I could even learn to accept and love myself, even with all my imperfections and pain. The feeling of liberation is immense. I squeeze Mousso just a little more, and for a moment, we stand rocking each other back and forth.

When Mousso releases me, I turn to retrieve the gift I've prepared for her. The gift of money pales in comparison, but it is all I can offer her from my world. I hope it will ease her suffering in some way, that it will feed and nourish her, and in that, she will be granted some comfort in her life. She takes the bundle with quavering hands, and holds it in disbelief. It is probably more money than she has seen in her whole life. It will provide for her for a long time.

"*Barika, barika,*" she says through tears, repeating the word over and over. She bows her head. "Ohhh, *Allah barika...*" Her thin body shudders with sobs.

After a time, she takes my hands and blesses me, offering a series of benedictions. I do not know all the words, but I feel the intent behind them. The words are filled with compassion and kindness.

"*Amiina,*" I reply, and then offer my own benediction. "*Allah toro dööya.* May God give you comfort."

Famoudou rises from his chair and stands beside us, and then takes our hands in his. I look at the old man, my mentor and adopted father in this village. I think of my father and mother back home, and know how fortunate I am to still have them in my life. My thoughts turn to my sister and her family, to Kerri and all my friends back home. I love them all so much. And I never knew until now how much I *need* them.

"Daouda," he says, "you are free now. Go. Return to your home and family, and live your life. You will find your healing."

A twenty-year curse has been lifted from me. I have found the source, and now I only pray it will give me strength for what I know must come next.

43

IMPERMANENCE AND REBIRTH

IT'S RAINING IN AFRICA. The clouds have swelled to their maximum, and now they do not hold back. The torrents will last for many months. Life will be difficult for a time, but the village knows how to deal with it. The rain brings life, and the fields will be watered and fertile again. The river will rise and overflow its banks. Streams and ponds will form where once there was only dry earth, and when the water recedes, fish will be abundant in the remaining pools. It is all part of the ongoing cycle of change at the heart of life. Without change, nothing grows. Without death, nothing can be reborn.

It is not raining where I am. Outside my window, the sky is gray and snow is lightly falling. It's April, but Vermont winters are long. Spring has not yet returned to northern New England, but I have.

I stand in the one-bedroom Airbnb I've rented in Burlington. This is not home, but it'll do for now. I'm close. There is one final task before me on this journey of healing, a fearsome dragon which still stands before me. I know I must slay it before it destroys me.

I mustn't hesitate now. Act swiftly. Have courage.

The end is near. I close my eyes and see the beast before me. It has ruled my life for too long. For too many years, I have lived in fear of it.

I walk down the stairs and out the door. The cold air hits me. After months of relentless heat, the freezing air bites at my exposed skin. I have little in the way of clothing, for I have given it all away.

I am wide awake now. My body trembles, and I call upon the ancestors once more. They will give me strength. They will steady my hand.

I think back to all that took place in the village. I remember the feel of the worn blade in my hand as I returned to the earth a gift of life. Sacrifices must sometimes be made. It is the only way that life continues. We must learn to let go, for all things are ruled by the law of impermanence. Even our darkest nights of pain and despair are bound to it, and cannot endure forever.

Daouda, I tell myself, *it is time to let go of your old life. You have reached the end of your journey.*

I reach into my coat pocket for the plastic container I know will be there. I listen for the familiar rattle inside. There are plenty left. A lethal amount.

My courage is waning. I may only have this one chance. I falter momentarily, frozen by fear. The dragon's breath is hot on my face, and I comprehend its menacing power. Its appetite knows no limits. It *will* annihilate me.

Do it now. Strike the beast down.

Courage surges through me. All my love, my hatred, my fears, my pain—it all rises to the surface. I strike at the beast with everything I have. When I hear the plastic container rattle into the trash receptacle, I slam the door hard. It is a one-way door. There is no possibility of retrieving the pills. They are gone forever.

I stumble back, knowing I have only injured the dragon. It will inflict its pain on me yet. But I know I will survive. The well of the source is deep.

For the next several weeks, I do not leave the apartment. I've told no one I am back in the States. My body is wracked with withdrawal symptoms, and I don't want anyone to see me like this. After more than a decade of constant narcotics use, the dragon will not leave its lair willingly. But I am not done fighting.

I'm doing this for you, I tell myself, *because I love you. You are worth it.*

The pain of withdrawal is worse than anything I have ever experienced. It makes me feel hollow. My bones ache. I'm feverish, and it's worse than the flu, worse even than the malaria I suffered through during past trips. Even my skin is painful to the touch. The soft blanket I lie beneath scratches my skin like sandpaper. I occasionally think death would be much easier, and wonder if I have made the right choice, or even if I can endure it. I cannot blame Erik for not wanting to go through this. But he and I had different paths to take. In the end, perhaps it was he who saved me.

For two full weeks, I eat nothing. I drink only water. I have no energy to find food. My body goes into a state of dormancy. It must conserve its resources, and it begins to burn the toxins that have built up in my body over a decade of abuse. Even bacteria are not safe from my body's relentless quest for fuel. The tables have turned. While I sleep, the klebsiella that hide deep in the tissues of my spine become my body's food.

I pass in and out of dream state both day and night, and am thankful when sleep overtakes me. It is my only relief. Always, I dream of Africa. I see Famoudou and Lanciné, and am often visited by Mousso. On several occasions, I awake in the darkness and think I see the ghost of Sako Gbè standing before me. My heart races, but not with fear. I welcome the visit from an esteemed elder. He stays with me, a silent reminder that I am never alone.

Each morning, I pray to the ancestors for the strength to go on.

I awake one morning to see the sun shining brightly outside my window. While I slumbered, spring arrived. The colors outside seem more vibrant than I ever remember colors could be. The buds on the trees are beginning to open, and the verdant leaves are dazzling. The blue of the sky is richer than any blue I have ever seen.

I am surprised to notice that I feel refreshed, despite not having eaten in two weeks. The withdrawal symptoms have finally passed. I rise cautiously, expecting the pain to drag me back down. But it doesn't.

I stand easily, and walk to the window. I raise it, and refreshing air rushes in. The smell of spring hits me, and my olfactory senses come alive. This time, it is no dream. The pain is gone.

I dress and head for the city park. I'm weak from fasting, and I walk slowly. But as I do, I'm simply drunk on the sensory inputs I'm receiving. Smells are overpowering, and they send blissful memories rushing headlong into my awareness. Every smell carries a memory of childhood with it. It's almost too much. In the park's gardens, trillium and lilies and sweet alyssum are starting to blossom, and their scents carry me back to the days of my youth.

I'm shocked, too, at the depth of my emotions. I see lovers walking hand in hand on the street, and it makes me want to cry. An old man on a park bench makes me marvel at growing old, wise from a lifetime of experience. I hope I might someday be an old man. An *elder*, even. Further along, a homeless woman asks me for spare change, and I apologize, for I have none. I have only love in my heart. I silently wish her all the love in the world. She smiles.

I'm swept away in the beauty of this new world around me. I've been reborn from the ashes of a life I had nearly given up on. And I'm startled to realize that my body feels altogether foreign to me, impossibly light, loose, and free from pain.

And I'm *hungry*.

I change my course and head into town. The City Market Co-op has a juice bar. I order something simple. I don't want to overdo it. When the flavors of watermelon and celery reach my taste buds, it is pure bliss. I have never tasted anything so rich. How can this be? I understand at this moment that, from now on, food will be my only medicine. The earth provides for us, and always has. And then I remember. There is something else I need.

I approach a young store clerk. She is pretty and full of spring cheer.

"Avez-vous du vinaigre de cidre?" I ask. They are the first words I have spoken to anyone in weeks.

She laughs. "What? Are you speaking French?" Then I remember I'm in America, and feel foolish. My brain searches its catalogue for the right words.

"Sorry. Apple cider vinegar. Have you some?" The words don't come out right, but they work.

"Of course. Right over here." She looks at me quizzically. "Hey, how'd you get so tan? You just get back from vacation or sumpt'n?"

I'm about to say something cryptic about the pathways of exile, and chuckle. "More like a spiritual retreat," I say instead.

She shrugs. "Well, I hope it was good. Winter's been *terrible* this year. My grandfather says his rheumatism's never been worse. Could barely get out of bed some days."

"That sounds dreadful."

She leads me to the aisle with various types of vinegar. I thank her, wish her a happy spring, and tell her I hope her grandfather feels better soon. I pick up the largest bottle of apple cider vinegar they have, and hold it in my hand. I wonder, *Will it work? Will it keep me out of pain?*

I know what Lanciné would say in response to these questions. But whether Allah wills it to work or not, I know it's time to go home. My real life is about to begin.

EPILOGUE

THE FIELD IS aglow with shades of green, amber, and sienna. The warmth of the late afternoon sun is pleasant, and I'm preparing to start a new drawing. This time, it's a different sort of portrait than I'm accustomed to. I study the plant's leaves, fully taking in its intricate design. Before I begin drawing it, I take out some tobacco leaves and place them on the ground as an offering. I introduce myself quietly, humbly.

So this is Artemisia, I think. I've probably seen it by the roadside a thousand times without ever knowing it.

Spend some time with it, the shaman said upon my arrival. *Don't rush. Get to know it awhile.*

For the next two hours, I invite the plant into my drawing, and it's like two old friends getting reacquainted after a long absence. As it comes to life on paper, I'm pulled into its dreamy world. Around me, thousands of artemisia plants sway and shimmer in the autumn breeze.

When I've completed the drawing, I'm tingling. Dusk is beginning to set, so I return to the shaman's small house in the woods. I find her sitting outside, stoking the fire, a lit cigar hanging from her hand. I quietly take the chair beside her, and wait for her to speak. She lingers, studying me closely.

"It's been a long time," she says.

"Yes, quite a few years now."

"And how has your pain been?" she asks.

"Fine," I respond without hesitation. "I'm healthy. Pain is mostly under control these days. I'm learning to manage it with diet and fasting. I no longer take any medicine. Well, unless you count plants as medicine—"

"I do count them as medicine," she says, smiling. "Powerful medicine."

I laugh at myself for saying it like that. "Well, you know what I mean. No drugs. Or painkillers. Food is my medicine now."

I explain to her how I've learned to listen to my body, and find out what to eat or avoid. A strict grain and sugar-free diet with lots of green plants and healthy fats, but low on carbs and with moderate animal protein, has brought me a vitality I haven't felt since my youth. I still drink apple cider vinegar daily. But by far, the most powerful tool in my arsenal is periodic fasting—something I discovered wholly by accident during my recovery in Burlington. Since then, a semi-annual fourteen-day fast resets my symptoms. Intermittent fasting the rest of the year is a crucial part of healing my damaged joints and gut. It may seem extreme, but it's much less extreme than a life of chronic pain—or injecting mutated hamster ovary cells.

"Fasting is a powerful tool for healing," she remarks. "The traditional peoples of the world have never forgotten this. It is a quite natural thing to do. Too bad people in the West have such a hard time accepting it."

I nod. Fasting is downright hard, and not for everybody. It needs to be done with guidance and knowledge, both of which are lacking in the West. Depriving ourselves of sustenance defies our survival instincts, but the results can border on the miraculous, for it is only during fasting that our body enters into deep cleansing modes. And the inner journey of quiet reflection one undergoes during the process is nothing short of a sacred trip back to the source.

"And you mentioned some plants?" she asks.

"Yes. There's artemisia, of course. Each variety has unique healing properties, as you know. But I also encountered a plant in Africa that intrigues me. A village healer we visited made a preparation of it."

I close my eyes and recall that day I saw the plant with star-shaped yellow flowers, and the turmeric-colored potion he made from the roots. I could have no idea at the time that this plant, *cryptolepis sanguinolenta,* was potent against klebsiella and other antibiotic-resistant bacteria. And as Lanciné informed me, a tea made from its roots is effective at treating malaria. It's apparently good at treating Lyme disease, too.

"I've only just begun learning about the gifts this plant offers," I say, "but I'm guessing I came across it for a reason."

"You're probably right. Very little happens by chance. But just remember, there is no shortcut to healing, and no silver bullet. Real healing requires dedication and sacrifice—and must take into account the spirit and heart, too."

I sigh. "Yeah, I'm beginning to learn this."

The heart does not heal overnight. I think back to my departure from Africa several years ago, and how the real journey of healing began *after* I returned. The hardest part was forgiving myself for all the years that I hid behind pain pills, and nearly lost myself to them. But when forgiveness came, the wounds of the past began to close. Julie's guidance and healing plants were instrumental in the process. Over time, I made peace with all that had happened, and I made peace with Kerri, too. It pleased me to know she was starting a new life. Love had returned to both our hearts, and that was enough for me.

My emotions rise to the surface. I'm about to get all misty-eyed, but the shaman clears her throat.

"There are still other matters to discuss, sonny. What about marijuana? Have you healed your relationship with this plant?"

I chuckle to myself about that one. Years ago, she told me that this plant was angry with me. Turns out she was right. New research has shown that marijuana—even high-grade medical strains—is host to a plethora of pathogens. These include none other than klebsiella, which is hardy enough to survive the flame. Every time I smoked marijuana, I was literally infusing my body with a fresh batch of klebsiella, which in turn triggered my body's painful autoimmune reaction.

Bacteria and bogeymen, I sigh. *One and the same?*

"Yeah," I say, "that plant was angry with me, alright. But I think I've healed that relationship now."

"Good."

She fans the flames with her feather wand, and we fall into a deep silence. The last of the season's cicadas hum lightly, and smoke swirls around us as she prays. When she looks up some time later, her face is again solemn.

"Your journey isn't over," she says. "This illness will always be with you, to remind you of your path. And there will be times when you fall off that path. The pain will come again. You must no longer see this as a curse, but as an opportunity to embrace the lessons it offers you. It is part of the pact you made when coming here to this lifetime."

I bow my head, for I feel the truth of her words. There are still days when the pain returns, though it's a shadow of what it once was.

"So, there's no end to this story, is there?" I ask.

She puffs on her cigar, and tendrils of smoke wisp beneath her old fedora. A wry grin appears on her face. "Ha! No story ever really ends, sonny. What fun would that be?" She cackles uproariously, and slaps my knee. "But at least now you've seen that real healing is possible."

I nod because now, I know. Not just that anything is possible, but that *everything* is possible. Rarely easy, and infrequently what we expect, but always possible—and very much worth all the pain.

When I think back now to Africa, and how she charmed me with her mystery and secrets, I understand that she was calling me to my true self. My *higher* self. In this life, I am an artist, and that is my calling. To live a life of creativity is to be in communion with angels and spirits. It is a high calling indeed, and I pray every day that I am worthy of it.

Four years after my return, I finally completed the series of drawings I started in the village, and put them all in my second book, *Drawing on Culture*. When I see those drawings, which survived in a little black portfolio case across the heart of Africa, I know it was all real, that it all happened. They are my proof I was there, that I met these people who infused my life with their gifts. One day, I hope to return the favor, to thank them each personally. I don't know how I will find them all again. Perhaps that is another adventure, for another time. Africa still beckons me, and I am forever bound to the village's law of reciprocity.

The shaman returns to her quiet prayers, and a breeze ruffles the trees above us. The leaves dance and shimmer in the fading light, and a deep sense of calm fills me. I think our visit is nearly over, for it's getting late. But then, the old woman's eyes snap open. Firelight illuminates her face. She looks alarmed.

"Well, this is highly unusual," she says.

My heart stops beating for a moment. "Oh?" I wonder if I should excuse myself and make a break for it while I still can. She speaks firmly, and I don't move.

"There is somewhere you must go. Someone needs to see you. Can you go on a journey?"

I sputter. The last time she sent me on a trip, it almost did me in. If I had to do it all over again, would I?

"Well, I...I..." I stammer, trying to think of any excuse not to. "I'm not sure that I'm ready to just pack up, and—"

"It's not that kind of journey, sonny," she says, rolling her eyes. "We'll stay right here. Just close your eyes and relax. You'll know what to do."

I'm not sure at all that I'll know what to do, but I ease back in my chair anyway. She leans forward and picks up a drum from beneath her chair. I close my eyes as instructed, and she beats the drum, softly at first. She finds her tempo, and the rhythm grows louder. It's slow and hypnotic. She maintains this beat for some time, and I drift into a peaceful awareness. Time bends and morphs, playing tricks on my mind. I have no idea what we're about to do, or if I'm even capable of taking the kind of journey she has in mind. My doubts prick at me like little mosquitoes. After what feels like a small eternity, I fear I should say something. But just before I can, a voice inside me speaks.

Have courage.

My last thought is of the *vodoun* adepts dancing in church one Sunday morning in Ghana, so many years ago. I remembered the woman in trance, with only the whites of her eyes showing. Her body was there, but she was *gone*. And then I'm gone too, washed in light, and all that tethers me to the world below is the faint sound of a drum beating somewhere in the distance.

AUTHOR'S NOTE

I am deeply saddened by the loss of my dear friend, Lanciné Condé, who passed away suddenly on September 5, 2021 at the age of 52. His legacy will live on through his music.

For updates on the Condé family in Guinée, visit:

davekobrenski.com/lancineconde

ADDITIONAL CONTENT

For additional content related to the book, including dozens of full-color photos from the story, please visit:

davekobrenski.com/fts

Or scan this code with a smartphone:

ABOUT THE AUTHOR

Dave Kobrenski is an artist and musician who loves a good adventure and travels to West Africa frequently. When he's not traveling, he makes art and music, builds flutes, writes and illustrates books, and hangs out with shamans and healers whenever possible.

Dave's first book is called *Djoliba Crossing*, and his book of drawings and essays from West Africa is called *Drawing on Culture*. Both books are available at davekobrenski.com/books and online wherever books are sold.

Dave lives in northern New Hampshire with his wife Karissa, his stepson Noah, and their three cats.

~

Sign up for news and exclusive content from Dave at:
davekobrenski.com/newsletter

Other Books by Dave Kobrenski:

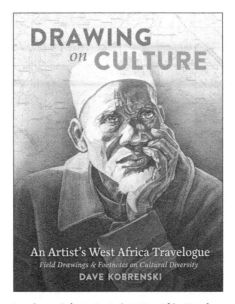

Drawing on Culture: An Artist's West Africa Travelogue

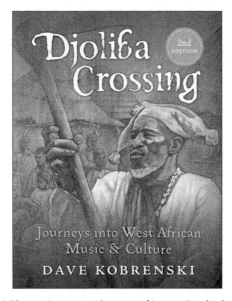

Djoliba Crossing: Journeys into West African Music and Culture